Xi Jinping's China

Also by Jayadeva Ranade

Rs. 1095.00 | 9789381904435 | Hardback

Forthcoming title by author

Cadres of Tibet

Rs. 1120.00 | 9789386288929 | Hardback

Xi Jinping's China

JAYADEVA RANADE

KW Publishers Pvt Ltd
New Delhi

ISBN 978-93-86288-90-5 Hardback
ISBN 978-93-86288-91-2 ebook

Published in India by Kalpana Shukla

KW Publishers Pvt Ltd
4676/21, First Floor, Ansari Road
Daryaganj, New Delhi 110002
Phone: +91 11 43528107
Marketing: kw@kwpub.in
Editorial: production@kwpub.in
Website: www.kwpub.in

Printed and Bound in India.

Dedicated to My Parents

Contents

Acronyms

CC	Central Committee
CCP	Chinese Communist Party
CDIC	Central Discipline Inspection Commission
CMC	Central Military Commission
CPEC	China-Pakistan Economic Corridor
CPPCC	Chinese People's Political Consultative Conference
CYL	Communist Youth League
MFA	Ministry of Foreign Affairs
MD	Military District
MR	Military Regions
MSD	Military Sub-District
NPC	National People's Congress
OBOR	One Belt, One Road
PAPF	People's Armed Police Force
PB	Politburo
PBSC	Politburo Standing Committee
PLASAF	People's Liberation Army Second Artillery Force
PLA	People's Liberation Army
PLAAF	People's Liberation Army Air Force
PLAN	People's Liberation Army Navy
PLARF	People's Liberation Army Strategic Support Force
PSB	Public Security Bureau
TAR	Tibetan Autonomous Region

1

China's Next Chairman—Xi Jinping

Tucked away virtually at the end of the communiqué issued on October 17 after the fifth plenary session of the Seventeenth Central Committee in Beijing, was a one-line paragraph announcing that China's Vice President, Xi Jinping, had been appointed Vice Chairman of China's Military Commission. The announcement confirms that Xi Jinping, viewed since 2007 as Hu Jintao's putative successor, is firmly on the path to taking over the three all-important posts of General Secretary of the Chinese Communist Party (CCP), President of China and Chairman of the Central Military Commission (CMC), after the Eighteenth Party Congress scheduled to be held in Beijing around October 2012, unless some drastic unforeseen event occurs. It simultaneously negates all speculative reports of factional infighting surrounding Xi Jinping's elevation to the top jobs. Xi Jinping's appointment was widely anticipated at the last Central Committee plenary session. His appointment now, however, indicates that he will have an apprenticeship of almost two years before he assumes supreme command of the People's Liberation Army (PLA).

The decision to combine the powers of the Party and Military was taken by Deng Xiaoping in 1987 when he anticipated that future generations of Party leaders would not possess military credentials and also not have the support of veteran cadres wielding sufficient authority over the military. These future leaders would, therefore, require greater authority to effectively command and control the PLA. Party General Secretary Zhao Ziyang was to be the first such leader, but that did not materialise because of the "Tiananmen Incident" one and a half years later. Jiang Zemin took over in November 1989 as Chairman of the Central Military Commission (CMC) without any preparatory period as the first Vice Chairman because of Deng Xiaoping's insistence that, during that troubled period, the Party must demonstrate its effective and visible command over the PLA. Deng Xiaoping was, however, present and able to intercede when necessary to support Jiang Zemin. The system of phased transfer of power was resumed with Hu Jintao's appointment as first Vice Chairman of the CMC in 1999 and later as Chairman of the CMC, replacing Jiang Zemin, in 2004. Hu Jintao became the first civilian Party leader to take over the reins of the CMC from a civilian predecessor without the benefit of a supportive veteran cadre present on the sidelines. Though Hu Jintao's appointment as CMC Chairman was delayed because of Jiang Zemin's reluctance to relinquish the post, Hu Jintao, in effect, took over as CMC Chairman two years after he had become the General Secretary of the Party.

In contrast to Jiang Zemin and Hu Jintao, neither of whom had any military credentials, Xi Jinping does have some experience in the PLA. After his graduation in Chemical Engineering from Qinghua University, Xi Jinping began work in 1969. He joined the Communist Youth League in 1971 and the CCP in 1974. Because of his father's position in the Party and PLA, Xi Jinping worked in the General Office of the State Council and CMC for almost three years from April 1979 till 1982 when he served as personal secretary to Geng Biao, Politburo member and China's Defence Minister and Secretary General of the CMC. Interestingly, during this period Xi Jinping was an officer in "active" service. Xi Jinping's military connections were sought to be buttressed in the official account of his career, released by Xinhua on the occasion of the announcement of his recent appointment. This stated that Xi Jinping had almost always been a member of the National Defence Mobilisation Committees in the various provinces to which he was posted. In that capacity, he would have attended meetings convened by the concerned Military Region and interacted with senior PLA officers. These periods of service together with his father's military associations have consolidated Xi Jinping's entrée into China's senior military hierarchy. Coincidentally, Xi Jinping's second wife, 47-year-old Peng Liyuan, is an accomplished Chinese folk singer who graduated from the Beijing Conservatory of Music and holds the rank of Major General in the PLA!

Xi Jinping, born on June 1, 1953, is the third child of Xi Zhongxun (1913-2002) and his wife Qi Xin. He has two elder sisters and a younger brother. Xi Zhongxun was a veteran Party cadre and one of the founders of a communist guerrilla army of north China and, during the epochal Long March in the mid-1930s, gave Mao Zedong and his troops shelter in the Ya'nan area. Xi Zhongxun was accused of plotting against Mao in 1962 and purged for the second time. He was later rehabilitated, but again purged during the Cultural Revolution and this time exiled to the countryside. Xi Jinping's life was scarred by the Cultural Revolution when, following his father's purge, he was sent to the countryside to be re-educated as a peasant and kept away from his family for several years. According to Xinhua, from 1969 to 1975, Xi worked as an "educated youth" sent to the countryside at Liangjiahe Brigade in his home province of Shaanxi where he served as party branch secretary. Xi Zhongxun, who was highly respected in the Party, was a friend and comrade of Deng Xiaoping's who rehabilitated him and appointed him Vice Premier. Xi Zhongxun, was the architect of the Special Economic Zones. Significantly, Xi Zhongxun opposed the crackdown by the People's Liberation Army at Tiananmen in June 1989. Also, among the websites shut down by the authorities in late 2009, when the conservative viewpoint on handling minorities began to gain ascendance, were some operated by NGOs and cadres with more liberal viewpoints associated with the late Party General Secretary Hu Yaobang and Vice Premier Xi Zhongxun, father of current Chinese Vice President Xi Jinping.

As the son of a senior Party cadre, Xi Jinping is a "princeling." The "princelings" constitute a fairly powerful grouping in the Party and military apparatus in China. They have also been assiduously cultivated and promoted by Hu Jintao especially in the PLA. Xi Jinping can currently bank on the support of a number of senior military cadres who are also "princelings." These include: Ma Xiaotian, Deputy Chief of General Staff of the PLA; Li Jinan, Director of the PLA's powerful General Political Department; Wu Shengli, Commander of the PLA Navy and CMC member; Xu Qiliang, Commander of the PLA Air Force and CMC member; Peng Xiaofeng, Political Commissar of the Second Artillery; Liu Yuan, Political Commissar of the Academy of Military Sciences; Zhang Youxin, Commander of the Shenyang Military Region; and Zhang Haiyang, Political Commissar of Chengdu Military Region. Xi Jinping will additionally benefit from the Party's strengthened grip over the PLA brought about by Hu Jintao. Hu Jintao launched successive and thorough year-long "education" campaigns throughout the PLA for three consecutive years to instil the concept that the Party exercises "absolute" control over the army. He also augmented the powers of the General Political Department and political commissars by giving them veto authority over PLA officers' promotions. Hu Jintao has simultaneously, since his term as Vice Chairman of the CMC, built up a core of loyalists in the senior echelons of the PLA. He is thus far estimated to have promoted over 50 officers to the rank of General and a number of others in grade promotions to senior appointments while awaiting rank promotions that come in routine course. This consolidation of civilian political control over the PLA will help Xi Jinping too.

Additionally, Xi Jinping has supporters in the top echelons of the CCP which include Song Ping, Zhu Rongji, Li Peng, Hu Jintao, Zhou Yongkang and the former Head of the CCP CC's Organisation Departmment, He Guojiang. Other supporters include some of the "princelings" in the Party. Whether Xi Jinping's elevation finally to the top posts will signal a change in China's domestic and foreign policies is debatable. Prior to this appointment and in an indication that he is being groomed for the top jobs, Xi Jinping had visited countries viewed by China as important, including Japan, Australia, Mongolia, Myanmar and Bangladesh as well as countries in Latin America and Europe. The communiqué mentioning Xi Jinping's appointment particularly dwelt on the international political situation and the challenges that are likely to confront China. It contained a suggestion that the review of China's Asia policy, that had begun late last year, had either been finalised or was nearing finalisation. Xi Jinping's military affiliations and pronounced linkages with senior PLA officers suggest that the military will continue to receive high budgetary allocations. The emphasis on modernisation of the PLA will remain and the focus on "integrated joint operations" and fighting "short duration regional wars under hi-tech informatised conditions" will continue. Xi Jinping's tenure will, therefore, probably see continuation of the present policy which combines diplomacy with a strong suggestion of military muscle.

While Xi Jinping has not yet visited India, he has met Indian officials and leaders in Beijing. For example, on August 8, 2008 Xi Jinping met Congress President Ms. Sonia Gandhi and her son, Rahul, in Beijing when they had gone to see the Summer Olympics. He had then thanked India for taking "effective" steps to ensure smooth passage of the Olympic torch relay in New Delhi and for backing Beijing's efforts to stage a "unique and well-run" Games. Xi Jinping said India had ensured the success of the Indian leg of the Olympic torch relay in New Delhi and "for that, we express our deep gratitude." The reference was to the threats by pro-Dalai Lama Tibetan protesters to sabotage the torch relay in New Delhi on April 17. The following month, on September 8, he met M. K. Narayanan, then India's National Security Adviser and Special Representative, who was in Beijing to attend the 12th Sino-Indian meeting on the boundary issue. During the meeting, Xi Jinping appreciated the all-round development of China-India relations. He pledged that China was committed to developing the strategic and cooperative partnership of peace and prosperity with India, adding that friendly Sino-Indian relations would benefit both Asia and the world as a whole. "The two sides should view the bilateral ties from a strategic and long-term perspective, and expand the common ground and properly handle the differences so as to push forward the long-term and stable relations," he added. On the boundary issue, Xi Jinping hoped that under the guidance of the leaders of both countries, a fair and reasonable framework acceptable to both sides would be worked out at an early date through equal consultation and friendly dialogue. He concluded with the remark that "both should maintain peace and tranquillity in the border area before the boundary issue is resolved." More recently on May 28, 2010, Xi Jinping met visiting Indian President Ms. Pratibha Patil and Foreign Secretary Ms. Nirupama Rao at a reception in Beijing to mark the 60th anniversary of establishment of ties.

Xi Jinping is well versed with Taiwan issues and developed connections with numerous Taiwanese businessmen during his almost seventeen years in Fujian and Zhejiang provinces. He also headed the Leading Group on Hong Kong and Macau. His wife visited Taiwan for eight days as part of a cultural delegation in 1997 and his brother-in-law has been living for some years in Taiwan's southern Chiayi county.

Xi Jinping met North Korean "leader" Kim Jong-il during the latter's visits to Beijing in 2008 and subsequently. An oblique suggestion of North Korea's desire to continue the present level of bilateral relations during Xi Jinping's upcoming term was contained in a congratulatory message. The official North Korean newspaper *Rodong Sinmun* published the message issued on the occasion of Xi Jinping's appointment to "the important post." In domestic matters pertaining to the minorities, though Xi Jinping has experience of remote and poor provinces and can be expected to encourage their development, he is unlikely to introduce relaxation in national policies and programmes. Xi Jinping's presence at both the national work conferences held in the first half of this year, on Tibet and Xinjiang where certain tough measures were approved, were in fact specifically pointed out in official "Xinhua" news agency despatches. It is nevertheless interesting that Xi Jinping's father, Xi Zhongxun, was an interlocutor for the Dalai Lama's Special Envoy Lodi Gyari in the 1980s and apparently carried a photo of the Dalai Lama. Prior to that he had some association with the 10th Panchen Lama, Tibet's second most important religious leader. Such links, however, are unlikely to influence Xi Jinping's stance on Tibet as that will have wider implications for the six million Tibetans and also for the peace and stability of China and the border regions.

On domestic political issues, as on most others, Xi Jinping has been very circumspect. He has not commented on issues like political reform. However, his father's "liberal" thinking and viewpoints could have left an imprint. At the same time, Xi Jinping is a Party apparatchik who has been a beneficiary of the system. Xi Jinping is unlikely to do anything that could weaken the Party or its monopoly on power, though he might tinker on the edges of limited and gradual political reform. Xi Jinping is credited with pushing economic reforms and has earned a reputation for "getting things done." His management of the prestigious Summer Olympics was appreciated. These views could be reflected in the ensuing economic reform policies.

(The article was published in Centre for Air Power Studies, New Delhi, October 25, 2010).

2

Xi Jinping's Leadership Style and China's Likely Policy Direction

China's new leader, Xi Jinping, has moved remarkably quickly to outline his personal vision for the country and this has attracted attention inside China and abroad. In doing so he has departed from the usual norm for China's top leaders, who wait at least two and a half to three years before spelling out their concept and trying to translate it into a "guiding ideology" for the country. In the process, he has set himself apart from all the other members of the Politburo Standing Committee (PBSC). The alacrity with which Xi Jinping has moved signals not only his self-confidence, but implies a high degree of assurance of backing from China's veteran leaders. It is another indicator that he and his predecessor, Hu Jintao, shared a close, collaborative partnership.

Xi Jinping's attempt to demonstrate that he will have a visibly different style of leadership came within a month of his being appointed General Secretary of the Chinese Communist Party (CCP) and Chairman of the powerful Central Military Commission (CMC) by the 18th Party Congress, which was held in Beijing from November 8 to 14, 2012. The 18th Party Congress additionally approved his appointment as President of China at the forthcoming National People's Congress (NPC) session presently scheduled to bc hcld from March 5, 2013.

Xi Jinping's "southern tour," or "nanxun," early in December 2012, was aimed at multiple audiences and emitted a multiplicity of messages. It hinted at the acknowledgement of popular dissatisfaction in some areas as well as the impatience in certain quarters at the slow pace which threatens to stall economic reforms. The main themes in Hu Jintao's Work Report to the 18th Party Congress, as well as in Xi Jinping's first two speeches immediately after conclusion of the Party Congress to the Politburo's first "collective study session" and the CMC meeting, were reflected in Xi Jinping's tour to Guangdong province. The Work Report and Xi Jinping's speeches all stressed the need for cadres to follow a frugal work-style, be close to the people, and eradicate corrupt practices—the latter especially singled out as having assumed serious proportions threatening the very existence of the CCP. Hu Jintao had, on at least three earlier occasions, warned of the threat to the CCP's existence from the high incidence of corruption. The widespread practice of cadres buying luxury cars, expecting lavish banquets during inspection visits, and leading a profligate lifestyle, had come in for pointed critical mention at three gatherings organised in Beijing earlier this year by the children of powerful and extremely influential veteran cadres, or "princelings." Significantly, these "princelings" are all associated with Xi Jinping and have been supportive of him.

Xi Jinping has kept the focus on combating corruption as publicised in his remarks on December 24-25, 2012, to Chen Changzhi, Chairman of the Central Committee of the China Democratic National Construction Association (CDNCA). Recalling Mao Zedong's comment in 1945 to Huang Yanpei, a former Chairman of this non-communist party, that governments will never be slack at work if they are under the supervision of the people, Xi Jinping said Mao's warning remains valid. Quoting an ancient Chinese proverb that "things must have gone rotten before insects can grow," Xi Jinping urged the Party to stay clean and self-disciplined.

The Hong Kong media and Hong Kong's Phoenix TV, which were the first to report on Xi Jinping's visit—prominently picked up four days later by the Mainland China media—publicised that Xi Jinping was accompanied by his wife and that his entourage travelled in minibuses escorted by police but without disrupting normal traffic. He was photographed waving to, and on occasion mixing with, the common people.

Xi Jinping's first visit outside Beijing after taking over as Party Chief was a 4-day (December 7-11, 2012) inspection tour of the wealthy southern province of Guangdong. From December 7, he visited the Shenzhen and Zhuhai Special Economic Zones (SEZ), Shunde and Guangzhou. Chinese commentators promptly compared this with Deng Xiaoping's "nanxun," or "southern tour" of 1992, which Deng Xiaoping undertook to give a push to the economic reform process that had then threatened to stall. Xi Jinping used the trip to deftly play up his and his family's association with Deng Xiaoping by laying a wreath at the Deng Xiaoping Statue in Lotus Hill Park. He also called on four retired cadres who had accompanied Deng Xiaoping on his "southern tour."

In the months leading up to the 18th Party Congress, a series of articles in the official Chinese media had debated the advantages of accelerated economic reforms. Hu Jintao's Work Report, with the entire drafting process of which Xi Jinping was closely associated, contained 86 references to "reforms," considerably more than the 70 in Premier Wen Jiabao's Report to the National People's Congress (NPC) earlier this March, indicating that the economic reform process with the objective of achieving "common prosperity" would definitely continue. Accelerated or radical reforms are unlikely, however, as Xi Jinping will do nothing that threatens stability or upsets the powerful and strongly entrenched interests in the State-owned Enterprises (SoE). Xi Jinping's tour also took place just weeks before the important annual Central Economic Work Conference opened in Beijing on December 16. As anticipated, the Central Economic Work Conference side-stepped important issues such as income redistribution.

It is interesting that Hu Deping, son of the popular former General Secretary Hu Yaobang, is a supporter of Xi Jinping and has been supportive of Wang Yang, till recently the Party Secretary of Guangdong. In the middle of this year Hu Deping identified Guangdong as the province which could be expected to resolve the contentious issue of peasant's property rights and land reforms. Adhering to practice, Wang Yang accompanied Xi Jinping throughout the 4-day tour. Soon after the tour Wang Yang was replaced on December 18 by a cadre on the career fast track, 1963-born Hu Chunhua, also known as "little Hu" and who was elevated at the recent Party Congress to the Politburo. Among other places, Hu Chunhua served in Tibet (1983-97) before being appointed First Secretary of the Communist Youth League (CYL) and later as Party Secretary of Inner Mongolia in November 2009. He is a protégé of Hu Jintao.

Xi Jinping's selection of Guangdong for his first tour outside Beijing also had personal overtones. His father, Xi Zhongxun, who was Guangdong Governor and Party Secretary from 1978 to 1981 before becoming Vice

Premier, had established the Shenzhen Special Economic Zone and been Political Commissar of the Guangzhou Military District. Xi Jinping visited his 86-year-old mother, Qi Xin, who lives in Shenzhen.

Xi Jinping's tour, however, did not have just economic content but included visits to PLA bases including the 124th division of the 42nd Army in Luofushan, Huizhou and the PLA Navy's South China Sea fleet, where he boarded the destroyer "Haikou." In Zhuhai, he visited the China Aviation Industry General Aircraft Co., which manufactures military and civil aircraft. At all these places, he made speeches expressing pronounced nationalist sentiments. China's official news agency "Xinhua" reported Xi Jinping as emphasising that "whatever time and whatever circumstances, [the army] must listen to the Party and follow the Party." He asked PLA officers and non-commissioned officers to adopt "real combat criteria" in military training and intensify such awareness among soldiers. Xi Jinping reiterated that the PLA's core task was to improve its ability to wage regional wars in the information age and conduct diversified military operations. Xi Jinping's visit to China's leading IT companies, like Tencent, hinted at the close collaboration between the PLA and IT companies, of which there is a concentration in Guangdong's Dongguan county.

The other important area which Xi Jinping has chosen to stress unusually early in his term could become his contribution to the CCP lexicon in case, towards the end of his first term in 2017, it is introduced into the Party Constitution along with "Mao Zedong Thought," "Deng Xiaoping's Theory," Jiang Zemin's "Three Represents" and Hu Jintao's "Outlook on Scientific Development." This is the "Chinese Dream," which blends his concept of the country's future with the probable key thrust areas for his administration. Promptly after conclusion of the 18th Party Congress and Xi Jinping's mention of it in a speech in late November while visiting a museum exhibition called the "Road to Revival," the "Chinese Dream" is being referred to by high-ranking Party cadres with increasing frequency, including in their interactions with foreigners when comparisons with the "American Dream" are not infrequent. It has become a hot topic on Sina Weibo and Chinese Television. Xi Jinping defined the "Chinese Dream" as "achieving the great revival of the Chinese nation," which resonates with definitive nationalist overtones. Party cadres say it envisages: Chinese people with higher incomes, better living conditions or environment and a strong Chinese nation. Achieving the "Chinese Dream" implies inclusive growth and co-opting the country's ethnic minority nationalities. Blogs posted by some "netizens" are, however, critical and question whether this is a dream of the 1.3 billion Chinese people or only the Chinese leaders. Others hope that China does not become a society where only money matters.

Significantly, Xi Jinping tasked a team of confidants, where Wang Huning is said to have had a leading role, almost three years ago to formulate the "Chinese Dream." The formulation appears to weave together crucial aspects of Xi Jinping's policies. The "Chinese Dream" is unambiguous that economic reforms will be pursued while retaining the emphasis on "common prosperity." Sensitivity to the need for maintaining social stability simultaneously places curbs on radical reforms. Reports emanating from Beijing that China's incumbent leadership favours an 8 per cent annual rate of growth and that the recent Central Economic Work Conference avoided tough reform initiatives directed at income redistribution—despite a rapidly rising gini coefficient—or State-owned Enterprises (SoE) because of their influence, lend credence to this. Hu Jintao's Work Report to the 18th Party Congress for the first time ever included a section on the "Ecology," or environment, and this finds an echo in the "Chinese Dream." Popular dissatisfaction with polluted rivers, adulteration and food safety would have been contributory factors. The clear references to a strong Chinese nation and "achieving the great revival of the Chinese nation" have nationalist overtones and figure often in Xi Jinping's speeches. They refer to the modernisation of the PLA and implicitly recall the humiliation suffered by China at the hands of foreigners in the past, in turn, underscoring China's unwillingness to compromise on issues that are seen by Beijing as impinging on national sovereignty or territorial integrity.

In addition to these overt moves that have raised popular expectations, Xi Jinping has been equally quick in asserting control over the Party's supervisory apparatus. Meng Jianzhu's elevation to the PB and appointment as Head of the Party's apex security body, the Central Politics and Law Commission, indicates that Xi Jinping, instead of any other PBSC member, will exercise direct supervisory control over matters relating to internal security and Intelligence.

Little noticed has been the expansion and strengthening of the Secretariat of the CCP's 18th Central Committee (CC). The Secretariat of the 18th CC has been enlarged to include seven members and, unlike for the past couple of decades, is a visibly influential body that includes a member of the Politburo Standing Committee (PBSC) and four members of the Politburo (PB). This suggests a more proactive role for the Secretariat, which reports directly to the CCP CC General Secretary. Its membership points to its orientation and Xi Jinping's likely priority areas in his first term.

The inclusion of Liu Yunshan, PBSC member who continues to oversee the propaganda and culture portfolios, as the senior most member in the Secretariat implies that political and ideological education accompanied by controls on the media and internet will be a priority. Liu Yunshan will be an influential voice on matters relating to initiatives in culture and China's "soft power." He will have a say on matters concerning Tibet and Tibetans because of his experience in shaping a decisive role for the Party's propaganda apparatus during the 2008 riots. Liu Qibao, PB member and Director of the CCP CC Propaganda Department, will probably reinforce Liu Yunshan's conservative views. Zhao Leji, Head of the CCP CC's Organisation Department who entered the PB at the 18th Party Congress and was formerly Party Secretary of Shaanxi Province, is included in the Secretariat along with Li Zhanshu, PB member and Director of the powerful CCP CC General Office and third generation "Red revolutionary" cadre. Zhao Hongzhu, PB member, ex-Party Secretary of Zhejiang Province and a former PLA officer, represents the CDIC in the Secretariat indicating that rooting out corruption will receive priority. This appears to be reinforced by the appointment of PBSC member Wang Qishan as Chairman of the expanded CDIC, which for the first time includes younger cadres born in the 1950s and 1960s. Yang Jing, a Mongol, is the sole minority cadre.

The inclusion in the Secretariat of Du Qinglin, a former Vice Chairman of the CPPCC and Director of the UFWD, is interesting. At 67 years, Du Qinglin should have been on the verge of retirement but has instead been inducted into the Secretariat. Viewed together with the appointments of 67-year-old Guo Jinliong, who served many years in Tibet, as Beijing Party Secretary; Chen Quanguo, who reports circulating in Beijing claim was appointed Tibet Autonomous Region (TAR) Party Secretary at Xi Jinping's behest; and Ling Jihua as Director of the UFWD; Du Qinglin's inclusion in the Secretariat could indicate an impending initiative aimed at Tibet and Tibetans.

Finally, Xi Jinping has very quickly begun assembling his personal team, or brains trust. Key figures among them who have so far been identified are: Li Shulei, 49 years old and former Vice President of the Central Party School. He has been appointed Xi Jinping's Political Secretary. Li Shulei knows Xi Jinping from his days in Xi'an, Shaanxi and was brought to Beijing by Xi Jinping in December 2007 as Vice President of the Central Party School. The other individual is 60-year-old Liu He. Fluent in English, Liu He has been drafted into Xi Jinping's personal staff as the speech writer for economic issues. Once a soldier with the PLA's 38th Group Army, Liu He was Deputy Director of the Leading Group for Financial and Economic Affairs and has been involved in drafting Five Year Plans since the 8th Five Year Plan (1991-95). Wang Huning, promoted to the PB at the 18th Party Congress and fluent in French, is the third individual being relied upon by Xi Jinping and is credited with having been tasked by Xi Jinping three years ago to formulate the "Chinese Dream." According to some reports he was closely involved in drafting Jiang Zemin's "Three Represents." His wife, Zhou Qi, is the daughter of a former Vice Minister of State Security. Born in 1955, he has been a close associate of Hu Jintao and accompanied him on virtually all his tours. Xi Jinping is also expected to tap the reputed liberal Chinese economist Sun Liping, who was his doctoral adviser, for advice on economic issues.

(The article was published in Centre for Air Power Studies, New Delhi, January 11, 2013).

3

The Bo Xilai Affair

The Bo Xilai affair is probably the single most cataclysmic event in the history of the Chinese Communist Party (CCP) since at least June 1989. In many ways, in fact, it has inherently more ominous portends. It is the first serious event to have disrupted the CCP since the vacuum created by the absence of a veteran leader of unquestioned authority. The PLA has also been considerably buffeted by the incident.

The incident, additionally, revealed numerous weaknesses within the CCP apparatus. Most significantly, its domestic security machinery—which is at the heart of all authoritarian and communist regimes—was shown to have been penetrated. Complementing this was the revelation that Party discipline had become lax with even members of the CCP nomenklatura flouting with impunity the Party's strict regulations, concerning unauthorised contact with foreigners. Equally significant was that the Party's sensitive Central Propaganda Department and its subordinate bureaus in the provinces, which supervise and closely virtually guide several times a day the Party's narrative on various developments, stayed aloof and in a state of watchful wariness for over a month between February 6 and March 16, 2012. This was a clear indicator that both contending factions were powerful enough for the middle and lower ranking cadres to be uncertain of the outcome of the struggle. The crisis was exacerbated by the absence of a veteran leader whose authority could not be challenged.

A major weakness in the CCP's security apparatus, revealed by Chongqing Police Chief Wang Lijun's failed attempt to defect to the US on February 6, has noticeably not attracted comment. There is little doubt that Wang Lijun had a clandestine relationship with American Intelligence officers. Instead of seeking shelter at the British Consulate in Chongqing, Wang Lijun chose to drive over four hours and 300 km to the US Consulate in Chengdu. A highly placed official in a communist state is most unlikely to arrive unannounced at a foreign diplomatic mission and seek asylum unless he has reason to believe that he will be afforded sanctuary. That he stayed at the US Consulate overnight and instructions were sought from Washington point to Wang Lijun's being "known" to US Consulate officials.

Bloodlines of candidates, patron-protégé linkages, mentor-mishu connections and rancorous relationships that had lain apparently dormant for decades, have all been at play. The main issues are not ideology or pace of reform, but the ambition of the large numbers of cadres aspiring for the unusually numerous vacancies that are to become available at the 18th Party Congress in October this year. So many openings have not become available at one time for decades, thus increasing the number of hopefuls. The new entrants will lead China through this decade. For some aspirants this Congress is the last chance for promotion before the age criteria, announced at the 17th Party Congress, compels them to retire once they reach the age of 67 years.

The causes for the Bo Xilai affair can be traced back to at least the 15th Party Congress when Bo Xilai's father's ambitions for him were revealed. At that time his father, Bo Yibo, lobbied hard for his younger son's entry to the CCP Central Committee (CC). The effort was repeated some years later at the 16th Party Congress. It was much later and during Jiang Zemin's term that Bo Xilai was appointed Governor of Liaoning and, thereafter, transferred to the centrally administered Chongqing Municipality. Bo Xilai was appointed to the CCP CC Politburo at the 17th Party Congress. This move fuelled Bo Xilai's aspirations for a position in the CCP CC's all-powerful, 9-member, Politburo Standing Committee (PBSC). The well informed Hong kong-based newspaper "Ming Pao" had reported that during a closed door meeting of the CCP CC's Organisation Department in January 2011, Vice President Xi Jinping had actually listed Chongqing Party Secretary and Politburo member Bo Xilai as among those earmarked for elevation.

Reports subsequently anonymously "leaked" by the authorities to China's official media, after Bo Xilai's ouster in mid-April as Party Secretary of Chongqing, played up Bo Xilai's ambitious nature. They alleged that he had secretly harboured higher ambitions and was even plotting to oust Xi

Jinping to take over the posts of China's President, CCP CC General Secretary and Chairman of the Central Military Commission. He and his brothers had attended the same special Beijing No. 4 School as Xi Jinping, Liu Yuan and other "princelings" where he was referred to as "big brother" and, therefore, it was hinted, resented the prospect of having to now be subordinate to Xi Jinping.

Sixty-two-year-old Bo Xilai was a candidate who stood out among the hopefuls. He came of impeccable "Revolutionary Red" lineage and was the son of Bo Yibo, one of the so-called "Eight Immortals." He had independent patronage linkages and had assiduously built an independent support base. He had a proven track record of competence at the Centre as Commerce Minister when he impressed foreigners—especially Americans—during negotiations with his memory, grasp of the subject and fluency in English. He had done well in the provinces and was popular in Dalian and Chongqing. In the centrally-administered Municipality of Chongqing, he smashed the underground triads and mafia, reduced income disparities, eased the restrictive hukou system to allow for freer movement of rural folk to urban areas, and boosted economic growth to 16.4 per cent. His policies were eulogised as the "Chongqing Model." Even China's "liberal economists" who were otherwise apprehensive about pro-Mao sentiments, like Sun Liping—who was Chinese Vice President Xi Jinping's doctoral adviser—in March 2012, lauded his performance and cautioned leaders against dismissing as incorrect all the policies followed by Bo Xilai. Cleverly, Bo Xilai had additionally tapped into the reservoir of pro-Mao nostalgia and sentiment that had begun to permeate the country to enhance his appeal. He gained the support of the neo-Maoists and various neo-Maoist websites. He was conscious that he had missed elevation to the PBSC at the last Congress by a slender margin and was this time leaving nothing to chance.

In his anxiety to secure a place in the PBSC, Bo Xilai overstepped limits. He gave a public demonstration of his influence by organising lavish celebrations for the Party's 90th founding anniversary in Chongqing, which were attended by many senior Party cadres including at least 6 members of the PBSC. Regardless of whether they all supported him or were hedging their bets, it was clear that Bo Xilai was rising and widely considered as having a very good chance to enter the PBSC. Cadres would have recalled that at an "internal" conference of the CCP CC's Organisation Department in January 2011, Vice President Xi Jinping had identified Bo Xilai as one of the upwardly mobile cadres. Pointedly, however, President Hu Jintao, Premier Wen Jiabao and the Director of the General Office, Ling Jihua stayed away from these celebrations in Chongqing.

Prominent supporters of Bo Xilai in the Party include China's powerful Security Czar Zhou Yongkang, PBSC member in charge of Propaganda, Li Changchun, and China's former President Jiang Zemin. This support became evident in the decision to take the 52-year-old Chief of the Chongqing Public Security Bureau, Wang Lijun, away to Beijing under the escort of Vice Minister Qiu Jin of the Ministry of State Security instead of keeping him in the jurisdiction of the Party's Central Discipline Inspection Commission (CDIC). It was followed by Chongqing Mayor Huang Qifan's public statement during the NPC plenum on March 5, 2012, recounting that Wang Lijun had sought sanctuary in the US Consulate in Chengdu and had to be talked into leaving peacefully by the Mayor and other colleagues. The Mayor's statement seemed to suggest that he was taking responsibility for the actions of his direct subordinate and deflecting responsibility away from Bo Xilai. Later, a Xinhua despatch announced that PBSC member Zhou Yongkang would supervise the work in Chongqing.

In the PLA, the Director of the PLA's powerful General Political Department (GPD), General Li Jinai, has been a supporter of Bo Xilai and attended the Party's 90th founding anniversary celebrations in Chongqing. The Political Commissar of the Second Artillery Zhang Haiyang is a childhood friend. Bo Xilai had nurtured relations with the 14th Army, founded by his father, and visited them in Yunnan in late February this year, after the Wang Lijun incident became public. He cultivated relations with the Chengdu Military Region by making substantial contributions to personnel welfare. Demonstrating his close relationship with the PLA, when Hu Jintao was in Hawaii on November 10, 2011, to attend the APEC Summit, Bo Xilai staged a large "defence mobilisation" military exercise in Chongqing where he invited Defence Minister Liang Guanglie and other southwestern Party and military leaders.

Bo Xilai's policies paid off and he succeeded in building a wide popular support base. However, his brash style, in violation of the low-key norm approved by the CCP, attracted adverse attention. His success in building an independent base was viewed by the Party Centre as a potential alternate power centre, which could threaten the Party's cohesion and unity. An alternate power centre would be a source of serious discomfiture to Party General Secretary and China's President Hu Jintao and Vice President Xi Jinping, and had to be neutralised.

As the dust settles it is becoming clearer that the move to prevent Bo Xilai's entry to the PBSC was premeditated and carefully planned. The individual chosen as the instrument was the flamboyant, 52-year-old ethnic Mongol Police Chief who had served with Bo Xilai in Liaoning and been hand-picked by Bo Xilai to be Police Chief of Chongqing. Wang Lijun, who was passionate about police work and fully enjoyed its perquisites, was appointed Vice Mayor in charge of Public Security of Chongqing. In a short while he helped Bo Xilai become popular by cleansing the Municipality of the triads. Wang Lijun was manipulated to investigate Bo Xilai so that Bo Xilai could be embarrassed into giving up the race. In case he resisted, Bo Xilai would be threatened with disciplinary action on charges of corruption. But Wang Lijun, either because he exceeded his brief, or feared for his life, or some other reason, strayed from the script and made an abortive attempt to defect to the US. This action immediately sealed Wang Lijun's fate and stunned the Party. There is very little doubt that Wang Lijun, who has been held at an undisclosed location, will probably be awarded the death penalty which will later be reduced to life imprisonment with hard labour.

Official accounts reveal that Wang Lijun was tasked to investigate the activities of Bo Xilai's wife, BoguKailai and particularly the murder of British businessman Neil Percival Heywood. He briefed Bo Xilai on his progress in the enquiry and it is from then that things began to go wrong for him. Bo Xilai divested him of the public security portfolio and within a week, on February 6, Wang Lijun made his bid for asylum in the US Consulate in Chengdu.

A small-time British businessman and fixer who had been educated in Harrow, UK, Neil Percival Heywood was found dead on November 15, 2011, in a dingy room at the three-star "Lucky Holiday Hotel" resort in Chongqing.

Forty-one-year-old Heywood stayed in China for nearly 21 years till his death and is reported to have helped Bo Xilai and his wife secretly stash the commissions earned abroad. Reports suggest that after BoguKailai had fallen out with French lawyer Patrick Devillers in 2005 or 2006, Neil Heywood stepped in to take his place as her main business agent. Friends of Heywood and acquaintances of BoguKailai say she had a sexual relationship with Devillers and possibly also with Heywood. Bogu Kailai is herself considered a competent and astute lawyer, who proved her calibre in cases in the US. She authored a book in 1998 entitled "Uphold Justice in America" that later became a TV serial. Incidentally, BoguKailai was herself a "princeling" being the daughter of renowned PLA General Gu Jingsheng. Suspicion continues to cloud some aspects of Neil Heywood's involvement. Firstly, official Chongqing police reports stated that when Heywood's body was discovered he was dead of "excessive alcohol consumption." However, his expatriate friends claim he was a teetotaller except very occasionally when he got totally intoxicated, usually over week-ends. Heywood was not doing well financially and his reclusive lifestyle raised queries among the expatriates in China who knew him. There were questions as to his source of income. Finally, the response of the British Embassy in Beijing was intriguing. They initially chose not to react to news of Heywood's death and did not send a representative to enquire into the circumstances, giving rise to suspicion that they wanted to keep the matter quiet as Heywood was linked to British Intelligence. It was only after the issue caused a stir in Beijing and got the attention of British Parliamentarians that the British Embassy took interest in the matter. Heywood's Chinese wife, Wang Lulu, was said to have been pressured by the Chongqing authorities to agree to, and authorise, a quick cremation without an autopsy and was so distraught when she arrived in the city that she sent her brother with a British consular official to identify the body. Reports claim that almost every single staff member at the Lucky Holiday Hotel was replaced over the following month and all current employees warned not to discuss the incident with anyone.

The drama that was to stun the CCP began to unfold within a week of Wang Lijun being divested of the public security portfolio by Bo Xilai. On February 6, 2012, Wang Lijun drove 300 km to the US Consulate at Chengdu and sought political asylum. As soon as his absence was detected, the Chongqing and Chengdu armed police surrounded the US Consulate. Chongqing Mayor Huang Qifan accompanied by a couple of officials went to the US Consulate where they had lengthy discussions with Wang Lijun. The next day (February 7) Wang Lijun was taken away to Beijing by air under the escort of Vice Minister Qiu Jin of the Ministry of State Security after he "voluntarily" left the US Consulate. For the CCP, which goes to great lengths to conceal the true crimes of those who defect or are guilty of espionage, Wang Lijun's action was unforgivable. His timing was also drastically wrong. Granting Wang Lijun political asylum on the eve of Xi Jinping's visit to the US would have jeopardised US relations with China. This the US does not want and Wang Lijun's request was turned down. That Wang Lijun had backers in Beijing is indicated by the initial reports claiming he had suffered a nervous breakdown and was being given "vacation-style treatment." But confirmation that Wang Lijun's supporters were not sufficiently strong and that the Party Centre was unwilling to condone such a serious breach of discipline came from China's President Hu Jintao. In an "internal" briefing on March 3 to CCP cadres who were delegates to the CPPCC conference, Hu Jintao labelled Wang Lijun a "traitor."

Wang Lijun's aborted attempt to defect to the US brought into public glare the intense infighting underway in the highest reaches of the CCP. Though a serious tussle had begun in the Party's top echelons, including retired veteran cadres, on what was to be done with Bo Xilai, it was evident that all were unanimous in the view that Party unity was paramount. The Party's core united around the Party Centre. This facilitated Hu Jintao and Wen Jiabao's efforts to muster support to remove Bo Xilai from Chongqing, dismiss him from the PB and CC and punish him. But opposition was tough and negotiations were intense as evident from the fact that no decision or announcement was forthcoming from February 6 when Wang Lijun's aborted defection became public knowledge till March 3. This indicated the strength of the forces ranged against Hu Jintao and Wen Jiabao. Also indicative was the failure of the authorities to snuff out the hundreds of thousands of blogs and microblogs circulating in China's cyberspace reporting on the events concerning Wang Lijun and Bo Xilai. It was only on March 15, at his last

NPC press conference as Premier, that Wen Jiabao cautioned Party authorities to learn from the developments in Chongqing. The next day it was announced that Bo Xilai had been replaced as Party Secretary of Chongqing and Vice Premier Zhang Dejiang, also a "princeling," posted in his stead.

Around this time Vice President Xi Jinping, publicly revealed the gravity of the situation for the CCP and his support to Hu Jintao, and cautioned Party cadres against taking sides. In a lengthy article in the Party's theoretical journal *Seeking Truth* on March 16, 2012, Vice President Xi Jinping urged cadres to "safeguard the purity of the party." He insisted that "we must resolutely stop and combat any wrong political tendencies that veer from the party's basic lines" and asserted that "leading cadres must resolutely uphold the Party's principles, charter, goals and policies." The article was publicised by the official news agency Xinhua the following day. Ultimately Hu Jintao, Wen Jiabao, Xi Jinping and Li Keqiang secured a decision to remove Bo Xilai. After weeks of further wrangling and negotiation, Hu Jintao, Wen Jiabao and Xi Jinping scored a signal success and initiated proceedings to dismiss Bo Xilai from the CCP's CC which was announced on the evening of April 10, 2012. The following day an unsigned, front-page editorial in the authoritative Party paper, *People's Daily*, asserted that "China is a socialist country under the rule of law. The dignity of its laws and authority cannot be damaged." It added,"Regardless of an individual's stature, anyone who breaks the law will be punished. There is no preferential treatment in the eyes of the law."All of China's official media front-paged the article the next day. This could be the prelude to Bo Xilai being put on trial and punished, though the severity of the punishment is probably yet being negotiated. The blunt message sent out by the Party is that no threat to the CCP's cohesion, unity and primacy would be tolerated.

Old loyalties undoubtedly played an important part and old scores were settled. Hu Jintao and Wen Jiabao are both protégés of Hu Yaobang, and Xi Jinping also had family ties to him. While Wen Jiabao was the more overt supporter of Hu Yaobang, all three had mantained links with Hu Yaobang's family and annually visited their residence. Some reports claim Qiao Shi played an important role in ensuring the decision against Bo Xilai. The warnings issued by Hu Deping, Hu Yaobang's son, during at least three public gatherings of "princelings" and liberal economists in Beijing since last year, had relevance. It was Wen Jiabao too who fired the first public salvo against Bo Xilai at the press conference on the last day of the NPC plenum in mid-March when he cautioned Chongqing's leadership to "learn lessons" from the Wang Lijun incident and mentioned the possibility of another Cultural Revolution. The irony of Bo Xilai's father, Bo Yibo, having been among Hu Yaobang's harshest critics during a five-day criticism session at the time of the "Anti-Bourgeois Liberalisation Campaign" in 1987, just two years before Hu Yaobang's death, cannot be missed.

Once the decision was taken, the Party moved swiftly to contain damage and diminish Bo Xilai's popularity by putting out a steady stream of stories about his and his wife's corruption. A *People's Daily* article of April 12 hinted at serious political implications by suggesting that Bo Xilai's wife, BoguKailai, may be holding a foreign passport. It referred to corrupt officials who "commit crime abroad or transfer dirty assets abroad, and some even secretly acquire foreign citizenship or dual citizenship." A former Ming Pao journalist has alleged that Gu Kailai holds a Hong Kong ID and Singapore Green Card. She was detained pending investigations into the death of British national Neil Heywood who, according to unconfirmed reports, had intimate relations with her of which Bo Xilai was aware. In any event, Bo Xilai and she were estranged. The decision to charge BoguKailai for the murder of Neil Heywood was taken on July 6, 2012 when it was also decided—perhaps for better optics—to shift the venue out of Bo Xilai's possible influence to the Hefei Municipal People's Court. As anticipated, the trial was swift, lasting a mere seven hours, and on August 20, 2012, the court announced that BoguKailai was "sentenced to death with a two-year reprieve" for "intentional homicide." She was deprived of political rights for life. Her bodyguard, Zhang Xiaojun, who had earlier served her father, was sentenced to nine years in prison. Indirectly acknowledging the wide international interest that the case had attracted, China's authoritative English-language weekly, Beijing Review, published a full account of the case. It is very unusual, but not rare, for death sentences to be awarded to high-ranking cadres or their spouses. The last such occasion was in 1995 when Yan Jianhong, the wife of Guizhou Party Secretary, Liu Zhengwei, was put to death for corruption. Reports at the time in the Hong Kong media claimed that Jiang Zemin intervened to ensure that an example was made of Liu Zhengwei's wife, but Liu himself was spared the death penalty. His career, however, never recovered.

Functionaries of the CCP CC's Propaganda Department, who had stayed inactive for a few weeks waiting to see which leadership group got the upper hand, swung into action after Xi Jinping's article of March 16. Chongqing Radio and TV were directed to curtail the "red"programmes started by Bo Xilai in February 2011. On April 12, Xinhua disclosed that between mid-March and early April, China had shut down 42 websites and deleted more than 210,000 online posts in a crackdown on "internet-based rumours." A few better known neo-Maoist websites and portals began to feel the effect and Utopia and maoflag.com websites were shut for "maintenance." Chongqing Satellite Television station resumed its broadcasting of popular drama series and news programmes during prime time on March 26, as publicised by the state-run newspaper *China Daily*. Many policies associated with Bo Xilai, like the revolutionary themes from the Mao Zedong era, were suppressed and the Chongqing television singing programme that featured Maoist anthems, called Daily Red Songs, were reduced to a weekly show. Chongqing Daily, on March 28, publicised City Propaganda Chief, He Shizhong's call to municipal propaganda workers to "firmly avoid movement-style (propaganda) methods" and "resolutely maintain a high degree of uniformity" with the CCP's Central Committee.

Support for Bo Xilai, however, continues to be voiced. Within a week of its activities being suspended the neo-Maoist website Utopia demonstrated unusual pugnacity and, on April 12, posted a banner which read: "However you shut us down or censor us, we Utopia will always support Bo Xilai!" Popular resentment at the action against Bo Xilai, though quickly quelled, surfaced when protests occurred in Chongqing on April 10-11 and banners eulogising Bo Xilai and demanding his return to Chongqing were unfurled on April 12, 2012. On Bo Xilai's birthday in July, anonymous individuals painted slogans in favour of Bo Xilai on walls in Chongqing. More recently on August 20, 2012, Reuters reported that when BoguKailai's trial commenced, neo-Maoist websites expressed support for Bo Xilai alleging that "he and his wife are victims of a plot that has opened a dangerous schism between them and the Communist Party." They also circulated online a very unusual petition signed by 1,644 persons, including two retired central government officials, calling for the impeachment of Premier Wen Jiabao. Neo-Maoist Websites like "Red China" have been active throughout this period. Han Deqiang, a lecturer at the Beihang University School of Business Management, neo-Maoist and supporter of Bo Xilai, was quoted as saying, "I believe there are too many doubtful points about the case" and that "this whole incident was intended to eradicate Bo Xilai's Chongqing model." He added, "They have destroyed a ray of hope for the Chinese Communist Party." According to Reuters, another supporter of Bo Xilai's and TV commentator, Sima Nan, said, "Bo Xilai can't be shut away like Yang Baibing was, because now is the era of the Internet, and so controlling opinion is so much more difficult."

The Party Centre did not lose sight either of Bo Xilai's fairly wide support in the PLA, implying that his links in the PLA were being investigated and negotiations over his future must have been tough. At least four leading articles and editorials were published in the *Liberation Army Daily* and *People's Daily* between February and April 12, exhorting the PLA to unite "more closely around the Party centre with comrade Hu Jintao as General Secretary" of the Party. The PLA was urged to adhere to the principle of "absolute loyalty" to the Party. On March 25, hours before Hu Jintao departed for Seoul, the *Global Times* website headlined an article urging all PLA troops to be "more tightly united around the Party Centre, the CMC and Chairman Hu (of the CMC)." On March 27, a *Liberation Army Daily* article candidly declared: "new developments have arisen as profound changes have taken place in the world, nation, and the Party. … We should ensure that all troops resolutely follow the command of the Party Central, Central Military Commission, and Chairman Hu."

Separately, inspecting troops in late March in the Lanzhou Military Region and Shaanxi Military District, Guo Boxiang, CMC Vice Chairman, asked for "greater stress on building the forces ideologically and politically" and greater emphasis on "maintaining the security and stability of the military forces."

The following listing by the Jamestown Foundation of some articles published this year, together with some additional instances of public demonstrations of loyalty to Hu Jintao, are illustrative.

People's Daily (June 25) carried an article by the Jinan Military Region Political Commissar exhorting military cadres to more aggressively challenge mistaken ideas about the PLA's political role in the face of growing pluralism in Chinese society.

Liberation Army Daily (LAD, June 17) urged military officers to be steadfast in their loyalty to the Chinese Communist Party (CCP). The implication was that many officers were insufficiently committed to the Party's continued rule.

On May 23, the Beijing Military Area Command held its 10th Party Congress, during which Hu Jintao demanded that military officers remain "absolutely obedient" and loyal to the Party. Senior PLA officers attended, including the CMC Vice Chairman Guo Boxiong, who cancelled a five-day visit to Japan and South Korea in order to attend.

An LAD editorial (May 15) encouraged soldiers to recognise the "conspiracy" behind efforts to separate the army from the Party, and need to adhere to the fundamental political system that places the CCP above the army.

An LAD (April 6) editorial asserted the need for the PLA to be firmly aligned with the Party to ensure political stability, because historical experience demonstrated that ideological competition intensified whenever the CCP faced a crucial moment of reform.

On April 6, high-ranking PLA officers publicly expressed loyalty to President Hu Jintao.

LAD (March 19) published an article declaring that the PLA must resist the "three mistaken ideas" about China's military development. It said it is necessary to "always put ideological and political construction first" because this is essential for strengthening the PLA.

Xinhua (March 13) publicised China's President Hu Jintao's speech. It said that "every soldier in the military must be aware that development while maintaining stability is the priority. Hu stressed that the PLA and armed police must focus on national defence and army building, and adhere to the fundamental requirement of making progress while maintaining stability."

Significantly, the *Liberation Army Daily* (LAD) article published on June 17, 2012 for the first time implied there were "sub-loyalties" in the PLA. Indirectly underscoring the sensitivity of the current period it said, "that the problem of loyalty is of special importance in the year of the 18th Congress, when 'enemy forces' are spreading rumours … ." Warning readers about "fake loyalty" the article urged personnel to be "aware of people just pretending to be loyal, who feign loyalty, but do not really mean it." Clearly indicating the leadership's concern, a few months earlier at the NPC session in March 2012, Premier Wen Jiabao had, for the first time, pointedly declared "we will run the armed forces with strict discipline." By July 2012, at least five central task force teams had conducted investigations in the jurisdiction of the 13th and 14th Group Armies associated with Bo Xilai.

Separately, a "study campaign" was launched throughout the PLA, affiliated military establishments and Party-run institutes, in late July this year to disseminate CMC Chairman Hu Jintao's "important" speech of July 23. Study sessions were held in establishments like the National Defence University (NDU) and the X'ian Politics Institute. The speech was delivered at an unprecedented national seminar, convened in Beijing for principal leading Party and military cadres at the provincial and ministerial level, in the run-up to the upcoming 18th Party Congress.

These themes were stressed again on the occasion of the PLA's 85th anniversary on August 1 this year. Lengthy articles eulogising the PLA's history and role in building the country "under the leadership" of the Chinese Communist Party (CCP), were front-paged by the Jiefangjun Bao *(Liberation Army Daily)*, official news agency Xinhua and other official Chinese media. Each of them emphasised that the PLA is the Party's army and owes it "absolute loyalty" and obedience. They warned that "hostile foreign forces" were spreading propaganda intended to weaken this relationship and that this needs to be combated. Other articles pointed to the inextricable close links between the Party and PLA and mentioned that over the years the CCP had strengthened its bonds with the PLA by establishing Party cells in each PLA company.

Controls on the Party's and national security apparatus were simultaneously sought to be tightened. Reports in this period revealed that 3,000 public security cadres had been sent for "political re-education." Early this April, a national conference of heads of county public security organisations was convened in Beijing.

Despite the success of Hu Jintao, Wen Jiabao, Xi Jinping and others in ousting Bo Xilai, there is strong evidence that the influence of the neo-Maoist, or "Left," forces has not diminished. Widespread opposition to aspects of the reform programme, corruption and the Party's drift from purist principles, remains and fuels the neo-Maoists. Bo Xilai too still has voluble supporters. Importantly, Bo Xilai was not the leader of the pro-Mao or neo-Maoist sentiments, but had tried to co-opt their support. While the neo-Maoists may have, therefore, lost an important leading representative, they remain fairly influential and active at various levels in the CCP and PLA. Senior Party cadres are trying todifuse opposition and impress on middle and junior level Party cadres the necessity of reforms. The spate of articles, including some signed commentaries, in China's official media like the *People's Daily, Global Times, Liberation Army Daily,* Qiushi *(Seeking Truth),* Xinhua, etc., clearly show that the neo-Maoist forces continue to wield considerable influence. The promotions in early August 2012 of officers to the General staff rank, for example, included some from the 14th Group Army, which was viewed as under Bo Xilai's influence. Similarly, senior Party and PLA cadres associated with, or from areas described as under, Bo Xilai's influence have been selected as delegates to the 18th Party Congress. A prominent example is General Zhang Haiyang, Political Commissar of Second Artillery.

Finally, the delay in framing charges against Bo Xilai and bring him to trial reveals that intense, protracted bargaining is still underway in the highest cchclons of the CCP. Though the case erupted into the public glare on February 6, and he was removed from his post in mid-March, Bo Xilai has since then been kept under detention at an undisclosed location and there has been no official communication regarding his fate. BoguKailai's trial for homicide and the sentence awarded to her clears the way for the framing and announcement of charges against Bo Xilai, but with the most serious charge having been dealt with, Bo Xilai is likely to be charged with violation of Party discipline.

The charges against Bo Xilai and severity of his sentence will indicate the influence still exercised by his supporters.

It is unlikely that the influence of neo-Maoist, or "Left" forces will soon diminish markedly and Xi Jinping could well have to contend with renewed bouts of opposition. The incident has had an impact on the PLA. An immediate fallout will be greater stress on political reliability while making appointments to top posts in the Central Military Commission and the PLA's senior levels, as also increased political control over the PLA. Relevant is that all ten PLA officers promoted as General this July were Political Commissars. China's security apparatus will also be subject to special attention and "political education."

(The article was first published in "The 18th National Congress of the Communist Party of China: A major turning point for China," by Pentagon Press for ICWA. This article was republished in Centre for Air Power Studies, New Delhi, July 26, 2012).

4

China's Eighteenth Party Congress: Trends and Analysis

The Chinese Communist Party's (CCP) week-long (November 8-14, 2012) 18th Congress, which concluded on November 14, 2012, marked an important milestone in the evolution of the CCP. It saw the smooth transfer of power to leaders of the next generation despite the severe political disruption caused by the unbridled ambition of Bo Xilai, the now ousted former Politburo (PB) member with unimpeachable "Red Revolutionary" lineage. The disruption, however, impacted on the composition of the Politburo Standing Committee (PBSC) where the preference was for stolid apparatchiks bound by traditional Party ideology and discipline. The Party Centre was also able to ensure that an acceptable political document was approved, namely, Hu Jintao's Work Report, a key Congress document which was drafted from the beginning under Xi Jinping's leadership. Most importantly, the Congress oversaw the handover of power to a pair of new leaders who had not been selected by "Long March" veterans, and a set of PBSC and PB members who have entirely different academic and social backgrounds than their predecessors and all of whom grew and joined the CCP during the tumultuous Cultural Revolution years.

18th Party Congress: An Introduction

Indirectly acknowledging the growing popular discontent caused by a variety of factors including corruption, rising income inequality, pollution and food adulteration, the 18th Party Congress opened in the Great Hall of the People in Beijing on November 8, 2012, amidst unprecedented high security. There were 1,704 journalists covering the event attended by 2,280 Delegates and 20 special invitees like Song Ping, Qiao Shi, Li Peng and Jiang Zemin, who also cast votes. Heating was turned up in Beijing since the end of October for the comfort of the 2,270 Delegates and 1.4 million "volunteers" were mobilised for security work in Beijing. Irate "netizens" complained that over 660 persons had been assigned to protect each Delegate. China sealed its borders with Myanmar, India and Nepal and put security forces on higher vigil in the Tibet and Xinjiang-Uyghur Autonomous Regions. The opening and closing ceremonies were marred, however, by news of the self-immolation of five Tibetans across China's Tibetan populated areas on November 7 and some more on the closing days of the Congress.

Reflecting the CCP's increased strength of 82.6 million, 2,270 Delegates, each representing 38,000 Party members, were selected for the 18th Party Congress. Fifty additional Delegates represented "businessmen." The CCP's changing complexion was evident in the inclusion among the Delegates of 160 of China's 1,024 wealthiest men. The number of Delegates representing the People's Liberation Army (PLA) registered a slight increase at 251 against 249 for the 17th Congress. Hinting at the deleterious impact of the Bo Xilai incident on the PLA, China's official news agency "Xinhua," while reporting that the PLA's list of Delegates had been finalised, specifically observed that all 251 had been hand-picked for their blemish-free political reliability and record.

The strength of the Party's 18th Central Committee (CC) registered a marginal increase from 371 to 376. The average age of the new 18th CC, however, dropped to 56.1 years with 166 of the 205 full members born in the 1950s. The number of women reduced to 33. There are 39 ethnic minorities represented in the CC, though the number of Tibetans in the CC has dropped from 2 to 1. Interestingly, the number of Tibetans among the alternate members of the CC, at the same time, rose to an all-time high of 4.

Notable is the reduced size of the PBSC, from 9 to 7. Reliable reports circulating in Beijing claimed that the size of the PBSC was conclusively decided only on November 14 evening. The reduced size meant that unlike in the earlier PBSC no leaders from the successor "sixth generation" were inducted, though at least 9 potential candidates for the top jobs are present in the PB. Ethnic minorities are not represented in the PBSC or PB, perhaps suggestive of an increased emphasis on political reliability and loyalty to the Party.

The seven-member Politburo Standing Committee (PBSC) led by 62-year-old Xi Jinping with Li Keqiang comprises dependable apparatchiks who adhere to the Party line and discipline and will neither brook any violation. Four of them are "princelings."

Liu Yunshan is a conservative and has been uncompromising in controlling and implementing the Party's approved narrative even when it meant excising portions of speeches made by President Hu Jintao and Premier Wen Jiabao. He effectively managed the propaganda apparatus during the riots in Tibet in 2008 and drove a wedge between the Han majority and Tibetans. As PBSC member he continues to oversee Propaganda, Culture and Education, implying that strict policing of the media and cyberspace will continue combined with strenuous propagation of Party ideology. He is also President of the Central Party School and Executive Secretary of the influential 18th CCP CC Secretariat, indicating he could be appointed Vice President by the National People's Congress (NPC) this March, when Xi Jinping is confirmed as President.

PBSC member Zhang Dejiang (b.1947), a "princeling" and son of former PLA Major General Zhang Zhiyi, is a disciplinarian and was educated in economics in North Korea. He will be appointed NPC Chairman this March and is likely to be the link between the Chinese and North Korean leadership. Yu Zhengsheng is another "princeling" and as CPPCC Chairman will guide matters relating to China's ethnic minority nationalities and non-communist parties with a firm, conservative hand. His record is that of an orthodox Party administrator.

The appointment of Wang Qishan, a "princeling" and son-in-law of former PBSC member Yao Yilin, as Chief of the Party's anti-corruption watchdog body, the Central Discipline Inspection Commission (CDIC), has prompted persistent speculation in Beijing that a crackdown on corruption will get underway early in 2013. Hong Kong's *South China Morning Post* observed on November 26 that Wang Qishan's skills would be put to the test as "the state will collapse if the Party does not tackle corruption, but the Party will collapse if the anti-corruption push is too hard." Wang Qishan is respected internationally as a tough economic administrator. The appointment of Wang Qishan as CDIC Chief removes a potential rival in economic administration to Li Keqiang, and will dilute efforts to reduce the economic empires of the SoEs.

The new Executive Vice Premier in charge of Economic issues, Zhang Gaoli, is fond of large government guided projects and has a reputation of working with powerful business interests rather than challenging them. He is unlikely to downsize SoEs. At the same time, he has the reputation of being a stern taskmaster and is credited with promoting the retail sector as a way of creating jobs other than in the construction and manufacturing sectors.

All of them except Xi Jinping and Li Keqiang will step down in 2017, reinforcing the assessment that they have been inducted into the PBSC to strengthen Party ideology, and provide stability and continuity to the Party at a time when it has been severely bruised by the Bo Xilai incident.

The other important facet of power for the CCP is the PLA and here too the power transition was smooth. In a major departure from past practice, except for the top post of Chairman of the Central Military Commission (CMC), China's top military leadership line-up was formally announced before the Chinese Communist Party's (CCP) 18th Party Congress opened. The unusually early announcement of key appointments, including those of the Beijing Military Region Commander and Commander of the 38th Group Army based at Baoding, both of whom have traditionally been individuals in whom the Party Chief reposes confidence, indicates that Hu Jintao and Xi Jinping are firmly in charge of the PLA and that Hu Jintao's influence will continue. It confirms earlier indications that Hu Jintao and his designated successor had a close, collaborative working relationship, undoubtedly facilitated by Hu Jintao's friendly ties with Xi Jinping's father, Xi Zhongxun. In apparent confirmation of reports emanating from Beijing since July 2012, that Hu Jintao was reluctant to retain office, Hu Jintao handed over charge of the powerful post of Chairman of the CMC to Xi Jinping on November 11. The authoritative *Global Times*, a subsidiary of the official Party mouthpiece *People's Daily,* on November 18, 2012, heaped fulsome praise on Hu Jintao for setting a "healthy" precedent. Xi Jinping declared that "Chairman Hu's important decision fully embodies his profound thinking of the overall development of the Party, country and military. The decision also embodies his exemplary conduct and nobility of character."

The theme for the Congress had been set a day earlier with Party spokesman Cai Mingzhao asserting that "inner-Party democracy" would be promoted but that "the leading position of the CCP in China is a decision made by history and the people." A banner wrapped around the inner walls of the room in the Great Hall of the People reading, "Hold high the banner of socialism with Chinese characteristics, use Deng Xiaoping Theory, the Three Represents and the Scientific Outlook on Development as our guidelines!" echoed the sentiment.

Hu Jintao's Work Report

Important political documents relating to the Party Congress are: Hu Jintao's 30,000-character, 12-part, Work Report to the 18th Party Congress and Xi Jinping's speeches of November 16 and 17, 2012.

Hu Jintao's Work Report had a strong undercurrent of Marxist and Maoist ideology. It included references to Marxism-Leninism-Mao Zedong Thought, twice mentioned the "Four Cardinal Principles"—a phrase coined by Deng Xiaoping but usurped by the "Leftists"—and spoke of strengthening "core socialist values." He used the phrase associated with Mao Zedong of "let a hundred flowers bloom and a hundred thoughts contend" and spoke of continuing to adapt Marxism to China's conditions. The Report mentioned reform 86 times and called for doubling GDP by 2021 from 2010 levels. The Report said, "economic entities under all forms of ownership have equal access to factors of production in accordance with law … and are protected as equals," but the emphasis was noticeably on "common prosperity" and economic policies that benefit peasants and rural folk. Emphasising gradual reform it cautioned that "in economic structural reform how to strike a balance between the role of the government and that of the market…" must be examined. Taking note of popular discontent, an entire portion of the 12-part report discussed "social management," the euphemism for domestic security. It also simultaneously addressed popular concerns. For the first time ever a Work Report contained a section on "Ecology" and referred to the need for "resource conserving" and need for an "environmentally friendly society." It was acknowledgement of popular concern and the efforts of the 3,000 environmentalist groups in China. As anticipated an entire section dealt with "Defence" and emphasised that the "most important" task for the armed forces "is to win a local war in the information age." It said, "China should strengthen the armed forces, protect its maritime interests and be prepared for 'local war' in the information age." "We should enhance our capacity for exploiting maritime resources, resolutely safeguard China's maritime rights and interests and build China into a maritime power." Other areas of equal importance were identified as cyber and space.

Hu Jintao's Work Report made some important observations on corruption and political reform. Referring to corruption, he was explicit in his warning that "if we fail to handle this issue well, it could prove fatal to the Party and even cause the collapse of the Party and fall of the state." On political reforms, which were advocated by "liberal" Chinese intellectuals in a series of articles and speeches in the months before the 18th Congress, Hu Jintao was categoric in imposing limits. He said, "reform of the political structure is an important part of China's overall reforms. We must continue to make both active and prudent efforts to carry out the reform of the political structure and make people's democracy more extensive, fuller in scope and sounder in practice." Setting out the Party line, he declared that, "we will take neither the old road of closed door and ossified politics, nor the wrong path of changing our banners." As usual there was minimal reference to foreign policy issues in the Work Report, where only Hong Kong and Taiwan were mentioned by name.

Xi Jinping's first speech as Party General Secretary to a "collective study session" of the Politburo was also high in ideological content. Xi Jinping, incidentally, has a doctorate in Marxist Philosophy. It emphasised the need to "uphold and develop socialism," "uphold and develop socialism with Chinese characteristics as the focus, priority..." and "make sure the 18th CCP National Congress guidelines become a powerful ideological weapon." He asserted that "the theoretical system of socialism with Chinese characteristics is the latest achievement in applying Marxism in China. In contemporary China, to uphold the theoretical system of socialism with Chinese characteristics is to truly uphold Marxism." Xi Jinping clarified that the CCP will be the sole ruling party in China for a long time. Stating that the CCP's task is to "make the Chinese people rich, build a strong and prosperous country and rejuvenate the great Chinese nation," Xi Jinping declared, "our Party will always be a strong leadership core in the historical course of upholding and developing socialism with Chinese characteristics." He listed "combating corruption" and "preventing degeneration" as priority tasks. He has followed this up over the past couple of weeks, including over the New Year, by often citing quotes and excerpts from Mao's poems.

Speaking at an enlarged meeting of the Central Military Commission (CMC) on November 16, Xi Jinping stressed the need to "take ideological and political building as the top priority in army building" and ensure the Party's "firm grip over the troops ideologically, politically and organisationally." He reiterated the importance of "the Party's absolute leadership over the armed forces." Xi Jinping announced the criteria for promotions in the PLA: "The military must promote and appoint cadres based on their political performance and guarantee that 'guns' are always controlled by reliable people with loyalty to the Party." He ordered the military to "always put the country's sovereignty and security first, comprehensively improve the military's deterrent power and capability of real combat to protect China's sovereignty, security and development interests at an information-based age." He pledged to enhance the anti-corruption effort and called on senior military officers to take the lead in obeying rules and regulations for self-discipline. A circular issued on December 4 detailed stringent guidelines restricting the hospitality and entertainment offered to senior PLA officers visiting subordinate formations.

18th Party Congress: Three Messages

The 18th Party Congress has sent out three clear messages. These are of: continuity, reassertion of the Party's traditional orthodox values and discipline, and retention of focus on domestic issues including gradual economic reforms leading to "common prosperity." Domestic security will receive greater attention of the Party General Secretary. The issue of the restive ethnic minorities, and particularly Tibetans, will be a high priority. This portends an increase in China's activities in Nepal and among Tibetan Buddhists.

On issues concerning sovereignty or maritime and land territorial claims, the new leadership, many of whom have been moulded by adversity during the Cultural Revolution and are mentally tough, will be less flexible and less willing to compromise. China will not reconcile from its stance on claims in the South China Sea and push the limits to attain its objective, but stop short of triggering conflict. It will exert military pressure including using economic levers.

For Beijing, the issue is not merely one of territory, but of regaining its status as the pre-eminent power of the region. To reinforce this the New Year celebrations organised by the CCP in Beijing's Great Hall of the People on January 1, 2013, staged "The First Annual 'Ocean China' New Year's Concert," when the audience was assured that the ocean was "China's blue-coloured territory." Xi Jinping's "Chinese Dream" outlines his ambitions. The new seven-member PBSC exudes these themes.

China's neighbours, including India and Japan, should be prepared for increased pressure.

(The article was published in Institute of Peace and Conflict Studies, New Delhi, January 2013).

5

China's New Leadership: Internal and External Implications of a Fresh Agenda

With the conclusion of the 18th Party Congress (November 8-14, 2012) and 12th National People's Congress (March 5-17, 2013), the Chinese Communist Party (CCP) successfully completed an important transfer of power to new leaders who will guide it through the present decade. The conferences, popularly referred to as the "Big Two," additionally approved senior level Party and Government appointments which clearly outline the new Chinese leadership's agenda.

These personnel appointments viewed along with the first speeches after their appointment of Chinese President Xi Jinping and Premier Li Keqiang on March 17, 2013, reveal that the economy, domestic security and modernisation of the armed forces will be a priority. China will persist with its foreign policy objective of trying to establish dominance in the Asia-Pacific, while insulating and preserving its relationship with the US and strengthening ties with Russia.

What is likely to be the agenda of the new Chinese leadership? What are the likely implications of this new agenda, especially on China's reforms process, military modernisation and foreign policy?

The New Team and a Fresh Agenda

Though Premier Li Keqiang referred to "reform" twenty-nine times in his speech in contrast to the outgoing Premier Wen Jiabao, who mentioned it in his Work Report in one brief paragraph, he ensured that there was pronounced emphasis on the rural sector and "common prosperity." This especially includes improving wages and living standards of farmers, peasants and workers and expanding coverage of education, medical, health and social security benefits.

Steps to alleviate the plight of migrant workers were touched upon. Document No.1/2013, issued by China's State Council, as in the past ten years, was on Agriculture and rural policies.

Reforms: The Divide between the Bureaucracy and Civil Society

Important in China's domestic debate regarding "reform" is the article by Xi Jinping's Doctoral Adviser and Tsinghua University Professor, Sun Liping, in the *Economic Observer* on March 4, 2013. It appears indicative of the Chinese leadership's thinking. He assesses that there is "deep division" between government officials and civil society in how they view "reform." While the former interprets reform as making systemic changes, civil society judges it on the basis of efficiency. Observing that vested interests opposed to reform remain sizeable but presently dormant, he cautioned that they would re-emerge stronger after some years. Asserting that reforms are only a means to an end, Sun Liping suggested that "building a society that is just and fair" could be the basis of a new approach.

The New Cabinet with an Economic Focus

The new 25-member Cabinet has eight individuals with a background in economics and the new Finance Minister, 61-year-old Lou Jiwei, has particularly strong credentials as a reformer and in economic structural reforms. He was hand-picked by veteran CCP leader Zhu Rongji, who earned the nickname "One-Chop Zhu" because he streamlined and drastically reduced business approval procedures. While he was Mayor of Shanghai, Zhu Rongji selected Lou Jiwei as Deputy Director of the city's Economic Structural Reform Office. Later as Vice Premier in 1993, he appointed Lou Jiwei to head the Macroeconomic Department of the National Economic Structural Reform Commission.

The other key appointment is that of Xiao Jie as one of two Deputy Secretaries General of the State Council. Selected by Premier Li Keqiang with whom he has a long association, Xiao Jie received a Doctorate from the Research Institute of Fiscal Science of the Ministry of Finance and later served for two decades in the Ministry of Finance, including as Vice Minister before being appointed Director of the State Administration of Taxation.

There are other reformers in China's new team of managers of the national economy. Well regarded central banker, Zhou Xiaochuan, despite his 63 years of age, has not only been retained as Governor of the People's Bank of China but promoted to the prestigious national position of Vice Chairman of the Chinese People's Political Consultative Conference (CPPCC). Similarly, 68-year-old Chen Yuan continues as Chairman of the China Development Bank, which he has headed since 1998 and been elevated as CPPCC Vice Chairman. Both are reputed for their forward-looking outlook and expanding their bank reserves and operations. CPPCC Vice Chairmen are, incidentally, permitted to continue in office till 70 years of age while Ministers and Provincial Governors retire at 65.

The powerful National Development and Reform Commission (NDRC) has been strengthened with its Minister Xu Shaoshi, Executive Vice Minister Jie Zhenhua and two Vice Ministers Liu He and Wu Xinxiong all members of the CCP's 18th Central Committee. Liu He is additionally a member of Xi Jinping's "brains trust" and his speech-writer on economic subjects. Between 1991and 1995, Liu He studied in Seton Hall University, New Jersey and later obtained a Masters in Public Administration from the Kennedy School of Government, Harvard University, USA. Vice Minister Wu Xinxiong, who headed the State Electricity Regulatory Commission since 2011, now heads the new National Energy Administration and expectations are that the coming months will see a reduction in energy subsidies.

Others in the team of pro-reform economists are Xiao Gang, who has been transferred from being Chairman of the Bank of China to head the China Securities Regulatory Commission where he is expected to push the pro-market policies introduced by his predecessor. The elevation of Vice Commerce Minister Gao Hucheng in the same Ministry indicates a preference for expertise and continuity in this important position. Gao Hucheng has 36 years of experience in foreign trade issues and was a commercial officer in the Chinese Embassy in the Congo in 1977. As Commerce Minister he will be part of the Party's "Leading Small Group on Foreign Affairs."

The country's security apparatus, at the apex of which is the Central Politics and Law Commission now headed by Meng Jianzhu, a member of the

Politburo (PB), will report directly to President Xi Jinping. Former Minister of Public Security (MPS) Meng Jianzhu was elevated to the Politburo at the 18th Party Congress. He has worked closely with Politburo Standing Committee (PBSC) member Liu Yunshun.

State Councillor Guo Shengkun is the new MPS Minister, but lacks a background in security, investigative or police work. This will facilitate control by Xi Jinping. Two new MPS Vice Ministers, Yang Huanning (55 years) and Li Dongsheng (57 years) however, have the right credentials and will strengthen the Ministry. All three are members of the 18th Central Committee, indicating the importance accorded to the MPS. The NPC session this March further increased the budget for domestic security to US$ 123.5 billion, which makes it higher than the national defence budget for the third consecutive year. The security apparatus is simultaneously being strengthened across the country as evident from the number of cadres with experience in police and security work who have been promoted at the recent NPC to senior positions in at least ten provinces.

Strengthening of the cyber control mechanism, especially interception and deletion of messages, blogs, tweets and re-tweets, will receive particular attention. The "Golden Shield" programme, on which over US$ 1.6 billion has already been spent, will be upgraded. This will accompany tightened controls on the media imposed by the Party's Central Propaganda Department under the supervision of PBSC member Liu Yunshun. The suspension in March of Deng Yuwen, Deputy Editor of Xuexi Shidao, the Central Party School's theoretical magazine, is an example. He wrote an Op-Ed this February that China should abandon North Korea. Liu Yunshun is also President of the Central Party School.

Modernising the PLA

The modernisation of China's People's Liberation Army (PLA) remains a priority with continued double-digit increases in the national defence budget. In addition to the emphasis on "winning local wars under conditions of informationisation" and "Integrated Joint Operations," indications are that there will be a noticeable push in the acquisition of advanced high-technology weaponry and development of the indigenous defence industry. China will continue to design and develop new missiles, nuclear submarines, stealth fighters and bombers, and jet engines. The appointments of General Chang Wanquan, former Director of the PLA's General Armaments Department (GAD), as Defence Minister, and General Zhang Youxia, the sole battle-experienced member of the Central Military Commission and supporter of acquiring advanced military technology, as the new Director of the PLA's GAD, strongly suggests that an increased share of the defence budget will now go to arms procurement and indigenous development of advanced weapons.

The appointment of General Ma Xiaotian as PLA Air Force (PLAAF) Commander means that modernisation and upgradation of the PLAAF will continue. There also appears to be increased discussion in Chinese military literature of the role of the PLA Navy (PLAN) and "Military Operations other than War" (MOOTW), confirming that planning is underway for increasing the PLAN's operational range and reach.

The effort to acquire modern defence technology and weapons will see increased cooperation with Russia which remains the largest supplier of defence materials to China. This was an important agenda item for Xi Jinping during his recent visit to Russia and meeting with Russian President Putin. China is understood to have offered to invest billions of US dollars in down payments in Russia's defence industry for upgraded weaponry. Agreements for the purchase of advanced defence equipment were also signed.

Efforts to further strengthen Party control over the PLA will simultaneously continue. Chinese President and CMC Chairman Xi Jinping has repeatedly emphasised the importance of the PLA being "absolutely loyal and obedient" to the Party and, in his first speech to a meeting of the enlarged CMC after taking over as Chairman in November 2012, declared that political reliability will be the determining criteria for officers' promotions.

A Forceful Foreign Policy?

China's foreign policy will become more vigorous as Beijing tries to counter what it perceives are US-led efforts to contain its rise. Its relations with the US will remain the most important bilateral relationship and Beijing will try and insulate it from damage. As recent developments and personnel appointments show, Beijing will at the same time try to safeguard its influence and interests especially in the Asia-Pacific. The PLA will be used to reinforce Chinese diplomacy. China will not yield on its maritime territorial claims in the region, which it perceives not only as a territorial issue but the recognition of which by world powers would mean acknowledgement of China's pre-eminent position in the region.

China's stance is underscored with the symbolic visit at the end of March 2013, by a 4-vessel PLAN flotilla to James Shoal—claimed also by Malaysia, Brunei, the Philippines, Taiwan and Vietnam—about 80 kilometres off Malaysia's coast. Most recently on April 3, 2013, the Vice President of the Chinese Institute of International Studies (CIIS), a think tank under the Chinese Ministry of Foreign Affairs, warned Manila to prepare for a rough four years for seeking international arbitration to sort out contested territorial claims. Earlier in March 2012, the Director of China's State Oceanic Administration, Liu Cigui, renewed China's claim to South Korea's Ieodo, a submerged rock south of Jeju Island, and followed it up within months with cartographic aggression. China's actions occur despite the escalating tension with Vietnam, the Philippines and Japan and appear intended to stake out the extent of China's maritime claims.

The contours of China's foreign policy under the new leadership are discernible in recent senior appointments. The promotion of erstwhile Foreign Minister 62-year-old Yang Jiechi as State Councillor replacing Dai Bingguo is important. Dai Bingguo has been China's pointsman for negotiations with important countries especially the US, Russia and the UK, and is China's nominee to the Special Representative-level talks with India on the border issue. Viewed by foreign diplomats as less hardline than Dai Bingguo, Yang Jiechi is an expert on American affairs, a fluent English speaker and graduate of the London School of Economics. His effort to keep Sino-US relations in good repair will be supported on the ground by the new Chinese Ambassador to USA, Cui Tiankai. Cui Tiankai, who has also been Ambassador to Japan, is a postgraduate from the School of Advanced International Studies, Johns Hopkins University, USA. The Minister of State Security (MOSS), Geng Huicheng, who continues in his job since 2007 is also, interestingly, an America expert. Before his promotion as Minister he headed the Chinese

Institute of Contemporary International Relations (CICIR), which is a think tank of the Ministry of State Security (MOSS).

Wang Yi, a fluent Japanese speaker and former Ambassador to Japan and Head of China's Taiwan Affairs Office, is China's new Foreign Minister. A consummate diplomat and skilled negotiator, he is credited with conducting the secret talks with then Chief Cabinet Secretary Shinzo Abe, which helped break the impasse in Sino-Japanese ties in 2001-2006 and facilitated Shinzo Abe's visit as Prime Minister to Beijing in October 2006. The Taiwanese, who have welcomed his elevation, credit him with giving Taiwan diplomatic space by allowing it to join the WHO. Wang Yi's appointment would be intended to not only reduce tensions with Japan, but nudge Tokyo towards accepting China's claims. It is expected that Wang Yi and Shinzo Abe, who have interacted in the past, have kept up contact. The appointments reflect the importance Beijing attaches to its relations with the US and this region, especially in the present context.

China, Myanmar and Nepal

China's apprehension, that the US will undermine its influence in countries where it has strategic investments, is indicated in the unusual appointment of a Special Envoy for Myanmar, and new Ambassadors to Myanmar and Nepal. Seventy-one-year-old Wang Yifan, a former Vice Foreign Minister in charge of Asian Affairs, was recently appointed Special Envoy for Myanmar. He brings additional heft to his assignment as a close relative of Qiao Shi. Qiao Shi was a PBSC member, Chairman of the Central Politics and Law Commission, head of the CCP CC's International Liaison Department (ILD) and a supporter of the popular deceased Party General Secretary, Hu Yaobang.The efforts of Yang Houlan, who was transferred at the end of February 2013 from Kathmandu to Myanmar in recognition of good work done, will be reinforced by Wang Yifan. Yang Houlan has been succeeded in Nepal by Wu Chuntai who was Deputy Director General in the Department of External Security Affairs in the Ministry of Foreign Affairs. His main task is to curb and control the activities of Tibetans in Nepal and inside India. Beijing's concern is that at some stage the US may use Tibetans to destabilise China.

In an attempt to prevent any sudden chill in India-China relations which could push India closer to the US, there has been a noticeable suspension in the past many months of anti-India rhetoric by Chinese officials, analysts and China's controlled media. China is also believed to have for the first time posted an Ambassador of the rank of Vice Minister to India.

This agenda of the new leadership reflects the policies and programmes of Xi Jinping and his Premier, Li Keqiang. They are influenced by the growing dissatisfaction and increasing incidence of popular protests, as well as the determination of the leaders to preserve the CCP's legitimacy and supremacy. The maintenance of social stability and ensuring "China's rise" are essential prerequisites.

(The article was published in the Institute of Peace and Conflict Studies, New Delhi, April 2013).

6

China's New Central Military Commission after the 18th Party Congress and its Implications

This is a crucial year for China, when large-scale changes at the top leadership echelons of the Chinese Communist Party (CCP) as well as the People's Liberation Army (PLA) will be approved at the 18th Party Congress scheduled to be held in Beijing in October 2012. The changes coincide with rising domestic discontent, inner-Party rivalries and increased turbulence in China's neighbourhood.

Both the CCP and PLA are in the midst of transformational change. The CCP's composition is changing as it dilutes purist principles, encourages the growth of private business, and admits wealthy individuals, businessmen and younger members. The PLA's requirements are similarly changing. In its advance towards becoming a professional technology-based military force, it is emphasising recruitment of better educated, technically qualified personnel and has established linkages with over 100 universities to qualitatively upgrade the calibre of officers and technical capabilities of its personnel. The changes coincide with the spread of pro-Mao nostalgia in the country and resentment against corruption. At least two PLA Generals of impeccable, prestigious "Revolutionary" lineage have spoken out strongly against corruption namely, Mao Xinyu, Mao Zedong's grandson who is a Major General in a PLA think tank and General Liu Yuan, former Chinese President Liu Shaoqi's son. The CCP and PLA have also both been buffeted by the recent factional infighting centring on the Bo Xilai affair. By July 2012, at least five central task force teams were conducting investigations in the jurisdiction of the 13th and 14th Group Armies associated with Bo Xilai. This could adversely blight the promotion prospects of some senior officers and has given prominence to the issue of the

PLA's loyalty to the Party. An article in the *Liberation Army Daily* (LAD) on June 17, 2012 for the first time seemed to imply there were "sub-loyalties" in the PLA. It said, "the problem of loyalty is of special importance in the year of the 18th Congress, when 'enemy forces' are spreading rumours, etc."

It then warns about "fake loyalty" and to be "aware of people just pretending to be loyal, who feign loyalty, but do not really mean it." Earlier, at the NPC session in March 2012, Premier Wen Jiabao had pointedly, and for the first time, declared, "we will run the armed forces with strict discipline." An official campaign was simultaneously launched against "depoliticising of the military, separating the Chinese Communist Party from the military, and nationalising the military." These fears are related directly to suggestions that the PLA should be an army of the State and not the CCP. Though initially voiced by the foreign media, the thought has been picked up by some Chinese intellectuals like the prominent and outspoken Chinese economist, Han Zhiguo, who has a following of over three and a half million on Sina Weibo. At a gathering in Beijing on January 18, 2012, he said that "reform had come to a dead end" and advocated, among other things, "nationalisation of the PLA."

Senior Party and PLA leaders apprehend that such sentiments could strike a chord with the better educated younger officers now joining the PLA. The sensitivity of the topic is evident in the summary dismissal on June 3, of Yu Chen, Editor of the Chinese newspaper *Southern Metropolitan*, for allowing a comment on the paper's official micro-blog mocking the CCP's insistence on retaining control over the PLA.

Almost a dozen instances of official media articles exhorting PLA personnel to be "absolutely loyal" to the Party and public expressions by PLA Generals of fealty to Hu Jintao have been recorded this year. It is in this backdrop that the CCP Central Committee (CC) will, at the upcoming 18th Party Congress this October, approve new appointments to China's all-powerful Central Military Commission (CMC). Political reliability will be the paramount requirement. The appointments will impact on the PLA's doctrine, policies and future direction. The Party Congress will usher in a new Central Military Commission (CMC), with seven of the current ten uniformed members retiring as they reach the mandated retirement age of 70 years. The two uniformed Vice Chairmen of the CMC who will retire are General Xu Caihou and General Guo Boxiong.

While China's Vice President Xi Jinping, ranked first among the present three CMC Vice Chairmen would, in the normal course, be expected to take over as CMC Chairman from Hu Jintao, this now seems unlikely. The unsettled domestic political situation emphasised by repeated exhortations by senior military officers and the official media urging the PLA to be "absolutely loyal" to the Party and rally "more closely" around "Chairman Hu Jintao," makes it probable that Hu Jintao will retain the position of Chairman of the Military Commission for at least another year.

Normally two of the three CMC members who do not retire will replace the two CMC Vice Chairmen who retire while the third should be appointed Defence Minister. Born in 1945, PLA Navy (PLAN) Commander Wu Shengli, assessed as favoured by Hu Jintao, is tipped to become a Vice Chairman. However, he is at the retirement age of 65 years and unless promoted retires in 2015. General Chang Wanquan, presently Director of the General Armaments Department (GAD) is another candidate for the position of CMC Vice Chairman and, given the importance attached to defence R&D and weapons indigenisation, he seems sure to be appointed. Third in seniority is PLA Air Force Commander Xu Qiliang, born in 1950, who is also assessed as a candidate for CMC Vice Chairman. In case Hu Jintao continues as CMC Chairman, however, Xu Qiliang's promotion could be deferred. Vice Chairmen of the CMC, incidentally, retire at 70 years while Military Region Commanders, with whom PLAAF and PLAN Commanders and heads of principal PLA departments are equated, retire at 65 years.

There is reliable indication that General Chen Bingde, who retires as PLA CGS, has recommended that the CMC undergo a symbolic generational change-over. He has proposed that only those born in 1949 or after, in other words those born in the People's Republic of China, be inducted into the CMC. In case this is accepted, then PLAN Commander Wu Shengli retires in 2015.

While Air Force General Ma Xiaotian (born in 1949) is widely considered a front-runner for the job of PLAAF Commander, a recent reliable input suggests otherwise. It asserts that Ma Xiaotian, presently a PLA Deputy Chief of General Staff (DCGS), a "princeling" closely connected to Hu Jintao and Xi Jinping and with a high-profile record of service, will be appointed Defence Minister and concurrently Vice Chairman of the CMC. If this materialises it will mean that the number of Vice Chairmen in the CMC will have been enhanced and Ma Xiaotian would have benefited from a double promotion. It would be the first time also that a PLAAF officer will officially interact on behalf of the PLA with foreign militaries and, more importantly, influence formulation of the defence budget. A consequence would be that Xu Qiliang, who is senior, gets elevated as CMC Vice Chairman giving the PLAAF an unprecedented three representatives in the CMC, unless Xu Qiliang is concurrently PLAAF Commander.

In case Ma Xiaotian is not appointed PLAAF Commander and Xu Qiliang is elevated as CMC Vice Chairman, then the Commandant of the Academy of Military Sciences and former PLAAF Deputy Commander, Air Force Lt. General Liu Chengjun (b.1949) is viewed as Xu Qiliang's successor.

General Liu Yuan (b.1951), son of China's former President Liu Shaoqi and friend of Xi Jinping, is currently Political Commissar of the PLA's General Logistics Department (GLD). He is a likely choice for CMC Vice Chairman to replace General Xu Caihou, who oversees political work in the PLA. Liu Shaoqi was, incidentally, Mao Zedong's key planner during the Sino-Indian conflict in 1962. General Liu Yuan commands prestige in the Party and PLA and has in recent months spoken out strongly against corruption in the PLA. But for him to be appointed CMC Vice Chairman would mean that he would also receive a double promotion. He has apparently been told, though, that he would be moving into the CMC and could end up being appointed Director of the PLA's General Political Department (GPD) and consequently a CMC member.

The other contender for the posts of CMC Vice Chairman as well as GPD Director is General Zhang Haiyang, presently Political Commissar of Second Artillery and also a "princeling." His chances might have been adversely affected because of his association with Bo Xilai, but his father, General Zhang Zhen, is alive and could try to intercede. He is also the son-in-law of Major General Sun Keji. Reports claim, however, that Zhang Haiyang has been implicated in a corruption scandal and might even face trial.

Another contender for the post of Director GPD is Vice Admiral Liu Xiaojiang (b. 1949), PLAN Political Commissar and former "mishu" to Admiral Liu Huaqing. His wife is the daughter of former popular Party General Secretary Hu Yaobang, who is respected by Hu Jintao and Premier Wen Jiabao. Liu Huaqing and Hu Yaobang were both opposed to Jiang Zemin. These connections give him a distinct edge in case he does not compete with General Liu Yuan.

New Commanders will be appointed to the People's Liberation Army Air Force (PLAAF), People's Liberation Army Navy (PLAN) and Second Artillery. The four principal departments of the PLA headquarters, namely, the General Staff Department (GSD)—whose head is the PLA Chief of General Staff (CGS) and equated with the head of the armed forces of other countries—General Political Department (GPD), General Armaments Department (GAD) and the General Logistics Department (GLD), will have new Directors. All are members of the CMC. Distinguishing the new CMC will be the increased representation of the PLAAF, and possibly even PLAN, in the CMC. Once the new PLAAF and PLAN Commanders are appointed, they will automatically assume their positions in the CMC. It was CMC Chairman Hu Jintao who, for the first time in 2004, appointed the PLAAF and PLAN Commanders as members of the CMC. Their predecessors, if still in service as in the case of the PLAAF, would have been elevated as Vice Chairmen of the CMC. Hu Jintao also introduced changes in the structure of the GSD to include officers from the PLAAF and PLAN at senior levels.

Selections for the posts of Commanders of the PLAAF, PLAN and Second Artillery as also the four General Departments of the PLA are normally from a pool of approximately 37 senior officers deployed in the 7 MRs, 7 MRAFs, 3 PLAN Fleets, and the Deputies in the PLA HQ General Departments. This number has increased, however, since Hu Jintao took over as CMC Chairman and began promoting officers to higher grade posts without waiting for them to get the corresponding Military rank. Additionally, if Political Commissars are counted, then the numbers increase. With the current emphasis on intensified ideological and political education and enhanced political control over the PLA, however, Political Commissars will be considered for higher rank and increased authority, but not be given operational command. In the running for the post of PLA CGS to replace General Chen Bingde is Commander of the Shenyang Military Region, General Zhang Youxia (b.1950), a "princeling" who was promoted full General in July 2011. He is one of the few Generals with battle experience, having participated in the Sino-Vietnam war. He initially adopted a tough line against the Philippines in the recent dispute over Scarborough Reef. He is reputedly close to Xi Jinping. Another contender is General Fang Fenghui (b.1951) who, as Commander of the sensitive Beijing Military Region, is trusted by Hu Jintao. He is a technocrat with command experience, including in the digitalised battlefield. General Li Shiming (b. 1948), Commander of the Chengdu Military Region and exercising operational jurisdiction over Tibet and the areas across the border with India, is also in the reckoning. He was appointed full General by Hu Jintao in 2010. All contenders are members of the 17th CCP CC. Vice Admiral Sun Jianguo (b.1952), Deputy CGS and former "mishu" to General Chen Bingde and Chief of Staff of PLAN (2004-6), is a leading candidate for the post of PLAN Commander. He is a nuclear submariner. These changes, however, will not mean a reduction in the primacy of the PLA ground forces, or PLAA as they are designated since China's Defence White Paper, 2010. Of the 57 senior General Officers in the PLA, for example, 37 are from the PLAA. In the Military Regions (MR) also, it is the Military Region Commander who heads the command and the head of the PLAAF Military Region Air Force, for example, is designated a Deputy MR Commander. The PLAA which has considerably larger manpower also receives a larger proportion of the budget in real terms.

These changes in the CMC will have implications for India and China's other neighbours as the new appointees would redefine China's military doctrine, strategy and the PLA's role in safeguarding national and territorial interests. The induction of additional representatives from the PLAAF and PLAN in the highest military body will mean greater emphasis on coordinated planning and conduct of Integrated Joint Operations (IJO). This will be reinforced by the composition of the CMC which will, for the first time, be weighed heavily in favour of undoubtedly politically reliable yet professional officers with operational backgrounds.

Those tipped as the new PLAAF and PLAN Commanders have operational credentials. The South China Sea Fleet is being equipped for a large operational role spanning the South China Sea, the Malacca Strait and the Indian Ocean. The first China-built aircraft carrier will be incorporated in this fleet. The presence of two senior PLAAF officers in the CMC guarantees that the PLAAF will receive adequate funds to pursue its modernisation programme. It is assessed that ten per cent of the defence budget will be spent on aircraft procurement and R&D. PLAN representation in the CMC will ensure continued allocation of a larger percentage of the defence budget for PLAN, and the Navy's modernisation programme will proceed apace. PLAN and PLAAF are both expected to assume a more operationally assertive posture. Meanwhile, the new PLA Chief of General Staff (CGS) will certainly have an operational background which would mean increased attention at high levels to the Sino-Indian border and China's other unsettled frontiers. Finally, of the sixteen identified "princelings" in the PLA's senior echelons, for the first time there will be three, or even four, in the CMC. Like in the CCP, they will influence national strategic policy giving it a harder inflexible edge and, additionally, be Xi Jinping's core supporters. As in the CCP's highest bodies, officers appointed to the CMC will belong to the "Cultural Revolution Generation" and likely to have a tougher, more nationalistic mindset. Overall, the PLA's political clout and representation in the Party is likely to remain unchanged with two seats in the PB while in the CC they will probably continue to retain 24 seats.

(The article was published in Centre for Air Power Studies, New Delhi, July 26, 2012).

7

Chinese Communist Party, Army and Eighteenth Central Committee

China's veteran communist leadership has traditionally had close ties with the People's Liberation Army (PLA) and ensured that they retain a tight grip over it. The role and importance of the PLA in communist China has grown steadily in importance over the years and its importance for the Chinese Communist Party (CCP) was brought into sharp focus during the Tiananmen "incident" in 1989. As veteran cadres, most of whom had gained their initial experience and grown while in the communist Armies, began disappearing from the scene the need was felt for tightening the CCP's control and grip over the PLA. This became more pronounced as Party apparatchiks with little or no experience of service in the PLA began entering the Party's top echelons. The present-day statements of senior Chinese Communist Party (CCP) leaders, that the "Party must firmly control the gun," reinforce their view of the need for enhanced political control over the PLA.

Deng Xiaoping's far-sighted move of establishing a Central Military Commission (CMC) under the Chairmanship of the General Secretary of the Chinese Communist Party (CCP) was with the objective of strengthening Party control over the PLA. The arrangement by which the prospective Party Chief was positioned as Vice Chairman of the CMC, so that he gains influence and establishes his authority before taking over as General Secretary of the CCP Central Committee (CC), usually five years later, effectively placed the PLA subordinate to the Party.

CCP CC General Secretaries Jiang Zemin and Hu Jintao both focused on the PLA, but Hu Jintao especially extended political control and expanded the CCP and Communist Youth League's (CYL) presence in the PLA. There are presently at least 90,000 cells of the CCP, comprising five members each, in the PLA. Political Commissars in the PLA have simultaneously been given an enhanced role and authority and their inputs now impact significantly on the career prospects of the PLA's operational officers. Political Commissars are now given training specific to the new kind of wars anticipated and their exposure to the different services and military regions/commands have been made more expansive.

The CCP and PLA leadership has identified, with concern, new vulnerabilities in the PLA. As greater numbers of better educated personnel and college graduates join the PLA, their potential susceptibility to "hostile" foreign propaganda is considered to be greater. This "hostile" foreign propaganda, which was troublingly noticed to have been articulated in the run-up to the recently-concluded 18th Party Congress by some of the more "liberal" Chinese economists calling for political reform, argues that the PLA should be an army of the State and not subservient to the CCP. The issue of factional "sub-loyalties" in the PLA was also, significantly, raised for the first time in a *Liberation Army Daily* (LAD) article published on June 17, 2012. Prompted by these considerations the Party and CMC jointly launched three successive year-long "political education" campaigns in the PLA to counter this propaganda. The latest such campaign was launched this year. The growing popular discontent, combined with the political fallout following the ouster of former Politburo member Bo Xilai including his efforts to make inroads into the PLA, has added to the Party leadership's concern. A Xinhua dispatch, which reported that the PLA had finalised selection of its 251 Delegates to the 18th Party Congress (November 8-14, 2012), specifically mentioned that their political records were free of blemish. The high number of Political Commissars in the list of Delegates reflected the importance of the Party's representatives in the PLA.

Within days of taking over as CMC Chairman, Xi Jinping signalled his intention of continuing this trend. At an enlarged meeting of the CMC on November 16, 2012, he stressed that "we must unswervingly adhere to the Party's absolute leadership over the armed forces" and ensure that the "Party has a firm grip over the troops ideologically, politically, and organisationally." He called for "... serious political discipline and organisational discipline."

PLA representatives have representation in the CCP's CC and Politburo (PB), thereby reinforcing the Party's control over the PLA since the PLA officers also have a ranking in the Party hierarchy. Over the past few years, the PLA has had two representatives in the PB, and PLA representatives account for between 18 and 20 per cent of the total CC membership. This has remained unchanged at the 18th Party Congress, indicating that there has been no visible gain in the PLA's political influence. Analysis of the PLA officers "elected" to the 18th CC reveals interesting data.

The number of PLA representatives in the PB remains at two and these are the two Vice Chairmen of the CMC, Xu Qiliang and Fan Changlong. Excluding these two Vice Chairmen, there are a total of 65 officers representing the PLA and People's Armed Police Force (PAPF) who are Full and Alternate Members of the CC. Of the total PLA/PAPF strength in the 18th CC, 41 are Full Members and 26 are Alternate Members.

All members of the Central Military Commission are CC members while the two Vice Chairmen, Xu Qiliang and Fan Changlong are members of the PB. Of them, Xu Qiliang is the former Commander of the PLA Air Force (PLAAF) and represents, for the first time ever, the PLAAF at the level of CMC Vice Chairman. The former Director of the GAD, Chang Wanquan, who has been retained as a Member of the CMC, is also a member of the CC, reinforcing reports that he is likely to take over in March 2013 as China's next Defence Minister. Commanders of all Military Regions, except Chengdu, are Full Members of the 18th CC. Similarly, the Political Commissars of all seven Military Regions, except the Lanzhou Military Region, are Full CC members. Non-inclusion of these two individuals could be indicative of their imminent retirement. Interestingly, the Commanders of the Tibet and Xinjiang Military Districts are both Full Members of the 18th CC. The parity maintained between the Commanders of Military Regions and their Political Commissars, with the inclusion of both as Full members of the 18th CC, is reflective of the Party's political control over the PLA/PAPF. The inclusion of 24 Political Commissars as members of the CC—18 as Full Members and 6 as Alternate Members—underscores their important role.

The 18th Party Congress appears to have made a determined effort to elect new representatives from the PLA to the CC. Of the 41 Full Members of the CC, 26 have been elected for the first time. The advent of first-timers is, however, most noticeable among the Alternate Members of the CC. Of the 26 Alternate Members, 23 have been identified as newcomers. Eleven of the Full CC members are below 50 years of age while the rest are mainly in their early 60s. A larger number of the Alternate CC Members are in their mid-50s, except for the present Chiefs of Staff of 2nd Artillery and the Nanjing MR and President of the NDU who are younger. In view of their numerical superiority, the PLA ground forces have the majority representation. There are 9 representatives of the PLA Air Force (PLAAF) and 5 of the PLA Navy (PLAN). Seven "princelings" have been identified among the 67 CC Members. None of the PLA's CC members, Full or Alternate, has been identified as belonging to an ethnic minority nationality and there is only one female among them. At least 8 of those inducted as Alternate Members of the CC clearly appear destined for long tenures or higher office.

Appendix

List of PLA/PAPF Members of the 18th Central Committee

(41 Full Members; 26 Alternate Members)

(* denotes First-Time as Full or Alternate Member; (xx) Age as in 2012)

Full Members of 18th CC

1. Xu Qiliang (62), PLAAF, Vice Chairman, CMC
2. Fan Changlong (65), Vice Chairman, CMC
3. Chang Wanquan (63), former Director, GAD and likely Defence Minister
4. Fang Fenghui (61), Director, GSD
5. *Wang Guangzhong (59), Deputy Director, GSD
6. *Sun Jianguo (60), Deputy Director, GSD
7. *Qi Jianguo (60), Deputy Director, GSD
8. Zhang Yang (61), Director, GPD
9. *Jia Tingan (60), Deputy Director, GPD
10. *Du Jincai (60), Deputy Director, GPD & PLA Secretary for Discipline Inspection
11. *Wu Changde (60), Deputy Director, GPD

12. Zhao Keshi (65), Director, GLD
13. Liu Yuan (61), Political Commissar, GLD
14. Zhang Youxia (62), Director, GLD
15. *Wang Hongyao (61), Political Commissar, GLD
16. Ma Xiaotian (63), Commander, PLAAF
17. Tian Xiusi (62), Political Commissar, PLAAF
18. Wu Shengli (67), Commander, PLAN
19. Liu Xiaojiang (63), Political Commissar, PLAN
20. *Wei Fenghe (58), Commander, 2nd Artillery
21. Zhang Haiyang (63), Political Commissar, 2nd Artillery
22. *Liu Yazhou (60), Political Commissar, NDU
23. Liu Chengjun (62), President, AMS
24. *Sun Sijing (61), Political Commissar, AMS
25. *Wang Jiaocheng (60), Commander Shenyang MR
26. *Chu Yimin (59), Political Commissar, Shenyang MR
27. *Zhang Shibo (60), Commander, Beijing MR
28. *Liu Fulian (59), Political Commissar, Beijing MR
29. *Cai Yingting (58), Commander, Nanjing MR
30. *Zhang Weiping (57), Political Commissar, Nanjing MR
31. *Xu Fenlin (59), Commander, Guangzhou MR
32. *Wei Liang (59), Political Commissar, Guangzhou MR
33. *Zhu Fuxi (57), Political Commissar, Chengdu MR
34. *Liu Yuejun (58), Commander, Lanzhou MR
35. *Zhao Zongqi (57), Commander, Jinan MR
36. *Du Hengyan (61), Political Commissar, Jinan MR
37. *Tian Zhong (56), Commander, North Sea Fleet
38. *Yang Jinshan (58), Commander, Tibet Military District
39. *Peng Yong (58), Commander, Xinjiang Military District
40. Wang Jianping (59), Commander, PAPF
41. *Xu Yaoyuan (60), Political Commissar, PAPF

Alternate Members of 18th CC

1. *Yin Fanlong (59), Deputy Director, GPD
2. *Qin Yinhe (61), Deputy Director, GLD
3. *Liu Sheng (56), Deputy Director, GAD

4. *Niu Hongguang(61), Deputy Director, GAD
5. *Gao Jin (53), Chief of Staff, 2nd Artillery
6. *Dr. Yang Xuejun (49), President, NDU
7. *Gao Jianguo (58), Director Political Department, Shenyang MR
8. *Wang Ning (57), Chief of Staff, Beijing MR
9. *Yang Hui (49), Chief of Staff, Nanjing MR
10. *Wu Changhai (58), Director Political Department, Nanjing MR
11. *Yi Xiaoguang (54), Deputy Commander, Nanjing MR & Commander, Nanjing MR AF
12. *Zhang Jianping (56), Deputy Commander, Guangzhou MR & Commander, Guangzhou MR AF
13. Ai Husheng (61), Deputy Commander, Chengdu MR
14. *Fan Chengui (57), Director Political Department, Lanzhou MR
15. *Zheng Qunliang (58), Deputy Commander, Jinan MR & Commander, Jinan MR AF
16. *Wang Jun (59), Deputy Commander, Jinan MR
17. Wang Jian (58), Deputy Political Commissar, Jinan MR
18. *Niu Zhizhong (57), Head of Logistics, PAPF
19. *Zhang Ruiqing (57), Political Commissar, Beijing Municipal PAPF
20. *Pan Liangshi (55), Commander, 39 Gp Army under Shenyang MR
21. *Jiang Weilie (57), Commander, South Sea Fleet
22. Dr. Ms. Chen Zuoning (55), Master Engineer, PLA General Logistics No. 56 Research Institute
23. *Prof Ma Weiming (52), Naval Engineering University
24. *Xu Linping (55), Commander 38 Gp Army under Beijing MR based in Baoding
25. *Dr. He Fuchu (50), President, Military Medical Science Academy
26. *Cao Qing (60), Head, Central Security Bureau under CCP CC General Office (former Security Chief of Marshal Ye Jianying)

(The article was published in Institute of Peace and Conflict Studies, New Delhi, December 2012).

8

Impact of Leadership Changes in China on Security and Defence Fields in the Country

The disturbed domestic security environment provided the backdrop to China's 18th Party Congress held from November 8 to 14, 2012. It included the widespread popular dissatisfaction caused by the publicised high incidence of corruption, growing income inequality, worker lay-offs, rising prices, etc. This has persisted over the past couple of years. The pervasiveness of this dissatisfaction, in fact, prompted China's largest and Government think tank, the Chinese Academy of Social Sciences (CASS), to warn last year that the people are losing confidence in the government and that they view cadres as being in league with real estate businessmen. This popular dissatisfaction manifested itself in a spate of mass protests that totalled 180,000 in 2011 and, according to confidential estimates, could increase at between 8 and 12 per cent annually.

The serious concern this is causing the Chinese leadership was reflected in the higher budgetary allocations for two successive years for domestic security. Significantly, the budgets for domestic security for the last two years (US$ 111 billion in 2012 for domestic security and US$ 106.4 billion for national defence) have been higher than the national defence budgets for the first time ever! The budgets for 2013 will be announced at the National People's Congress (NPC) session scheduled to be held in early March 2013. Linked to this popular dissatisfaction is another worrying feature for China's leadership and this is the apparently ebbing confidence of Chinese in their country and government. Contents of a recent report of the Party's anti-corruption watchdog body, the Central Discipline Inspection Commission (CDIC) now headed by Politburo Standing Committee (PBSC) member Wang Qishan, were recently commented upon by the independent mainland

Chinese weekly *Economic Observer*. It claimed that US$ 1 trillion, equivalent to 40 per cent of Britain's annual gross domestic product, had been smuggled out of China illegally in 2012. While this figure is disputed by analysts, they nonetheless describe the flow of money as dramatic. Beijing University Professor Li Chengyan suggested that about 10,000 officials had absconded from China with as much as US$ 100 billion. The CDIC disclosed that 1,100 government officials had fled China during last year's national holidays in October and that 714 had been successful in getting completely away.

Separately, China's International Emigration Report (2012), as publicised by China's official news agency Xinhua in January 2013, revealed that in China 27% of business owners with personal assets of more than 1 billion yuan (US$ 160 million) have emigrated while 47% are considering emigration. It added that in the past three years at least 17 billion yuan (US$ 2.7 billion) of capital has flown abroad.

The political disruption caused by the now ousted Politburo member of impeccable "Red lineage," Bo Xilai, is another major event that has impacted on the CCP and personnel selection at its highest echelons. The Bo Xilai incident shook and stunned the CCP and prompted its leadership to scrutinise the political reliability and loyalty of cadres and take steps to ensure that they operate within the strict bounds of Party discipline. The manner in which Wang Lijun, Chief of the Public Security Bureau of the centrally-administered Chongqing Municipality, easily gained access to the US Consulate in Chengdu in his failed bid to defect to the US, rang alarm bells in Beijing especially as it showed that a member of the Party's nomenklatura of the rank of a central Vice Minister was susceptible to the blandishments of a foreign intelligence organisation. The inference that he was in regular touch with US "diplomats" is unmistakable.

The Party's reaction to these developments was clearly reflected in the selection of Delegates to the 18th Party Congress and selection of members to the 18th Central Committee (CC), 25-member Politburo (PB) and the reduced 7-member Politburo Standing Committee (PBSC). The declared emphasis was on the loyalty and political reliability of cadres. There is not one member of China's ethnic minority nationalities in the PB or PBSC. With specific reference to the Tibetans, they appear to have been particularly affected with not a single Tibetan among the PLA's 251 Delegates to the 18th Congress and neither a single representative among the PLA's contingent of officials included in the 18th Central Committee. Only one Tibetan figured among full members of the 18th CC.

Special attention was focused on the country's public security apparatus. In the wake of central investigations revealing that Bo Xilai had successfully penetrated the public security apparatus and acquired influence, approximately 3,000 public security cadres were summoned to Beijing for "political re-education" in the immediate aftermath of the Bo Xilai incident. Again prior to convening of the 18th Party Congress, 1,400 county-level public security chiefs were imparted "special" training. The susceptibility of the country's public security apparatus to penetration was highlighted also in the case involving the escape to the US Embassy in Beijing of the blind dissident activist Chen Guangchen. Public security personnel deployed to guard the blind dissident activist's residence were officially acknowledged as complicit in his escape.

The importance attached to domestic security has heightened in recent years as Beijing has assessed that the international environment surrounding China is becoming adverse. The thinking of senior echelon Chinese Communist Party cadres is reflected in an article authored last year by Zeng Shengquan, Director of Sichuan's Provincial Public Security Department. He wrote in Gong'an Yanjiu that: "hostile foreign and domestic forces manipulate, incite speculation about, and directly provoke contradictions within our people in increasingly prominent ways. Their methods fall into three main categories:

"Taking advantage of our instabilities to stir up trouble. The economic transition and social transformation that have accompanied our country's reform and development have brought about a profound adjustment of the pattern of interests and, objectively speaking, have provided the conditions for hostile elements to meddle. They seize on some controversial and sensitive domestic issue, 'rights protection' incident, or judicial case and openly meddle, wantonly speculate, and attempt to instigate the ignorant against the party and the state, damaging our excellent situation of prosperity and stability. This approach is quite insidious and concealed, and public security organs must be highly vigilant."

"Meddling in our mass incidents to intensify contradictions. This specific stage of our country's economic and social development exhibits a wide range of social contradictions and major disputes; if these are improperly handled, they can easily lead to mass incidents. Hostile forces do everything in their power to meddle in our country's internal mass incidents in a vain attempt to exacerbate the situation, scale, destruction, and impact; the incidents in Guizhou's Weng'an County and Yunnan's Menglian County are typical examples. This approach is bound to aggravate the antagonism of these contradictions and the seriousness of the resulting consequences. Public security organs must guard against this."

"Seeking every opportunity to directly create chaos. An increasingly powerful China creates great uneasiness for the hostile forces both inside and outside its borders. They directly rouse their domestic forces into action and take advantage of the portion of the masses that do not know the truth; increasingly common incidents of vandalism, arson, and other destructive activities."

Complicating these concerns was the apparent sympathy of PBSC member and the country's Security Czar, Zhou Yongkang, for Bo Xilai. There additionally appeared to have been some laxity in supervision over the extent of Zhou Yongkang's powers. The visible fallout of this has been the downgrading of the position of Chairman of the Party's apex security apparatus—the Central Politics and Law Commission—from that of a PBSC member to a PB member. With the retirement of Zhou Yongkang at the 18th Party Congress, the Minister of Public Security, Meng Jianzhu was elevated to the PB and appointed Chairman of the Central Politics and Law Commission. Meng Jianzhu had, incidentally, worked in close coordination with Liu Yunshan, then Director of the Party's Propaganda Department and now a PBSC member. The downgrading of the position of Chairman of the Central Politics and Law Commission to that of a PB member implies that Meng Jianzhu will henceforth report directly to CCP CC General Secretary Xi Jinping, who will thus exercise tighter control over the security and intelligence apparatus.

The appointment earlier in February of former Guangxi Communist Party Secretary, 1954-born Guo Shengkun as Minister of Public Security, also hints at further dilution of the authority of the Minister of Public Security and possible enhancement of the Party Chief's authority and control over the security apparatus. Meanwhile, there are credible reports that as part of a government restructuring the Ministry of State Security is being relegated to the Departments directly under the State Council and is likely to be renamed the National Security Bureau. The proposal for restructuring and reduction of over 27 government departments down to 18 is likely to be considered at the NPC session this March.

While Guo Shengkun would have had experience of supervising public security work in the Guangxi-Zhuang Automonous Region, he lacks direct experience of security work and knowledge of law. Guo Shengkun, a Han and native of Jiangxi province, joined the CCP in 1974. He is a graduate from the Jiangxi Institute of Metallurgy, a Professor of Engineering and a PhD in Management. His background has been in State-owned Enterprises (SoE) and, during an interview in 2010, he described himself as a politician with a background in business. He also said that "the government should seek to maximise the interests of the public, which are based on the principles of equity and justice." The latter sentiment could position him to guide the proposal for abolition of the 350 "reform-through-labour" camps, which have been functional in China since 1957, through the NPC this March. Opinion about his appointment is divided though. Professor Zhu Lijia, of the Chinese Academy of Governance in Beijing, said Guo's previous role as Guangxi's party chief would also have given him some familiarity with such matters, while Professor Hu Xingdou, a Beijing-based commentator, said a public security minister should have the legal knowledge to ensure the security system was run properly, and he was not sure that Guo had it.

The new leadership installed at the 18th Party Congress will continue the policies of its predecessor with increased emphasis on security and propaganda.

PLA

There is greater continuity in leadership and doctrine of the PLA, but the new Chairman of the Central Military Commission (CMC), Xi Jinping, has already indicated that political reliability will be an area of increased emphasis.

Appointments to key military posts were announced on October 25 and later on November 6, in both cases before even commencement of the 18th Party Congress on November 8 in Beijing, thus signalling that competing interest groups in the Chinese Communist Party's (CCP) highest echelons had reached agreement on major personnel issues with regard to the PLA. It additionally conveyed that the matter relating to ousted Politburo member and "princeling," Bo Xilai, had basically been settled. Xi Jinping's emphasis on the political reliability of PLA officers, however, reveals that suspicions continue to linger in the aftermath of the Bo Xilai episode. Bo Xilai has since been stripped of Party membership and currently awaits trial with reports stating that his mother-in-law, Fan Chengxiu, has hired a couple of lawyers to fight his case.

The announcements implied too, that ongoing investigations of People's Liberation Army (PLA) personnel had been completed. Earlier this August while releasing the list of 251 PLA Delegates to the 18th Party Congress, it was specifically stated that all Delegates had a blemish-free political record. This assertion hinted that while those closely associated with Bo Xilai, like Generals Liu Yuan and Zhang Haiyang, might not be promoted they would probably neither be punished. The failure to promote General Liu Yuan, who is the son of former Chinese President Liu Shaoqi and is close to Xi Jinping, is significant and indicates that lineage has failed to provide immunity. Interestingly, although a PLA Delegate to the Party Congress, General Liu Yuan failed to attend the opening ceremony of the 18th Party Congress in Beijing on November 8, though he appeared later. Generals Liu Yuan and Zhang Haiyang are both, incidentally, members of the 18th CC.

The unusually early announcement of key appointments was also clear indication of Hu Jintao being firmly in charge of the PLA and signalled that his influence will continue. It reinforces the assessment that Hu Jintao and Xi Jinping had worked in close coordination over the past few years.

In addition to the entire top echelon of the PLA, appointments to the crucial Military Commission's Secretariat, which continues to be an entirely civilian body, were additionally effected. Xi Jinping would have been consulted and concurred in all these appointments, especially as all but two of the newly appointed senior officers will serve coterminus with him. Doubts about how close the coordination was between Hu Jintao and Xi Jinping would have been removed when, in December 2012, Xi Jinping appointed Chen Shiju as Head of the CMC General Office. Chen Shiju, a civilian, was the Head of Hu Jintao's office. Hu Jintao's decision to relinquish the post of Chairman of the

Central Military Commission (CMC) should be viewed in this backdrop, as also in the context of reports emanating from Beijing at least since July 2012, that he had indicated his preference to step down from all posts.

According to an unusual disclosure on November 18, 2012, by the authoritative *Global Times*, a subsidiary of the official Party mouthpiece *People's Daily*, the handover of the post of Chairman of the Military Commission was completed only on November 15, at an enlarged meeting of Central Military Commission. The *Global Times* article, again unprecedentedly, heaped fulsome praise on Hu Jintao for voluntarily stepping down and setting a "healthy," new precedent. In confirmation of earlier indications that Hu Jintao and his designated successor were working closely together, China's new supremo, Xi Jinping, declared: "Chairman Hu's important decision fully embodies his profound thinking of the overall development of the Party, country and military. The decision also embodies his exemplary conduct and nobility of character." He pointedly added that Hu Jintao "has pushed China's military development one giant step forward based on achievements made under the leadership of Chairman Mao Zedong, Chairman Deng Xiaoping and Chairman Jiang Zemin." Hu Jintao, in turn, asserted that Xi Jinping was qualified and ready to lead the People's Liberation Army (PLA).

Xi Jinping, at the same meeting, took visible charge and laid down his criteria—visible also in the new appointments—for the PLA. He effectively set at rest the debate about "more Red than Expert" by declaring that: "The military must promote and appoint cadres based on their political performance and guarantee that 'guns' are always controlled by reliable people with loyalty to the Party." He ordered the military to "always put the country's sovereignty and security first, comprehensively improve the military's deterrent power and capability of real combat to protect China's sovereignty, security and development interests at an information-based age." Allegations of rampant corruption in the PLA found resonance when Xi Jinping pledged to enhance the anti-corruption effort within the armed forces and called on senior military officers to take the lead in obeying rules and regulations for self-discipline.

The main features of China's new Military leadership are clearly: the professional background of all the Members and both Vice Chairmen of the Military Commission; the increased number of "princelings," or members of the "Red Nobility" led by the Chairman of the Military Commission Xi Jinping; and the implicit emphasis on Integrated Joint Operations (IJO), especially an enhanced operational role for the People's Liberation Army (PLA) Air Force (PLAAF).

Additionally, the PLAAF for the first time ever has two representatives in the Military Commission—CMC Vice Chairman Xu Qiliang and PLAAF Commander and concurrent Military Commission Member General Ma Xiaotian. The PLA's representation in the CCP Central Committee's (CC) Politburo (PB) remains unchanged at 2, with the presence of General Xu Qiliang and General Fan Changlong. The presence of Xu Qiliang, however, ensures an additional voice for the PLAAF in the Party's second highest body. This can be expected to ensure a more prominent role for the PLAAF, including in IJOs, and enhanced funding. All other members of the CMC are members of the 18th CC.

Almost as if on cue, the official English-language *China Daily* reported on November 15, 2012, that China has a long-term plan until 2030 to develop advanced aviation engines. US$ 1.6 billion has been earmarked for the first phase to fund research and development of engines till 2015. An AVICS official said, "During the first phase, which will conclude by the end of 2015 if everything goes well, we will strive to ensure our air force's aircraft be equipped with proper engines and to lift our development capability to that of the developed countries' level in the 1980s." In the second phase China will substantially narrow the technological gap between it and the developed countries and that in the "near future all of the PLA air force's third-generation aircraft use domestically developed engines." "Our ultimate goal is to guarantee that China can develop its own aviation industry without being disrupted or contained by anyone else."

The PLA has in recent years been trying to upgrade its doctrine, tactics and armaments as also indigenous research and development of weaponry. Emphasis has been given to Integrated Joint Operations (IJO) and transportation of battle-ready armed and fully equipped troops across long distances. There has been repeated mention of the need to prepare for a short "local war" under "conditions of informationsation" using overwhelming firepower. This was reiterated in Hu Jintao's Work Report to the 18th Party Congress. Similarly, the South China Sea will remain an area of active concern where China will continue to establish its dominance. This too found mention in Hu Jintao's Work Report when he, for the first time in a Work Report, emphasised that China would be a maritime power. The recent appointments reveal that China's new military leadership will focus on both these crucial areas.

The appointment as Vice Chairman of the Central Military Commission (CMC) of the former Commander of the People's Liberation Army Air Force (PLAAF), Xu Qiliang, was announced on November 6, 2012. A professional aviator and advocate of robust modernisation of the PLAAF, Xu Qiliang was born in March 1950. With his appointment the PLAAF now for the first time ever has two representatives in China's highest military body. Xu Qiliang is a "princeling" and is loyal to Hu Jintao.

The other new Vice Chairman of the CMC is General Fan Changlong, till now Commander of the Jinan Military Region (MR). He is the oldest PLA officer to be appointed to the Military Commission and should normally be tipped to retire at the next Congress in 2017.

General Fang Fenghui, who was born in 1951, has been appointed Director of the PLA's General Staff Department (GSD), a post loosely equated with that of Army Chief. A graduate of China's elite National Defence University (NDU), he is reputed to be a technocrat with command experience including in the digitalised battlefield. More importantly, when Fang Fenghui was appointed Military Region Commander in 2007, he was the youngest officer in the PLA to hold that rank. In a sign of the trust that Hu Jintao reposed in him, Fang Fenghui was the beneficiary of a double promotion when he was appointed Commander of the sensitive Beijing Military Region.

General Fang Fenghui exemplifies the new generation of professionally savvy officers. Apart from his command-and-control skills, he is a much-published author on military strategy, particularly in the areas of computer-aided war games and the synchronisation of different branches of the military forces. One of his favourite mottos is that "radically changing times demand innovation in strategic theories." Hu Jintao was said to be very impressed with Fang Fenghui's orchestration of the 2009 military parade in Beijing, which marked the 60th anniversary of the People's Republic of China's (PRC) founding. Last year, Fang Fenghui won praise when he supervised complicated large-scale manoeuvres involving more than 30,000 soldiers from the Beijing, Lanzhou and Chengdu MRs.

The appointment of General Zhang Youxia, born in July 1950, as Director of the General Armaments Department (GAD), is another that points to an officer's professional background being a factor in his selection for higher office. Long a proponent of modernisation of the PLA's weaponry, Zhang Youxia has now been empowered to implement suitable policies. In 2009, General Zhang Youxia was quoted in the Party newspaper *"People's Daily"* as saying: "The fires of war are burning throughout the world. In this area the gap between the Chinese military and foreign militaries is growing day by day. This is a real problem." As GAD Director, General Zhang Youxia will now supervise overseas procurement and armaments research.

He is also the only officer in the Central Military Commission with combat experience. He participated in the Laoshan battles of the 1979 Sino-Vietnam border war as Commander of the 119 Regt, 40th Division, when he was wounded. General Zhang Youxia is the son of General Zhang Zongxun, regarded as one of the "Ten Anti-Japan Generals" of the CCP and a "princeling." He is loyal to Hu Jintao, but also close to Xi Jinping.

Born in 1947, General Zhao Keshi, the new Director of the General Logistics Department (GLD), owes his promotion to Hu Jintao. The oldest among the Generals appointed to the top posts recently, General Zhao Keshi was also only a Chief of Staff when he was picked by Hu Jintao in 2007, and appointed Commander of the Nanjing Military Region, thereby benefiting from a double promotion.

Born in 1951, General Zhang Yang, the new Director of the powerful General Political Department (GPD) was apparently appointed at Hu Jintao's behest. He was earlier Political Commissar of the Guangzhou Military Region. Zhang Yang was an old "partner" of Fang Fenghui in the Guangzhou Military Region. When Fang Fenghui served as the Chief of Staff in Guangzhou from 2003 to 2007, Zhang Yang was Director of the Military Region's Political Affairs Department from 2004 to 2007. His appointment as Director of the powerful GPD increases General Fang Fenghui's authority in the PLA and is in line with the criteria spelt out recently by Xi Jinping for evaluating PLA officers.

Born into a military family in August 1949, General Ma Xiaotian, the new PLAAF Commander, joined the PLA in 1965 and the CCP in 1969. Reputedly a flamboyant and proficient fighter pilot, Ma Xiaotian did very well in his course at the NDU. He has been a member of the 16th and 17th CCs. Known to be an outspoken officer with hawkish views on China's territorial disputes in the East and South China seas, he has handled the Intelligence and Foreign Affairs portfolios of the PLA as Deputy Chief of PLA General Staff for 5 years. He has experience of Tibet while in the Lanzhou MR. He succeeded Xu Qiliang as the PLA's Deputy Chief of General Staff in 2007 when Xu Qiliang was made Commander of the PLAAF and has now again inherited Xu Qiliang's post.

In May 2012, when China and the Philippines were locked in a stand-off over the South China Sea's Scarborough Shoal, Ma Xiaotian told the Hong Kong-based Phoenix TV, "the South China Sea issue is none of the United States' business; it's just [territorial] disputes between China and its neighbouring countries." He added that "the PLA is able to protect China's maritime territories," but "at the moment China is not preparing to resort to military means—that would be the very last option."

At the annual Shangri-La Dialogue in 2010, Ma Xiaotian told US Pacific Commander, Admiral Robert Willard, that China would not accept any surveillance by US ships and planes in the South and East China seas, and that Washington's arms sales to Taiwan were "creating obstacles" for Sino-US military-to-military exchanges. He reiterated concerns about Cold-War era alliances and called for more equal, trusting relationships.

Most predictable was the direct elevation of 1954-born General Wei Fenghe as Commander of the Second Artillery, or China's strategic missile force. Wei Fenghe served as chief of staff of the Second Artillery from 2006 to 2010 and was involved in the intercontinental ballistic missile testing in 1989. He is a professional soldier and has spent his entire career with the Second Artillery. He joined the PLA and CCP in 1970 and was an alternate member of the 17th CC.

Admiral Wu Shengli, PLA Navy (PLAN) Commander born in August 1945, lost out in the latest round of promotions, but has been retained as PLAN Commander. Wu Shengli is the son of Wu Xian, a former Vice Governor of Zhejiang Province, and a "princeling." Wu Shengli finally did not make the cut despite his proximity to Hu Jintao, and there is a possibility a new PLAN Commander could be appointed by 2014.

Finally, General Chang Wanquan continues to be officially listed as a Member of the Military Commission indicating that he will probably be China's new Defence Minister.

The South China Sea will be an area of active interest for China's new leadership and its military. This is clear from the pronouncements of at least two of the recently appointed top officials. General Zhang Youxia, in the initial stages itself adopted a tough line against the Philippines in the dispute over Scarborough Reef. Similarly, the new PLA Air Force (PLAAF) Commander General Ma Xiaotian, has made unequivocal pronouncements on the subject. Interestingly, both Zhang Youxia and Ma Xiaotian are "princelings." Xi Jinping and Xu Qiliang are the other two "princelings" in the CMC. While reports suggest that Xi Jinping had not been attending meetings of the newly constituted "Office to Respond to the Diaoyu Crisis" since his appointment as CCP CC General Secretary, there is credible reporting to indicate that steps being taken now to counter Japan had been enumerated by this Office earlier.

Military modernisation will remain fast-paced with special attention to development of high-tech indigenous Defence R&D, "informationisation," the PLAAF, PLAN and Second Artillery. Xi Jinping has paid constant attention to the PLA since taking over as Chairman of the CMC. During his southern tour, for example, he included visits to PLA bases including the 124th division of the 42nd Army in Luofushan, Huizhou and the PLA Navy's South China Sea fleet, where he boarded the destroyer "Haikou." In Zhuhai, he visited the China Aviation Industry General Aircraft Co., which manufactures military and civil aircraft. At all these places he made speeches expressing pronounced nationalist sentiments.

Xi Jinping's repeated references to the humiliation heaped on the Chinese by foreigners, the "China Dream" and assertions that there will be no infringement of China's sovereignty and territorial integrity, all make apparent that there will be less flexibility and a reluctance to agree to concessions on issues of sovereignty or territorial disputes. Pressure on Japan and India could increase.

(The article was published in Centre for China Analysis and Strategy (CCAS) and C3S Paper No. 1108, March 5, 2013).

9

China's New Development Strategy: Emphasising Domestic Consumption, Human Resources and R&D

In another demonstration of their firm grip, President Hu Jintao and Premier Wen Jiabao recently launched an entirely new development path. The Five-Year Plan (2011-15) together with this year's "Report on the Work of the Government" and Report of the National Development and Reform Council (NDRC), outline China's new economic and development strategy. If it succeeds, then by 2015, China will be on a qualitatively higher plane than most other countries.

Chinese Economic Model: An Analysis

In 2005, Hu Jintao and Wen Jiabao had successfully formulated and effected a major policy shift away from Deng Xiaoping's philosophy of "allowing some to get rich first" to that of "common prosperity." Their new policy saw a marked rise in the popularity of the Chinese Communist Party (CCP) among the masses. This has been particularly noticeable among rural residents.

Hu Jintao and Wen Jiabao have, in another bold move, this time discarded the economic model followed by China for the past three decades. They have sought to anticipate the requirements of the current decade and ensure China a place on the emerging economic high table. Programmes are being initiated across China to boost domestic consumption and upgrade human resource skills with a pronounced emphasis on science and technology, while at the same time trying to balance this effort with the compulsions of retaining the CCP's popularity and support among the masses.

The main features of the new policy orientation are: converting China from being the "world's manufacturer" to becoming the "world's consumer";

upgrading its scientific and technological capabilities with an emphasis on innovation; expanding educational coverage; and improving the living conditions and increasing the wages of the people, especially those in the rural areas.

The ten-day Fourth Plenary Session of China's National People's Congress (NPC), which convened in Beijing in March 2011, approved plans for a change in the country's economic orientation. The reports presented for approval include, "Report on the Work of the Government," "Report on the Implementation of the Central and Local Budgets for 2010 and on the Draft Central and Local Budgets for 2011," and "Report on the Implementation of the 2010 Plan for National Economic and Social Development and on the 2011 Draft Plan for National Economic and Social Development," prepared by the National Development and Reform Council (NDRC). The CCP's Central Committee's (CC) Politburo had earlier deliberated on each of these reports for six months.

What Is the Agenda?: An Understanding

The above reports presented at the NPC plenum, including the "Report on the Work of the Government," which Wen Jiabao took two hours to read, signal that China will switch to a development path which gives greater emphasis to: scientific and technological innovation; upgrading of peoples' skills and education; boosting domestic consumption; and expansion of social insurance and health benefits to the majority of people in the rural and urban areas. Wen Jiabao particularly appreciated the "major breakthroughs" in "cutting-edge science and technology such as the manned space mission, the lunar exploration programme and supercomputers."

The economic development path now outlined by these reports moves China away from the export and investment-led model to one that is driven by Chinese consumers. The Twelfth Five-Year Plan (2011-15) envisages three major shifts. The manufacturing model that has promoted exports and investment-led growth is now to be replaced by a labour-intensive services model. This will include wholesale and retail trade, domestic transport and supply-chain logistics, health care, leisure and hospitality. This is expected to boost job creation as well as give the benefit of cleaner and greener growth.

The second feature will be enhancement of wages especially of those in the rural sector, which are planned to increase annually at 7 per cent in real terms. Wages in the rural sector are currently 30 per cent less than those in urban areas. The plan is to introduce reforms and tax policies that will increase rural purchasing power, broaden rural land ownership, and use technology to raise agricultural production. The reports insist that shrinkage of cultivable land will not be allowed and foodgrain production will not only be maintained at 500 million tons but enhanced by 50 million tons. In an attempt to address the problems of the 15-20 million people who migrate from rural to urban areas, it was felt there will be need to revise the "hukou" system, which restricts movement of people away from their birthplace.

The third aspect is intended to promote domestic consumption by accelerating building of the social safety net to reduce fear-driven high savings. This includes policies and subsidies to encourage rural residents to purchase domestic appliances and goods. Social security, pensions, medical and unemployment insurance schemes are to be expanded substantially, with basic pension insurance and medical insurance systems expected to cover the entire population by the end of the Plan period. These measures, it is anticipated, will lessen the impact of continuation of the "one-child" policy. Last year basic medical insurance covered 432.06 million urban residents, an increase of 30.59 per cent over the previous year, and 835 million rural residents or 96.3 per cent of the population. The government has also decided not to allow the Consumer Price Index (CPI) to rise above 4 per cent and will ensure availability of grain and essential food items in rural and urban areas. The increase in CPI from this year's 3.1 per cent has been attributed to international market pressures.

The upgradation of science and technology and scientific innovation is being given special attention. Provision has been made for a 12.5 per cent increase in the budget allocated for science and technology in 2011 raising it to 194.41 billion Yuan. Of this 25.719 billion Yuan has been earmarked as funds for basic research, increased investment in the State Natural Sciences Fund, key national laboratories and basic research institutes, and programmes for independent R&D on major scientific equipment. A sum of 99.063 billion Yuan has been set aside for research in cutting-edge technology.

Education will play a major role in this effort to transform China's economic profile from being a mere manufacturer to an innovator and producer of high-technology goods for export. Accordingly, in 2011, spending on education is planned to reach 4 per cent of GDP and gross enrolment ratio in secondary education is expected to reach 84 per cent. Plans call for increasing enrolment in the current year to 6.75 million undergraduate students and 560,000 graduate students (against the 6.618 million undergraduate and 538,000 graduate students in 2010) in regular institutions of higher learning.

Other measures including appropriate amendment of China's taxation, fiscal and insurance policies will be implemented to facilitate Chinese companies to "go global." China will continue to "guide" foreign investments towards high-end manufacturing, high-tech industries, modern service industries, new energy and environmental protection industries.

As if to affirm this emphasis on science and technology, a Xinhua dispatch in mid-March publicised a report of the Chinese Academy of Science and Technology for Development (CASTED), which ranked China twenty-first among the world's forty most innovative countries. China ranked first in terms of number of research personnel and export of high-tech products, fourth in total R&D investment and third in the number of authorised patents.

Twelfth Five-Year Plan: Highlights

The highlights of the Twelfth Five-Year Plan are: population will be controlled below 1.39 billion, or natural growth rate will be kept under 6.5 per cent; the economic growth rate is targeted to be 7 per cent and GDP should exceed 55 trillion Yuan (RMB), up from the 39.8 trillion Yuan in 2010; rate of urbanisation will be 51.5 per cent; value added output of emerging strategic industries will account for 8 per cent of GDP; coastal regions will transform from being the "world's factory" to the hub of R&D, high-end manufacturing and service sector; spending on R&D will rise to 2.2 per cent of GDP; foreign investment will be welcomed in agriculture, high-tech and environment protection industries and nuclear power will be developed more efficiently with preconditions of ensuring safety; "construction of large-scale hydropower plants will gain momentum in southwest China"; the country's optical cables will extend to 10.95 million km and the number of Internet access ports will rise to 223 million, an increase of 1 million and 35 million respectively; length of high-speed railway will increase by 13,000 km to reach 45,000 km with total length touching 99,000 km; length of highway network will reach 83,000 km; China will open six new airports to air traffic, including a new airport being built at Beijing, bringing the total to 181; and China will build 36 million affordable apartments for low-income people. Premier Wen Jiabao spoke specifically of expanding use of the RMB in cross-border trade and investment and making it convertible under capital accounts.

The emphasis on innovation, science and technology and space research will impact on China's defence preparedness. As China's GDP grows to an estimated 55 trillion Yuan by 2015, there will be consequential double-digit hikes in the defence budget. China will step up acquisition of high-tech weaponry and hardware, which will have attendant implications. China's enhanced ability to develop high-tech weaponry and Space weapons will be backed by steadily increasing financial support and an enhanced reservoir of trained human resources. These factors along with intensified training in joint integrated operations and increased emphasis on informationisation to prepare the PLA to fight and win local wars, will need to be factored in by India and China's neighbours.

The CCP's sensitivity to issues concerning the people was noticeable in the recent NPC session which discussed issues of concern to ordinary people, including high prices of apartments and the distress this causes to younger citizens. The government, therefore, decided to build large numbers of low-cost houses and at least 10 million low-cost apartments in Beijing.

Problems of the ordinary Chinese individuals and particularly of those in the rural areas have been the focus of the Party leadership. Premier Wen Jiabao's blunt warning at the NPC that rising prices, gap between the rich and poor, and corruption could "even hit the government's control of power" encapsulated the underlying sentiment of the leadership visible in all the reports that were presented. This was symbolised at the NPC session in March 2011, with the presence of three Deputies representing the over 200 million migrant workers in China. The Chinese Communist Party (CCP) leadership has already taken major initiatives to ameliorate the living and working conditions of rural migrant workers by extending them greater benefits including payment of wage arrears, access to health and social insurance. The NPC session was assured by the Premier that cases of rural residents eligible to settle in cities would be taken up gradually.

A major step in this direction is the socio-economic experiment with far-reaching implications, which the Party leadership approved and which has quietly been underway since 2003. The pilot reform project was initiated in a municipality of Chengdu, capital of China's southwestern province of Sichuan. It was made public within days of the conclusion of the NPC session. It would have helped that the Party Secretary of Sichuan, 1953-born Liu Qibao, is reputed to be a close associate of President Hu Jintao and aspirant for a post in the Politburo to be constituted in 2012. The experiment has been praised by renowned Chinese economist, Li Yining and Nobel laureate, Mundell.

A lengthy Xinhua dispatch, describing these pilot reforms, said the Party Central Committee had identified developing agriculture, raising farmer income and developing the rural economy as the most important element of Party work. This includes facilitating the free movement of labour between urban and rural areas. Other noteworthy features of this reform programme are: granting farmers "the right to contract land on a legal, voluntary and paid basis." This innovative policy is said to have generated funds for the village community and farmers individually thereby raising their standard of living. It has facilitated living in a "centralised manner" in relative comfort with all modern amenities. It has also converted the farmer's land and house into assets which he can parlay into capital.

To do this, the programme implemented a "rural ownership system" in which the villagers" receive "ownership certificates" confirming their rights to land and houses with the assistance of the Party branch of the village. The authorities plan that urban and rural residents will be permitted free migration starting 2012. Farmers will be allowed to work and live in cities without losing their land holdings and houses. This pilot reform project is to now be extended to a number of other counties.

Economic changes that have occurred in China over the past thirty years were reflected in the NPC. At least 70 NPC Deputies accounting for almost US$ 70 billion in wealth were among the private businessmen and entrepreneurs represented at the NPC and Chinese People's Political

Consultative Conference (CPPCC) sessions. They would have received some comfort when the NDRC report reiterated that "non-public sector" (a euphemism for the private sector) would be encouraged and government will create "an institutional environment for economic entities under all ownership forms to use factors of production on an equal basis in accordance with the law, compete as equals in the market and be equally protected by the law."

Wang Wenbao, Vice Chairman of the All-China Federation of Industry and Commerce, in the CPPCC urged "earnest implementation" of the central government's policies to encourage and support development of private business. He recalled that by the end of 2010, China had 42 million private and self-employed businesses and that China's private sector created more than 75 per cent of the jobs, 60 per cent of the GDP and 50 per cent of the total tax revenues.

Conclusion

These economic plans have far-reaching implications. A major change will be in the communist philosophy that has guided communist China's progress in the past six decades. Dilution of purist communist ideology moved forward with the acceptance of private business as part of the economic landscape and is being further legitimised by membership of the CCP. The suggestion now is to place these private businesses on an equal footing with the State-owned Enterprises (SoE). Further dilution of purist communist principles has also been effected with the reform initiative in Chengdu where "ownership" certificates are being granted to farmers, rural and urban residents for their house and land.

The emphasis on R&D and science and technology, if successful, will launch China on to a higher, more advanced level in innovation, manufacturing and defence. China's indigenous GPS system the Beidou is expected to be operational by 2025 and Beijing has recently unveiled ambitious, capital-intensive plans to use Space Stations to harness solar energy by 2050.

Finally, China's trading partners, including countries like South Korea, European nations and the US, will be keenly watching implementation of China's new economic plans in the expectation that increased domestic consumption will facilitate export of goods by them. China has, in the meantime, accelerated "internationalisation" of the RMB (Yuan). Efforts are underway to allow cross-border direct investment in RMB this month and, once implemented, the rules will expand channels for overseas-acquired RMB funds to flow back into the country thereby giving a push to the RMB's internationalisation drive. Foreign investors will then be permitted to make direct investments in China with RMB legally obtained overseas. This will also reduce Beijing's dependence on the US Dollar because of its huge holdings of US debt.

Though there are no indications of a serious threat to the CCP's position, nevertheless, vulnerabilities with the potential to derail China's ambitious developmental strategy exist. These include the potent mix of: rising unfulfilled popular aspirations, growing restiveness of the ethnic minorities who mainly reside in China's vulnerable border regions, and increasing anger at the rapaciousness of Party and Government cadres and neglect of environmental issues. China's leadership has so far successfully tackled these issues, but their task is now more complicated with the rapidly growing usage of Internet and mobile telephones.

(The article was published in the Institute of Peace and Conflict Studies, New Delhi, September 2011).

10

China's Twelfth National People's Congress: An Analysis of the Composition and Content

The first session of the Twelfth National People's Congress (NPC) held in Beijing from March 5 to 17, 2013 completed the final phase of transfer of power to China's top leadership, which was elected at the 18th Party Congress last November. Controls were predictably tight as 2,987 Deputies converged on Beijing for the event.

The Chinese Communist Party's (CCP) central Propaganda Department issued firm 10-point guidelines to China's media listing prohibited topics and cautioning them to use only verified reports released by Xinhua. Guangdong's provincial propaganda department cautioned journalists not to "debate or pass judgement on the results of the election in your coverage." Despite strengthened controls on Internet usage, China's "netizens" posted thousands of critical remarks and 100 Chinese "intellectuals" urged the Government to immediately ratify the International Covenant on Civil and Political Rights (ICCPR).

As per tradition, the Chinese People's Political Consultative Conference (CPPCC), a largely advisory body which includes non-Chinese Communist Party (CCP) entities and with a membership of about 2,200, met a day earlier. Its new Chairman, Politburo Standing Committee (PBSC) member Yu Zhengsheng, presided. Twenty-three persons were appointed to the prestigious post of CPPCC Vice Chairman. In accordance with new directives, arrangements were frugal and the CPPCC announced that its paperless proceedings would save Yuan 2 million, or US$ 321,200 in expenses.

National People's Congress: The Composition

The NPC session attended by 2,986 delegates—Shao Zhanwei, Mayor of Hangzhou, died during the proceedings on the opening day—approved the appointment in single-candidate elections of Xi Jinping as President, Li Keqiang as Premier, Li Yuanchao as Vice President and Zhou Qing as President of China's Supreme People's Court. A "princeling" and member of the Politburo, Li Yuanchao, will rank after all 7 PBSC members. He did a year's course in 2002 in Harvard. Formerly Head of the CCP CC Organisation Department, 62-year-old Li Yuanchao is unlikely to continue after the next Party Congress.

In addition to the 13 Vice Chairmen appointed by the NPC, on March 16, it approved the Premier's recommendation for 4 Vice Premiers, 5 State Councillors and 25 Ministers. The Vice Premiers are: Zhang Gaoli, PBSC member as Executive Vice Premier; Liu Yandong (f), PB member and former head of UFWD; Wang Yang, former Party Secretary of Guangdong and Politburo (PB) member; and Ma Kai, PB member, former head of the National Development and Reform Commission (NDRC) and Deputy Chairman of the Tibet Work Leading Group. At least three of the Vice Premiers are cautious and unlikely to push reforms, which appears in accordance with Premier Li Keqiang's gradualist economic agenda.

The five State Councillors are: Yang Jing, an ethnic Mongol, Politburo (PB) member and long-time close associate of Li Keqiang who has been appointed Secretary General of the State Council. The Secretary General manages the daily work of the State Council as the Premier's right-hand man. This is the first time that someone from China's ethnic minority nationalities has been appointed to this powerful position; General Chang Wanquan as Defence Minister; former Foreign Minister Yang Jiechi as replacement of Dai Bingguo; Guo Shengkun, who continues as Minister of Public Security (MPS); and Wang Yong, with a background in the Party's anti-corruption body, the Central Discipline Inspection Commission (CDIC).

Of the 25 Cabinet appointments, two fewer than earlier, 14 are holdovers. The more important include Xu Shaoshi, till now Minister of Land and Natural Resources, as Head of the powerful NDRC; Lou Jiwei, head of China's sovereign fund the "China Investment Corporation," as Finance Minister;

Gao Hucheng, former Vice Minister for Commerce, elevated as Commerce Minister; Zhou Shengxian, who continues as Minister of Environmental Protection despite opposition from NPC Deputies; and Wang Zhengwei, Deputy Party Secretary and Chairman of Ningxia-Hui Autonomous Region as Head of the State Ethnic Affairs Commission. Geng Huichang, an America expert and former Head of the Ministry of State Security (MoSS) think tank, "China Institutes for Contemporary International Relations" (CICIR), continues as Minister of MoSS. Zhou Xiaochuan has been retained as head of the People's Bank of China (PBoC).

Important are the senior appointments in China's foreign policy establishment, which will shape China's foreign policy. Sixty-two-year-old former Foreign Minister Yang Jiechi replaces Dai Bingguo as State Councillor. Dai Bingguo has been China's pointsman for negotiations with the US, Russia and the UK, and is China's nominee to the Special Representative-level talks with India on the border issue. Yang Jiechi is an expert on American affairs, fluent English speaker and graduate of the London School of Economics. Foreign diplomats view him as less hardline than Dai Bingguo.

Fifty-nine-year-old Wang Yi, a fluent Japanese speaker and former Ambassador to Japan and Head of China's Taiwan Affairs Office, is China's new Foreign Minister. A consummate diplomat skilled at negotiations, he is credited with conducting the secret talks with then Chief Cabinet Secretary Shinzo Abe, which helped break the impasse in Sino-Japanese ties in 2001-6 and facilitated Shinzo Abe's visit to Beijing as Premier in October 2006. The Taiwanese, who have welcomed his elevation, say he gave Taiwan diplomatic space by allowing it to join WHO. Both appointments reflect the importance Beijing attaches to these countries, especially in the present context.

National People's Congress: The Content

Chinese Premier Wen Jiabao, his image dented by disclosures about the vast sums amassed by his family's corruption, presented his final "Report on the Work of the Government" on the opening day of the NPC on March 5. The 29-page "Report" spelt out China's achievements and targets for the coming year. Popular concerns were reflected in the Report. Interestingly, while Wen Jiabao referred to "Deng Xiaoping Theory," Jiang Zemin's "Three Represents" and

Hu Jintao's "Scientific Outlook on Development" he made no mention of Mao Zedong! He was careful in reading his 100-minute-long Report and did not once refer to "political reform." Reforms were mentioned only in one brief section of the Report. The oft-made comment, that "without commensurate political reform, economic reform cannot succeed," was missing.

Extolling last year's achievements, like the Beidou Satellite Navigation System, commissioning of China's first aircraft carrier the "Liaoning" and the XXIX Olympics, China's Premier highlighted that China is now the world's second largest economy with a GDP of 51.9 billion Yuan.

Among the Report's highlights were the retention of last year's economic growth target of 7.5 per cent, assurance of creating nine million jobs during the year, bringing down inflation to 3.5 per cent from last year's 4 per cent, keeping unemployment below 4.6 per cent, and promoting equitable growth including between rural and urban residents and in urban centres.

Farmer's property rights were mentioned for the first time in a Government Work Report, suggesting enhanced protection of their rights. The Report stressed that the main purpose of the country's land reform system is "to protect farmer's property rights and interests" which is central to China's rural stability and long-term development." It added, "we should always protect farmer's legitimate property rights and keep them motivated."

Popular deceased Party General Secretary Hu Yaobang's son, Hu Deping, had last year publicly stressed the need for properly settling issues related to farmers' land rights. He spoke out after the clashes last year at Wukan village, Guangdong, and was supportive of Guangdong Party Secretary Wang Yang. Hu Deping is a strong supporter of Xi Jinping.

Equitable distribution of income, a theme repeatedly emphasised by Hu Jintao, received special mention in the Premier and NDRC's Reports. The Premier described the income distribution system as "a basic system of vital importance for social and economic development, and an important cornerstone of the socialist market economy." He emphasised that there is need to "narrow the income gap so that the fruits of development are more equitably shared by the people."

A separate paragraph was devoted to the Law on Regional Ethnic Autonomy and infusing "new vitality into the cause of promoting unity and progress of ethnic groups in China." There was apparent emphasis on accelerating "leapfrog" development of the Tibet and Xinjiang Autonomous Regions, including in the NDRC Report. Specific mention was made of expanding print, TV and Radio coverage in these regions. Noteworthy is the appointment of cadres with experience of working in minority regions, or minority issues, to senior positions in the CPPCC and NPC.

The armed forces and, particularly, China's maritime interests, received pointed attention. The Premier declared that "new progress was made in strengthening national defence and the armed forces." There had been "major achievements" in the "revolution in military affairs with Chinese characteristics" and the military had "greatly enhanced their ability to carry out their historic mission... and accomplished a number of urgent, difficult, and hazardous tasks." He exhorted the armed forces to "resolutely uphold China's sovereignty, security and territorial integrity and ensure its peaceful development," adding that they "provide a firm guarantee." His remarks differed from last year and absent was the emphasis on the People's Liberation Army (PLA) being "absolutely loyal" to the Party. The routine mention of "winning local wars under information age conditions" was also missing, but these figured in Xi Jinping's first speech after the NPC on March 17.

Pronounced focus on China's maritime interests was evident, however, in the remark that "we should strengthen comprehensive marine management... and safeguard China's maritime rights and interests." This was amplified in the restructuring of departments from which the restructured State Oceanic Administration emerged considerably strengthened.

The Ministry of Finance "Budget Report" and NDRC's "Draft Plan for National Economic and Social Development," were presented later that day. The budget for medical and health care increased substantially by 27.1 per cent over last year. Both Reports referred to, inter alia, expanding medical, old-age pension and education coverage in rural areas, enhancing foodgrain subsidies for farmers and raising grain production.

The trend of double-digit increases for National Defence was continued with a 10.7 per cent rise, bringing the allocation for defence to Yuan 720 billion, or US$ 116 billion.

In contrast to expectations that there could be an easing in security controls, especially abolition of the 300 "Reform through Labour camps," the focus on strengthening stability remained. The budget for domestic security was enhanced by 8.7 per cent to Yuan 769.1 billion, or US$ 123.5 billion, making it the third successive year when the domestic security budget is higher than that for national defence.

Similar sensitivity to public concern was evident in the restructuring proposal approved by the NPC, which meshed with the assurances in Premier Wen Jiabao's Work Report. It addressed public concerns regarding the Railways, where there was widespread public outcry of corruption after the high-speed train disaster at Wenzhou in July 2012, adulteration of foodstuffs and medicines, and criticism of the "one-child" policy. Though initial plans called for reducing Government departments from 27 to 18, the NPC finally approved abolition of only two departments. The Ministry of State Security (MoSS), NDRC and State-owned Enterprises (SoE) remain untouched.

Under the restructuring, the Ministry of Transportation takes overall policy and planning functions and oversees rail, road, water and air transportation. A new National Railway Bureau is to be established under its management together with a new China Railway Corporation. The Ministry of Railways has been abolished.

A National Health and Family Planning Commission (NHFPC) takes over all functions of the Ministry of Health and the National Population and Family Planning Commission. The Ministry of Health and the National Population and Family Planning Commission have been abolished. There is an implication that the "one-child" policy, introduced since 1971, could gradually be relaxed.

A new General Administration of Food and Drugs (GAFD) has been established. The State Administration of Food and Drugs and the State Council's Office of the Food Safety Committee are abolished.

The propaganda apparatus has emerged more powerful with the formation of the National Commission for Press, Publications, Radio, Films and Television. GAPP and SARFT have been abolished. At a conference on March 19, Luo Shugang, deputy chief of the CCP's Propaganda Department, said the merger would improve "management of ideology."

Affirming China's maritime ambitions and claims, the State Oceanic Administration (SOC) has been appreciably strengthened. It takes over all executive maritime oversight responsibilities as well as personnel of the Ministry of Public Security, Ministry of Agriculture and Customs Administration. The SOC will be managed by the Ministry of Land and Resources.

The SOC's new responsibilities include development of the seas, exercising maritime authority, overseeing and managing exploitation of the seas and ensuring environmental protection. The SOC will take professional guidance from the Ministry of Public Security. A high-level National Maritime Committee (NMC), to formulate national strategy for developing the seas and coordinating important maritime matters has been established. The SOC will be the NMC's executive arm.

The National Energy Administration (NEA) takes over the State Electricity Regulatory Committee (SERC) but remains under the NDRC. The SERC will be abolished. This could be a prelude to the gradual reduction of energy subsidies on coal, natural gas and petrol, as demanded by two of the 118 powerful and wealthy State-owned Enterprises (SoE), namely, Sinopec and PetroChina.

There were some interesting sidelights at the NPC session. Fang Xingyuan Feng, a researcher at the Chinese Academy of Social Sciences (CASS), revealed that a number of CPPCC members held foreign passports, while Hong Kong's *Oriental Daily News* claimed that the high number of such officials is "turning the NPC and CPPCC sessions into a UN session!" The number of billionaires in the NPC and CPPCC increased by 17 per cent over last year to 83 US Dollar billionaires. Thirty-one in the NPC have assets worth more than US$ 1 billion while there are 52 in the CPPCC, which additionally includes 24 "princelings."

Deputies initiated suggestions for reforms on issues of public concern such as soil pollution, illegal house purchases and child abuse. CPPCC Deputies submitted over 500 suggestions.

The issue of China's troubled minorities surfaced obliquely with reports filtering in during the NPC of clashes involving Uyghurs in Korla town in the Xinjiang-Uyghur Autonomous Region. The Party's Propaganda Department promptly prohibited the Chinese media from reporting on it.

Interesting was the composition of the 20-strong Tibet Autonomous Region (TAR) delegation to the NPC, which included six non-Tibetans. Three are members of the TAR administration, namely, Party Secretary Chen Quanguo, Deputy Party Secretary Wu Yingjie and the Commander of the People's Armed Police in Tibet, General Guo Yili. Of greater interest are the three who are neither concerned with, nor resident in, Tibet. Prominent are Chang Xiaobing, Chief Executive of China's second largest telecom company, China Unicom Hong Kong Ltd., and Wang Huning, PB member and member of the powerful 18th Central Committee (CC) Secretariat. He has been included in earlier TAR delegations. In addition to 4 senior cadres with a background of TAR, two Tibetans have been appointed Vice Chairmen to the CPPCC and NPC and the Chinese-appointed Panchen Lama is a member of a CPPCC Standing Committee. These are indicators that issues pertaining to Tibet are high on Xi Jinping's agenda.

The NPC has clearly signalled that the CCP will be unchallenged, economic reforms will be gradual and the PLA and security apparatus will continue to be strengthened. Finally, it amply clarified that there would be no easing of the Party's political control. Wang Shengjun, outgoing President of the Supreme People's Court, declared in the NPC that the Party has unquestioned leadership over the judiciary and urged judges and other "judicial workers" to profess "total loyalty to the Party, country, Constitution and law."

(The article was published in the Institute of Peace and Conflict Studies, New Delhi, March 2013).

11

Third Party Plenum

The Four-day (November 9-12, 2013) Third Plenary session of the 18th Central Committee (CC) of the Chinese Communist Party (CCP) concluded in Beijing on November 12, 2013. It was attended by 204 Full Members and 169 Alternate Members of the 18th CC, which comprises 205 Full Members and 171 Alternate Members. Standing Committee members of the Central Discipline Inspection Commission (CDIC), leading officials from relevant departments, some grassroots-level delegates to the 18th CCP National Congress as well as experts and scholars were present at the plenary session as non-voting delegates.

The days leading up to the 18th CC's Third Plenum witnessed stark reminders of the spreading domestic discontent and unceasing restiveness among Tibetan and Uyghur minorities in the Tibet Autonomous Region (TAR) and Xinjiang Uyghur Autonomous Region (XUAR). The discontent has ensured that domestic security issues dominate the agenda of the CCP leadership headed by Xi Jinping and boosted the domestic security budget to over US$ 110 billion, or more than the national defence budget. Most alarming was the incident on October 28, described by Chinese security authorities as a "terror attack" by armed Uyghur "terrorists" from Xinjiang who bypassed the heightened security measures and drove an SUV into the gate of the Forbidden City in the heart of Beijing. On November 6, small bombs were detonated outside the CCP headquarters in Taiyuan, capital of Shanxi province. The CCP CC's plenary meeting was also not held in the Great Hall of the People but in a PLA-owned hotel in Beijing.

The Plenum, while further strengthening Xi Jinping's position, effectively sent out three clear messages. First, that Xi Jinping is China's paramount leader and he personally steered the slew of economic reforms approved at this Plenum. Second, that the CCP, conscious of its sagging popularity and widespread popular dissatisfaction, is agreed on the need to promote comprehensive economic reforms to create jobs, further improve entrepreneurial opportunities for the people and boost the national economy to ensure that the country realises the "Chinese Dream" and ranks among the world's most advanced countries by 2020. Third, the Plenum recognised the need to strengthen security coordination with the initial focus on domestic security and accelerate military reform and modernisation.

In Beijing, there was an unmistakable air of public optimism that surrounded this Plenum. In addition to China's official media a number of Chinese observers, economists and analysts described it as a crucial Party meeting next in importance only to Deng Xiaoping's 11th CC Plenum in December 1978, which approved the "open-door and reform" policy. Sentiment was prevalent that steps to commence implementation of the wide-ranging reforms that had been announced would begin early. This was reinforced soon enough with the disclosure that it had been decided to set up a "Leading Small Group for the Comprehensive Deepening of Reform," to oversee implementation of the reforms. Other steps followed. The popular perception of Xi Jinping as a "person of the masses" and decisive leader who gets things done contributed to this air of optimism.

Xi Jinping's leadership role and direct involvement in drafting the reforms was clarified in official reports detailing the timeline for preparation of the draft which was finally approved at the Third Plenum on November 12, 2013. This was underscored by the release on November 15—within three days of the conclusion of the Plenum—of the self-explanatory "Xi Jinping's Explanation of the CPC Central Committee Decision on Several Major Issues on the Comprehensive Deepening of Reforms" and the lengthy "CCP Central Committee Decision Concerning Some Major Issues in Comprehensively Deepening Reform."

Official reports that gave the timeline of drafting of the reform proposals stated that the Politburo (PB) set up a 60-member drafting group headed by Xi Jinping in April 2013. Before its first meeting on April 24, the drafting group had sought the opinions of all Party and government organisations down to the level of Autonomous Regions and received 118 proposals. At the meeting on

April 24, Xi Jinping asked members to "make a strategic plan for deepening reforms across the board" and produce a "landmark document that will meet public expectations." The first draft was submitted to the seven-member Politburo Standing Committee (PBSC) on July 25 which, after a number of amendments, was circulated to more than 100 departments across the country. By September 4, the group had received 2,564 proposals of which over 40 per cent were included in the final document. After discussing the draft with the non-communist parties, the PB decided to submit it to the 18th CCP CC's Third Plenary session where it was accepted after a vote on November 12. The document containing over 300 reform measures was released to the public on November 15, 2013.

The "Explanation" of the proposal is usually offered to the CC plenum by the PB or PBSC member in charge of the subject, which in this case should have been expected to be Premier Li Keqiang. It was Xi Jinping, however, who presented his 11,000-character "Explanation" to the 18th CC plenary session. Xi Jinping disclosed that he had chaired the group preparing the draft of the Decision along with PBSC Members Liu Yunshan and Zhang Gaoli as the Deputies. Significantly, Premier Li Keqiang was not included.

The 3,490-word Plenum Communiqué further confirmed Xi Jinping's imprimatur on the Third Plenum and his standing in the CCP leadership by declaring that "comrades in the entire Party, (who) must closely revolve around the Party Centre with Comrade Xi Jinping as General Secretary to forge ahead" and "realise the Chinese Dream of the great rejuvenation of the Chinese nation!" The Communiqué, of course, paid the mandatory obeisance to China's pantheon of "veteran revolutionary" leaders and urged that "we must hold high the magnificent banner of Socialism with Chinese characteristics, take Marxism-Leninism, Mao Zedong Thought, Deng Xiaoping Theory, the important 'Three Represents' thought and the Scientific Development view" as the guide.

The Communiqué identified four major areas where the Third Plenum had approved decisions. Important was the discussion on the "mixed economy," where it stated: "The core issue is to straighten out the relationship between the government and market, allowing the market to play a decisive role in allocating resources and improving the government's role." This is the first time that the role of the market was described as "decisive." Earlier it used to be described as "basic." Chinese analysts interpret this as a clear indication that the authorities will let the free market play a bigger role in the economy.

The role of public and non-public sectors in the economy was also discussed with both described as "important components." This was accompanied by a strong endorsement of the role of the private sector. In the context of the urban-rural divide there was a suggestion that the "hukou," or household registration, system would be reformed. The Communiqué made special mention of "further widening investment access, accelerating the building of free trade zones and expanding the opening up of inland and border regions."

As anticipated there was little, or no, discussion concerning political reforms. On the contrary the 21,548-character, 60-section "CCP Central Committee Decision concerning Some Major Issues in Comprehensively Deepening Reform" approved by the Plenum on November 12, and released on November 15, specifically declared that "The most important matter is persisting in the leadership of the Party." It emphasised the need to "strengthen and improve the Party's leadership over comprehensive deepening of reform." It dealt at length with the Party's leadership role and its importance. The Xinhua report on the Plenum Communiqué was more categorical and asserted that the CCP's leadership role must be adhered to. Both documents asserted the Party's premier role and referred to it over 25 times.

The Decision also stressed the role of ideology and propaganda and dwelt at length on the role of propaganda and culture in building "socialist core values." It made it evident that the Party's role in media, cinema, etc., would be strengthened and become more pervasive. It similarly emphasised the need for the Party to promote "socialist core values" and "love for the motherland" among students. In its mention of the role of media and cinema, it was implicit that stringent controls would continue.

The lengthy 21,548-character, 60-section "CCP Central Committee Decision Concerning Some Major Issues in Comprehensively Deepening Reform," approved over 300 reform proposals. Most are ambiguously worded but some are specific, indicating that they would be taken up earlier. Some of the more important proposals that were approved are briefly highlighted below.

The CC Plenum tackled the issue of reform of the monopolistic, extremely wealthy and powerful State-owned Enterprises (SoE), which have been the subject of public discussion for years. Confirming that they have a dominant role in the socialist economy, the Third Plenum announced some concrete decisions that directly affect the SoEs. These include that they will now pay a percentage of their profits to the State and this percentage will rise to 30 per cent by 2020. This dividend to the State will be used for public welfare like health insurance and social security. Three other equally crucial reform measures are that: (i) SoEs will begin to "reasonably" increase the proportion of persons hired directly from the open market; (ii) SoEs will "strictly standardise" the salaries, duty remuneration, duty expenses and professional expenses of SoE management personnel. The authority to determine the "reasonable" amount appears to have been left to the SoEs; and (iii) other enterprises including private, are permitted to acquire shares in SoEs. While an attempt has been made towards reform of the SoEs, the measures approved by the Third Plenum are really small, tentative steps that do not dilute their grip over national resources or dominant position in the national economy.

The Plenum mandated a definite move towards prices being determined by markets and specifically authorised reform in the competitive pricing of water, oil, natural gas, electricity, traffic, telecommunications, etc. It also urged formulation of a marketised withdrawal system where the fittest survive and enterprise bankruptcy systems are perfected.

On financial market systems, it has encouraged domestic and international entities by permitting "non-government capital" to sponsor the establishment of small and mid-size banks. It said procedures for foreign investments should be streamlined by implementing a "management model for foreign investment with pre-entry national treatment and the negative list." It said the qualification accreditation programme should be reduced and changed "from certification before licensing to licensing before certification." Recent anecdotal evidence from Beijing-based foreign businessmen suggests that action to reduce the number of bureaucratic procedures especially in the financial sector have already begun to be implemented.

Renminbi (RMB) exchange was specifically referred to in the Decision, with a call for acceleration of interest rate marketisation and towards realisation of convertibility of RMB capital accounts. Action towards implementation was quick with Zhou Xiaochuan, the progressive Governor of the People's Bank of China (PBoC), quoted by *China Daily* (November 20) as saying within days after the Third Plenum that "China is poised to take yet another step in making the yuan a free floating currency." Separately, PBoC Deputy Governor Yi Gang said that a ceiling on deposit rates offered by the bank would be phased out.

The reform measures said that government control over micro-level matters should be reduced and examination and approvals must be cancelled without exception for all economic activities that market mechanisms can effectively regulate. It asked governments to transfer what can be handled by localities to them. A separate reform measure approved the reduction in the number of government departments and called for some separation of the Party from the government.

Tax revenue systems are to be improved and the proportion of direct taxation will be progressively increased. VAT will be enhanced along with tax on high-energy consumption and high pollution products. An individual Income Tax system is to be established and the legislation of bills to tax real estate and levy a tax for environmental protection is to be accelerated.

Describing the recently inaugurated China Shanghai Free Trade Trial Zone, reportedly promoted by Premier Li Keqiang, as a "major measure," the Decision approved by the Plenum urged more openness with the Hong Kong Special Administrative Region (SAR), Macau SAR and Taiwan. Governments were asked to "broaden inland border openness" and develop transportation links to forge "foreign economic corridors" as well as develop the "Silk Road economic belt" and the "Sea Silk Road."

The Plenum directed that the system of protecting property rights must be perfected, adding that "property rights are the core of ownership systems." It instructed that "property rights in the public economy may not be violated, property rights in the non-public economy may equally not be violated." It asserted that the State protects economic property rights and legal interests in all sorts of ownership systems.

Reform measures approved by the Plenum stressed innovation at all levels including industry and schools. It urged development of IPR and technology markets and raising the proportion of young and middle-aged talents in the science and technology sector.

Alleviation of the condition of peasants and gini coefficient remained a priority with the Plenum substantially enlarging the property rights of peasants and demanding that they be endowed with more property rights. Their membership rights in collective economic organisations are now to be guaranteed along with their rights over homestead land. It demanded forward movement on peasant housing, property rights, mortgage, guarantee and transfer and added that "property-type income channels for peasants" should be expanded.

In addition, the sale, rent or lease of land by the rural collective, including for construction, has now been permitted on the same terms and prices as for State-owned land. The Plenum's Decision directed that land expropriation be reduced and measures for its expropriation be standardised with guarantees for affected peasants. Mechanisms are to be created to ensure the reasonable allocation of profits from increased land values to the State, collective and individual, while increasing the profit to the individual.

The existing structure of town and country was described as a "main obstacle" restraining urban and rural development. The Plenum approved reforms that allow "peasants to equally participate in the process of modernisation and jointly share the fruits of modernisation." More categoric was the instruction to "change people transferred away from agriculture into townspeople, progressively change people transferred away from agriculture who meet conditions into urban residents. Innovate population management, accelerate household registration system reform, completely lift restrictions on settling in administrative townships and small cities, lift restrictions on settling in mid-size cities in an orderly manner, rationally determine conditions for large cities, strictly control the scale of the population in especially large cities."

The last mentioned reform relaxes, but does not abolish, the hukou, or household registration system with cadres largely continuing to retain their powers. It does, however, facilitate the migration of rural workers to urban areas. Together with the other reform measures it boosts the revenue earnings of rural residents by allowing monetisation of their holdings and ameliorates the living conditions of rural migrant workers by granting them housing and social security benefits as admissible to urban residents. The move is estimated to add up to 40 million rural migrant workers to the labour force.

The Third Plenum relaxed the stringent family planning norms introduced by Deng Xiaoping in the late 1970s and permitted families in which either of the parents is a single child to have a second child. The relaxation is intended to reverse the effects of the low fertility rate—which has dropped to 1.6 since 1992—and maintain China's young labour resources. There was a drop in China's working age population for the first time in 2012 when the number of people aged between 15 years and 59 years fell by 3.45 million. Ageing has been another consideration. China's National Committee on Ageing has estimated that people aged above 60 years will number over 200 million by the end of 2013 and over 400 million by 2033. The impact of the relaxation will, however, be minimal as the fast development of the economy and high cost of living has seriously discouraged younger people in China from having children.

The Plenum approved the measure to abolish the "laojiao," or reform-through-labour, system in vogue in China since 1957. The decision followed through on Premier Li Keqiang's announcement at the National People's Congress (NPC) session earlier this March that work was underway on a plan to abolish the "laojiao" system by the end of the year. The system will officially end once it is approved by the next NPC, China's version of a Parliament, in March 2014.

There was a modicum of judicial reform, but no substantive steps. Barely a month before the Third Plenum the official website of the Supreme People's Court posted a paper demanding an end to corruption in courts and asking officials to stop interfering in the courts' decisions. The paper asked that courts be allowed to independently exercise judicial authority based on constitutional principles and that all forms of local and departmental protectionism should cease.

The drive against corruption and "people's" supervision over government were addressed. The anti-corruption body, namely, the Central Discipline Inspection Commission (CDIC) gained more powers with the Plenum approving that the CDIC and the Party's Organisation Department would have the authority to appoint the Secretaries and Deputy Secretaries of subordinate

Discipline Inspection Committees (DIC) in provinces, Autonomous Regions, etc., so as to dilute the influence of local government authorities over the DICs. DICs will also henceforth supervise the functioning of DICs subordinate to them concurrently with the concerned government body. The subordinate DICs have been mandated to report clues and investigations to the higher level DIC. China's official news agency "Xinhua" disclosed that the Third Plenum had also expanded a two-year trial programme to now cover the entire PLA and authorised the CDIC to oversee top military officers to ensure they are doing their jobs properly and are incorruptible.

Similarly, the supervisory role of the National People's Congress (NPC) has been strengthened with people's governments being instructed to report to the People's Congresses at the same level before publishing major policy decisions.

Reforms touching mainly on the domestic security apparatus have definitively enhanced Xi Jinping's authority. They have additionally increased his direct control over the security apparatus. The section dealing with domestic issues and innovation of the social management system included the decision to establish a State Security Committee, also called the National Security Committee (NSC), which will be headed by Xi Jinping. It is assessed as likely to have the same status as the Central Military Commission and the two "Leading Groups" on National Security and Foreign Affairs. It will include representatives from the PLA, PAPF, MPS, MoSS, Ministry of Commerce, MFA, the CCP CC's Propaganda Department and the CCP CC's International Liaison Department (ILD). The Plenum also approved, as part of these reforms, the enhancing of the strength of public security forces especially for Internet security and safeguarding secrets on the Internet.

Xi Jinping explained that the NSC is necessary to strengthen the "unified leadership of State security work." This committee will combine planning and coordination components. Referring to formation of the security committee, Chen Xiangyang, Deputy Director of the China Institutes of Contemporary International Relations (CICIR) a think tank of the Ministry of State Security, wrote in the official English-language *China Daily* that "the country is witnessing frequent social disputes. Meanwhile, hostile forces at home and abroad, including separatism, extremism and terrorism, are looking for opportunities to undermine social stability." "China," he said,"is faced with a more severe security situation." The head of China's official foreign policy think tank said that the new NSC will focus on the "Three Evils" (terrorism, separatism, and religious extremism) in addition to coordinating international strategy, particularly on maritime issues. A Japanese newspaper reported in end-November that a 60-member secretariat had been established and the new NSC was establishing "hotlines" with six countries. With these reforms it is anticipated that the US$ 110 billion domestic security budget will appreciably increase.

Far-reaching and major military reform measures were approved by the Third Plenum. In an entire separate section on military reform and modernisation, interesting was the mention of the need for "building a line of people's troops that heed the Party's command." Also, the Plenum, while referring to the need to strengthen and perfect military strategies and build modern military force systems, referred to "prominent contradictions and problems."

Among the new military reforms proposed are the streamlining of personnel and reorganisation of military leadership structures including at the level of the Military Commission, General Headquarters and all services. It said that Joint Operations outfits and Joint Theatre Operations Command Systems would be set up under the Military Commission along with "new type combat units." The implication is that the Military Regions are likely to be replaced by Theatre Commands on the US pattern. The "new type combat units" could refer to formations integral to the Theatre Commands which are highly mobile, self-contained, cyberwarfare-capable troops well-armed with advanced, lethal weaponry. There have been indicative hints in China's military newspapers and magazines for some years now that both these are under consideration.

The Plenum Decision called for continuing joint operations training in the armed forces and accelerated establishment of integrated "informationisation commands." Improvement and streamlining of PLA Logistics is to receive special attention together with national defence science and technology research and the research and development of advanced armaments. Reforms approved by the Plenum clearly indicated that the PLA, especially the ground forces, will be subjected to a further downsizing in personnel strength—particularly of non-combatants—and that the role, strength and budgets of the PLA Air Force (PLAAF), PLA Navy (PLAN) and Second Artillery will be enhanced. There will be impetus on regularising the rank of NCOs and policies for the welfare and rehabilitation of veterans. There is focus also on improving the calibre of recruits and training in military schools and academies.

The reforms suggest that more officers from the PLAAF, PLAN and Second Artillery can be expected to be deployed in the General Staff Department (GSD), General Logistics Department (GLD) and General Armaments Department (GAD) to improve Integrated Joint Operations, facilitate coordination in integrated logistics, and promote development of advanced weaponry specific to these three services.

Indication that work to implement the reforms approved at the Third Plenum had commenced was evident in the article written by General Xu Qiliang, former PLAAF Commander and presently Vice Chairman of the Central Military Commission (CMC) in the *People's Daily* on November 22. Confirming that more importance would be given to the PLAN, PLAAF and Second Artillery, he said they would be strengthened and their role enhanced and that non-combatant units and personnel would be reduced. Reports circulating in military circles in Beijing over the past two years have mentioned plans to reduce PLA strength by 800,000 personnel.

Steps to implement some of the reforms approved at the Third Plenum have already commenced in the economic sector and the PLA. The Party too has initiated action. Interesting in this context is an 8-point directive on cadre evaluation policies issued on December 6, 2013, by the powerful CCP CC Organisation Department to provincial authorities. This instructs provincial authorities not to rely simply on economic development statistics for promotion purposes; warns against political "show" projects undertaken by cadres to raise their profiles; and asks for more comprehensive evaluation of local cadres, taking into consideration the longer-term cost-benefit analysis of their performance.

Nevertheless, the CCP leadership under Xi Jinping faces numerous and tough challenges. In addition to the economic difficulties which observers have underscored, the seemingly intractable restiveness of the country's minority nationalities and widespread popular discontent accentuated by the 400 million active "netizens," pose a serious challenge. This is exacerbated by the political divisions that are beginning to surface. The publicised announcement last month of a "political" party, with the officially discredited and ousted Politburo member Bo Xilai as its patron, is an example. They will expect the support of the nearly 30 million Cultural Revolution-vintage Party cadres. Additionally, the powerful group of "Red Descendants," or children of veteran CCP leaders, who influence leadership decisions are divided on the future course that the Party should take and have begun to voice their differences.

The Third Plenum of the 18th CCP CC is nonetheless a major attempt at boosting China's economy and lifting the country up to the ranks of the world's advanced nations by 2020. The continuing emphasis on rapid modernisation of the PLA and its technological capabilities with particular attention to enhancing the role and capabilities of the PLA Navy, PLA Air Force and Second Artillery, or strategic strike force, is intended to enable realisation of "China's Dream" and add muscle to its diplomacy. This is of direct relevance to China's neighbours. The important objective is to ensure that the Chinese Communist Party retains its legitimacy and position as the country's unchallenged, solitary ruling political party when it celebrates its hundredth anniversary in 2021.

(The article was published in the Institute of Peace and Conflict Studies, New Delhi, November 2013).

12

China: The Fifth Plenum of the 18th CCP CC (October 26-29, 2015)

The four-day (October 26-29, 2015) eighth session of the 18th Chinese Communist Party Central Committee's (CCP CC) Fifth Plenum has, as expected, further strengthened and consolidated Party General Secretary Xi Jinping's authority and position. The 5,923-character Communiqué issued promptly after the Fifth Plenum on October 29, 2015, exuded confidence as it firmly set out the path for reforms with the focus on all-round development and asserted China's goals for the next five years including that of "building a moderately prosperous society by 2020." There were, interestingly, few references to "stability" despite the steadily growing number of popular protests which China officially estimates at more than 500 each day, and the "Chinese Dream" unveiled by Xi Jinping at the 18th Party Congress in November 2012 was enshrined in the Plenum Communiqué.

The Fifth Plenum of a CC traditionally discusses and approves the crucial issue of leadership appointments. This includes nomination of Party cadres for elevation to top Party and military posts at the next Party Congress, in this case the 19th Party Congress due in 2017. In view of the slowdown of the economy and recent hiccup in the stock market attributed to manipulations, including by "foreign investors," this plenary session also deliberated on economic issues including approval of the Thirteenth Five-Year Plan (2016-20). The Plenum was attended by 199 Central Committee members and 156 alternate Central Committee members and was presided over by CCP CC General Secretary Xi Jinping. Exhibiting responsibility for the Thirteenth Five-Year Plan (2016-20), Xi Jinping also gave the "Explanation" of the "Proposals" of the Discussion Draft to the Plenum.

In a strong suggestion that leadership issues would be discussed, the state-run *Global Times* on October 8, 2015, just days before the Fifth Plenum convened in a Beijing hotel, publicised a very unusual report posted on a WeChat site operated by the Party-owned *Beijing Daily*. Applauding Xi Jinping's initiative in effecting personnel reshuffles and launching the severe anti-corruption campaign, the state-run *Global Times* quoted Zhang Xixian, a Professor with the Central Party School, as saying, "The large-scale reshuffle helped select leaders of both action and bravery, as China needs such leaders to tackle the economic problems and ensure a strong start during the 13th Five-Year Plan (2016-20) period." The WeChat post on the Beijing Daily website disclosed that "more than half of the CCP CC members selected during the 18th Party Congress in 2012 have been moved to different positions or were removed from their current jobs ahead of the Fifth plenary session." Asserting that such a "large-scale reshuffle is extremely rare in the history of the CCP, a result, said observers of the anti-graft campaign, which has been of unprecedented severity," the WeChat post "revealed that a total of 104 out of the 205 CPC Central Committee members have been promoted, demoted or expelled from their positions since 2012."

Illustrative is the unprecedentedly vigorous and intensive anti-corruption campaign steered by the Party's Central Discipline Inspection Commission (CDIC) led by Xi Jinping's school friend, fellow "princeling" and Politburo Standing Committee (PBSC) member, 67-year-old Wang Qishan. It has penetrated the deepest corners of the Party, government and the People's Liberation Army (PLA) and felled over a hundred senior cadres of the level of central Vice Minister or Minister. Reports have disclosed that a total of 4,300 officers, or 30% of the PLA's officer cadre, have been arrested, or placed under investigation, on charges of corruption. This includes dozens of Generals.

Since his appointment in November 2012, Chinese President and Party General Secretary Xi Jinping has rapidly consolidated his authority and appointed loyalists to crucial posts. He has emerged as the most powerful leader since Mao Zedong and today overshadows all others in the seven-member PBSC. His authority is set to be further boosted with the Fifth Plenum approving the promotion of cadres selected by Xi Jinping. While he will try and promote his nominees to the 373-member CC to build an enduring power base and ensure elevation of his protégés to the Politburo (PB) and PBSC at the 19th Party Congress in 2017, Xi Jinping might quite possibly try to replace those retiring from the Politburo (PB) with a couple of his nominees belonging to the successor sixth generation. There is speculation in Beijing that the Fifth Plenum was to consider approving an extension for 67-year-old Wang Qishan, CDIC Chairman and PBSC member and allow him to continue in the 19th PBSC.

Decisions on some important appointments in China's military establishment, including cases relating to at least three "princelings," are due. The plenary session will need to decide on whether to now replace present PLA Navy (PLAN) Commander, Admiral Wu Shengli, a "princeling" who has reached 70 years which is the retirement age for a CMC member, or retain him till 2017. There has additionally been persistent speculation—in fact since the 18th Party Congress—of the elevation to the apex Central Military Commission (CMC) of General Liu Yuan, Political Commissar of the PLA's General Logistics Department (GLD) and son of former Chinese President Liu Shaoqi. General Liu Yuan, who has spoken out strongly against corruption in the PLA even before the 18th Party Congress, is a close friend of Xi Jinping and, like him, a "princeling." His promotion could mean either expansion of the CMC or creation of a new position in it. There is speculation also that 65-year-old General Zhang Youxia, also a "princeling" and close friend of Xi Jinping, is likely to be elevated at the next Party Congress in 2017 to the CMC as Vice Chairman. Zhang Youxia, a hardliner on issues concerning national sovereignty and territory and a staunch advocate of equipping the PLA with advanced defence technology and equipment, is one of the few PLA officers at that level with actual battle experience having fought in the Sino-Vietnam war in 1979. Xi Jinping's father, Xi Zhongxun and Zhang Youxia's father, General Zhang Zongxun also worked together in 1947 in the PLA's Northeast Army Corps as Political Commissar and Commanding Officer respectively.

While decisions on leadership appointments will largely be under wraps till the next Party Congress, the 5,923-character Communiqué issued after the Fifth Plenum formally approved the PB's elevation of Central Committee Alternate Members Liu Xiaokai (b. 1962), Chen Zhirong (b. 1957) and Jin Zhenji (b. 1959) as full Central Committee members. All three are ethnic minority cadres belonging to the Miao, Li and Korean ethnic minorities respectively. The Plenum also accorded formal approval to the CDIC's report "concerning grave disciplinary violations" of Ling Jihua, Zhou Benshun, Yang Dongliang, Zhu Mingguo, Wang Min, Chen Chuanping, Chou He, Yang Weize, Pan Yiyang and Yu Yuanhui, and endorsed the PB's decision expelling Ling Jihua, Zhou Benshun, Yang Dongliang, Zhu Mingguo, Wang Min, Chen Chuanping, Chou He, Yang Weize, Pan Yiyang and Yu Yuanhui from the Party.

The Thirteenth Five-Year Plan (2016-20) is important for China as it will cover the crucial stage when China crosses the "middle-income trap" to a higher stage of development. It comes at a time of growing economic difficulty and when official Chinese estimates are that approximately between US$ 300 billion to US$ 400 billion could be "illegally" taken out of China in 2015, reflecting continued lack of confidence in the country's economy. The official "2015 Graduate Study Abroad Situation Report" also revealed that the proportion of Chinese students returning compared to the numbers leaving China for foreign study has climbed steadily over the past 15 years and has now reached 75%. It added, however, that "many students are having great difficulty finding employment from which they can earn a good income, especially difficult since they had to send so much money for tuition overseas. Eighty per cent of the returned students earn less than 10,000 RMB per month." The article concludes that "this situation is making students and their families look at graduate study abroad more critically and to realise that they shouldn't just do to go along with a fad."

These issues were discussed at the Fifth Plenum together with probably lowering of China's growth target, accelerating state-sector reforms and redoubling efforts to reduce pollution. To invite public attention to the Thirteenth Five-Year Plan (shisanwu) the CCP CC's Propaganda Department took the unusual step of releasing a quick-tempo animated cartoon video. Earlier in September, the CCP CC's Propaganda Department issued a notice (No. 320 of 2015) to the *People's Daily*, Xinhua News Agency, *Guangming Daily*, *Economic Daily*, *China Daily*, China National Radio, China Central Television, China Radio International, China News Service, and subordinate media outlets listing "guidelines" for reporting on economic issues. The "guidelines" instructed them to "continue to deepen their study and transmission of the spirit of General Secretary Xi Jinping's series of important speeches, revolving around the strategic positioning of the 'Four Comprehensives' combined with deep concern for public opinion." It explained that the "guidelines" were intended to strengthen economic propaganda and channel public opinion preparatory to promoting the discourse on "China's bright economic future and the superiority of China's system, as well as stabilising expectations and inspiring confidence." The official media was asked to: (i) properly interpret economic data by using reports of the National Bureau of Statistics, the China Banking Regulatory Commission, and other relevant organisations; (ii) correctly report on new changes in economic market conditions; and (iii) closely follow economic market conditions.

Describing the Thirteenth Five-Year Plan (shisanwu) as a "decisive stage" in China's development, the Plenum Communiqué, which as usual omitted details of growth rates or targets that are expected to filter out separately, emphasised the goal of building a "moderately prosperous society by 2020." There was indication that the campaigns promoting austerity and against corruption would continue. It also pointed to the importance of agricultural modernisation and ideological and political work. There was noticeable emphasis on "innovation," construction of "strategic scientific laboratories" and implementing the "Internet Plus" action plan.

Interesting was the Communiqué's reference to the "new normal" while referring to economic development and call for reduced government interference in the setting of prices. Interestingly, the draft of the Plan posted on government websites and Baidu before the Plenum convened had mentioned that the Renminbi (RMB) would appreciate at 2% annually for each year of the Plan, but that portion of the draft has since been deleted. The Plenum simultaneously stressed that economic development "must persist in the dominant position of the people," thereby suggesting that the powerful and wealthy State-owned Enterprises (SoE) will continue to have an important role in the national economy. It took positive note of the "relatively rapid and stable economic development and social stability." Among the important points were: maintaining "a high-medium economic growth rate" which, basing their analysis on the 12th Five-Year Plan approved at the NPC, experts assess the Plenum would have approved in the range of between 6.5% and

7%; doubling the 2010 GDP and average incomes of rural and urban residents by 2020; and "letting industry march to a high-end economic level." It called for implementation of "China Manufacturing 2025," which is designed to create more skilled jobs and promote innovation in areas like pharmaceuticals, aerospace and new energy. The Plenum indicated that priority would be given to "implementing a strong network country strategy" and expanding the railway network. Strengthening of the security and military establishments was mentioned.

The Proposals approved by the Plenum did focus on the necessity of curbing emissions, "clean" technologies and a green environment. A cloud was cast over these statements, however, by the disclosures around the same period in the official statistics released by the Chinese government. These asserted that China has actually been consuming 17% more coal each year than reported, translating into the release into the atmosphere of almost a billion more tons of carbon dioxide annually. The new figures add about 600 million tons to China's coal consumption in 2012.

The Plenum Communiqué also enshrined Xi Jinping's vision of China's Dream and insisted there must be "a firm basis for the realisation of the second centenary struggle objective and the Chinese Dream of the great rejuvenation of the Chinese nation."

The Plenum document, which fully endorsed the policies and actions of the Party under Xi Jinping's leadership, concluded with a call to "the entire Party and the people of all ethnicities in the entire country to unite around the Party Centre with Comrade Xi Jinping as General Secretary ever more closely, to have one heart among the ten thousand masses ..."!

(The article was published by the Centre for China Analysis and Strategy and Institute of Peace and Conflict Studies, New Delhi, March 2015).

13

China's Sixth Plenum Designates Xi Jinping as "Core" of the Leadership

After four days (October 24-27, 2016) of deliberations at the military-owned Jingxi Hotel in Beijing, 197 full members and 151 alternate members attending the Sixth Plenary session of the Chinese Communist Party's (CCP) 18th Central Committee (CC) under the chairmanship of Chinese President Xi Jinping agreed that Xi Jinping would henceforth be designated the "core" (hexin) of the Party Centre, or fifth generation leadership. The decision, contained in the over 6,000-word Plenum document, however, clearly seemed to hold back from granting Xi Jinping unfettered authority by equally carefully emphasising "collective leadership" and asserting that "no party organisation or individual should suppress or undermine intra-party democracy."

The Plenum document clarified that in addition to the 197 members and 151 alternate members of the Central Committee, also present were members of the Central Discipline Inspection Commission (CDIC), relevant responsible comrades, some of the Party's 18 representatives of grass-roots comrades, and experts and scholars. Interesting was the Plenum document's tone, which continued the emphasis of the 18th Party Congress on the Party's supremacy, Party discipline and stability and underlined the importance of the Four Basic Principles and Marxist ideology. The Sixth Plenum document issued on October 27, 2016, said, "Comrade Xi Jinping as the core has taken the lead in setting an example, firmly promoting comprehensive and strict party governance. ..." It "called on the comrades of the whole party to unite closely around the Party Central Committee with Comrade Xi Jinping as the core and ... firmly establish the awareness of the political situation, the overall situation, the core consciousness and the awareness of the Party Central

Committee." Stressing the need for strict observance of Party discipline and norms, it used the term "strict" at least 15 times. There was indication that the campaigns against corruption and rectification of the Party would continue and the need for "supervision" was stressed and mentioned at least 40 times.

Coined by Deng Xiaoping, author of China's "Four Modernisations," the term "core of the Party Centre" was at the time intended to reinforce the pre-eminent political authority of Jiang Zemin who had been brought in from Shanghai and appointed as Party General Secretary in the midst of the Tiananmen turmoil in June 1989. Deng Xiaoping had then described Mao Zedong as the "core" of the first generation of leaders, Deng Xiaoping himself as representing the "core" of the second and Jiang Zemin as the "core" of the third generation of leadership. Hu Jintao, in large part because of his differences with Jiang Zemin who was reluctant to yield authority even after retirement and exercised considerable influence till very recently, was not described as the "core" of the fourth generation of leaders. By ascribing the position of "core" of the fifth generation to Xi Jinping, the Sixth Plenum decision has now affirmed Xi Jinping's decisive pre-eminent political status and placed him alongside Mao Zedong and Deng Xiaoping.

The effort to make Xi Jinping the "core" of the fifth generation of leadership has been deliberate. According to Wu Zhong of *Asia Times*, this was first suggested by Politburo member Wang Huning at a high-level Party meeting this January. Most significant, however, was the statement made in August 2016 by Li Zhanshu, Director of the CCP CC's powerful General Office and Xi Jinping's hand-picked confidant, who asked Party cadres to "staunchly … safeguard General Secretary Xi Jinping as the 'core'."

This was followed by all five Commanders of the People's Liberation Army's (PLA) newly-created Military Zones pledging loyalty to Xi Jinping. At least 15 provincial Party Secretaries have also endorsed Xi Jinping as the "core" leader. In fact, then Hubei Party Secretary, 1956-born Li Hongzhong, at a meeting of the Hubei Province Party Standing Committee on January 15, 2016, asserted that "the Politburo and its Standing Committee are the core leaders [hexin] of the party, General Secretary Xi Jinping is the core leader of the party centre. To proactively maintain the authority of the party centre means maintaining the leading core of General Secretary Xi Jinping." Li

Hongzhong was subsequently moved to the higher profile position of Party Secretary of Tianjin in September 2016.

A propaganda effort to build Xi Jinping's image as the "core" of the fifth generation was noticeable in the months preceding the Sixth Plenum with references in articles in China's state-controlled official media. The *People's Tribune*, which is affiliated to the official Party paper, *People's Daily*, on October 18 called for a "strongman" or "Great Leader." The following day, General Liu Yazhou, Political Commissar of the PLA's National Defence University (NDU) and a "princeling" close to Xi Jinping, wrote in the CCP CC Propaganda Department's journal Dangjian and asked for a "mature and strong core of the leadership." The day the session concluded on October 27, there was a more direct commentary in the *People's Daily*. It claimed that endorsing Xi Jinping as the "core of the party centre" embodied the common wish of "the party, the military, and all ethnic groups."

The title of "core" of the leadership will give Xi Jinping greater political authority at a time when China is beset by various problems as well as a slowdown in economic growth, worker lay-offs and widespread growing popular protests. In the context of domestic politics, it affirms Xi Jinping's standing within the CCP, diminishes challenges to his authority and will facilitate him override objections from other factional groupings. As Xi Jinping's acolytes have told *Caijing* magazine, Xi Jinping is ushering in a "new 30 years" which will put today's China on the threshold of a third era comparable to those begun by Mao Zedong and Deng Xiaoping! Xi Jinping has already announced the deadlines for two of the biggest national endeavours in recent years, namely, achieving "China's Dream" by the CCP's centenary in 2021 and the geo-economic initiative of "One Belt, One Road" (OBOR) by 2049 in time for the 100th anniversary of the People's Republic of China!

The Sixth Plenum decision will strengthen Xi Jinping's efforts to rectify and reform the 88-million strong CCP where 1 million members have already been punished, and also push ahead with the campaign against corruption which has made him popular with the common man. In a manner, the 348 members of the Party Central Committee have accorded their approval to the tough policies being implemented by Xi Jinping since the 18th Congress in November 2012. Noteworthy in this context is the Plenum's assertion "that the people of Hong Kong should not be allowed to stand up to the people."

To that extent the Sixth Plenum could facilitate Xi Jinping's attempts to induct cadres of his choice to the Central Committee (CC), Politburo (PB) and Politburo Standing Committee (PBSC) at the 19th Party Congress next October-November. Almost 90 vacancies are expected to arise in the Central Committee because of members reaching the retirement age, their dismissal on various charges of corruption or indiscipline, and death. Crucial are the eleven vacancies in the PB of which five are in the PBSC.

There are also inescapable foreign policy implications. The endorsement of Xi Jinping's policies since the 18th Congress, and assertive statement regarding the calls for "independence" in Hong Kong, include China's assertive foreign policy. China, it is assessed, will continue to stay focused on establishing sovereignty over the 3 million square kilometres of the South China Sea that it claims. Neither is there likely to be any softening in its stance on reunification with Taiwan. Similarly, any change in China's attitude towards India is very unlikely.

(The article was published in Centre for China Analysis and Strategy, New Delhi, October 31, 2016).

14

China: Document Number 9 and the New Propaganda Regime

Upset by the apparent indiscipline in the country's media and cultural space over the past couple of years, where ideas viewed as seeming to challenge the Chinese Communist Party's (CCP) authority were being openly aired, the new CCP leadership under its General Secretary Xi Jinping decided in January 2013, soon after its installation, to impose stringent regulations governing the propaganda and cultural organisations. The "Bo Xilai affair" had also severely jolted the Party and it is not without coincidence that the campaign to reform and control the media and cultural organisations coincides with the Party's severe "mass-line" campaign, which focuses on restoring adherence to the Party's ideology, traditions, values and discipline.

The parameters for "reform" of China's propaganda and cultural organisations are based on a tough speech delivered by Xi Jinping at the National Ideology and Propaganda Work Conference in Beijing over August 19-20, 2013, when he stressed the need for stringent controls over the country's Propaganda apparatus. These were promptly concretised later that month in the Party Document No. 9. The contents of Xi Jinping's speech, available elsewhere but only excerpts of which have been publicised by China's official media, were reinforced in a hard-hitting article published by the Party's authoritative theoretical magazine Qiushi *(Seeking Truth)* on October 16, 2013, and later repeated by China Central Television (CCTV). The Qiushi article calls for ideological uniformity, warns against "anti-China forces" who are attempting to "Westernise" China with the aim of destabilising it, and attacks those who have been proposing "neoliberal economic and constitutional governance reforms."

Propaganda and culture have traditionally been considered exceptionally important by authoritarian governments and communist regimes, including the CCP. The importance of the CCP Central Committee's (CC) Propaganda Department rests in its authority to control and shape the Party's narrative, particularly in an environment where the media is virtually entirely owned by the state. The collapse of the erstwhile Soviet Union further emphasised to the CCP the importance of political education as well as the need for effective controls on media and cultural organisations. Advent of the Internet and its rapid spread in China where the number of registered Internet users touched 500 million by July 2013, has made the task of the CCP CC's Propaganda Department more difficult despite the recruitment of an estimated 2 million "informal" Internet censors, or monitors, also known by the token amount they are paid namely, "Ten centers."

Controls over the media had slackened, especially in the uncertain political climate prior to the 18th Party Congress. An atmosphere of apparent laxity had allowed the airing and spread of fairly "liberal" ideas, which are anathema to communist regimes, in China's media, cultural and cyberspace over the past year or two. In China these included the advocacy of "democracy," demands for civil rights and freedoms for individuals, suggestions for the armed forces being moved out from under Party control and being placed under the State, etc.

An example of this laxity was evident as recently as on October 18, 2013, when a Guangzhou newspaper, the *New Express* challenged the CCP CC's Propaganda Department to demand the release of one of its journalists, Chen Yongzhou. Chen Yongzhou had exposed the apparent wrongdoings of a company owned by a provincial government. *New Express* was supported by other commercial media and bloggers despite the CCP CC Propaganda Department's instructions not to report on the incident. On October 26, however, the CCP CC's Propaganda Department enforced its writ and China's official media began reporting that Chen had confessed to being bribed to print disinformation and he was paraded on China Central Television (CCTV) in a prison uniform. By the following day, *New Express* had been cowed into publishing an apology for its earlier statements.

The CCP leadership's concern at the growing indiscipline in the media was accentuated by fears of US-led efforts to destabilise China. As the CCP, under the leadership of former Chinese President Hu Jintao, assessed that US-led efforts to destabilise China's communist regime particularly through the so-called "Shadow Internet" had intensified, the importance of the CCP CC's Propaganda Department increased over the past years.

In March 2011, Wu Bangguo, then a member of the Politburo Standing Committee (PBSC) and Chairman of China's version of a parliament, the National People's Congress (NPC), announced that there were five things China would never do. These were:

(i) no multiparty democracy (bu gao duodang lunliu zhizheng);
(ii) no ideological pluralism (bu gao zhidao sixiang duoyuanhua);
(iii) no separation of powers or bicameral legislature (bu gao "sanquan fenli" he liangyuanzhi);
(iv) no federalism (bu gao lianbangzhi); and
(v) no privatisation (bu gao siyouhua).

There has been no departure from these "Five Dont's" in the Party's official line over the years.

Clear indication of the mood within the Party was available at the sixth plenary session of the 17th CCP CC, held in October 2011, which listed propaganda and culture as the solitary item on its agenda. This was followed by the elevation of Liu Yunshan, a hardliner and then Director of the CCP CC's Propaganda Department and Politburo (PB) member, to the 7-man ruling Politburo Standing Committee (PBSC) at the 18th Party Congress held in November 2012. Liu Yunshan was credited with overseeing the dramatic rejuvenation of the Party's propaganda from an ineffective policy of lax control to an energetic policy aimed at actively shaping public discourse. He proactively managed the propaganda apparatus during the 2008 riots in Lhasa and successfully drove a wedge between the majority Han population and Tibetans. Liu Yunshan retained charge of the propaganda and culture portfolio after his promotion to the 7-member PBSC, indicating that the new Party leadership's views on propaganda and culture remain unchanged and continue to be restrictive. His influence is demonstrated by his presence next to Xi Jinping in official photographs of all propaganda-related functions.

Soon after the sixth Plenum in October 2011, then Chinese President Hu Jintao declared in a signed essay in the January 2012 issue of the CCP theoretical magazine Qiushi *(Seeking Truth)* that: "we must clearly see that international hostile forces are intensifying the strategic plot of westernising and dividing China, and ideological and cultural fields are the focal areas of their long-term infiltration." He asserted "we should ... take forceful measures to be on guard and respond." His essay indicated approval of the major policy initiatives announced at the October plenum. Vice President Xi Jinping reinforced this on January 4, 2012, adding that ideological control and political education in universities needs to be strengthened.

Xi Jinping as CCP CC General Secretary and President of China presided over his first meeting of the National Conference of Chiefs of Propaganda Departments in January 2013, which endorsed the assessment that efforts were being made to undermine and overthrow the CCP. The conference directed Propaganda officials at all levels to tighten media control and ensure proper enforcement of the "Seven No's." On May 13, 2013, the CCP CC's Propaganda Department issued a document summarising the main conclusions of the meeting of Propaganda Chiefs and entitled "Report on the Current Situation of the Ideological Front." The May 13 document identified seven "dangerous" topics, namely, universal values, press freedom, civil society, civil rights, errors of the Chinese Communist Party (CCP), crony capitalism and judicial independence.

Simultaneously, in May 2013, the CCP issued an internal circular to all Party Committees entitled, "On the Current Situation in the Ideological Domain", which listed "Seven Things That Should Not Be Discussed." Zhang Xuezhong, a Professor of Political Science at Shanghai's East China University divulged the contents of this document on his Sina Weibo microblog. Zhang Xuezhong's post was soon deleted from Weibo before the topic was censored. His posting listed the seven topics on which universities and the media were to discourage discussion.

The seven things are:

(i) universal values;

(ii) freedom of the press;

(iii) civil society;

(iv) civil rights;

(v) historical mistakes by the Party;
(vi) Party-elite capitalism; and
(vii) judicial independence.

Implementation of measures to exercise tighter and more effective control over media outlets began after this conference from around May 2013. A Report to the Centre for International Media Assistance (October 22, 2013) quoted from the annual report of the Hong Kong Journalists Association's (HKJA) issued in July 2013, and pointed out that a series of personnel and structural changes were underway in many media outlets in Hong Kong to ensure increased compliance with the Party "line." Examples mentioned include the *Sing Pao Daily News*, where a veteran Xinhua News Agency journalist was appointed as publisher. Special internal groups were established at three Beijing-owned, or pro-Beijing, newspapers namely the *Ta Kung Pao*, *Wen Wei Po*, and the *Hong Kong Commercial Daily*. Their members are mostly from the mainland and they are tasked with vetting and approving the articles that these media outlets are considering publishing.

Around the same time, following Xi Jinping's comments of January 2013, efforts commenced to intensify the "ideological and political" training of young university teachers. An "Opinion" jointly authored by the CCP CC's Organisation Department, Propaganda Department and Ministry of Education was published by the official Party newspaper, *People's Daily*, on May 28, 2013. It asserted that "a few young teachers are lost in their political beliefs. They have fuzzy ideals and beliefs, their occupational and professional ethics are fading. ... They cannot serve as role models for others." It listed 16 areas where emphasis was necessary for enhancing "ideological and political" training. A key feature was deepening of education in "the theoretical systems of Marxism, Leninism, Mao Zedong Thought, and socialism with Chinese characteristics." These areas of concern are reflected in the Document No. 9.

The Document No. 9, issued in August 2013, is a detailed prescriptive guideline for regulating China's propaganda and cultural organisations. Describing the current ideological situation as "complicated" and the struggle as "fierce," it lists seven "incorrect ways of thinking." These include: advocating Western constitutional democracy thereby negating the current leadership and government system led by the CCP; advocating "universal values" in a bid to substitute the core value system of socialism with Western values; advocating "new liberalism" with the aim of dismantling State-owned Enterprises (SoEs) and changing China's basic economic system; challenging the Party's control of the media and the system for managing the press and publications; and, trying to deny the CCP's history and the history of the People's Republic of China, including the "scientific value and guiding role of Mao Zedong Thought."

It said these "incorrect thoughts and views" had seeped into China via the Internet and underground channels. Internal Internet fora, blogs, weibo, conferences, seminars and university classes were listed among the platforms used for such "infiltration." It was adamant that "anti-China forces in Western countries and domestic dissidents" are continuously "infiltrating China's ideological domain and challenging mainstream ideology."

The Document accused some Western embassies and consulates in China, media organisations and NGOs of spreading Western values and views and "cultivating so-called anti-government forces." In an implicit reference to the Bloomberg and *New York Times* reports, which revealed the extent of wealth amassed by the families of former Chinese Premier Wen Jiabao and Xi Jinping respectively, it accused them of "spreading political rumours and smearing Party and national leaders." The Document warned that "Western anti-China forces" will persist in encouraging change and continue to point the "spearhead of Westernisation, separatism and 'colour revolution' at China." In conclusion, it was unequivocal in demanding "that the power of leading the press and media is always controlled by the hands of those who are at one with the Central Committee of the Party with Comrade Xi Jinping as General Secretary."

Coinciding with the issue of Document No. 9, media organisations were informed that all journalists in China will be vetted and issued fresh press accreditation cards after they pass an examination to ascertain their political reliability. Directions were issued summoning the first batch of 250,000 journalists to report for a 3-month training programme where subjects include "theories on socialism with Chinese characteristics," and the "Marxist view on journalism." The journalists have been directed to reject ideas of democracy and human rights, which are described as values propagated by the West and targeting China's Communist Party. They are taught that the United States is "trying to undermine" China. They have also been told not to write articles favourable to Japan while discussing territorial and historical issues between the two countries. Similar instructions have been given with regard to the Philippines and Vietnam.

Promptly after issue of Document No. 9 by the CCP CC Propaganda Department, new restrictions were imposed limiting the number of foreign programmes that a television station could telecast. These were limited to only one in a year. The programmes cannot be telecast during the prime-time viewing hours from 7.30 p.m. to 10.00 p.m. Television stations have additionally been mandated to allocate a minimum of 30 per cent of their total programming time to the telecast of public-interest programming, such as documentaries, education and "morality-building" programmes. New musical talent shows which are mostly copies of those in the West and which have become very popular in China, are limited to one every three months.

The CCP leadership's concern about China's ethnic minority nationalities is manifest in Document No. 9 which, pertinently, makes particular mention of efforts to "manipulate and stir up Tibetans to self-immolate, create violent and terrorist incidents and in Xinjiang, use ethnic and religious issues for separatist and disruptive activities." Tibet, where Party surveillance and control has been increased over the past two years, has been quick to feel the impact of Document No. 9 and the recently launched "mass-line" campaign.

This latest campaign aimed at propaganda and cultural organisations has been authorised at the highest echelons of the CCP and is intended to re-emphasise the Party's ideology and reinforce Party control. It is a broad spectrum campaign that aims to regulate and control media and cultural organisations, while proactively challenging perceived Western-led attempts to undermine the CCP's authority and ruling position. This campaign to reform and tighten the CCP's control over the media, including "new media" and culture, needs to be viewed together with the "mass-line" campaign now underway in China. Both are long-term campaigns.

(The article was published in the Institute of Peace and Conflict Studies, New Delhi, November 2013).

15

China's Defence White Paper 2013

China issued its eighth biannual Defence White Paper entitled, "The Diversified Employment of China's Armed Forces," on April 16, 2013. The last White Paper, pertaining to 2010, was published in 2011. China's Defence White Paper 2013, is a 47-page document with five sections and 3 short appendices listing: joint exercises and training with foreign armed forces from 2011 to 2012; participation of China's armed forces in international disaster relief and rescue (2011-12); and China's participation in UN peacekeeping operations (2011-12).

The Defence White Paper 2013 makes it apparent that the Asia-Pacific region currently dominates Chinese military thinking. This Defence White Paper is at once an expression of the Chinese leadership's self-confidence and its confidence in the capabilities of its armed forces. After the ritual assertion that China will "not seek hegemony, behave in a hegemonic manner or engage in military expansion" and brief token acknowledgement of the importance of international cooperation, it states clearly that the military build-up and modernisation will continue. There is discernible emphasis on expanding the capabilities and operational reach of the People's Liberation Army Navy (PLAN) and PLA Air Force (PLAAF) together with increased investment in domestic R&D to upgrade the indigenous defence industry.

China started to fall in line with international practice on matters relating to military transparency since 1998, when it first began to publish Defence White Papers. Issued with the twin objectives of meeting international demands for a degree of transparency with regard to its defence modernisation programme as well as wanting to stay engaged with the international community, China has, of late, also begun using the Defence White Papers to publicise its national objectives and world view, albeit in a very cautious way. In this, it follows the practice of other nations.

Though they avoid specifics, China's Defence White Papers nevertheless do offer an insight into the broad thinking of senior echelons of the Chinese political and military leadership associated with matters of national defence. Unlike Western documents that also focus more on detail and specific capabilities, China's Defence White Papers gloss over specifics and reveal few details of expenditure or weapons acquisitions or manufacture. China's record of transparency in these matters remains opaque, though there has been slight incremental improvement over the years. As could be expected in a country where the armed forces are subordinate to the ruling political party, namely, the Chinese Communist Party (CCP), China's Defence White Papers blend political thinking with the broad plans for the armed forces. The leadership's thinking on a range of issues including: the future plans and role of the armed forces; anticipated areas of conflict; levels of suspicion of other countries; areas of China's interest; and the extent of military cooperation with foreign nations, are discernible in the present Defence White Paper 2013. China too uses the Defence White Papers as instruments of politics and diplomacy.

China's world view outlined in the latest Defence White Paper clearly highlights its preoccupation with the developments in the Asia-Pacific region, especially the role of the US, and identifies potential anticipated threats to China's ambitions. In the initial two paragraphs of its first Section captioned, "New Situation, New Challenges and New Missions," the Defence White Paper singles out the Asia-Pacific region as having become "an increasingly significant stage for world economic development and strategic interaction between major powers." Hinting at Beijing's concern about US interference it says, "The US is adjusting its Asia-Pacific security strategy, and the regional landscape is undergoing profound changes." A blunt, yet thinly veiled, comment follows in the very next paragraph with the assertion that "Some country has strengthened its Asia-Pacific military alliances, expanded its military presence in the region, and frequently makes the situation there tenser." The implied reference to the US is unmistakable.

The next sentence in the same paragraph makes specific mention of Japan as one among "some neighbouring countries" that are taking actions to exacerbate the situation and cites its "making trouble over the issue of the Diaoyu islands" as example. Affirming that the threat from the "three forces" of terrorism, separatism and extremism is increasing, this White Paper in language almost identical to that used in the Defence White Paper of 2010, describes "Taiwan independence separatist forces" as "still the biggest threat to the peaceful development of cross-Straits relations." Security risks to China's overseas interests, it concludes, are on the rise.

Clarifying the role of the armed forces as "to win local wars under the conditions of informationisation," it listed among the tasks for the armed forces the containing of "separatist forces," safeguarding border, coastal and territorial air security, and "protecting national maritime rights and interests" and "national security interests in outer space and cyberspace." Significant are the independent references to the armed forces providing "reliable support for China's interests overseas" and "firmly safeguarding China's core national interests." These "core national interests" are neither defined nor elaborated.

Of particular concern to China's neighbours with unresolved, or overlapping, territorial claims are the portions relating to the PLAN and PLAAF in the section on "Building and Development of China's Armed Forces." The PLAN, it affirmed, will accelerate its pace of modernisation and develop advanced submarines, destroyers and frigates and develop blue-water capabilities of conducting mobile operations. It described the development of an aircraft carrier as having a "profound impact on building a strong PLAN and safeguarding maritime security." Interestingly, the release of this Defence White Paper coincided with the official disclosure the same day—incidentally also PLA Navy Day—that China's new aircraft carrier "Liaoning" would go on a long voyage on the high seas later this year. Separate reports suggest it could sail from its present berth at Qingdao's military dock within about 3 months up to Okinawa or Guam.

The PLAAF, it said, is developing advanced weaponry and equipment such as new-generation fighters, new types of ground-to-air missiles and radar systems, improving its early warning command and communications networks and "raising its strategic early warning, strategic deterrence and long-distance air strike capabilities." There is no mention of the 3-phase R&D effort underway to indigenously develop advanced jet engines for the PLAAF, disclosed in mid-March 2013 and for which a huge budgetary allocation has already been made.

A novel feature of China's Defence White Paper this year is the disclosure of troop strengths of the PLAA, PLAN and PLAAF. It was accompanied by a sketchy outline of the deployment of their formations and, in the case of the PLAA, the identifying numbers of the Combined Armies located in each of the seven Military Regions (MR), which the Defence White Paper called Military Area Commands (MAC). The PLAA's troop strength was disclosed as 850,000. Listing the MRs in order of seniority, it disclosed the following Combined Army deployments: Shenyang (16th, 39th, and 40th); Beijing (27th, 38th, and 65th); Lanzhou (21st and 47th); Jinan (20th, 26th and 54th); Nanjing (1st, 12th and 31st); Guangzhou (41st and 42nd); and Chengdu (13th and 14th). The disclosure in the White Paper 2013 confirms the deployments estimated by foreign analysts.

The total strength of the PLAN was stated to be 235,000, while that of the PLAAF was declared to be 398,000 with an Air Command at each of the MRs. This official revelation of troop strengths has helped correct international estimates that were in use till now. These estimates placed the PLAN's total strength as ranging between 255,000 and 290,000 with that of the PLAAF ranging between 300,000 and 330,000. China's Defence White Paper 2013, now shows that estimates for the PLAN were low while those for the PLAAF were high. China's strategic missile force, or the PLA Second Artillery Force (PLASAF), continues to stay shrouded in secrecy and no details of its strength or deployments have been disclosed.

A close reading of this Defence White Paper reveals certain possible policy level statements. Specifically, these pertain to the use of missiles and nuclear weapons. It described China's strategic missile force, namely the PLA Second Artillery (PLASAF), as a "core force for China's strategic deterrence." It disclosed that the PLASAF will use nuclear missiles to launch a counter-attack either independently or in conjunction with "the nuclear forces of other services." It added that the PLASAF's conventional missile force can shift "instantly" from peacetime to wartime readiness "and conduct conventional medium- and long-range precision strikes." Absent in the White Paper were the routine references to non-first use of nuclear weapons by China, though while referring to the PLASAF's role the terms "strategic deterrence" and "nuclear counter-attacks" were repeatedly used. The assertion that the PLASAF will use its nuclear missiles in conjunction with those of other services makes clear that all the services of the PLA are operationally nuclear capable. That the PLASAF will engage in conventional conflict is made clear in the White Paper, which raises the risk of miscalculation by the adversary.

As in the Defence White Paper 2011, which used the acronym for the first time, this White Paper also refers to the PLA's ground forces as the PLAA. There has, however, been scattered mention of the PLAA in China's official media through 2012. The Defence White Paper 2013 similarly placed the PLAA, or PLA Army, first followed by the PLAN, PLAAF, PLASAF and the People's Armed Police Force (PAPF). Details of the role and functions of the PAPF, militia and border militia, and the Hong Kong and Macao garrisons are additions in this year's White Paper.

Repeated usage of the acronyms PLAA, PLAN, PLAAF and PLASAF indicates that these services are increasingly acquiring independent identities and coming out from under the dominance and control of the PLAA or the PLA's ground forces. The composition of the new Central Military Commission reinforces this view. The moves would be part of the leaderships' effort to professionalise the armed forces, inculcate "service pride" in each service and encourage each of them to generate their own doctrines, or theories, of war and battle plans.

Nevertheless as the large number of PLAA personnel present among the Delegates and Deputies to the 18th Party Congress and 12th NPC reveals, the status and influence of the PLA ground forces remains unaffected, though they have probably dropped more to the level of "primus inter pares." Furthermore, the Military Region Commanders are all from the ground forces and the PLAAF and PLAN personnel are placed under their command. PLA General Departments too continue to be staffed mainly by personnel from the ground services and they are the ones who plan, formulate and issue central directives.

China's Defence White Paper 2013 touched on the other roles of the armed forces including Military Operations Other Than War (MOOTW), joint exercises and training with foreign forces and international disaster relief.

It dwelt at some length on the contribution of the Chinese armed forces to international peacekeeping where Africa came into focus.

Finally, this Defence White Paper contained two references to India in one paragraph and in the same context. This was in the context of the observation that "since January 2012, independent deployers such as China, India and Japan have strengthened their convoy coordination."

(The article was published in the Institute of Peace and Conflict Studies, New Delhi, April 2013).

16

China's Defence White Paper 2015

On May 26, 2015, China's Ministry of National Defense (MND) issued its ninth White Paper entitled 'China's Military Strategy'. This 9000-character (in Chinese or 6,393 words in English), 6-chapter long White Paper is the first ever to have been issued which solely discusses China's military strategy. Reflecting Beijing's self-confidence, the White Paper spells out China's expanded 'national interests' and role envisaged for its armed forces which, it asserted, must "effectively secure China's overseas interests". Outlining the PLA's role, the White Paper says "national security is more vulnerable to international and regional turmoil, terrorism, piracy, serious natural disasters and epidemics, and the security of overseas interests concerning energy and resources, strategic sea lines of communication (SLOCs), as well as institutions, personnel and assets abroad, has become an imminent issue".

Important is the White Paper's assessment of China's domestic security situation. Unlike in 2013, this White Paper makes specific mention of Tibet indicating the upgraded importance of the Tibet issue to the Chinese Communist Party (CCP) leadership. The toughly-worded paragraph in the White Paper emphasises that "China faces a formidable task to maintain political security and social stability. Separatist forces for "East Turkistan independence" and "Tibet independence" have inflicted serious damage, particularly with escalating violent terrorist activities by "East Turkistan independence" forces. Besides, anti-China forces have never given up their attempt to instigate a "color revolution" in this country. Consequently, China faces more challenges in terms of national security and social stability".

The PLA is predictably enjoined to "firmly follow the goals of the Chinese Communist Party (CCP)", "resolutely safeguard China's sovereignty, security and development interests", and provide a "strong guarantee for realising the

Chinese Dream of achieving the great rejuvenation of the Chinese nation". Unlike those issued earlier, this White Paper includes none of the purportedly conciliatory references to the 'Five Principles of Peaceful Coexistence' or 'harmonious world'.

China's first officially described White Paper was issued nearly 20 years ago in November 1998, and was simply called "China's National Defense." Thereafter, in a bid to build its credentials as a 'responsible' major power which is transparent on defence issues, China has issued defence-related White Papers almost every two years. The series of white papers are official statements of Chinese government policy and usually provide Beijing's official view of the contemporary international and regional situation, relations with Taiwan and a statement of the major elements of China's defense policy. Most of the White Papers contained only general information regarding China's military policies or the People's Liberation Army (PLA), except for those issued in 2011 and 2013, which included new details of China's force structure and strength, organization, doctrine and the national defense mobilization system.

China's White Papers of 2011, 2013 and the current White Paper of 2015, all reveal that efforts continue to formalise the identities of the different services and distinguish between the PLA's ground forces and the PLA Air Force (PLAAF), PLA Navy (PLAN) and the PLA Second Artillery (PLASAF). The White Paper of 2011, in fact, for the first time referred to the ground forces as the PLA Army (PLAA) and this practice is continued in the subsequent White Papers. The White Paper of 2013, titled "Diversified Employment of China's Armed Forces," also for the first time ever officially provided details of the force strengths of the PLAA, PLAAF, PLAN and PLASAF.

The latest White Paper reflects Beijing's continuing concern about its periphery and, while acknowledging that the international environment is generally peaceful, dwells on the likelihood of "immediate" and "potential threats of local wars". It notes that "small-scale wars, conflicts and crises" continue to recur in some regions. It identified the "international competition for the redistribution of power, rights and interests" as a new threat confronting China. Others were listed as including increased terrorist activities and complex and volatile "hotspot issues, such as ethnic, religious, border and territorial disputes".

Pertinent is the assessment in Chapter I of the White Paper which, while reiterating China's maritime territorial claims, conveys a thinly veiled warning to countries in the region. It observes that "as the world economic and strategic center of gravity is shifting ever more rapidly to the Asia-Pacific region, the US carries on its "rebalancing" strategy and enhances its military presence and its military alliances in this region. Japan is sparing no effort to dodge the post-war mechanism, overhauling its military and security policies....On the issues concerning China's territorial sovereignty and maritime rights and interests, some of its offshore neighbors take provocative actions and reinforce their military presence on China's reefs and islands that they have illegally occupied. Some external countries are also busy meddling in South China Sea affairs; a tiny few maintain constant close-in air and sea surveillance and reconnaissance against China. It is thus a long-standing task for China to safeguard its maritime rights and interests. Certain disputes over land territory are still smoldering. The Korean Peninsula and Northeast Asia are shrouded in instability and uncertainty. Regional terrorism, separatism and extremism are rampant. All these have a negative impact on the security and stability along China's periphery".

Declaring that "without a strong military a country can be neither safe nor strong", the White Paper focused on the Preparations for Military Struggle (PMS) and directed the armed forces to accelerate efforts to raise combat capability. Modifying the guidelines for PMS which had last been revised in 2004, it said emphasis would now be placed on "winning informationized local wars, highlighting maritime military struggle and maritime PMS". China's armed forces were mandated to conduct live-setting training, IT-based simulated training, and face-on-face confrontation training in line with real-combat criteria. Training in complex electro-magnetic environments, complex and unfamiliar terrains, and complex weather conditions are to be intensified. It said the PLAA will improve combat readiness with combined arms and ensure agile maneuvers and effective response. The PLAN will continue to perform regular combat readiness patrols and maintain a military presence in relevant sea areas. The PLAAF will maintain vigilant and efficient combat readiness with all-dimensional response and full territorial reach while observing the principles applicable in peacetime and wartime. It disclosed that the PLASAF will maintain an appropriate level of vigilance in peacetime and remain action-ready.

The White Paper listed the strategic tasks for China's armed forces. These include to:

- deal with a wide range of emergencies and military threats, and effectively safeguard the sovereignty and security of China's territorial land, air and sea;
- resolutely safeguard the unification of the motherland;
- safeguard China's security and interests in new domains;
- safeguard the security of China's overseas interests;
- maintain strategic deterrence and carry out nuclear counterattack; and
- strengthen efforts in operations against infiltration, separatism and terrorism so as to maintain China's political security and social stability.

The White Paper additionally detailed some of the enhanced capabilities that China's armed forces will acquire in the coming years. This includes aero-space and cyber capabilities. Stating that the new tasks of the PLA ground forces require "mobile operations" and "multi-dimensional offense and defense", it said the PLA Army (PLAA) will "continue to reorient from theater defense to trans-theater mobility", build small, multi-functional and modular units and "elevate its capabilities for precise, multi-dimensional, trans-theater, multi-functional and sustainable operations". The importance of integrated joint operations (IJO) was underscored.

The PLA Navy (PLAN)'s role has been considerably expanded from one of "offshore waters defense" as at present to the combination of "offshore waters defense" with "open seas protection." The PLAN has accordingly been tasked to build a "combined, multi-functional" marine combat force structure. Earmarked for enhancement is the PLAN's "strategic deterrence and counterattack" capability.

The White Paper similarly added a definitive offensive role for the PLA Air Force (PLAAF). It said the PLAAF will "endeavor to shift its focus from territorial air defense to both defense and offense, and build an air-space defense force structure". The PLAAF will also boost its capabilities for "strategic early warning, air strike, air and missile defense, information countermeasures, airborne operations, strategic projection and comprehensive support".

The PLASAF, it said, will continue to have nuclear and conventional missiles in its inventory and accelerate development of independent innovations in weaponry and equipment. It was tasked to improve the force structure by combining nuclear and conventional capabilities. The White Paper said the PLASAF will strengthen its capabilities for strategic deterrence and nuclear counterattack, and medium- and long-range precision strikes.

The People's Armed Police Force (PAPF) came in for mention with the White Paper highlighting its role in effectively maintaining social stability and contingency response, counter-terrorism operations etc. The indication is that the PAPF will acquire more and modern equipment and that the domestic security apparatus will continue to receive high budgetary allocations.

While the PLAN already receives a proportionately larger share of the defence budget, this latest White Paper highlights the importance of the maritime domain and goes well beyond the White Paper of 2013 in emphasising the importance of naval power. Appearing to set the stage for the next round of military reforms, it unambiguously declared: "The traditional mentality that land outweighs sea must be abandoned, and great importance has to be attached to managing the seas and oceans and protecting maritime rights and interests". China, it said, must "develop a modern maritime military force structure commensurate with its national security and development interests, safeguard its national sovereignty and maritime rights and interests, protect the security of strategic SLOCs and overseas interests....so as to provide strategic support for building itself into a maritime power".

The importance accorded to these issues by China's leadership was immediately visible when Beijing deputed Admiral Sun Jiangguo, PLA Deputy Chief of General Staff and a potential successor to Admiral Wu Shengli as Commander of the PLAN, to lead a large Chinese delegation to the Shangri La Dialogue held in Singapore just three days later on May 29-30, 2015. Though Admiral Sun Jiangguo delivered a mildly worded speech from a prepared text, he declined to respond to any questions regarding the South China Sea disputes from representatives of other participating nations and requested them to separately discuss issues bilaterally with the PLA delegation.

China's effort to build the PLAN's maritime capability has accelerated after the 18th Party Congress and articulation by Chinese President Xi Jinping of the muscular 'China's Dream'. Just months earlier in May 2012, Beijing had begun to issue new Chinese passports sparking protests internationally. The passports appeared to be a re-statement of China's perceived territorial limits and mirror the extent of the Chinese nation as envisioned in the maps published by Beijing in 1954, and which continue to be taught in China till today. The map, which is part of a textbook titled "A Brief History of Modern China", claims to show nineteen of "the Chinese territories taken by the Imperialists in the old Democratic Revolutionary Era (1840-1919)". These include Nepal, Bhutan, Burma (Myanmar) and in India the state of Sikkim and territories in the north-east comprising the former states of Assam, NEFA and Nagaland, as well as the Andaman Islands.

The latest White Paper also removes the ambiguity in the previous White Paper regarding use of nuclear weapons. It categorically states "China has always pursued the policy of no first use of nuclear weapons" and "China will unconditionally not use or threaten to use nuclear weapons against non-nuclear-weapon states or in nuclear-weapon-free zones, and will never enter into a nuclear arms race with any other country". It did, however, say China "will optimize its nuclear force structure....and survivability and protection, and deter other countries from using or threatening to use nuclear weapons against China".

The White Paper makes clear that China perceives this as "an important period of strategic opportunity" during which it can realize "the Chinese Dream of great national rejuvenation". Its focus and tone have undoubtedly aroused concern among China's neighbours and especially the countries which have unresolved territorial, including maritime, disputes with China.

China's insistent push for its strategic geo-economic initiative of 'One Road, One Belt' (New Silk Road Economic Belt and Maritime Silk Route) strongly suggests it is intent on becoming a global maritime power. A US estimate claims that China has plans to increase its Navy to 351 ships by 2020. Release of the White Paper, 2015 also coincides with the growing tensions in the South China Sea and Beijing's testy relations with the US.

The White Paper is of direct relevance to India. It comes in the backdrop of the appreciably and recently visibly upgraded Sino-Pakistan strategic relationship which has impinged on India's sovereignty and territorial integrity and Beijing's continuing intransigence on tackling the issue of the disputed border or intrusion by PLA troops.

It confirms that the PLA continues to rapidly build capability to win local wars. The focus is on acquiring the capability to rapidly move, by land or air, units of well-armed and well-equipped troops from locations across China to the borders. The White Paper additionally states that the PLAA and PLAAF will increase patrolling along the borders and the PLAN will enhance force projection activities in the South China Seas and increase its visibility in the oceans.

Of particular importance is the apparent upgradation of the Tibet issue and references to the "separatist forces" of "Tibet independence", "serious damage" they have inflicted and "formidable task" of maintaining security. Relevant are the observations that among the new threats that China confronts, are the "international competition for the redistribution of power, rights and interests"; that "certain disputes over land territory are still smoldering"; the existence of "hotspot issues, such as ethnic, religious, border and territorial disputes"; and the likelihood of "immediate" and "potential threats of local wars". These highlight Beijing's continuing concern of the situation on its periphery. The reference to "international competition for the redistribution of power...", however, hints that Beijing views India as a longer term challenge.

(The article was republished in the Indian Strategic Studies, New Delhi, June 2015).

17

Xi Jinping and China's Major Military Reforms—2015

Chinese President Xi Jinping's public announcement downsizing the People's Liberation Army (PLA) at the grand military parade on September 3, 2015, was a major event. It signalled that the final stages of reform and reorganisation of the PLA would begin now that internal consensus had been reached. Despite the transparently thin attempt to package the 300,000 personnel troop reduction as a move towards promoting peace, the troop reduction is actually part of a long-planned effort to streamline and strengthen the PLA and fashion it into a high-tech, lethal, "informationised" force capable of defending China's national interests at home and abroad while expanding China's strategic space.

These reforms have direct implications for India and countries in the region, with whom China has territorial disputes or who have borders with it. They will undoubtedly monitor the reforms closely.

Plans for military reforms and restructuring were finalised earlier and downsizing the PLA is part of the final phase. After the release for internal circulation of the "PLA's Development Outline for Cultivating Armed Forces Talent before the Year 2020" (referred to only as the "Outline"), which spelt out plans for restructuring the PLA, official documents described the five-year (2011-15) period as "crucial" in the PLA's development.

The plans received a substantive push when the Chinese Communist Party's (CCP) Third Plenum, which was held in November 2013, approved proposals for major organisational restructuring and technological upgradation of the PLA. Within days after the Third Plenum, CMC Vice Chairman and former PLA Air Force (PLAAF) Commander, Xu Qiliang, asserted that the reforms will be implemented, that non-combatant personnel would be "eliminated," and that the reforms will enable the PLA to "win wars."

On March 15, 2014, China's authoritative official news agency, Xinhua, announced the creation of a new "Small Leading Group for Deepening Reform of National Defence and the Military." It was set up as a sub-committee of the Central Military Commission (CMC) under the chairmanship of Xi Jinping assisted by two Deputy Chairmen who were also the Vice Chairmen of the CMC, namely, General Fan Changlong and General Xu Qiliang. Names of the other members have not yet been disclosed, but outspoken General Liu Yuan, a high-ranking "princeling" close to Xi Jinping and Political Commissar of the PLA's General Logistics Department (GLD), is probably one member.

Implementation of the reforms has been delayed by institutional resistance and the PLA's downsizing is now expected to be completed only by 2017. Among the factors prompting resistance were reports that consequent to the reorganisation of Military Regions (MR) and PLA Headquarters in Beijing, a number of Generals and senior officers would be rendered redundant and transferred to Beijing. This meant loss of authority and perquisites, such as housing, which they currently enjoy. The different services also resisted downsizing of their personnel strengths and reduction in their share of the budget.

At least two signed articles in the *Liberation Army Daily* (LAD) on September 9, 2015, publicised the existence of resistance to reforms inside the PLA. The first article cautioned that implementation of the reforms would be difficult and "would require an assault on fortified positions to change mindsets and root out vested interests, and that the difficulties would be unprecedented." Advocating their implementation, which it asserted were essential, the article observed that "if these reforms failed, measures still to come would be nothing more than an empty sheet of paper."

Reiterating that implementing military reforms would be difficult, another article in the same paper said that as reforms begin to be implemented, "there could be significant structural contradictions and an accumulation of institutional obstacles." Its author, Ma Depao, was associated with the Academy of Military Sciences (AMS) till 2006, but is now probably with the PLA Daily.

In this backdrop, the presence on the podium of Hu Jintao and Jiang Zemin, Chinese President and Chairman of the Central Military Commission (CMC) Xi Jinping's two immediate predecessors, was significant. Their presence next to Xi Jinping was intended as assurance—to domestic and foreign audiences of support for Xi Jinping and his plans to reform and restructure the PLA. Jiang Zemin's presence was particularly significant since a large number of the PLA Generals and senior officers under arrest, or under investigation, on charges of corruption are closely associated with Jiang Zemin or his protégés. Rumours were also circulating for some months in official circles in Beijing that Jiang Zemin was either already under house arrest, or likely to be detained soon.

A compromise regarding military reforms was undoubtedly reached before Xi Jinping announced the downsizing of the PLA on September 3, 2015. In addition to support for the reforms from his fellow "princelings" and loyalists in senior echelons of the PLA, support would additionally have come from the younger, more professional officers. Resistance would have been diluted by the vigorous campaign against corruption launched by the Central Discipline Inspection Commission (CDIC) in the PLA and efforts at "education" by the PLA's General Political Department (GPD), with both efforts facilitated by the 40 per cent hike in salaries and allowances awarded to PLA personnel last year.

The troop reduction of 300,000 announced on September 3, 2015, is far less than the 800,000 envisaged in 2011. In April 2011, the Beijing-owned Hong Kong based *Wen Wei Po* newspaper publicised plans for reducing the PLA's size by 800,000 personnel. While the report was denied by China's Defence Ministry, Professor Han Xudong of China's National Defence University (NDU), commenting on the *Wen Wei Po* report to *Global Times*, a subsidiary of the authoritative CCP newspaper *People's Daily*, disclosed that *Wen Wei Po's* report was the personal opinion of a retired PLA General formerly in charge of downsizing. He added, though, that the Defence Ministry's denial did not mean there would be no reductions in the future. Hinting at the extent of personnel cuts, he elaborated that since the US has a 1.4 million army and India a 1.2 million army, a 1.5 million strength for the PLA would be adequate.

Separately, Chinese military officers commenting on the *Wen Wei Po* report on background to *Jane's*, said the central authorities were working out targets for future downsizing, but big cuts are unlikely. Reductions, they said, could be expected in 2-3 years. However, they would not affect the PLA's capabilities as it would extensively use Information Technology and science and technology for advanced modern weaponry. PLA personnel would be better educated, better trained and more proficient. These comments as well as appearance of the report in *Wen Wei Po* together with excerpts from the "PLA's Development Outline for Cultivating Armed Forces Talent before the Year 2020," provided insights into the PLA's restructuring plans.

Commenting on the personnel cuts announced in September 2015, retired Major General Xu Guangyu, a Senior Consultant at the Chinese Military Disarmament Control Council and an expert on Chinese contemporary military affairs, justified the need for reforms and said, "these reductions are an effort to stay on this path and increase quality not numbers." Colonel Yang Yujun, spokesman for China's Ministry of National Defence (MND), clarified that troops to be disbanded are those "equipped with outdated armaments and office staff and personnel of non-combat organisations." Separately, the authoritative official news agency Xinhua said on September 3, 2015, that, "Non-combat units and administrative staff will be cut, and units with older weapons and equipment will reportedly be targeted for demobilisation."

After a meeting of the CMC on September 10, 2015, the two Vice Chairmen of the CMC, General Fan Changlong and General Xu Qiliang, travelled to all seven Military Regions (MR) to explain the reform plans to middle and lower ranking military officers. Simultaneously, senior officers of the PLA's four principal general departments, namely, the General Staff Department (GSD), General Political Department (GPD), General Logistics Department (GLD) and General Armaments Department (GAD), the PLA Air Force (PLAAF), PLA Navy (PLAN), Second Artillery Force (SAF) and the People's Armed Police Force (PAPF), were instructed to express support for the reforms.

The proposed reforms, described as the most extensive and wide-ranging till now, are likely to introduce changes in the rank structure to bring them on par with international practice. Reports indicate that the new Theatre

Commanders would be of lower rank than the present MR Commanders to reduce their political influence and Senior Colonels are to be designated as Brigadier General. The ranks of Second Lieutenant and Lieutenant will be readjusted with possible introduction of a rank of Lieutenant Commander.

It is certain that the PLA's four principal General Departments (GSD, GPD, GLD and GAD) and the Ministry of National Defence (MND) will be restructured. Equally certain is that non-combat units and administrative staff will be cut and units with older weapons and equipment will be targeted for demobilisation. This could result in the demobilisation of a number of Group Armies (GA) whose inventories have a preponderance of older systems. The GA's being accorded lower priority by the PLA—evidenced by their not having Special Forces and Army Aviation Brigades/Regiments—could similarly be earmarked for demobilisation.

Based on official reports, which state that Beijing perceives less external threat from the northern sector, analysts assess that three GAs from this area would be demobilised. These are likely to be: 27th GA, Beijing MR; 40th GA, Shenyang MR; and 47th GA, Lanzhou MR. If the cuts are deeper then possibly the 14th GA in the Chengdu MR and 20th GA in Jinan MR could be demobilised. Chinese media reports indicate that the PLA troop strength in the southern sector—southwest facing India and the southeast responsible for a Taiwan crisis, as well as the South China Sea and Vietnam—would not experience major cuts.

Reports suggest the restructuring will result in the establishment of four or five Theatre Joint Commands. There have been indications in China's official media since at least 2011 and in the official Defence White Papers issued since 2013, that the PLA is contemplating switching to Theatre Commands and discarding the present system of Military Regions (MR). The increasing number of long-range, trans-MR Integrated Joint Operations (IJO) being conducted by the PLA, particularly since 2007, have been a pointer.

Based on Chinese media and other reports, the following outline of the proposed restructuring of the PLA emerges.

- The existing 7 MRs will be replaced by 4 Theatre Joint Commands. These will be a Northeast Theatre Command created by merging the Shenyang and Beijing MRs; a Northwest Theatre Command centred on the Lanzhou MR; a Southwest Theatre Command consisting of Chengdu MR; and a Southeast Theatre Command formed by merging the Guangzhou, Nanjing and Jinan MRs; or

- That the 7 MRs will be consolidated into 5 Theatre Joint Commands. In this case the Theatre Commands would be: Northeast Theatre Command comprising Shenyang and Beijing MRs; Northwest Theatre Command consisting of Lanzhou MR; Southwest Theatre Command comprising Chengdu MR; and a Southeast Theatre Command that incorporates the Guangzhou and Nanjing MRs. This version claims that there will also be a Reserve Joint Command based on Jinan MR, which will provide forces to other Theatres as required and perform other allotted tasks. Yet another option being mentioned is that the Beijing and Shenyang MRs will be merged into a separate Joint Command with responsibility for defence of the capital and protection of the border with North Korea. In such a case, the Southeast Theatre Command will include the Nanjing, Guangzhou and Jinan MRs. This version provides for one additional Command thereby implying that fewer troops/units would be demobilised.
- Surprisingly, the reports claim that the Theatre Joint Commands would not directly command troops, which will be under the individual PLAA, PLAN, PLAAF commands in each Theatre except in times of war. In times of war the troops will be placed under a Joint Command which is to be established in each Theatre.
- The personnel strength of the PLA ground forces, for the past few years being officially referred to as PLAA, will be reduced to 360,000. China's Defence White Paper issued in 2013 had disclosed the PLAA's troop strength as 850,000.
- Both versions state that the personnel strengths of the PLAN and PLAAF will increase but make no mention of the secretive strategic force, namely, the Second Artillery. This could be because the strength of the Second Artillery has increased by 10,000 personnel over the past year.
- In the reorganisation of the PLA's 4 General Departments, the GSD will be upgraded and include high-ranking officers from all service branches. It

will be a higher echelon organisation than the other General Departments. It will be entrusted with planning functions and provide advice to the Chairman of the CMC and be modelled on the US Joint Chiefs of Staff. Also, the GLD and GAD will be merged into one GLD.

- The PAPF will be transformed into a National Guard and will additionally absorb a considerable number of the demobilised PLA personnel.
- The number of military academies will be reduced from the present 150 to 29.

Retired PLA Major General Xu Guangyu was quoted by the official state-run *Global Times* on September 6, 2015, as separately speculating that the ratio of ground, air and naval forces would finally be 2:1:1, a dramatic shift from the current estimate of about 4:2:1.

Meanwhile, the US-based Chinese news service Boxun reported that restructuring of the existing 150 military academies has already begun under the supervision of General Liu Yuan, Political Commissar of the PLA's General Logistics Department (GLD) and close associate of Xi Jinping. General Liu Yuan, who is the son of former Chinese President Liu Shaoqi and a ranking "princeling," supports the military reforms pushed by Xi Jinping and has publicly spoken out against corruption in the PLA. Boxun said the 150 academies are to be reduced and merged into 29 academies, with the remaining being transferred to the local civilian administration. Only military academies catering solely to the PLA, like the Army Non-commissioned Officer Academy, the Officer College, Staff and Command College, Logistics College, Military EngineeringCollege, Armaments and Equipment College and Strategic Artillery Academy are to be retained.

Institutes like the National Defence University (NDU), the Defence University of Science and Technology, the Military Museum, PLA Archives, Military Academy of Medical Sciences, Engineering Design Institute, armaments research institutes affiliated with the general headquarters and military service branches, and science and technology and academic research organisations, will all be incorporated into the national defence administrative system. A major reform measure is that officers of these establishments will be demobilised and no longer have military ranks, but be designated as civilian personnel. The National Defence University (NDU) will, however, continue to be responsible for training senior military cadres.

The reform and restructuring of the PLA essentially orients the Theatre Joint Commands as per their primary task. It is intended to concentrate firepower and troops trained for a specific type of warfare within a single Theatre for ease of rapid deployment. Land and sea warfare forces are to be grouped separately. For example, the Shenyang and Beijing MRs to be merged into the Northeast Theatre Command and the Jinan, Nanjing and Guangzhou MRs to be absorbed in the Southeast Theatre Command have a mainly maritime role. The primary objective of these Theatre Joint Commands will be to enable China to establish dominance over the East China Sea and South China Sea and stand up to a US-Japan alliance. Reports suggest that by 2020, the Theatres will be reinforced by three aircraft carrier combat groups with the existing aircraft carrier "Liaoning" deployed in the East China Sea, and the other two aircraft carriers in the South China Sea. The time frame for creation of the Theatre Joint Commands is five years.

The backdrop for these military reforms is the assessment of China's political and military leaders of the international situation and environment around China. Significant for India is the PLA spokesman's statement to the Hong Kong-based Chinese language newspaper, *Wen Wei Po*, on May 27, 2011. Stating that the strength of 2.3 million is appropriate for the PLA, he justified it because of the "vastness of Chinese territory, the difficulties of the tasks required for defending maritime interests and the endless number of national development interests which are putting new requirements on army building." The spokesman added that "China is currently facing an unsafe world and increasing uncertainty. The West is recovering while the East is anxious and the North is stable while the South is tense, dangerous situation on China's borders is increasing. There is also the possibility that the actions by outsiders will bring about complex changes."

The annual conference on the "Global Military Situation" organised by the PLA's prestigious Academy of Military Sciences (AMS) on January 9, 2015, also discussed the regional security situation in the Asia-Pacific, Europe and the Middle East. It was attended by over 150 senior PLA officers and experts including from the CMC, the four General departments, NDU and the Commandant and Political Commissar of the AMS.

The conference concluded that "unprecedented changes are taking place in the global military situation; military force in international relations is more widely used; and the situation in the Asia-Pacific has worsened."

Based on these and similar high-level official assessments, the reforms are intended to streamline the PLA and equip it to effectively defend China's claimed maritime domain and "fight and win wars." Chinese President Xi Jinxing, who as secretary (mishu) to Chinese Defence Minister Gang Biao in 1979 had a ringside view of how Deng Xiaoping thoroughly reformed the PLA, will guide implementation of these far-reaching reforms designed to make China strong and realise "China's Dream."

For India, it is pertinent that both versions of the restructuring proposals mention that Lanzhou and Chengdu MRs, which are oriented for military operations against India, will be retained as reinforced, independent Theatre Commands. While safeguarding Chinese investments in the northern areas of Pakistan could be a factor for the Lanzhou Theatre Command, the indication is clearly that China will maintain an "offensive" posture towards India.

(The article was published in Centre for China Analysis and Strategy, New Delhi, November 2015).

18

Major Structural Reforms in PLA: Brief Initial Assessment

The crucial phase of the major military reforms—described as "far-reaching and unprecedented"—that were publicly announced on September 3, 2015 by Xi Jinping, who is concurrently the General Secretary of the Chinese Communist Party (CCP), President of China and Chairman of the Central Military Commission (CMC), began to be implemented over New Year's Eve. While the reforms have yet to be fully implemented, an initial assessment of the difficulties in implementation and their scope would perhaps be useful.

Though plans had been drafted in 2011, it took Xi Jinping and his predecessor, Hu Jintao, considerable time and effort to build requisite consensus in the People's Liberation Army (PLA) to begin this phase of the reforms involving structural reorganisation and personnel downsizing. In addition to setting up the "Small Leading Group for Deepening Reform of National Defence and the Military" in March 2014, a lengthy front-page commentary in the *People's Liberation Army Daily* and *People's Daily* quite unusually separately disclosed that,"Chairman Xi went into offices and visited colleges, went to the plateaus, visited the borders, sat in driving seats and cockpits, taking the pulse of reform with soldiers." It added that the Leading Group for Defence and Military Reform collected opinions from more than 900 current and former senior officers and experts, issued questionnaires and received thousands of online suggestions. Between March and October 2015, there were more than 800 meetings about reform covering almost 700 military bases and units. Both the Vice Chairmen of the CMC had also travelled in September 2015 to all seven military regions to explain the reforms to the middle and lower ranking PLA officers. China analyst Peter Mattis recently quantified the efforts as entailing 860 seminars, 900 officer surveys, and several party plenary conference work reports. Resistance in the PLA to downsizing the 2.3 million strong army has apparently been considerable, including at senior levels where many of the approximately 1,144 serving PLA General Staff officers apprehend being deprived of functional posts and attendant perquisites.

On December 31, 2015, on the occasion of conferring flags on the newly created PLA General Command of Army, PLA Rocket Force and PLA Strategic Support Force, Xi Jinping outlined the future direction of the PLA in an official speech known as "Xun Ci"—literally translated as "admonishing words." Xi Jinping is only the second Chinese communist leader to give a "Xun Ci" since the founding of the People's Republic of China (PRC). The other leader to have delivered a "Xun Ci" to the military in China's 67-year history was Mao Zedong, who did so in 1952 and 1953. Xi's decision to deliver the "Xun Ci" is a sign of his confidence and indicates that he is consolidating authority to implement the plans for major military reform.

The substantive contours of these reforms are fast becoming clearly visible. On January 1, 2016, the Central Military Commission headed by Xi Jinping issued the full text of the 4,993-character "Guideline on Deepening National Defence and Military Reform."

The "Guideline" clearly emphasised the political nature of the PLA and its subordinate relationship to the Chinese Communist Party (CCP). The central features of these are: strengthened political and ideological education; expansion of the Chinese Communist Party (CCP) organisation in the military; strict political discipline, organisational discipline and personnel discipline; financial discipline and discipline regarding secrecy; strict action against "political and organisational liberalism"; thorough implementation of the resolutions of the Party's 18th Congress and the Third, Fourth and Fifth Plenum, Marxism-Leninism, Mao Zedong Thought, Deng Xiaoping Theory, the important thought of "Three Represents" (of Jiang Zemin), the guidance of Scientific Development Concept (of Hu Jintao) and the teachings of Chairman Xi Jinping's series of "important speeches."

The "Guideline" asserts that the main objective of the reforms is to equip the PLA for "Theatre battles"—in other words to replace the existing military regions with Theatre Commands. Simultaneously, it said a joint operational command system would be established and military-civilian integration would be promoted. Asserting that the PLA will have the capability of "winning the information war" and effectively carrying out "mandated missions by a military system with Chinese characteristics," the "Guideline" asserted that these reforms would be achieved by 2020. This coincides with Xi Jinping's declared objective of the "Two 100s" (namely, well-off society by 2021 and fully developed nation by 2049) to realise "the Chinese dream of the great rejuvenation of the Chinese nation."

The "Guideline" also disclosed that while in 2015 the focus was on organising implementation of the leadership and management system and reforming the joint operational command system, in 2016 the reforms will focus on downsizing the PLA and its organisation, reforming the "military combat force structure" and institutions, and basically completing the reforms. The period between 2017 and 2020 is to be devoted to making further adjustments to specific areas of reform and optimising and improving the reforms that have been implemented. Attention will be paid to the development of military and civilian integration.

Underscoring the need for reorganising the command structure, the "Guideline" stipulated that there is "need for a joint operational command at the CMC level and at the theatre level, a two-level operational command system; and an integrated command system for peacetime and especially a main and capable strategic and tactical command system." Outlining the Theatre Command configuration, it said the reform will establish a three-tier "CMC-battle zone commands-troops command" system and an administration system that runs from the CMC through various services to the troops. Its main features are:

- Regarding military scale and structure, the focus will be on fewer but better troops with "Chinese characteristics" and a switch from quantity to quality and greater efficiency. There will be a reduction of military personnel by 300,000, whereby 2.3 million troops will be reduced to two million. There will be a proportionate reduction in the number of non-combatant personnel and institutions. Old equipment will be eliminated and there will be developments in new equipment. Separately, the

Washington Times reported on January 7, 2016, that as part of downsizing the PLA and structural reforms, the PLA Culture Work Units under the PLA's General Political Department (GPD) had been dismantled after 63 years. Earlier in 2013, there were credible reports that Major General Luo Yuan favoured the closure of the PLA's Song and Dance Division under the PLA's General Political Department (GPD). Xi Jinping's wife, Peng Liyuan, is incidentally a Major General in this division!

- Depending on the strategic tasks and operational requirements and the need to enhance functions and create more synergy, the structure of the reserve forces and militia will be optimised;
- New military academies will be built for training new military personnel; there will be emphasis on military training and practice to improve early, middle and higher three-tier training system; the size and structure of colleges and universities will be optimised;
- The human resources policy and military personnel classification system will be revised and adapted to establish a rank-dominated hierarchy and promote professional military service officers, non-commissioned officers, and civilians. Military wages, housing, insurance and other systems will be reformed.
- Reforms will focus on civil-military integration, developing a high level of civil-military integration, focusing on market-led demand and effective institutional policy incentives;
- The armed forces command system will be strengthened under the centralised leadership of the CMC; and
- The system of Military Law, especially rules and regulations in the military counsel system, military justice, discipline inspection, supervision and inspection system, will be reformed.

On January 2, 2016, the state-run *Global Times* summarised the contents of the "Guideline on Deepening National Defence and Military Reform" released by the Central Military Commission on New Year's Day. Justifying the reforms the *Global Times* observed, briefly:

- "China's national interests and current international situation are constantly changing, so is the task of the Chinese army. Hence, the PLA and relevant mechanisms have to be adjusted accordingly to keep up with the pace of China's rise";

- "the task that confronts China's armed forces is arduous and more than just safeguarding the nation's maritime and land territories … As China's international cooperation grows, more Chinese enterprises go global and the country embraces greater responsibility to maintain regional and world peace, a strong Chinese army is needed";
- "China must have a strong military ... China doesn't need to worry about military aggression. But there is more about national security ... During China's rise, friction with the US has gone beyond broad geopolitics. If China has a big gap with the US in terms of military prowess, this will affect its international position and other countries' attitude toward China";
- "with a strong army, China can be more politically appealing, influential and persuasive, and will make it easier to network. As we gain more trust from other countries, many of them will no longer be dependent on the US for security and on China for economic benefits";
- "moreover, our military strength has to be demonstrated to the world. The army needs to be able to fight battles and provide real deterrence. The supreme art of war is to subdue the enemy without fighting."

It noted that on December 31, 2015, at a ceremony in Beijing attended by all its members, the CMC had announced establishment of the PLA General Command of the Army, the PLA Rocket Force and the PLA Strategic Support Force. Xi Jinping conferred military flags to all the three new organisations on the occasion and also announced the names of the Commanders and Political Commissars of the new organisations indicating that they are now formal, separate and independent entities.

Generals Li Zuocheng and Liu Lei were appointed Commander and Political Commissar of the PLA's General Command of the Army, the Commander and Political Commissar of the PLA Rocket Force are General Wei Fenghe and General Wang Jiasheng respectively and General Gao Jin has been appointed Commander of the new PLA Strategic Support Force and General Liu Fulian as its Political Commissar.

Establishment of these organisations, it was stressed, was "to realise the Chinese dream and the dream of a strong military, and a strategic initiative to build a modern military power system with Chinese characteristics."

Xi Jinping described the PLA Rocket Force as, "China's core strategic deterrence power" and asked the new Rocket Force to develop "nuclear deterrence and counterstrike capability which is credible, reliable, medium- and long-range precision strike ability, as well as strategic check and balance capacity to build a strong modern Rocket force." Some Chinese language news sources have speculated that the Second Artillery was restructured due to the realisation that it would be unable to adapt to the future strategic needs of the PLA and to simplify the process of three-dimensional combat missions. The new force, they say, might integrate the missions of strategic nuclear submarines and strategic bombers. The suggestion is apparently that the new Rocket Force will control and have in its inventory missiles with range of over 300 km and control and coordinate SSBNs and strategic bombers.

Xi Jinping said that the "PLA Strategic Support Force is a new-type combat force to maintain national security and an important growth point of the PLA's combat capabilities." The indication is that its responsibilities could include technical reconnaissance, electronic warfare, space-based warfare, innovation and missile R&D. Suggesting that it would cater to the requirements of all the different services, Yao Yunzhu, a Senior Researcher at the PLA Academy of Military Science, said the establishment of the Strategic Support Force will integrate the support forces of different services to improve efficiency and save costs.

The PLA's General Command of the Army appears to effectively be the headquarters of the ground forces—since 2011 described in official Chinese documents including the Defence White Papers as the PLA Army (PLAA). It will likely absorb some of the functions of the erstwhile General Political Department, General Logistics Department and the General Armaments Department while some would be merged into the CMC. The "Guideline," however, also indicated that these PLA General Departments would remain. Lou Yaoliang, Head of Military Strategy Studies at National Defence University (NDU), described establishment of the PLA's General Command of the Army as a "highlight," adding that modernisation of the ground force had been hindered till now by the more than 20 PLA central departments in charge of various aspects of the ground force. He observed too that "establishment of the Army Headquarters also means the PLA has begun to change its long-held Army-centred mentality."

Separately, on January 6, 2016, Hong Kong's *South China Morning Post* claimed to have obtained the list of Commanders of the new Theatre Commands/Zones appointed to top PLA posts consequent to the restructuring and reorganisation. It described the appointments as temporary. According to this report General Fang Fenghui will head the newly created Joint General Staff; Xu Fenlin will be Deputy Chief of Joint General Staff; Li Zuocheng will be PLAA Chief; Sun Jianguo will be PLAN Commander; Yi Xiaoguang will be PLAAF Commander; Wei Fenghe will be Chief of the new Rocket Force; Gao Jin is to head the new Strategic Support Force; Liu Yuejun will be Commander of the East Combat Zone; Wang Jiaocheng will head the South Combat Zone; Song Puxan will be Commander of the North Combat Zone and Han Weiguo will be Commander of the Central Combat Zone.

According to this, all Military Region Commanders are being accommodated in the new Theatre Commands except for the former Commander of the Nanjing Military Command, 61-year-old General Cai Yingting, who was a secretary to the late CMC Vice Chairman Zhang Wannian, a close aide to Jiang Zemin. He has been moved as President of the PLA Academy of Military Science (AMS).

While the substantive parts of this crucial stage of the military reforms are being implemented fairly rapidly, there appears to be, however, continued unease in the middle and lower ranks of PLA officers. Indicative is the publication of at least twenty articles relating to the military reforms from September 3, 2015 until now, by the official PLA Daily.

(The article was published by Centre for China Analysis and Strategy (CCAS) and Vivekananda International Foundation (VIF), New Delhi, January 2016).

19

PLA Reform, Reorganisation, Restructuring and Implications for India

In a clear demonstration of his authority and confidence over the New Year, Chinese President Xi Jinping began implementing the crucial second phase of military reforms announced earlier on September 3, 2015. The reorganisation and restructuring of the 2.3 million-strong People's Liberation Army (PLA), described by Chinese analysts as the most "extensive" ever and which has been on the drawing board since well before 2011, is the most critical reform initiative taken by Xi Jinping since he took over in November 2012. It is also only the second time in the history of the People's Republic of China (PRC) that the PLA—a powerful, vital part of communist China's power structure—is being radically reformed. Designed to qualitatively upgrade the PLA's capabilities and structure, the objective is to prepare the PLA to assist the Chinese Communist Party (CCP) realise the "China Dream" and protect China's overseas national interests. There are clear implications for India as well.

A blend of compromise, coercion and consultation preceded implementation of the reforms, clear contours of which are now visible. The appearance of veteran CCP leader Jiang Zemin on the rostrum at the "grand military parade" on September 3, 2015, was suggestive of high level compromise. So also was the discarding of original plans to downsize the PLA by 800,000 personnel and opt instead for reducing troop strength by 300,000. Official Chinese reports additionally disclosed that the Leading Group for Defence and Military Reform collected opinions from more than 900 current and former senior officers and experts, received thousands of suggestions, held 860 seminars and prepared several Party plenary conference work reports. These efforts sought to assuage the concerns of numerous senior PLA officers, including the more than a thousand Generals, who remain apprehensive that the reforms could threaten their jobs and perquisites.

Implementation has moved rapidly since the beginning of January 2016. Creation of two new services, namely the PLA Army (PLAA) and the PLA Strategic Support Force, along with their separate Headquarters and Commanders, have been formalised. The Second Artillery, or strategic force, has essentially been renamed the PLA Rocket Force. Fifteen organisations including major departments like the General Staff Department (GSD), General Political Department (GPD), General Logistics Department (GLD) and the General Armaments Department (GAD) have been absorbed directly into the Central Military Commission (CMC). Of these, the Political Department is already receiving noticeably more importance, indicating that the CCP leadership is determined to ensure that PLA officers are "politically reliable" and that the PLA remains the Party's army.

Other departments directly under the CMC are: CMC General Office, CMC Equipment Development Department, CMC Training Management Department, CMC National Defence Mobilisation Department, CMC Discipline Inspection Commission, CMC Political and Legal Affairs Commission, CMC Science and Technology Commission, CMC Strategic Planning Office, CMC Reform and Formation Office, CMC International Military Cooperation Office, CMC Audit Office, and the CMC General Affairs Administration.

The PLA Rocket Force and PLA Strategic Support Force were created on December 31, 2015. The PLA Rocket Force, which appears essentially to be a new name for the Second Artillery, will control and retain in its inventory the various missiles presently available with the Second Artillery. Chinese President and CMC Chairman Xi Jinping described the PLA Rocket Force as "China's core strategic deterrence power" and asked that the new Rocket Force develop "nuclear deterrence and counterstrike capability which is credible, reliable, medium- and long-range precision strike ability, as well as strategic check and balance capacity to build a strong modern Rocket Force." To that extent, the existing ambiguity regarding deployment of nuclear and conventional missile systems remains. It is also yet to become clear whether the new Theatre/Zone Commanders—who are senior to the former MR

Commanders—will exercise operational authority over PLA Rocket Force elements deployed within their jurisdiction.

Some Chinese language news sources speculate that the Second Artillery was restructured due to the realisation that it would be unable to adapt to the future strategic needs of the PLA and to simplify the process of three-dimensional combat missions. They assess that the new Rocket Force might integrate the missions of strategic nuclear submarines and strategic bombers.

Xi Jinping described the "PLA Strategic Support Force as a new-type combat force to maintain national security and an important growth point of the PLA's combat capabilities." The role of the new PLA Strategic Support Force includes high-technology warfare and space, cyber and electronic warfare. It is likely to additionally include technical reconnaissance, innovation and missile R&D. Suggesting that it would cater to the requirements of all the different services, Yao Yunzhu, a Senior Researcher at the PLA Academy of Military Science (AMS), said the establishment of the Strategic Support Force will integrate the support forces of different services to improve efficiency and save costs.

On January 8, 2016, Hong Kong's well informed "Tung Fang Jih Pao" quoted Beijing-based military commentator Song Zhongping, a retired military instructor at the PLA's influential Second Artillery Force, as disclosing that the Strategic Support Force will be made up of an Internet Army, an Aerospace Army and Electronic Warfare Troops. Song Zhongping added that the new force would be equipped in the future with the "Shenlong" space plane. The unmanned "Shenlong" is being developed as a space weapons launch platform, as well as for surveillance, intelligence and early-warning missions.

The new PLA appointments appear to have followed the same criteria as Xi Jinping's earlier promotions with the emphasis on professional competence, experience in battle or Military Operations Other Than War (MOOTW) and political reliability. While the MR Commanders have been reshuffled, all except one have retained a command. General Liu Yuejun is Commander of the East Zone; General Wang Jiaocheng heads the South Zone; General Song Puxan commands the North Zone and General Han Weiguo is Commander of the Central Zone. Sixty-one-year-old General Cai Yingting, who was a secretary to the late CMC Vice Chairman Zhang Wannian—a close aide to Jiang Zemin—has been moved as President of the prestigious PLA Academy of Military Science (AMS). The description of these appointments "as temporary" suggests that some reshuffling, retirements and promotions should be expected in the coming months.

Those elevated to the new posts are: General Fang Fenghui, born in 1951 and till now head of the PLA's GSD, who has been appointed to head the newly created Joint General Staff. The youngest MR Commander at one time, he is an expert in the digital battlefield and an electronics enthusiast whose hobby is developing integrated military command software; 1953-born General Xu Fenlin, till now Commander of Guangzhou MR, is the new Deputy Chief of Joint General Staff; General Li Zuocheng, a battle veteran of the 1979 Vietnam War who is reputed to have preferred delayed promotions rather than buying his rank and was till recently Commander of the Chengdu MR, now heads the ground forces as Commander of the PLA Army (PLAA); 63-year-old Admiral Sun Jianguo, a submariner and a former President of the PLAN Submarine Academy, is the new PLA Navy (PLAN) Commander replacing Wu Shengli. He has been the front-runner candidate for the post of PLAN Chief since 2012; 1958-born General Yi Xiaoguang, who joined the PLAAF at the age of 16, takes over from Ma Xiaotian as PLA Air Force (PLAAF) Commander. A fighter pilot born into a family with a military tradition, he has been regarded a rising star of the PLAAF since his tenure as the DCOS in charge of Training and HQ Affairs when he was the second youngest PLAAF officer holding a Corps level post. He composed "The Chinese/English Manual for Jet Pilots" in 1992; General Wei Fenghe, erstwhile Commander of the Second Artillery, continues as Chief of the new PLA Rocket Force; and General Gao Jin is head of the new PLA Strategic Support Force. Born in 1959, both General Gao Jin's parents were PLA officers and he served in the Second Artillery throughout his career except since December 2014 when he was appointed President of the PLA Academy of Military Science. He became the youngest Regional-level Commander in the PLA when he was 55 years of age.

The newly created Joint General Staff seems to have been set up to plan and conduct Joint Integrated Operations (JIO), which have been repeatedly emphasised by China's leadership for almost the past decade. The posts of Chief and Deputy Chief of the Joint General Staff would, therefore, appear to be tenable by officers of the PLAA, PLAAF or PLAN. Similarly, the Zones, or Theatre Commands, could in future be commanded by officers from the PLAA or PLAAF or PLAN depending on the primary task of the specific Zone.

The Joint General Staff will additionally plan and coordinate the despatch of PLA troops abroad to safeguard China's national interests. Coinciding with the assertion in the 2015 Defence White Paper that the PLA would "adapt itself to tasks in different regions, develop the capacity of its combat forces for different purposes, and construct a combat force structure for joint operations," the same month China's National People's Congress (NPC) laid the basis for the military to claim that long-range overseas missions are a legally recognised operational mandate. Clauses 28 and 30 of the new National Security Law provide for "the protection of strategic energy supply channels, PRC citizens abroad, and other external interests." Chapter 7 of the National Security Law authorised police, intelligence officers, military or semi-military forces to carry out overseas anti-terrorism operations.

The reorganisation of the erstwhile seven Military Regions into five Theatre Commands, or Zones, is of interest to China's neighbours. The Guangzhou and Nanjing Military Regions remain untouched but have been renamed the South and East Zones. The North Zone includes the entire Shenyang MR and portion of the erstwhile Beijing MR. The Central Zone consists of Jinan MR and the remaining portion of Beijing MR. The Jinan MR is to demobilise more than 60,000 officers.

The usually well informed Hong Kong media mentions that each of the five new "strategic zones" will have less than 3,000 staff. The reports state that the North Zone will concentrate on Mongolia, Russia and Korea; the Central Zone will focus on protection of Beijing; and the South and East Zones will primarily be Maritime Commands responsible for maritime security and safeguarding the South China Sea and East Sea respectively. The implication is that Vietnam and Taiwan continue to be areas of concern to China's military leaders.

Of particular interest for India is the West Zone, which merges the erstwhile Lanzhou and Chengdu MRs. Comprising more than half of China's land area, 22 per cent of its population and more than one-third of China's land-based military, the newly constituted West Zone represents a strengthened military formation. The merger of the Lanzhou and Chengdu

MRs will improve joint planning, coordination and operations. Incorporation of the Qinghai region in the West Zone will facilitate the rapid induction and deployment of high-altitude acclimatised and trained troops into Tibet and across Ladakh. Establishment of the West Zone also reveals China's increased and abiding military interest in the region in addition to facilitating focus on "threats in Xinjiang and Tibet as well as Afghanistan and other states that host training bases for separatists and extremists."

Equally pertinent is the appointment of General Zhao Zongqi, till recently Jinan MR Commander, as Commander of the new West Zone. His credentials indicate he was hand-picked for this post. General Zhao Zongqi is fluent in Arabic and has experience of Tibet. He is a war hero, having participated in the Sino-Vietnam War in 1979 when he is reported to have often disguised himself as a Vietnamese to gather information. He served over 20 years in Tibet as Deputy Chief of Staff (1984-99) and Chief of Staff (1999-2004) of the Tibet Military District (TMD). Born in 1955, General Zhao Zongqi has foreign service experience and was posted in Tanzania as Defence Attaché. He has also been military consultant for a drama serial on the PLA in 2006. Incidentally, the new PLAA Chief General Li Zuocheng also has experience of Tibet having served in the Chengdu MR.

A number of factors will determine whether the reforms succeed and the PLA is strong and adequately competent by 2020 to achieve the goals set by China's leaders. China's neighbours would be aware that Chinese leaders have not wavered from their objective of "reunifying China" and that Xi Jinping's declared goal is to achieve China's Dream by 2020. Though the official *Global Times* justified the reforms as intended to overawe adversaries since "the supreme art of war is to subdue the enemy without fighting," there is a potential wild card. Xi Jinping, who was secretary (1979-82) to Chinese Defence Minister Geng Biao in the latter part of the Sino-Vietnam War, might be tempted to emulate Deng Xiaoping and "test" the new PLA once the reforms are completed.

(The article was published by Centre for China Analysis and Strategy (CCAS) and Vivekananda International Foundation (VIF), New Delhi, February 2016).

20

China's Focus on Military Activities in Tibet

China's People's Liberation Army (PLA) and the country's official military media have kept a discernible focus on the activities and exercises of the PLA formations deployed in Tibet in the past some months.

The recent round of promotions in the People's Liberation Army (PLA) by China's President and Chairman of the Central Military Commission (CMC) Xi Jinping, on the occasion of the 88th anniversary of the PLA on August 1, 2015, continues the emphasis on professionalism and preference for either battlefield, or other operational, experience for elevation to the higher ranks of the PLA. Included in the list are some officers with experience of service in Tibet and identified affiliations to Xi Jinping. The promotions are also indicative of Xi Jinping having begun to prepare for the 19th Party Congress in 2017.

The ten officers now promoted to the highest rank of General are: PLA Deputy Chief of Staff, Wang Guanzhong; Deputy Head of the PLA's General Political Department, Yin Fanglong; PLA Navy Political Commissar, Miao Hua; Commander of the Beijing Military Region, Song Puxuan; Commander of the Lanzhou Military Region, Liu Yuejun; Commander of the Jinan Military Region, Zhao Zongqi; Commander of the Chengdu Military Region, Li Zuocheng; and Political Commissar of the Nanjing Military Area Command, Zheng Weiping. The others promoted were Zhang Shibo, President of the PLA National Defence University (NDU) and Wang Ning, Commander of the People's Armed Police Force (PAPF).

Of the ten officers promoted, at least four are veterans with battle experience and service in Tibet. All four officers are assessed to be on track for further promotion. Zhao Zongqi participated in the Sino-Vietnam War in 1979 when he is reported to have often disguised himself as a Vietnamese to gather information. Born in 1955, Gen. Zhao Zongqi has studied Arabic and has experience of foreign service having been posted to Tanzania as a defence attaché. He has even served as a military consultant for a drama serial on the PLA in 2006. He has served twenty years in Tibet and is a member of the 18th CCP CC. PAPF Commander, Wang Ning, who has worked with Xi Jinping in Fujian, participated in the Sino-Vietnam War on the Yunnan border. A member of the Tibet Work Group, he has been promoted as General after only three years as Lieutenant General instead of the normal four. Particularly important currently for India among these latest promotions to the rank of General are the elevations of the Commanders of the Lanzhou and Chengdu Military Regions, both exercising operational jurisdiction across India's borders. While the Lanzhou Military Region's jurisdiction includes the Ladakh sector, the Chengdu Military Region covers the rest of the Sino-Indian border. Interestingly, both the Commanders were in position at the time of the intrusions in the Depsang Plains and the Chumar area in Ladakh in April 2013 and September 2014 respectively, and their promotions confirm the assessment at the time that the intrusions were deliberate, planned and premeditated actions. (Reference: "China Tests India in Ladakh," *New Indian Express* dated September 25, 2014; and "China Is Placing Key Generals on India Border Near Ladakh,"*Sunday Guardian*, dated January 31, 2015.)

Sixty-year-old General Liu Yuejun, Commander of the Lanzhou Military Region (MR), has a blemish-free political record confirmed by his membership of the 16th, 17th and now 18th Central Committees of the Chinese Communist Party (CCP). He is one of the few PLA officers at this rank with battle experience having fought in the Sino-Vietnam war (1979) and seen active duty in the Fakashan conflict. Liu Yuejun, was appointed to the present post in October 2012, and is significantly, like Xi Jinping, a "princeling." He additionally has solid military credentials as his father, Liu Yide was a Deputy Director of the Political Department of the 14th Group Army and his mother was a soldier. Liu Yuejun was also born in a military camp of the communist people's army. Consequent to his promotion as General, he will be a contender for elevation to a higher post at the next Party Congress in 2017.

The Commander of the Chengdu Military Region (MR), General Li Zuocheng, was earlier Deputy Commander of the Military Region. Li Zuocheng, who is 60 years old, also has battle experience and was awarded a first-class merit when he was 26 years old for leading a PLA company to victory during the month-long Sino-Vietnamese war in 1979. He suffered injuries to his right arm during the conflict. He too will be in the running for appointment to higher office at the next Party Congress. A possible disadvantage for Li Zuocheng, however, could be that he is neither a full nor alternate member of the Party's 18th Central Committee.

The promotions point to the attention being given by the Chinese leadership to the Sino-Indian border and to steadily enhancing and consolidating military preparedness in Tibet. In addition to preserving peace and stability in its restive southwestern autonomous region, Beijing is ensuring adequate military presence against India. Last year Major General Zhang Jiansheng was promoted and posted as a Deputy Commander of the Lanzhou Military Region. He was the first officer from the South Xinjiang Military District in the last 22 years to be promoted directly to Lanzhou and was Commander of Ali Military Sub-District (MSD) a decade ago. He brings to the Lanzhou Military Region Headquarters firsthand knowledge of the Tibetan plateau and the western areas of the Tibet Autonomous Region (TAR).

There has additionally been some interesting coverage of military matters relating to Tibet in China's official media in recent months. Among the disclosures is the reported—almost year-round—presence of J-10, J-11 and SU-27 aircraft in the Tibet region on either deployment or for exercises. Other reports have separately claimed that thirty-two J-10 fighter aircraft were positioned for the first time in Tibet at the airfields in Lhasa and Hoping through the winter (November 20-December 25, 2014) and that Chinese fighter aircraft flew more than 1,460 sorties last year.

An official Chinese media report in April 2015 claimed that the principle followed in the PLA's deployment in the Tibet region is that of "lighter in the front, and heavier at the back." It explained that there are three lines of defence. The first is the Border Defence Regiment, which is deployed nearest to the border; second is the Mountain Division whose objective is to safeguard Tibet; and the third comprises a division-level of Motorised Combat troops. Focusing on the need to augment rapid transportation capability in the Tibet region, the report observed that the third line of defence, or Motorised Combat troops, require a still faster mode of transportation for the troops.

This report also confirmed the strategic objectives of the dual-use road and rail transportation network being developed in the Tibet Autonomous Region (TAR). Observing that the troops are largely dependent on the construction of railway infrastructure, the report said that in August 2014, a new railway line from Lhasa to Shigatse had been officially operationalised. It noted that construction of a 402-km-long railway line from Lhasa to Linzhi began in December 2014. Stating that the Lhasa-Shigatse Rail line and Lhasa-Linzhi Rail line will connect the two extreme points of east and west in the region, it said this will enhance the PLA's "deployment ability" and "response capability." The Tibet region, it added, will in future become the centre of the Qinghai-Tibet Railway.

The report also referred to air power and transport and said that in the last few years China had successfully constructed a number of airports on the Qinghai plateau. It said that among them there are seven modern airports located in the TAR, where a significant number of J-10 and J-11 aircraft are deployed to create a "defence line" of air combat. It disclosed that there had also been a gradual rise in the number of J-10 aircraft deployed in the Gongga region, adding that the HQ-9, a Chinese made air defence missile, has been deployed to provide safety and security for the airports and railways as well as to guard against the threat posed by the deployment of Indian aircraft on the border.

One recent official Chinese bulletin, catering mainly to PLA personnel, discussed some of the military deployments in the TMD. Among the PLA Artillery Regiments deployed in the TMD, it disclosed that Unit 7761 of the 308 Artillery Regiment is deployed in Lhasa; Unit 77678 is based in Nixi, Bayi village in Linzhi County; and Unit 77625 is deployed at Duilongdeqing County of Lhasa Municipality. It also listed the deployment of a few other PLA units directly under the TMD.

Units Directly under Tibet Military District: 15th Engineer Brigade (Dazi, Lhasa); Unit-77619, 308 Artillery Regiment, Lhasa; Unit-77611, 65th Air Defence Division, Lhasa; Unit-77616, 16th Vehicle Regiment, Lhasa; Communications Battalion, Lhasa; Special Operations Division, Lhasa; Unit-77606, Lhasa.

52nd Mountain Division (Bayi village, Linzhi County), Unit-77675; Artillery Regiment (Nixi, Bayi village, Linzhi County) Unit-77678; 1st Battalion (Bujiu village, Linzhi County); 2nd Battalion (Yongjiu village,

Linzhi County); 3rd Battalion (Yongjiu village, Linzhi County); 4th Battalion (Bujiu village, Linzhi County).

53rd Mountain Brigade (Linzhi City, Milin County) Unit-77680; Artillery Regiment (Jiage village, Linzhi City, Milin County) Unit-77683; First Battalion (Wolong village, Linzhi City, Milin County); Second Battalion,(Gangga village, LinzhiCounty); 3rd Battalion (Linzhi County), 4th Battalion(Wolong village, Linzhi City, Milin County).

54th Armoured Brigade (High Plateau Cavalry—Due to the outstanding contribution to the completion of major tasks on January 13, 2010, the CMC Chairman Hu Jintao signed a circular note of merit) (Lhasa City, Duilongdeqing County), Unit-77625; an Artillery Regiment; a mechanised infantry First Battalion; mechanised infantry 2nd Battalion; a mechanised infantry 3rd battalion; Tank Battalion; Chemical Warfare Battalion.

Border Defence Regiment of the Military Sub-District under Tibet Military District (also the Independent Battalions): 1st Border Defence Regiment (Shannan City, Longzi County) Unit-77629: China-India and China-Bhutan Border.

2nd Border Defence Regiment (Shannan City, Cuona County) Unit-77635: China-India, China-Bhutan Border. Luoza County 5th Independent Battalion (Shannan City, Luoza County): China-Bhutan Border.

3rd Border Defence Regiment (Shigatse City, Tingri County) Unit-77639: China-India and China-Nepal Border.

5th Border Defence Regiment (Shigatse City, Saga County) Unit 77646: China-Nepal Border.

6th Border Defence Regiment (Shigatse City, Yadong County) Unit-77649: China-India and China-Bhutan Border. (Nathula outpost is the 1st outpost of South West; Zhangniangshe Outpost of the 6th Border Defence Regiment is the Yunzhong outpost.)

Gyantse 1st Independent Battalion (Shigatse City, Gyantse County) Unit-77655: China-India and China-Bhutan Border.

Gangba 2nd Independent Battalion (Shigatse City, Gangba County) Unit-77656: China-India Border. (Chaguola Outpost is the High Plateau Red Border Defence Troops.)

4th Border Defence Regiment (Chayu, Linzhi), Unit-77643: China-India Border.

Medog County 3rd Independent Battalion (Beibeng village, Linzhi City, Medog County); Medog Garrison, Mofan Battalion, Unit-77659: China-India Border; and the Milin 4th Independent Battalion (Nanyi Township, Linzhi City, Milin County): China-India Border.

Meanwhile, China continues to expand its strategic reach in this region and is extending its arterial communications network right up to India's borders. China's road and rail networks in Tibet are all dual-use strategic projects funded partially from the national defence budget. The Second Artillery, which has its own railway construction battalions, is often involved. Commenting that "high-speed rail lines are becoming a major transport force for the People's Liberation Army," the high-circulation, influential *China Youth Daily* (Zhongguo Qingnian Bao) said in January 2014 that "the Second Artillery (China's strategic missile forces) could use the high-speed rail network to quickly deploy short-range missiles in a certain strategic direction." Adding that the PLA has been using high-speed trains to move troops in exercises since 2009, the report said China "eventually will set up a high-speed network of eight lines extending in all directions." Observing that a typical military train includes 16 high-speed rail cars that carry 1,100 lightly armed soldiers, the news report forecast that "with the daily improvement in China's high-speed rail network, transferring a 100,000-person army 1,000 li [310 miles] might be possible within half a day in the future," and that the PLA will utilise high-speed rail to project "mobile combat forces in various strategic directions."

Official Chinese media reports have separately commented on China's plans to extend the Lhasa-Shigatse railway. Plans call for the strategic railroad network to radiate outwards from Lhasa to Kathmandu and further onward to Lumbini in Nepal. Survey work for the railway line from Shigatse to Kyirong on the Sino-Nepal border has been completed and construction work has already begun. Survey work is reported to be underway for extending this railway to Lumbini via Kathmandu. PLA railway engineers will be involved. PLA engineers can similarly be expected to be involved in construction of the second airport at Lumbini just across India's border, for which a US$ 60.7

million contract has been awarded to the Northwest Civil Aviation Airport Construction Group of China. China's military presence along India's borders and Beijing's involvement in India's immediate neighbourhood will be further strengthened consequent to the award of these contracts by Nepal.

An analysis of the military exercises conducted by the PLA in the last two years, except for the recent major exercises, is revealing. It suggests that the number of exercises reported to have been conducted by the Lanzhou MR slightly exceeded those by the Chengdu MR's Tibet Military District (TMD). During the military activities and exercises held since 2013, especially noticeable was the use of People's Liberation Army Air Force (PLAAF) aircraft and helicopters. Since November 2013, helicopters were noticed for the first time being used for regularly patrolling the borders across the Ladakh sector in the Ali MSD. Also, in December 2013 new recruits were for the first time flown by chartered civil aircraft from Kashgar to the Ali MSD with official reports publicising that henceforth troops will travel to this region only by air and not by road. From August 2014, PLAAF aircraft of the Lanzhou MR were reported to be engaging in "combat confrontation" exercises including in "low meteorological conditions." Beginning April 2015, J-11 and SU-27 aircraft of the PLAAF of Lanzhou MR came to notice regularly conducting exercises. A regiment of J-11 aircraft of the PLA Air Force (PLAAF) commenced night combat training in Tibet on August 9, 2015. China's official media reported that groups of J-11 heavy fighters were seen taking off from Lhasa's Gongga airfield at twilight on an August evening to engage in a "confrontation drill." China's official media additionally reported that the regiment "has begun paying much attention to the training of air battle at night," which has become a routine training programme in its annual training plan.

China also recently flight-tested its latest Z-18 (White Heron) military transport helicopter developed by the Changhe Aircraft Industry Group (CAIG) in Tibet when it broke a record by attaining an altitude of 9,000 metres and flying above Mount Everest. Capable of carrying 27 passengers with a 2-man crew, the Z-18 is the second Chinese military helicopter after the Sikorsky S-70C that can operate in the high-altitude Qinghai-Tibet Plateau.

Similarly, regiments of the Second Artillery, Rocket Artillery and Armoured Brigade deployed in the Tibetan Plateau conduct regular training and "live-fire" exercises under conditions of "informationisation." On July 28, 2015, a Regiment of the Second Artillery conducted a live-firing exercise with "new artillery guns" at a location in the Tibet Plateau and at heights between 3,700 metres and 4,800 metres. The troops "prepared an environment for actual war situations" and conducted an "exercise to address the problems of Combat unit mechanical failure, electrical problems, battle damage repair, and to enhance the soldiers' ability in battlefield command and also in practical use of equipments and to support the proper use of artillery. They also carried along 300 electrical equipments."

Apparently expanding the scope of the exercise, the PLA General Logistics Department (GLD) started its materials and POLs supply drill code-named "Supply Action-2015" in the Tibet Autonomous Region on August 8, 2015. Separately, China's official news agency Xinhua reported on August 10, 2015, that the PLA Chengdu Military Area Command started a joint military drill code-named "Joint Action-2015D" in late July 2015 that entered its "live fire" stage on August 10, 2015 "in a plateau area in southwest China's Sichuan Province." It disclosed this would be the first of five similar drills that will involve a total of more than 140,000 soldiers from over 140 PLA regiments of various types.

Continuing its emphasis on Integrated Joint Operations (IJO), designed for the rapid deployment of self-contained troops equipped with heavy fire power to areas along the border, the PLA plans to complete more than 100 joint exercises involving over 50 army corps this year. He Qimao, head of the Joint Drill Bureau of the PLA General Staff Department's Training Department, was quoted as saying that a "joint operation system" will be formed by the Chinese armed forces including army, navy, air force, artillery, armed police, intelligence, reconnaissance and electronic warfare.

The unsettled, disputed border with India, restiveness in Tibet and Tibetan areas and Beijing's determination to appoint a person of its choice as the XIVth Dalai Lama's reincarnation, are factors that will contribute to China continuing to keep its focus on Tibet.

(The article was published by Centre for China Analysis and Strategy (CCAS) and Vivekananda International Foundation (VIF), New Delhi, August 2015).

21

China in Transition

(*Valedictory Address at the Chennai Centre for China Studies on May 2014*)

I will focus on what is happening in China in the last year or two which, somehow to my fortune, has not been covered in depth! I will also, as the Chinese say that it takes a bold man to go against the current, put across a point of view that goes against the stream of the speeches which I have heard this morning. I do not take as benign a view of what China's ambitions are. While I do accept that we must seize whatever opportunity we find, at the same time I think we should not have a defeatist mindset, which is that they are already too powerful and we must make the best of what we can.

First, let me talk about the domestic scene in China which is very much like ours in India. I think it is undergoing a tremendous change. And Ambassador Ranganathan did pick up on something I am looking at. There was an incident involving Bo Xilai who is a former Politburo member. And I think even today people have not really grasped the extent to which that episode represented a political phenomenon—a phenomenon for change. Throughout 2012-13, in fact, we noticed a churning in Chinese politics such as we have not seen in the past. It was almost like an American style of political campaign that was going on there for part of the time! And Bo Xilai pulled out all stops in his attempt to enter the Politburo Standing Committee—he used the Maoist card by fanning revolutionary songs, engineering a revolutionary-style campaign and various other things. But, in the end, he was unsuccessful in his bid. But a couple of things did happen from his failed attempt. For one, we are seeing the reverberations even today when whole lots of people closely associated with him, including one of his closest supporters, Zhou Yongkang, who was the "Security Czar" and

Politburo Standing Committee member, along with a lot of his supporters have been rounded up and they are either in jail or awaiting charges. The latest rumour circulating in Beijing in the last three days is that Zhou Yongkang's own arrest is imminent. So, let us see whether it happens or not, but his eldest son has been picked up as has his brother-in-law.

The other thing that happened as a consequence of Bo Xilai's failed attempt was, if I put it like a journalist would, the "gathering of the clans." All "veteran" leaders of the Chinese Communist Party got together and they saw the bid for power as a threat to the Party—the Party Centre as it were—and they joined hands. They therefore packed the Politburo Standing Committee with Party stolid apparatchiks. The first fallout was that:

- there was no successor of the next generation who was selected, and among the younger cadres only Xi Jinping and Li Keqiang were brought in;
- second was that all these veteran leaders, regardless of the faction they represented, backed Xi Jinping one hundred per cent.

And here let me digress a little bit. I have always held for the last few years that there is no gap between Hu Jintao and Xi Jinping—and I think that is confirmed now. Xi Jinping and Hu Jintao, his predecessor, have operated very closely together. We can see that in the manner in which the top appointments in the PLA were effected even before the 18th Party Congress and this could not have been done unless both were on the same page. Further, the Beijing Party Chief was appointed by Hu Jintao months before the Party Congress and that appointment is always held by the person who has the confidence of the CCP chief and could not have been done unless Xi Jinping had approved it. Evidence is that the same man was promoted and continues. Also, the Tibet Autonomous Region Party Secretary was appointed many months earlier reportedly at the behest of Xi Jinping. What I think is the final point, and those of us who have been in the bureaucracy will understand, that Xi Jinping picked up Hu Jintao's personal secretary of the last 25 years and appointed him as the Head of his Personal Office in the Central Military Commission. That is a key appointment. No one does that unless he has absolute confidence in that man as well as good relations with that man's former "boss." So, that is the situation as I see it and that part of the transition has taken place.

We can see that Xi Jinping has emerged as probably the most powerful man in China today. Let me take a bit of risk here in the presence of people who are experts and say that, after Mao Zedong, we are for the first time seeing a leader as powerful—as overtly powerful—in China today. Deng Xiaoping was certainly powerful but he remained in the background. Today we have Xi Jinping. He is the Party Chief, he is the Military chief and he is the President of China and additionally he is the head of the Leading Small Group on Foreign Affairs and he is the Head of the Leading Group on National Security. He has captured the Chairmanship of the National Security Council, which was set up very recently at the Third Party Plenum. He has taken over the economic policy, which has not been done over, I think, for the last so many years and to that extent Li Keqiang was sidelined at the recently held Plenum. Xi Jinping has taken over that job. And he heads the Leading Group set up for the Comprehensive Deepening of Reforms. So he is, in fact, totally in charge. And it is this strength that he got which enabled him to pronounce on something which we referred to earlier this morning as the "China Dream." The "China Dream" has been in the air for quite many years, but he spelt it out. And it is not just a dream like an "American dream" which is an individual thing. It is a collective dream and it is muscular and robust. It is not a China Dream that talks only about putting money into the people's pockets—that is something everyone wants and is a laudable thing! He also talks about the rejuvenation of China and that is shorthand for the recovery of all the territories that China claims which is of the old Qing dynasty and which includes large chunks of India as it is today. So it is not an innocent dream. It also represents Xi Jinping's ambition to go down in history and to have his, shall we say his prescription, introduced into the Chinese constitution and Chinese lexicon within a year of his taking over power.

This Third Plenum unveiled 300 reforms, all of them aimed at transforming China from a country where things are "manufactured" to a country where things are "made." The difference being that innovation, science and technology, research and education are all being given a lot of emphasis. And a lot of money has been poured in that and continues to be poured into these sectors now. They also fixed a 7.5 per cent growth rate. They reiterated that China is a maritime nation, which was earlier stated at the 18th Party Congress. They also spoke about the "new Silk Route" and the "Maritime Silk Route." Both of which indicate the renewed thrust in western China and the remote, hinterland provinces. Of course, that does impact on us and I will come to that later.

This was at the conference on "peripheral diplomacy" that was held in the last week of October before the Third Party Plenum. It did not get much attention and was not much written about because, I think, everybody was looking at the Third Party Plenum. But this is the first time in the history of the People's Republic of China that such a conference has been held. It is important for two things:

- It fleshed out the policies China will actually follow with regard to its neighbours; and
- for the first time in its history, China decided to designate neighbouring countries as "friends" and "enemies." This has never happened before.

It was clarified by Prof. Yan Xuetong, Tsinghua University Professor known for his proximity to Xi Jinping. He clarified what was meant by this new policy. He said that "cooperative relations" are what China has with very good friends like Russia and some countries in Africa. Then, he said, a "competitive relationship" is what China has with countries like the US. He clarified while talking about the "new style of big power relations" that it is designed to ensure that the "competitive relationship" does not deteriorate into one of "confrontation." He was that explicit. Then he said we have a relationship of "confrontation" like with an enemy and he named Japan. And let me share one thing with you, in all the interactions with Chinese officials when Japan comes up for mention they go red in the face and thump the table!

Pieces of these policies are already being put into place. Though there were a lot of references to Myanmar, and I think a member of the audience asked about that, it didn't really come in for mention. For the first time since the time of Mao, China has again started playing a role in the internal affairs of another country—of course at that country's request—and that is in Myanmar. It has arranged three meetings so far when it has tried to broker a deal between the Myanmar Government, Army and the rebel factions in the North, which it had not done earlier. China of course has strategic stakes.

It is also supplying money and arms and ammunition to the ethnic Chinese groups.

Pakistan and Nepal have been identified in November, by the Vice Minister of the International Department of the Chinese Communist Party while on a visit to Kathmandu, as two other countries that have been designated as "friends" under this policy and who will benefit a lot from the largesse that China plans to give to them. So, if you hear anyone saying we should not be worried about what is happening in Nepal, I personally would discount it. I am worried. Forget the fact that we have cultural links with the Nepalese people. We are both supposed to be Hindus and they come to India for jobs, etc. That is fine, but once the rail link comes through—and it will come through—and if the Chinese establish a base in Lumbini which is just across the border, all this will change. The China Association of Buddhists are now learnt to have taken over the proposed redevelopment of Lumbini. I think we need to be very careful. I am not saying Nepal is going to become inimical, but it will certainly be something that should cause us some sleepless nights.

Underlying all this is something which I think is major and which Mr. Gopal and I were discussing last evening, namely, the jostling going on between the US and China.The United States has been the number one target for all these years and certainly since China's Modernisations started. And here I again come to Prof. Yue Xuetong. He said there is no trust between the two and, explicitly in writing and during a talk, that there has been no trust since 1989 between China and the United States. That is the basis on which the two start. There have been a number of articles written, particularly in the newspaper which caters to the public security apparatus in China, about what the US ambitions are. These they say are: to dismantle the Chinese Communist Party, introduce multiparty democracy and convert the present socialist command economy into a free-market economy. They have expressed a lot of concerns about that. Again, here I would come back to the Bo Xilai incident. They were convinced, as I am sure some of us with a similar background would be, that Bo Xilai's security chief would not have gone to the US consulate unless he had the assurance of sanctuary. He didn't get it, but that was because the timing was wrong. Xi Jinping was about to visit the US and the Americans did not want to queer the pitch. The Chinese remain quite worried.

China has been watching what the US can do and what its capabilities are. And they have been building an asymmetric capability to deter the US. They can't defeat them, but can deter them and delay them in the areas where it affects both countries—and that is the Asia-Pacific, the South China Sea and the East Sea. Here they picked on, if you recall, two countries, namely, the Philippines and Japan, both with security alliances with the US. The Chinese vessels came into waters claimed by the Philippines in the Scarborough Reef and the Philippines navy went to meet them though they are no match. America brokered a peace and Chinese vessels withdrew and the Philippines navy withdrew, but then the Chinese promptly came back and said this is ours. The US did nothing. All other countries in the region watched that. The Chinese then turned their attention to Japan and began needling them on the Senkaku Islands. There has been a lot of rhetoric by both the countries, but what is the role that the US has played—it has tried to broker a peace. In fact, during the last visit by a high-level interlocutor from the US to Beijing, he was told "why don't you carry on to Tokyo and talk to them. We are okay." That is the kind of confidence that the Chinese are displaying and on the sea that is the kind of aggression they display.

I was reading just last week that the Party Secretary of Hainan said that every day we get fishing vessels coming into our waters and we send them back, sometimes after negotiations. The point is it is happening everyday and they are pushing them back and that is the aggressiveness that China is displaying. One may call it aggression or call it assertiveness. Whatever it is, they are taking territorial boundaries very clearly. To my mind, at least since 2007, China has adopted a more assertive posture not only in the Sea of Japan or East China Sea but also with regard to other areas. The Asia-Pacific is the first test case where China and the US are both in fact pushing each other to assert influence. If you recall, some years ago the Chinese were, in fact, bold enough to suggest to the Americans that why don't we share responsibilities in this area. You take care of Hawaii and that side and we will take care of the waters on this side of Hawaii. We will share intelligence with you and you don't have to bother yourself and come into our area. The Americans obviously did not accept it, but that is the Chinese aim and they are continuously pushing for that. If you are not convinced by this let me dwell on another statement. On February 20, the present Chinese Ambassador to the US addressed an American audience and in that address he said, in polite language, words to the effect that you know we are in the Asia-Pacific, we belong to that region. We know that the US is an Asia-Pacific country. It will be in that region. We also know that the US is a very strong country. To digress a bit here, they assess that the US may not be on the decline. They are very strong and going to remain strong for years. That's what he said. He also said that China is more indigenous to the Asia-Pacific than America is and neither is it from Mars! This was to an American audience. This is the confidence with which China deals with countries like the United States on its own soil. What China does affects everyone. Us, it affects more.

What they are continuously doing on our borders is a matter of concern. I don't want to be jingoistic, but they certainly have claims on Arunachal, they have claims on J&K which has been spelt out. I have seen a couple of articles in their newspapers particularly the *China Youth Daily* where they talk about their claims on Ladakh and describe it as part of Tibet. I think, ladies and gentlemen, that is something we need to look at and not ignore.

As far as the international arena is concerned, certainly they are looking at maximising the opportunity from the current global economic downturn. They have gone one better now. They have developed plans for a rail link from Beijing to Madrid and have started trying to talk to the various countries along the route to make an investment. In some cases they have offered to buy their national debt in order to have the rail link going. That is the kind of thinking they have.

As far as the sea passage is concerned, they are building stakes there. They have been allotted deep seabed mining rights in the Indian Ocean just off Madagascar. That means they are going to be there for a really long time. A naval officer here said this morning that there is no need to worry. I think he is a bit out of sync. It is time for worry because they have 10 to 15 years' lead time before they have their presence and that is how much time we have to get ready for their presence. That's the way we should be looking at it and luckily that is the way the Naval Headquarters is looking at it.

There are, nevertheless, lots of problems that China faces. Domestically, I think, the Tibet problem is really worrying them. Xinjiang, too, but they are dealing with it as a terrorism issue and law and order issue. Tibet is more worrisome. Apart from that they are worried about the latest US initiative, which is the pivot. The pivot's military content also seems to have receded. It is the TPP and TPIP which has China worried. So far China has benefited from the WTO and international trade regime. With the TPP the standards are going to be raised and China is going to be disadvantaged. They realise this and are now talking about joining the TPP. We, on the other hand, are still nervous about the TPP. But, unless we get our act together, I think we are going to find ourselves even worse off. Pakistan has links with the Uyghur terrorists' actions and the Chinese authorities are aware of it. Some of them have mentioned it, but they try to play these down. In any case I don't think that this is something that is going to upset China's equation with Pakistan.

Finally, let me just conclude by saying that there were very pertinent issues raised here today. My intention is not to, as someone said, whine about what China is doing. My intention is just to alert you as to what China is doing and then to get you to think about what we can do to seize the opportunity that might present itself. I don't think enough work has been done on that. We need to sit down and quantify really what are the areas that we need to look at and where can we go. I am not talking about military terms. I am talking about economic opportunities and opportunities for building our influence in the area which is of acute importance to us.

(The speech was published in the Centre for China Analysis and Strategy, New Delhi, May 2014).

22

The 19th Congress of the Chinese Communist Party

The upcoming 19th Congress of the nearly 88-million strong Chinese Communist Party (CCP), to be held in Beijing in October/November 2017, is important not only for Xi Jinping and China, but potentially for China's neighbours and the world. It will consolidate the course on which China is set.

The standard preparations for the 19th Congress have been underway since last year. 2300 delegates representing the CCP's 88 million members divided into 40 blocs representing workers, farmers, peasants, soldiers, women, entrepreneurs etc. will be elected by June 2017. The CCP Central Committee (CC)'s General Office and groups in the CCP CC including veteran cadres, who though retired remain very influential, are finalising drafts of the report to be read by Xi Jinping. There are indications that the Party Constitution is likely to be amended and a major inclusion will probably be Xi Jinping's speeches and instructions as 'Xi Jinping Thought' or 'Xi Jinping Theory'. In July 2014 the authoritative Party theoretical journal 'Qiu Shi' (Seeking Truth) had called Xi Jinping as "one of China's greatest communist leaders" who had put forward "new thinking, new views and new conclusions". More recently the Head of the CCP CC General Office Liu Zhanshu stated in an internal address given in February and published on the social media account of the People's Daily's overseas edition on April 30, 2017, that Xi Jinping's key speeches formed a "complete theoretical system". He said "They cover all aspects of reform and stability, domestic and diplomatic affairs, military operations and party rule." No other CCP Chief has gained such stature yet!

Whether the People's Liberation Army (PLA) will retain its strength in the 19th Congress and the CC it elects is unclear. The PLA is being streamlined and reduced in size which means that the number of full and alternate members that it has in the CC could drop. The 7 Military Regions have since been replaced by 5 Theatre Commands. Also pertinent is that since last year Xi Jinping has pushed a trend for professionalising the PLA and quietly 'pushing it back into the barracks' as it were. Official reports last year publicised that 86 PLA officers of the rank of Major General and above had been dismissed for corruption. China's official news agency 'Xinhua' on March 27, 2017, stated that a total of 4,885 military officials were punished for disciplinary offenses in 2016. It quoted a PLA Daily commentary which called for strict scrutiny in personnel work and especially in the promotion and selection of military cadres. It asserted that "Malpractice, including spreading political rumours, reckless comments on the Party's theories and policies, and participation of illegal associations should all be prohibited and punished" and urged servicemen not to be distracted, and concentrate on building a strong military and maintaining a high degree of focus in combat training. The number of provinces which now have a PLA representative in their Provincial Party Standing Committee has drastically reduced. While Xi Jinping may not advocate a reduction in PLA representation at this Congress it is something that will happen definitely by the 20th Congress.

Like at the last Congress when in a departure from past practice appointments at senior levels of the PLA and Central Military Commission (CMC) were filled before the Congress, it seems that this could be the case this time too. The PLA Navy Commander and the Commander of the Southern Theatre – for the first time ever a PLA Navy officer – were appointed this January. Reports have been in circulation since early last year that decisions have already been taken regarding the next PLA Air Force (PLAAF) Commander and some other appointments.

The 19th CCP CC will witness a major personnel turnover. Over 200 vacancies, or exceeding 60 per cent, in the 376-member CC are anticipated – occasioned by deaths, people reaching the retirement age and dismissals on charges of corruption. It is assessed that 208 of the CC members are to retire in the normal course with another nearly 35 purged for corruption. If the retirement criteria informally decided at the 17th Party Congress stays in force then of the present 7 Politburo Standing Committee (PBSC) members 5 will retire as also 11 of the 25 Politburo (PB) members. The most important of these bodies is the PBSC and the selection of cadres for elevation to the PBSC will be the focus of the greatest attention not only of Xi Jinping but also of the Party 'elders'.

Reports have, however, been circulating in Beijing since the Sixth Party Plenum in October 2016, which designated Xi Jinping as the "core of the Party leadership", that Xi Jinping may retain 68- year old Wang Qishan, his school friend and current Chairman of the Central Discipline Inspection Commission (CDIC) that spearheads the anti-corruption campaign, in the PBSC. If so, then Xi Jinping will have ignored the informal rules in force since the 17th Party Congress that cadres of 67 years of age would be ineligible for elevation to the PB/PBSC. But such a change is under consideration for "special cases" as indicated by the remarks of Deng Maosheng, a Director with the Policy Research Office of the CCP CC, who in November 2016 described it as a "perceived convention only". He added that "the arrangement can be flexible with reference to circumstances" and that "'Seven up, Eight down' is not set in stone".

In case such an exception is made then PBSC member Liu Yunshun, who is exactly a year older than Wang Qishan, can also advance a claim. He has held charge of the powerful and important propaganda apparatus and formulated and enforced progressively tough control measures in academia, the official media, cultural scene etc. over the past decade. He also heads the important CCP CC Secretariat, which under Xi Jinping is very powerful. It opens the way also for Xi Jinping's continuance beyond the 20th Congress.

In addition reports are circulating in Beijing that the PBSC may be further downsized from the present 7 to 5 or even scrapped altogether. The latter would very obviously strengthen Xi Jinping's authority immensely and possibly undermine collective decision-making in the CCP. It would accelerate China's moving on its new trajectory where it is expanding its economic, strategic and diplomatic 'reach' well beyond its borders with OBOR, CPEC, SCO, AIIB etc. Xi Jinping's acolytes have been saying since 2013 that China under Xi Jinping has embarked on a new 30 year era like that of Mao Zedong and Deng Xiaoping before him.

Xi Jinping will try and induct as many of his protégés into the CC, PB, and PBSC. On the basis of appointments made by him so far, it is assessed that Xi Jinping's choice of cadres will largely be from among those of 'Red families' or 'Red nobility'; those with a military/security background; educated cadres who have served in difficult, remote or poverty-stricken provinces like Guizhou; and cadres not affiliated or aligned to factions of any surviving senior leaders. A number of those identified as Xi Jinping's protégés are younger cadres born in 1956 or after and many will be first time entrants to the CC. By February 2017, Xi Jinping had already promoted and positioned 130 cadres in important posts.

Some of Xi Jinping's key cadres can be considered as reasonably certain to enter the PBSC, like Liu Zhanshu. He is a third generation 'Red', has served in a poverty-stricken province and is a long time highly trusted confidant of Xi Jinping. He is already a PB member and if age is the criteria is just eligible for elevation as he was born in 1950 and is 67 years old. There are others like Ding Xuexiang (DOB: 1963) who is presently an alternate member of the 18th CC but is tipped to take over from Liu Zhanshu and could be promoted to the PB at the 19th Congress. Others include PB members Hu Chunhua (DOB: 1963) who is Party Secretary of the important Guangdong province; Sun Zhengcai (DOB: 1963) who is Party Secretary of Chongqing Municipality; and Vice Premier Wang Yang (DOB: 1955), all of whom were earmarked for higher office during Hu Jintao's tenure. Among other likely entrants to the PB are Huang Kunming (DOB: 1956) who is a princeling and an alternate member of the 18th CC and Li Shulei (DOB: 1964), reputedly a child prodigy and member of the 18th CC.

Finally, the 19th Party Congress has implications for China's neighbours and the world. If, as is expected, Xi Jinping emerges strengthened from the Congress then China's already assertive posture will be accentuated. There are signs, however, that some sections have differences with Xi Jinping on strategic issues. For example, when Xi Jinping initiated the request for a meeting with US President Donald Trump, retired PLA Major General

Jin Yinan, a national security strategy expert and former Director of the Institute of Strategy Study at the PLA's National Defence University, questioned the timing of the meeting in a posting on internet which received wide circulation inside China. China's push to dominate the South China Sea will nonetheless gather strength. For Xi Jinping it is important to enhance China's stature on the world stage.

The 'China Dream' and OBOR are flagship national projects identified with Xi Jinping. Their respective target dates are 2021, or the CCP's centenary and 2049, or the hundredth year of the founding of the People's Republic of China! Xi Jinping will strive to achieve both. This will imply greater pressure on countries to endorse the OBOR and a toughening of China's already assertive stance.

(This paper was published by Centre for China Analysis and Strategy (CCAS) in May 11, 2017).

23

Xi Jinping's Power Base

Since his appointment simultaneously to China's three top posts of General Secretary of the Chinese Communist Party (CCP) Central Committee (CC), Chairman of the Central Military Commission (CMC) and President of China at the 18th Party Congress in November 2012, Xi Jinping has steadily acquired and consolidated greater authority. In addition to the post of Commander-in-Chief of the People's Liberation Army (PLA) that he assumed on April 20, 2016, Xi Jinping heads a majority of the Central Leading Small Groups (CLSGs). He oversees the public security apparatus, the National Security Commission, Cyber Security, Military Reforms, Foreign Affairs and Economic Reforms. The CCP's Sixth Plenum in October 2016 further enhanced his authority when it designated him the 'core' of the leadership. Xi Jinping today holds more formal posts than any other leader in the CCP's history.

The 18th Party Congress also approved the 'China Dream' articulated by Xi Jinping and which clarified his vision for China. The deadline for achieving the 'China Dream', which includes the redressal of 'past humiliation' and 'recovery' of so-called 'lost territories', is the CCP's centenary in 2021. Soon thereafter in September 2013, Xi Jinping proposed his ambitious geo-economic strategic initiative called 'One Belt, One Road' (OBOR). Stretching from Beijing to Europe it seeks to link production centres in China with natural and other resource centres around the world over a China-built communications artery. China hopes to complete the OBOR by the country's hundredth founding anniversary in 2049, and establish China as a major global power. Xi Jinping's acolytes say that China has embarked on a new 30-year era like those earlier of Mao Zedong and Deng Xiaoping!

In this backdrop and with the 19th Party Congress scheduled to be held in October/November 2017, speculation has increased as to whether Xi Jinping will at that time induct a successor to the Politburo Standing Committee (PBSC) or keep leadership succession ambiguous, thus retaining for himself the option of continuing in office beyond the norm of two 5-year tenures. There is also speculation whether the retirement dates informally accepted by the Party and observed since the 17th Party Congress will stay in force or be disregarded.

Reports in circulation in Beijing for some months now suggest that PBSC Member Wang Qishan, a 'princeling' and close friend of Xi Jinping who heads the Central Discipline Inspection Commission (CDIC), which has felled large numbers of senior officials in the Party, Government, State-owned Enterprises (SoEs) and the PLA, may continue in the PBSC. Some reports speculate that Wang Qishan might be appointed Premier with Li Keqiang retained as PBSC Member but moved as Chairman of the National People's Congress (NPC).

Since November 2012 especially, Xi Jinping has effectively used the anti-corruption campaign to strengthen his position. He has simultaneously been assiduously handpicking cadres for key appointments to help him build a strong support base. These cadres and officials mainly comprise those who have worked with Xi Jinping in the Zhejiang or Fujian provinces and, to an extent, Shanghai. Xi Jinping appears to have a clear preference for: cadres without affiliation to any of the factions led by surviving veteran leaders; second generation 'Reds' or 'princelings'; cadres with a military or security background; and cadres with service in the poorer or remote provinces. Political reliability and commitment to Party ideology are important criteria. Xi Jinping's appointees earmarked for key slots are often noticed occupying the number two, or deputy, position before moving into the senior position when the vacancy occurs. Many of Xi Jinping's appointees are in the important central leading groups and the powerful CCP CC's General Office, Organisation and Propaganda Departments. Some occupy key positions in the Ministries of Public and State Security.

Brief bio-sketches of 20 of the important cadres loyal to Xi Jinping are listed below.

Li Zhanshu (栗战书), DOB: August 1950; Place of Birth: Pingshan County, Hebei Province

Li Zhanshu joined work in December 1972 and joined the Chinese Communist

Party (CCP) in 1975. He is a second generation 'Red cadre' and a 'princeling'. His uncle Jia Zhengtong, died during the War of Liberation in 1949 at the age of 26 less than a month after he got married. In an essay written in 2005 in memory of his uncle, Li Zhanshu described his father bringing the uncle's body back to their village on a cart and wrote "There is an endless yearning that dwells deep in my heart. No matter how time flies, my thoughts for him linger."

Li Zhanshu's ties with Xi Jinping go back to the 1980s, when Xi Jinping governed Zhengding county in Hebei province and Li Zhanshu was in charge of neighbouring Wuji county. During the time he and Xi Jinping were both county-level party chiefs in Hebei Province in the 1980s they often drank socially.

66-year old Li Zhanshu is today Xi Jinping's most powerful ally after anti-corruption chief Wang Qishan. He is almost certain to remain in the Politburo when many of its 25 members are replaced at the 19th Party Congress next year as they will have reached the mandatory retirement age. Under the existing Party norms, Wang Qishan, who is now 67, is due to retire at the 19th Party Congress.

Li Zhanshu is reported to be particular about work and once said in an interview that he abides by a "three nos" principle: No messing around with other people, no playing games, no loafing on the job. As Director of the General Office of the Central Committee, Li Zhanshu is tasked with assisting President Xi Jinping on a range of issues, including diplomacy, the economy and legal reforms. He is one of the most powerful Directors of the CCP CC's General Office in the past few decades. His predecessors did not have seats on the Politburo. He almost always accompanies Xi Jinping on domestic and overseas trips and, indicative of the deep trust he enjoys, travelled to meet Russian President Vladimir Putin before Xi Jinping visited Russia in March 2015. Commencing 2016, Li Zhanshu has begun to make official domestic trips, something very rare for a person in his position. He is also the Director of the General Office of the National Security Commission, recently created and chaired by Xi Jinping.

Ding Xuexiang (丁薛祥), DOB: 1963; Place of Birth: Nantong City, Jiangsu Province

Ding Xuexiang graduated from the Northeast Heavy Machinery Institute

(Yanshan University) and worked at the Shanghai Research Institute of Materials from 1982 to 1999. He joined government service in 1962 and joined the CCP in October 1984.

His first cadre position was as a Deputy Director on the Science and Technology Work Committee of the Shanghai Municipal Party Committee. He was Head of the Shanghai Party Committee's General Office in 2007 when Xi Jinping arrived as Shanghai Party Secretary. Ding Xuexiang won Xi Jinping's confidence in the 6 months they worked together and was soon promoted to the post of Secretary General of the Shanghai Municipal Party Committee. He was Secretary of Shanghai's Political Science and Law Committee for a year before Xi Jinping asked him to work directly for him in Beijing as Deputy Director of the CCP CC General Office.

According to an article in the Beijing Youth Daily in 2013, when Xi Jinping introduced the members of his Shanghai Municipality to the press in May 2007, he described Ding Xuexiang as "Here is another young man, and he was born after 1960."

When Ding Xuexiang was head of the Shanghai Party's General Office, he wrote an article for 'Secretary Work' magazine that laid out his philosophy for serving as an aide to leaders. He wrote: "The prosperity of a country depends on political affairs, and the achievement of political affairs relies on the work of the assistant. The general office of the party committee, as the think tank of the party committee and brain of the leaders, should place as its first priority its service of consultation." Secretaries must "plan with the heart of a commander despite having a post as a soldier. If you cannot do this, it will all be in vain, no matter how much additional effort you make and how much more work you do."

Ding Xuexiang began getting noticed from 2015 after he was spotted in the background of several of Xi Jinping's photos and amidst reports that he is known for quickly turning his bosses' public remarks on trips into official notices without referring to notes. A source has been quoted as describing him as someone who "boasts some remarkable traits, ranging from perfect writing skills to a famously strong memory." The same source added that Xi Jinping picked him because he knew he could rely on Ding Xuexiang to not discuss the President's private thinking with outsiders.

There is expectation that Ding Xuexiang, who is reputed to have Xi Jinping's ear, will replace Li Zhanshu as Director of the CCP CC's powerful General Office once the latter is promoted at the upcoming 19th Party Congress. He is an alternate member of the 18th CPC Central Committee.

Zhong Shaojun (钟绍军), DOB: 1960; Place of Birth: Quzhou City, Zhejiang Province

Zhong Shaojun is Xi Jinping's secretary on the Central Military Commission. He has been Xi Jinping's secretary (*mishu*) for over 12 years.

Zhong Shaojun is a civilian CCP cadre with a Master's degree from Zhejiang University and Doctorate Degree from Beijing's Tsinghua University. From 2007 to 2013, he was Director of the Political Group of the General Office of CCP Central Committee. He is Deputy Director of the General Office for the Central Military Commission and Director of Office for Xi Jinping Chairman of Central Military Commission since June 2013.

Zhong Shaojun's official biography designates him a Senior Colonel. A CCTV news clip from 2013 shows Zhong Shaojun visiting a satellite launch base in Gansu Province with Xi Jinping and wearing a green, short-sleeve People's Liberation Army (PLA) uniform with shoulder insignia designating him a Sr. Colonel.

Prior to this appointment, Zhong Shaojun, a native of Zhejiang Province, worked in the Province as a propaganda official when Xi Jinping was the Zhejiang Party Secretary. He was then transferred to Shanghai, where he worked under Ding Xuexiang in the General Office. Revealing the trust he enjoys and his proximity to Xi Jinping, Zhong Shaojun was transferred at the same time that Xi Jinping moved to posts in different cities.

Zhu Guofeng, DOB: around 1970; Place of Birth: Beijing

Little is publicly known about Zhu Guofeng except that he graduated from the prestigious Peking University. He is a confidante of Xi Jinping and also one of his secretaries (*mishu*). In footage from state television he was seen at a meeting with Xi Jinping and other world leaders during the Boao Forum for Asia in southern China in April 2013.

Chen Xi (陈希), DOB: 1953; Place of Birth: Putian City, Fujian Province.

Chen Xi joined the CCP in 1978, and graduated with a Master's degree from the Department of Chemical Engineering of Tsinghua University. He was a Visiting Scholar at Stanford University, California, USA. After spending almost 30 years at Tsinghua after graduation, Chen Xi served as a Deputy Party Secretary at Liaoning province and from 2011 as Executive Vice Chairman of the China Association for Science and Technology. He has been a member of the 17th CCP CC and is now a member of the 18th CC.

Chen Xi was Xi Jinping's classmate and roommate at Tsinghua University, Beijing college. His posting to Beijing came less than a year after Xi Jinping became General Secretary of the CCP and in 2013 he was promoted as Executive Deputy Director of the CCP CC's powerful Organisation Department, which oversees cadres' appointments at Vice Ministerial level or above. Within months of his appointment, the Organisation Department issued a 'landmark' document specifying selection procedures for promotion of cadres. It superseded the previous procedures introduced by Hu Jintao, whereby cadres were chosen based on internal voting.

Hu Heping, DOB: 1962; Place of Birth: Linyi County, Shandong Province.

Hu Heping studied in the Hydraulic Engineering Department of Tsinghua University in 1980 and joined the CCP in 1982.He obtained a Doctorate of Civil Engineering from the University of Tokyo. From 2008 to 2013 he was Secretary of the the CCP Party Committee of Tsinghua University. From 2013-2015 he was in Zhejiang Province and in 2015 moved to his third new position in two and a half years as Deputy Secretary of the CCP Shaanxi Provincial Committee and was appointed Governor in 2016. He is China's second youngest provincial governor.

For more than 10 years, Hu Heping was a Tsinghua University colleague of Chen Xi, who is now the first ranking Deputy Director of the Chinese Communist Party's powerful Organisation Department, which oversees cadres' appointments at vice-ministerial level or above.

Hu Heping is an alternate Member of the 18th CCP CC.

Huang Kunming (黄坤明), DOB: November 1956; Place of Birth: Shangkang County, Fujian Province

Huang Kunming joined work in December 1974 and the CCP in September 1976. He is a 'princeling' and his father, Huang Debiao was member of the PLA and the CCP.

Huang Kunming worked in Fujian Province from 1977-1999 and thereafter was posted to Zhejiang province, where he worked till October 2013. His term generally overlapped that of Xi Jinping.

59-year old Huang Kunming, is the second-most powerful man in the CCP CC's Propaganda Department. He was made Executive Deputy Director of the CCP CC Propaganda Department in late 2013, and concurrently as Office Director of the Central Spiritual Civilization Steering Committee. Two months after his appointment as Executive Deputy Director of the Propaganda Department, Xi Jinping delivered a hard-line speech about propaganda and ideology. Before moving to Beijing, Huang Kunming was Party Secretary of Zhejiang's capital Hangzhou for three years.

He was appointed provincial Propaganda chief in 2007, the last year of Xi Jinping's term as Party Secretary of Zhejiang Province. He mostly remained out of the spotlight until his promotion in 2014. In an article published in *People's Daily* in 2015, Huang Kunming said the "international environment is getting more complicated, as hostile Western forces intensify [efforts] to divide and Westernise us". Cadres must be "armed with the spirit [expressed] in Xi's speeches".

Huang Kunming, who is an alternate member of the 18th CC, is well positioned to be a candidate for the next Politburo in 2017.

Chen Yixin (陈一新), DOB: 1959; Place of Birth: Taishun County, Zhejiang Province.

A 'Cultural Revolution Rusticated Youth' in Zhangcun Commune, Lishui Prefecture, Zhejiang Province, Chen Yixin graduated from the Physics Department of Lishui Teachers Special School in 1981 with an associate degree and entered the work force in 1976. He joined the CCP in 1982.

Having spent his entire career in Zhejiang Province, Chen Yixin was Secretary of the Wenzhou City Party Committee from 2013-2015 when he is considered to have played a central role in helping it recover from its worst debt crisis in decades. Xi Jinping brought him as Deputy Director of the CCP CC's Central Leading Small Group (LSG) for Comprehensively Deepening Reform in the General Office. The LSG was created by Xi Jinping and is chaired by him.

Li Shulei (李書磊), DOB: 1965

A former child prodigy, Li Shulei was admitted to Peking University in 1978 at the age of 14. He obtained a degree in Library Science and a Master's and Doctorate in Literature before joining the Central Party School at 24. After two decades at the think-tank, he became the school's youngest Vice President at the age of 44.

Li Shulei was Xi Jinping's deputy in the Central Party School when Xi Jinping headed it from 2007 to 2012 as the Executive Secretary of the CCP CC's Secretariat. According to the Hong Kong and Taiwan media, Li Shulei wrote many speeches for Xi Jinping. The Hong Kong-based *Yazhou Zhoukan* reported that Li Shulei wrote Xi Jinping's speech to an arts and literature forum two years ago, in which the President demanded that the sector should serve the people and socialism.

In 2014, Li Shulei was transferred to head Fujian's publicity department, in a move widely interpreted as indicating that he is being groomed for senior positions. Prior to his transfer, Li Shulei had served only a few years in government – as deputy party chief in Xian, Shaanxi Province from 2004 to 2006, and Deputy County Secretary in Qinglong, Hebei Province, from 1992 to 1993.

51-year old Li Shulei, was appointed Secretary of Beijing's Commission for Disciplinary Inspection in 2015. His appointment to head Beijing's anti-corruption watchdog body at such a sensitive time suggests Li Shulei is a trusted man.

Li Shulei, who is a member of the 18th CCP CC, is well positioned for entry in to the Politburo at the 19th Party Congress.

Shu Guozeng DOB: 1956; Place of Birth: Hangzhou City, Zhejiang Province.

Shu Guozeng entered the work force in 1974 and is a member of the CCP. In Zhejiang Shu Guozeng was informally known as Xi Jinping's "facile writer". He served first as a mishu to Xi Jinping and was then promoted as

Deputy Director of the office of the Zhejiang Provincial Party Committee in 2004 by Xi Jinping when he was provincial Party Secretary. From 2008-12 he was Director of the Zhejiang Province Party School History and Research Office and from 2012-14 was Director of the Zhejiang Province Development and Research Centre. In 2014, he was promoted and appointed Deputy Director of the General Office of the Leading Group for Financial and Economic Affairs, which is chaired by Xi Jinping.

Shu Guozeng has no previous government experience outside Zhejiang. Shu Guozeng has shown a fondness for quoting Mao Zedong in articles he has published.

He now convenes quarterly meetings and provides an important forum for Xi Jinping to deliver decisions on economic issues. China's official media reports that unlike the annual Central Economic Work Conference – an event inherited from the Jiang Zemin and Hu Jintao era, where both the President and Premier delivered talks on economic affairs – Xi Jinping has been the only speaker at meetings of the leading group.

Liu He (刘鹤), DOB: 1952; Place of Birth: Beijing Municipality

Liu He is a 'princeling'. Having joined as a worker and cadre in the Beijing Wireless Factory from 1974-78, Liu He received a Master's degree in Management from the Industrial Economics Department of Renmin University in 1982. In 1992-93, he was a student at Seton Hall University, Business School, New Jersey, USA. From 1994-95 he studied in the John F Kennedy School of Government, Harvard University, Cambridge, Mass, USA where he earned a Master's in Public Administration and worked as a Researcher in the Mesan Project.

Xi Jinping and Liu He have been friends since they were in their teens and both graduated from Beijing 101 Middle School, which is the prestigious school attended by many children of senior Communist Party and military officials. Both also have a military background and Liu He once served with the PLA's 38th Army. They have served together in Fujian and Zhejiang provinces.

Liu He heads the General Office of the Central Leading Group on Finance and Economics and is Xi Jinping's chief economic advisor and writes Xi

Jinping's economic speeches. Liu He accompanies Xi Jinping on his travels. Once, introducing Liu He to senior US government officials Xi Jinping said "This is Liu He, this person is very important to me."

He is a member of the 18th CC and is likely to be admitted to the Politburo at the 19th Party Congress.

Cai Qi (蔡奇), DOB: December 1955; Place of Birth: Youxi County, Fujian Province.

Cai Qi joined work in March 1973 and joined the CCP in August 1975. From 1973-75, Cai Qi was a 'Cultural Revolution Rusticated Youth' in Xiyang Commune, Fujian Province. Cai Qi worked in Fujian Province from 1973 to 1999, as Deputy Director of the Fujian provincial party committee's General Office and thereafter served fifteen years in Zhejiang Province from 1999 when he became Mayor of the city of Quzhou. He moved to Beijing in 2014 as Acting Mayor of Beijing Municipality – a position held usually by individuals trusted by the CCP CC General Secretary..

When he was Executive Vice Governor of Zhejiang in 2013, Cai Qi quite unusually replied to a complaint made by the mother of a civil servant. After she wrote on Cia's social media page that her son needed to drink a lot of alcohol at official dinners, Cai Qi as Head of Zhejiang's Organisation Department, replied: "Tell me which department your son works in and he won't have to drink again".

Cai Qi is reputed to be an open-minded official who makes his views known to the public. He is one of the few CCP cadres who uses the social media and his account on the Tencent micro-blogging platform has more than 10 million followers. Cai Qi described himself as a "Bolshevik" online and, before his promotion and move to Beijing repeatedly quoted Xi Jinping's remarks on his Weibo account, referring to him as General Secretary Xi, '*Xi Dada*' (father) or Boss Xi! He stopped updating his account after his promotion. His colleagues in Zhejiang describe Cai Qi as a close ally of the President.

Meng Xiangfeng (孟祥锋), DOB: 1964; Place of Birth: Pingxiang, Hebei Province.

Meng Xiangfeng graduated from Jilin University with a Master's Degree and later obtained a Doctorate in Law from the Central Party School. Meng Xiangfeng's background extends across diverse fields, including cultural heritage and discipline inspection. He spent a year in the Party Committee of Hangzhou, capital of Zhejiang province.

He has served mainly in Liaoning Province where he was Director of the Supervision and Inspection Department of Liaoning Province from 2011 to 2013. He came to Xi Jinping's attention between 2002-2007 when he was in Zhejiang. Meng Xiangfeng is reported to have developed close personal relations with Xi Jinping when he was working in Zhoushan.

From March 2013 until April 2015 he was Director, National Administration for Protection of State Secrets (NAPSS), responsible for archiving classified Communist Party and government documents. He was handpicked by Xi Jinping and appointed Vice Minister for Public Security in charge of a working group specializing in 'Fox Hunt 2015'.

Following a three-year reshuffle of the top secretariat office, in September 2015, Meng Xiangfeng was appointed President Xi Jinping's deputy chief of staff.

Meng Qingfeng

59-year old Meng Qingfeng was Xi Jinping's deputy Police Chief when Xi Jinping was Party Secretary of Zhejiang Province. Meng Qingfeng was head of the Economic Crime Investigation Department under the Ministry of Public Security in December 2010. He was promoted to Assistant Minister of Public Security in November 2014 and Vice Minister of Public Security in 2015. Meng Qingfeng's new position got publicised within a month after his appointment when he publicly led a team at the China Securities Regulatory Commission to search for evidence of alleged market manipulation, and declared that the authorities would go after those responsible for the stock market slump.

Wang Xiaohong

Wang Xiaohong began his career in Fujian, where he remained until August 2013. Wang Xiaohong was Xi Jinping's subordinate during the latter's entire term in Fujian. In December 2014, Wang Xiaohong was Deputy Governor of Henan province in charge of the provincial public security department.

Wang Xiaohong served in Fujian for 34 years and held positions such as Director of the Minhou County Public Security Bureau and Director of the Fuzhou Public Security Bureau. He later became police chief of Xiamen, before moving to Henan province.

Wang Xiaohong was promoted to the post of police chief of Beijing in March 2014. The Police Chief of Beijing is a job entrusted to a person of the Party Chief's confidence. He was appointed Vice Minister of Public Security in May 2016.

A source has been reported as disclosing: "I have heard Wang served as a ban lang (the best man or head groomsman) at Xi Jinping's private wedding with Peng Liyuan, attended by only close relatives. They are so close to each other."

Chen Wenqing (陈文清), DOB:1960; Place of Birth: Renshou County, Chengdu, Sichuan Province.

Born in 1960, Chen Wenqing joined the CCP in 1983. He graduated from the Department of Law Southwest University of Political Science and Law and entered the work place in 1984.

He has served 12 years in the public security apparatus in Sichuan province and later was in Fujian province from 2006. He worked in the Central Discipline Inspection Commission. Chen Wenqing switched over to the Ministry of State Security (MoSS) in 1994, becoming Deputy Director at the Sichuan Provincial State Security Department (SSD). In 1998, Chen Wenqing took over leadership of the department and held the position until 2002, when he moved to head the Sichuan Provincial People's Procuratorate. In 2006, Chen Wenqing moved to Fujian, where he served until 2012 as both, Secretary of the provincial Commission for Discipline Inspection and as provincial Deputy Party Secretary. Following the 18th Party Congress at which Xi Jinping came to power, Chen Wenqing was brought to Beijing to become a Deputy Secretary of the Central Discipline Inspection Commission (CDIC).

He was appointed Minister of State Security in November 2016. He is a member of the 18th CCP CC.

Lin Duo, DOB: 1956; Place of Birth: Heze City, Shandong Province

Lin Duo was born in 1956 and entered the work force in 1974. He joined the CCP in 1975. Lin Duo earned his Master's Degree from the CCP CC's Central Party School in 1998.

He was Secretary of the CCP Xicheng District Committee of Beijing Municipality from 2006 to 2010. In July 2010, Lin Duo was appointed Vice Mayor and Acting Mayor of Harbin City, Deputy Secretary of the CCP City Committee, and Secretary of the Leading Party Group of Harbin City Government.

He is considered a protege of Central Discipline Inspection Commission (CDIC) Chairman Wang Qishan and was appointed Governor of Gansu province in April 2016. Lin Duo has never worked in the western province, nor has he been a governor of any province. His appointment, which made him a provincial cadre, effectively postponed his retirement for five years until 2021.

Wang Dongfeng (王东峰), DOB: 1958; Place of Birth: Xian City, Shaanxi Province

Wang Dongfeng joined the CCP in 1980 and entered the work force in 1981. From 1999-2001 he was a student at Xi'an Jiaotong University Shaanxi Province, Xi'an City. From 2000-2001 he was a student at the Central Party School.

From 2001-2004 he was in Shaanxi Province and then till 2013, he was Vice Director of State Administration for Industry & Commerce. He was appointed Deputy Secretary CCP Municipal Committee, Tianjin Municipality in 2013. He is a Member of the 18th CCP Central Committee, Central Commission for Discipline Inspection.

He was appointed Mayor of Tianjin Municipality in November 2016. He is a strong candidate for the CC in 2017.

Yang Zhenwu (杨振武), DOB: May 1955; Place of Birth: Xinle County, Hebei Province.

Yang Zhenwu joined the CCP in 1975 after graduating from Nankai University, Tianjin and entered the work force in 1978. He joined editing work in newspapers in September 1978.

After Xi Jinping's appointment as Party Secretary of Shanghai he appointed some "old friends" to the Shanghai Municipality Party Committee, including Yang Zhenwu as head of the Publicity Department. From 2009 to 2013, Yang Zhenwu was Director of the CCP Shanghai Municipality Party Committee Publicity Department. He was Deputy Director in People's Daily from 1989-2001; Editor-in-Chief of the People's Daily Overseas Edition from 2004-2006 and was appointed Editor-in-Chief of People's Daily in April 2013.

On May 16, 2016, Yang Zhenwu as Editor-in-Chief of the People's Daily authored a lengthy essay warning that the CCP could make a "historic mistake" if it fails to control new media and harness it for propaganda. He wrote: "To lose speech is to lose power."

Fu Zhenghua (傅政华), DOB: 1955; Place of Birth: Luanxian County, Tangshan, Hebei Province.

Fu Zhenghua entered the work force in 1970 and joined the CCP in 1973. A rising star in the security apparatus, Fu Zhenghua was promoted to Vice Minister of Public Security in 2013, after a stint as Beijing's political chief. He is now ranked first among the seven Vice Ministers in the Ministry of Public Security.

Known for his high-profile style, Fu Zhenghua made a name for himself after only 74 days as Beijing's police chief in early 2010 when he closed 'Heaven on Earth', a luxury nightclub suspected of providing sex. Within months of taking up his new job at the Ministry of Public Security, he started leading armed patrols by Beijing police forces. He had played a prominent role in persecution of the Falungong when Jiang Zemin was Party General Secretary.

In a surprise move the official website of the Central Politics and Law Commission announced on August 18, 2016, that Fu Zhenghua had been 'removed' as a member of the Central Politics and Law Commission. This has prompted speculation that he might have lost Xi Jinping's confidence. Fu Zhengua is not known to have worked directly under Xi Jinping, but is known to have played a leading role in bringing to justice former PBSC Member and Security Czar Zhou Yongkangon charges of corruption and abuse of power in 2013.

There are some other cadres assessed as close to Xi Jinping and who are not in central CCP organisations, but are among the aspirants for elevation at the upcoming 19th Party Congress. A few among the more important are: (i) 1955-born **He Lifeng**, who is alternate Member of the 18th CCP CC and presently Deputy Director of the National Development and Reform Commission. He was Xiamen's financial chief when Xi Jinping was the city's Deputy Mayor in charge of finance from 1985 to 1988. (ii) **Xia Baolong**, who was born in 1952, was transferred to Zhejiang in November 2003 as Deputy Party Secretary. He served under Xi Jinping who was then Party Secretary of Zhejiang. He was officially elected as Governor in January 2012 and on December 18, 2012, was promoted as Party Secretary of Zhejiang Province. The crack-down on Christians and burning of crosses last year was ordered by him. More recently, instructions were issued in December 2016 to regulate the activities of Tibetan Buddhist and other Buddhist monks and nuns in the province. He has been a member of the 15th, 16th and 17th CCs and is a Member of the 18th CC.; (iii) **Li Qiang** is Party Secretary of Jiangsu Province and an Alternate Member of the 18th CC; (iv) 1960-born **Chen Min'er**, who is Guizhou Party Secretary, is a member of the 18th CC and regarded as a member of China's Sixth Generation of leaders. (v) **Ying Yong** was born in 1957, and worked in Taizhou's public security and later Political and Legal Affairs Commission, before being appointed in November 2006, as President of the Zhejiang Provincial High Court. He was appointed Mayor of Shanghai in January 2017.; (vi) Hainan Governor **Liu Cigui**, who was born in 1955, served in China's State Oceanic Administration from 2011-2014 where he adopted an assertive stance on China's maritime claims including in the South China Sea ; (vii) born in 1968, **Fang Xinghai** graduated from Tsinghua University in 1986, and received a doctorate from Stanford University, USA in 1993. He started his career at the World Bank through the Young Professionals Program, subsequently returning home in 1998 to join the China Construction Bank. He is Vice-Chairman, China Securities Regulatory Commission; (viii) **Xu Lin**, born in 1963, has served in the Tibet Autonomous Region (TAR) from 1995-98. He was Director of the Shanghai Municipality Propaganda Department before being brought to Beijing in 2015 as Deputy Director of the Central LSG for Internet Security and Informationisation. In June 2016, he took over as Director of the Central LSG for Internet Security and Informationisation (known also as -- Central Leading Group for Cyberspace Affairs).; (ix) Chen Jining was born in 1964 and graduated from Tsinghua University.; (x) born in 1955, **Zhong Shan** is Vice Minister in the Ministry of Commerce.

(The paper was published by Centre for China Analysis and Strategy (CCAS) in January 2017).

24

18th CC Members

Name	中文名字	Primary bureaucratic affiliation	Bureaucratic affiliation at time of election to 18th CC (if different)	Job Titles	DOB
Yu Guangzhou	于广洲	Govt (Customs)		Director, General Administration of Customs.	1953年1月生
Xi Jinping	习近平	Central Party		CC General Secretary, Vice-President, CMC Chairman, Head of Party School	1953年6月
Ma Kai	马凯	Govt (State Council)		Secretary-General, State Council; State Councilor, State Council; President, China National School of Administration	1946年6月
Ma Biao (Zhuang)	马飚(壮族)	Prov (Guangxi)		Deputy Party Secretary, Guangxi; Chairman of Peoples Govt	1954年8月生
Ma Xingrui	马兴瑞	SOE		President and Party Secretary of China Aerospace Science and Technology Corporation (CASC)	1954
Ma Xiaotian	马晓天	PLA		CMC, Commander of PLA Air force	1949年8月
Wang Jun	王君	Prov (Inner Mongolia)	Prov (Shanxi)	Party Secretary, Inner Mongolia	1952
Wang Xia (f.)	王侠(女)	Govt (NPFPC)		Director, National Population and Family Planning Commission	1954
Wang Min	王珉	Prov. (Liaoning)		Party Secretary, Liaoning	1950

Name	中文名字	Primary bureaucratic affiliation	Bureaucratic affiliation at time of election to 18th CC (if different)	Job Titles	DOB
Wang Yong	王勇	Govt (SASAC)		Director + party secretary of SASAC (State-Owned Assets Supervision and Administration Commission)	1955
Wang Chen	王晨	Govt (Information Office)		Vice-head of CC Publicity Department. Director, International Communication Office of the Central Committee of the CPC. Director, State Council Information Office	1950
Wang Yi	王毅	Party (Taiwan Office)		Foreign Minister	1953
Wang Sanyun	王三运	Prov (Gansu)		Party Secretary, Gansu	1952年12月
Wang Wanbin	王万宾	NPC		Deputy Secretary-General of NPCSC	1949
Wang Yupu	王玉普	ACFTU		Vice Chairman of All-China Federation of Trade Unions	1956
Wang Zhengwei (Hui)	王正伟(回族)	Prov. (Ningxia)		Ningxia Deputy Secretary, Chairman Ningxia People's Government	1957
Wang Dongming	王东明	Prov. (Sichuan)	Central Party (Office for Central Org. Committee)	Party Secretary, Sichuan	1956年7月生
Wang Guangya	王 光亚	Govt (HK & Macao Office)		Director, Hong Kong and Macao Affairs Office of the State Council	1950
Wang Weiguang	王伟光	Academic		Vice-President and Deputy Party Secretary of CASS	1950
Wang Anshun	王安顺	Prov. (Beijing)		Deputy Party Secretary of Beijing, Mayor of Beijing, Chairman of Beijing CPPCC Municipal Committee	1957
Wang Zhigang	王志刚	Govt (MOST)		Secretary of the CPC Leading Group on Science and Technology. Deputy Secretary General, Ministry of Science and Technology	1958

Name	中文名字	Primary bureaucratic affiliation	Bureaucratic affiliation at time of election to 18th CC (if different)	Job Titles	DOB
Wang Qishan	王岐山	Central Party	Govt (State Council)	Member, PBSC; Secretary of Central Discipline and Inspection Commission, Vice Premier	1948年7月
Wang Huning	王沪宁	Central Party		Member, PB; Director of the Central Party Policy Research Office	1955年10月
Wang Guosheng	王国生	Prov. (Hubei)		Governor and Deputy Party Secretary of Hubei	1956
Wang Xuejun	王学军	Govt (State Letters and Complaints Bureau)		Deputy Secretary General of State Council. Director, State Bureau for Letters and Calls.	1952年12月出生
Wang Jianping	王建平	PAP		Commander of PAP	1953年12月
Wang Shengjun	王胜俊	Courts (Supreme Peoples Court)		President, Supreme People's Court	1946年10月生
Wang Hongyao	王洪尧	PLA		Political Commissar, General Armament Department	1951年11月生
Wang Xiankui	王宪魁	Prov. (Heilongjiang)		Governor + Deputy Secretary, Heilongjiang Province	1952年7月生
Wang Guanzhong	王冠中	PLA		Deputy Chief of the General Staff, Head Quarters of PLA General Staff	1953年2月生
Wang Jiarui	王家瑞	Central Party		Head of the International Liaison Department of the CPC Central Committee	1949年9月生
Wang Jiaocheng	王教成	PLA		Commander, Shenyang Military Region	1952年
Wang Xinxian	王新宪	CPPCC (China Disabled Persons' Federation)		Vice-Chairman of China Disabled Persons' Federation	1954年11月生
Wang Rulin	王儒林	Prov. (Jilin)		Party Secretary, Jilin Province	1953年4月生

Name	中文名字	Primary bureaucratic affiliation	Bureaucratic affiliation at time of election to 18th CC (if different)	Job Titles	DOB
Zhi Shuping	支树平	Govt (State Admin. of Quality Supervision, Inspection and Quarantine)		Director, State Administration of Quality Supervision, Inspection and Quarantine	1953年6月生
You Quan	尤 权	Prov (Fujian)	Govt (State Council)	Party Secretary, Fujian	1954年1月23日生
Che Jun	车俊	Prov (XAR)		Deputy Secretary, XAR. Secretary General and Political Commissar, Xinjiang Production and Construction Corps.	1955年7月出生
Yin Weimin	尹蔚民	Govt. (State Administration of Civil Service)		Director, State Administration of Civil Service	1 9 5 3 年 1 月生
Bayanqolu (Mongolian)	巴音朝鲁(蒙古族)	Prov (Jilin)		Deputy Party Secretary, Jilin. Chairman of Jilin CPPCC	1955年生
Bater (Mongolian)	巴特尔(蒙古族)	Prov (Inner Mongolia)		Deputy Party Secretary and Chairman of Peoples government, Inner Mongolia	1955年2月生
Lu Zhangong	卢展工	Prov (Henan)		Party Secretary, Henan	1 9 5 2 年 5 月生
Ye Xiaowen	叶小文	Central Party		Secretary of Leading Party Group of the Central Institute of Socialism, First Vice President	1950年8月生
Tian Zhong	田中	PLA		Commander, North Sea Fleet of PLA	1956年一
Tian Xiusi	田修思	PLA		Political Commissar, PLA Airforce	1950年2月
Padma Choling(Tibetan)	白玛赤林(藏族)	Provinces (TAR)		Deputy Party Secretary and Chariman of People's Govt, TAR	1951年10月生
Bai Chunli (Manchu)	白春礼(满族)	Academic		President of CASS	1953年9月生
Ling Jihua	令计划	Central Party		Director, United Front Work Department	1956年10月生

Name	中文名字	**Primary bureaucratic affiliation**	**Bureaucratic affiliation at time of election to 18th CC (if different)**	**Job Titles**	**DOB**
Ji Bingxuan	吉炳轩	Prov (Heilongjiang)		Party Secretary, Heilongjiang	1951年11月生
Zhu Xiaodan	朱小丹	Prov (Guangdong)		Governor + Deputy Secretary, Guangdong	1953年1月生
Zhu Fuxi	朱福熙	PLA		Commander, Chengdu Military Region	1955年7月
Quan Zhezhu (Korean)	全哲洙(朝鲜族)	Central Party		Deputy Director of the CPC Central Committee United Front Work Department. Secretary of CPC Leading Party Group and First Vice-Chairman of the All-China Federation of Industry and Commerce.	1952年3月
Liu Peng	刘鹏	Govt (Administration of Sports)		Director, State General Administration of Sports	1951年9月
Liu Yuan	刘源	PLA		Political Commissar, General Logistics Dept.	1951年
Liu He	刘鹤	Govt		Deputy Director, Office of Leading Group for Economic and Financial Affairs. Deputy Director, Development Research Center of the State Council	1952年1月
Liu Yunshan	刘云山	Central Party		Head of Party School. Member of Secretariat.	1947年7月
Liu Yazhou	刘亚洲	PLA		Political Commissar, National Defense University of the PLA	1952年10月
Liu Chengjun	刘成军	PLA		President, Military Academy of Sciences	1950年生
Liu Weiping	刘伟平	Prov. (Gansu)		Governor + Deputy Party Secretary, Gansu Province	1953年5月生
Liu Yandong (f.)	刘延东(女)	Govt (State Council)		Member, PB; State Councillor.	1945年11
Liu Qibao	刘奇葆	Central Party	Prov. (Sichuan)	Member, PB; Member of Secretariat. Director, Central Propaganda Department	1953年1月

Name	中文名字	Primary bureaucratic affiliation	Bureaucratic affiliation at time of election to 18th CC (if different)	Job Titles	DOB
Liu Xiaojiang	刘晓江	PLA (Navy)		Political Commissar, PLA Navy	1949年12月
Liu Jiayi	刘家义	Govt (Audit Office)		Auditor-General, National Audit Office	1956年8月
Liu Yuejun	刘粤军	PLA		Commander, Lanzhou Military Region	1954年9月生
Liu Fulian	刘福连	PLA		Political Commissar, Beijing Military Region	1953年生
Xu Dazhe	许达哲	SOE		President and Party Secretary of the China Aerospace Science and Industry Corporation	1956年9月生
Xu Qiliang	许其亮	PLA		Member, PB; Vice-Chairman, Central Military Commission.	1950年3月
Xu Yaoyuan	许耀元	PAP		Political Commissar, PAP	1952年12月出生
Sun Huaishan	孙怀山	CPPCC		Secretary of Party Committee and Deputy Secreatry-General, CPPCC	1952年6月
Sun Jianguo	孙建国	PLA		Deputy Chief of General Staff, Headquarters of General Staff. Secretary General, National Defense Mobilization Committee of China	1952年2月
Sun Chunlan (f.)	孙春兰(女)	Prov. (Tianjin)	Prov. (Fujian)	Member, PB; Party Secretary, Tianjin Municipality	1950年5月
Sun Zhengcai	孙政才	Prov (Chongqing)	Prov (Jilin)	Member, PB; Party Secretary, Chongqing Municipality	1963年9月
Sun Sijing	孙思敬	PLA		Political Commissar, Military Academy of Sciences	1951年12月生
Su Shulin	苏树林	Prov. (Fujian)		Governor and Deputy Party Secretary , Fujian Province	1962年3月生
Du Qinglin	杜青林	Central Party		Member of Secretariat. Vice Chairman, CPPCC	1946年11月生

Name	中文名字	Primary bureaucratic affiliation	Bureaucratic affiliation at time of election to 18th CC (if different)	Job Titles	DOB
Du Jincai	杜金才	PLA		Deputy Secretary, CCDI. Secretary, Central Military Commission Commission for Discipline Inspection. Deputy Director, General Political Dept of PLA	1952年
Du Hengyan	杜恒岩	PLA		Political Commissar, Jinan Military Region	1951年7月
Li Wei	李伟	Govt (DRC)		Director, Development Research Center of the State Council. Party Committee Deputy Secretary.	1953年8月生
Li Bin (f.)	李斌(女)	Prov. (Anhui)		Governor and Deputy Party Secretary, Anhui Province	1954年10月
Li Congjun	李从军	Central Party (Xinhua)		President, Xinhua	1962年3月出生
Li Dongsheng	李东生	Govt (MPS)		Vice-Minister, Ministry of Public Security. Deputy Secretary, Party Committee	1955年12月生
Li Liguo	李立国	Govt (Ministry of Civil Affairs)		Minister, Ministry of Civil Affairs	1953年生
Li Jiheng	李纪恒	Prov. (Yunnan)		Governor and Deputy Party Secretary, Yunnan Province	1957年1月生
Li Keqiang	李克强	Govt (State Council)		PBSC. Vice Premier, State Council	1955年7月
Li Xueyong	李学勇	Prov. (Jiangsu)		Governor + Deputy Party Secretary, Jiangsu Province.	1950年9月生
Li Jianhua	李建华	Academic		Deputy Director, Chinese Academy of Governance. Secretary, Party Committee.	1954年9月生
Li Jianguo	李建国	NPC		Member, PB; Vice-Chairman and Secretary-General of the Standing Committee of the 11th NPC.	1946年4月
Li Hongzhong	李鸿忠	Prov (Hubei)		Party Secretary, Hubei	1956年8月

Name	中文名字	Primary bureaucratic affiliation	Bureaucratic affiliation at time of election to 18th CC (if different)	Job Titles	DOB
Li Yuanchao	李源潮	Central Party		Member, PB.	1950年11月
Yang Jing (Mongolian)	杨晶(蒙古族)	Govt (Ethnic Affairs Commission)		Member of Secretariat. Vice-head of the United Front Work Dept. Director of the State Ethnic Affairs Commission	1953年12月生
Yang Chuantang	杨传堂	Govt (Ministry of Transport)		Minister of Transport	1954年5月生
Yang Jinshan	杨金山	PLA		Member of Party Standing Committee, TAR. Commander of TAR Military Region.	1954年8月生
Yang Dongliang	杨栋梁	Govt (Work Safety)		Director of the State Administration of Work Safety and Deputy Director of the Work Safety Committee of the State Council.	1954年1月生
Yang Jiechi	杨洁篪	Govt (MFA)		Minister of Foreign Affairs	1950年5月
Yang Huanning	杨焕宁	Govt (MPS)		Vice Minister of Public Security	1957年3月生
Xiao Gang	肖钢	Finance (PBOC)		Chairman, Bank of China	1958年出生
Xiao Jie	肖捷	Govt (Taxation)		Director, State Administration of Taxation	1957年6月
Wu Changde	吴昌德	PLA		Deputy Director, General Political Dept of PLA	1952
Wu Shengli	吴胜利	PLA (Navy)		CMC. Commander, PLA Navy	1945年8月
Wu Aiying (f.)	吴爱英(女)	Govt (MoJ)		Minister of Justice	1951年12月
Wu Xinxiong	吴 新雄	Govt		Chairman, State Electricity Regulatory Commission	1949年10月
He Yiting	何毅亭	Central Party		Executive Deputy Director, Policy Research Office of the CPC Central Committee	
Leng Rong	冷溶	Central Party		Director, Central Party Literature Research Center	1953年8月生

Name	中文名字	Primary bureaucratic affiliation	Bureaucratic affiliation at time of election to 18th CC (if different)	Job Titles	DOB
Wang Yang	汪洋	Prov (Guangdong)		Member, PB. Party Secretary, Guangdong Province	1955年3月12日
Wang Yongqing	汪永清	Govt (Public Sector Reform)		Committee member and Office Director, State Commission for Public Sector Reform	1959年9月出生
Shen Yueyue (f.)	沈跃跃(女)	Central Party		First Deputy Head, Central Organization Department	1957年1月
Shen Deyong	沈德咏	Courts (Supreme Peoples Court)		Party Leading Group Deputy Secretary and Vice-President, Supreme People's Court	1954年2月
Song Dahan	宋大涵	Govt (Legislative Affairs)		Director, State Council Legislative Affairs Office. Party Leadership Group Secretary.	1952年12月
Song Xiuyan (f.)	宋秀岩(女)	CPPCC (All China Womens Federation)		Party Leadership Group Secretary, Vice Chairwoman, and First Scretary of the Secretariat, All-China Women's Federation	1955年10月
Zhang Yang	张阳	PLA		CMC. Director, PLA General Political Department	1951年8月
Zhang Mao	张茅	Govt (Health)		Vice-Minister, Ministry of Health. Party Leadership Group Secretary	1954年2月
Zhang Yi	张毅	Prov. (Ningxia)		Party Secretary, Ningxia	1950年8月
Zhang Youxia	张又侠	PLA		CMC. Director, General Armament Dept.	1950年7月生
Zhang Shibo	张仕波	PLA		Commander, Beijing Military Region	1952年2月出生
Zhang Qingwei	张庆伟	Prov. (Hebei)		Governor and Deputy Party Secretary, Hebei Province	1961年11月
Zhang Qingli	张庆黎	Prov (Hebei)		Party Secretary, Hebei Province	1951年1月
Zhang Zhijun	张志军	Govt (MFA)		Executive Vice-Minster, Ministry of Foreign Affairs. Party Leadership Group Secretary	1953

Name	中文名字	Primary bureaucratic affiliation	Bureaucratic affiliation at time of election to 18th CC (if different)	Job Titles	DOB
Zhang Guoqing	张国清	SOE (NORINCO)		General Manager, China North Industries Group Corporation	1964年8月出生
Zhang Baoshun	张宝顺	Prov (Anhui)		Party Secretary, Anhui Province	1950
Zhang Chunxian	张春贤	Prov (XAR)		Member, PB. Party Secretary, XAR	1953年5月
Zhang Gaoli	张高丽	Central Party	Prov (Tianjin)	Member, PB.	1946年11月
Zhang Haiyang	张海阳	PLA		Political commissar, PLA Second Artillery Corps	1949年7月
Zhang Yijiong	张裔炯	Central Party		Executive Vice Director, United Front Department	1955
Zhang Dejiang	张德江		Prov (Chongqing)	Member, PBSC. State Council Vice Premier	1946年11月
Lu Hao	陆昊	Central party		1st Secretary of Secretariat of the CYLC Central Committee	1967年
Chen Xi	陈希	Academic		Vice Chairman, Party Leaderhip Grp Secretary and First Secretary of the Secretariat, China Association for Science and Technology	1953年9月
Chen Lei	陈雷	Govt (Ministry of Water Resources)		Minister, Ministry of Water Resources	1954年6月
Chen Quanguo	陈全国	Prov (TAR)		Party Secretary, TAR	1955年11月
Chen Qiufa (Miao)	陈求发(苗族)	Govt (Industry and Information Technology)		Vice-Minister, Ministry of Industry and Information Technology. Secretary of Party Leadership Group. Director, State Administration for Science, Technology and Industry for National Defense (SASTIND). Director, China Atomic Energy Authority. Director, China National Space Administration (CNSA)	1954年12月
Chen Baosheng	陈宝生	Central Party		Vice-President, CPC Central Party School	1956年5月

Name	中文名字	Primary bureaucratic affiliation	Bureaucratic affiliation at time of election to 18th CC (if different)	Job Titles	DOB
Chen Zhenggao	陈政高	Prov. (Liaoning)		Governor & Deputy Secretary, Liaoning Province	1952年3月
Chen Min'er	陈敏尔	Prov (Guizhou)		Deputy Secretary, Guizhou Province	1960年9月
Nur Bekri (Uygur)	努尔•白克力(维吾尔族)	Prov (XAR)		Deputy Party Secretary and Chairman of Peoples Government, XAR	1961年8月
Miao Wei	苗圩	Govt (MIIT)		Minister, Ministry of Industry and Information Technology	1955年5月
Fan Changlong	范长龙	PLA		Member, PB; Vice-Chairman, Central Military Commission	1947年5月
Lin Jun	林军	CPPCC		Chairman, All-China Federation of Returned Overseas Chinese	1949年7月
Lin Zuoming	林左鸣	SOE (China Aviation Industry Corporation)		President of China Aviation Industry Corporation	1957年5月
Shang Fulin	尚福林	Finance (China Securities Regulatory Commission)		Chairman of the China Securities Regulatory Commission	1951年11月
Luo Zhijun	罗志军	Prov (Jiangsu)		Party Secretary, Jiangsu Province	1951年11月
Luo Baoming	罗保铭	Prov (Hainan)		Party Secretary, Hainan Province	1952年10月
Zhou Ji	周济	Academic		President, Chinese Academy of Engineering	1946年8月
Zhou Qiang	周强	Prov (Hunan)		Party Secretary, Hunan Province	1960年4月
Zhou Benshun	周本顺	Central Party		General-Secretary of Central Politics and Law Commission. Deputy -Director, Committee for Comprehensive Management of Public Security	1953年2月

Name	中文名字	Primary bureaucratic affiliation	Bureaucratic affiliation at time of election to 18th CC (if different)	Job Titles	DOB
Zhou Shengxian	周生贤	Govt (Ministry of Environmental Protection)		Minister of the Ministry of Enviornmental Protection.	1949年12月
Zheng Weiping	郑卫平	PLA		Political Commissar, Nanjing Military Region	1955年生
Fang Fenghui	房峰辉	PLA		CMC, Chief of General Staff	1951年4月
Meng Xuenong	孟学农	Central Party		Deputy Secreatry, Work Committee of the Central Government Departments under the CPC Central Committee. President, Party School of Departments under the Central Committee	1949年8月
Meng Jianzhu	孟建柱	Central Party	Govt (Minister of Public Security)	Secretary of the CPC Central Committee Politics and Law Commission	1947年7月
Xiang Junbo	项俊波	Finance (China Insurance Regulatory Commission)		Chairman of China Insurance Regulatory Commission	1957年1月
Zhao Shi (f.)	赵实(女)	Other		Vice Chairwoman and Secretary of Party Leadership Group, China Federation of Literary and Art Circles	1953年8月
Zhao Zhengyong	赵正永	Prov. (Shaanxi)		Party Secretary and Governor, Shaanxi Province	1951年3月
Zhao Leji	赵乐际	Central Party	Prov (Shaanxi)	Member, PB; Member of the Secretariat.Head of the Organization Department.	1957年3月
Zhao Keshi	赵克石	PLA		CMC. Director of General Logistics Dept.	1947年11月生
Zhao Kezhi	赵克志	Prov (Guizhou)		Governor and Party Secretary of Guizhou Province	1953年12月
Zhao Zongqi	赵宗岐	PLA		Commander, Jinan Military Region	1955年
Zhao Hongzhu	赵洪祝	Central Party	Prov (Zhejiang)	Member, Secretariat; Deputy secretary, CCDI.	1947年7月

Name	中文名字	Primary bureaucratic affiliation	Bureaucratic affiliation at time of election to 18th CC (if different)	Job Titles	DOB
Hu Zejun (f.)	胡泽君(女)	Courts (Supreme People's Procuratorate)		Deputy Procurator General, Supreme People's Procuratorate	1955年3月
Hu Chunhua	胡春华	Prov (Guangdong)	Prov (Inner Mongolia)	Member, PB; Party Secretary, Inner Mongolia	1963年4月
Yu Zhengsheng	俞正声	Central Party	Prov (Shanghai)	Member, PBSC	1945年4月
Jiang Daming	姜大明	Prov (Shandong)		Governor and Deputy secretary, Shandong	1953年3月
Jiang Yikang	姜异康	Prov (Shandong)		Party Secretary, Shandong	1953年1月
Luo Huining	骆惠宁	Prov (Qinghai)		Governor, People's Government Qinghai Province	1954年10月
Qin Guangrong	秦光荣	Prov (Yunnan)		Party Secretary, Yunnan	1950年12月
Yuan Chunqing	袁纯清	Prov (Shanxi)		Party Secretary, Shanxi	1952年3月
Yuan Guiren	袁贵仁	Govt (Ministry of Education)		Minister of Education	1950年11月
Geng Huichang	耿惠昌	Govt (MPS)		Minister, Ministry of State Security	1951年11月
Nie Weiguo	聂卫国	Govt (Three Gorges Project)		Deputy Director, State council Three gorges project construction committee. Director, Office of the State Council Three Gorges Project Construction Committee	1952年8月
Li Zhanshu	栗战书	Central Party		Member of Secretariat. Director of the Central Committee General Office. Secreatry, Work Committee of the Central Government Departments under the CPC Central Committee	1950年8月
Jia Ting'an	贾廷安	PLA		Deputy Director, General Political Dept of PLA	1952年9月
Xia Baolong	夏宝龙	Prov (Zhejiang)		Party Secretary and Governor, Zhejiang	1952年12月生

Name	中文名字	Primary bureaucratic affiliation	Bureaucratic affiliation at time of election to 18th CC (if different)	Job Titles	DOB
Tie Ning (f.)		CPPCC (Chinese Writers Association)		Chairman of the China Writers Association	1957年
Xu Shousheng	徐守盛	Prov (Hunan)		Governor and Deputy Party Secretary, Hunan Province	1953年1月
Xu Shaoshi	徐绍史	Govt (Ministry of Land and Resources)		Minister, Ministry of Land and Resources	1951年10月
Xu Fenlin	徐粉林	PLA		Commander, Guangzhou Military Region	1953年7月
Gao Hucheng	高虎城	Govt (MOFCOM)		Vice-Minister and negotiator, Ministry of Commerce	1951年8月生
Guo Shengkun	郭声琨	Govt (MPS)	Prov (Guangxi)	Minister of Public Security	1954年10月
Guo Jinlong	郭金龙	Prov (Beijing)		Member, PB; Party secretary, Beijing.	1947年7月
Guo Gengmao	郭庚茂	Prov (Henan)		Governor & Deputy Party Secretary, Henan Province	1950年12月生
Guo Shuqing	郭树清	Finance (China Securities Regulatory Commission)		Chairman, China Securities Regulatory Commission	1956年8月
Huang Xingguo	黄兴国	Prov (Tianjin)		Mayor and Deptuy Party Secretary of Tianjin	1954年10月
Huang Qifan	黄奇帆	Prov (Chongqing)		Mayor and Deptuy Party Secretary of Chongqing	1952年5月
Huang Shuxian	黄树贤	Cetnral Party		Deputy Secretary, CCDI	1954年9月
Cao Jianming	曹建明	Courts (Supreme People's Procuratorate)		Procurator-General of the Supreme People's Procuratorate	1955年9月
Qi Jianguo	戚建国	PLA		Deputy Chief of the PLA General Staff	1952年8月
Chang Wanquan	常万全	PLA		CMC member.	1949年1月
Lu Xinshe	鹿心社	Prov (Jiangxi)		Governor and Deputy Party Secretary of Jiangxi Province	1956年11月生

Name	中文名字	Primary bureaucratic affiliation	Bureaucratic affiliation at time of election to 18th CC (if different)	Job Titles	DOB
Peng Yong	彭勇	PLA		Commander of XAR Military Region, Member of Party Committee for XAR	1954年1月生
Peng Qinghua	彭清华	Prov (Guangxi)	Prov (Hong Kong)	Director of the liaison office of the Central People's Government in Hong Kong SAR	1957年4月生
Jiang Dingzhi	蒋定之	Prov (Hainan)		Governor of Hainan Province and Deputy Secretary of the CPC Hainan Provincial Committee.	1954年9月
Jiang Jianguo	蒋建国	Govt (General Administration of Press and Publication)		Deputy Director of the General Administration of Press and Publication, Deputy Secretary of the General Administration of Press and Publication Leading Party Group.	1956年12月
Jiang Jiemin	蒋洁敏	SOE (Petrochina)		President of PetroChina Company	1955年10月
Han Zheng	韩正	Prov (Shanghai)		Member, PB. Party Secretary and Mayor, Shanghai	1954年4月
Han Changfu	韩长赋	Govt (Agriculture)		Minister of Agriculture	1954年10月
Jiao Huancheng	焦焕成	Govt (State Council)		Secretary General, State Council. Director of the Government Offices Administration of the State Council.	1949年10月生
Xie Fuzhan	谢伏瞻	Govt (Research Office of the State Council)		Director of the Research Office of the State Council.	1954年出生
Qiang Wei	强卫	Prov (Qinghai)		Party Secretary, Qinghai	1953年3月
Lou Jiwei	楼继伟	Finance (China Investment Corportation)		Chairman of China Investment Corporation (CIC), Chairman of Cetral Huijin Investment Ltd.	1950年12月
Xie Zhenhua	解振华	Govt (NDRC)		Vice-Minister of NDRC	1949年11月

Name	中文名字	Primary bureaucratic affiliation	Bureaucratic affiliation at time of election to 18th CC (if different)	Job Titles	DOB
Chu Yimin	褚益民	PLA		Political Commissar, Shenyang Military Region	1953年7月
Cai Wu	蔡武	Govt (Ministry of Culture)		Deputy Director of the Central Propaganda Dept; Minister of Culture.	1949年10月
Cai Mingzhao	蔡名照	Central Party		Editor, Peoples Daily	1955年6月
Cai Yingting	蔡英挺	PLA		Commander, Nanjing Military Region	1954年生
Cai Fuchao	蔡赴朝	Govt (SARFT)		Deputy Director of the Central Propaganda Dept; Director of SARFT	1951年4月
Luo Shugang	雒树刚	Central Party		Executive Deputy-director of Central Propaganda Dept; Director of Central Civilisation office	1955年5月生
Wei Liang	魏亮	PLA		Political Commissar, Guangzhou Military Region	1953年2月
Wei Fenghe	魏 凤和	PLA		Commander, PLA Second Artillery Corps	1954年2月

25

China's New Policy of Peripheral Diplomacy

A very important meeting which approved China's new policy for relations with its neighbours seems to have attracted little attention and comment, possibly because it was overshadowed by the anticipation surrounding the Chinese Communist Party (CCP) Central Committee's (CC) Third Plenum which was held a couple of weeks later in November 2013. All seven members of the CCP CC Politburo Standing Committee (PBSC) attended the entire two days (October 24-25, 2013) of this meeting, along with representatives of the various departments of the Central Committee, State Councillors, the Central Leading Small Group for Foreign Affairs and China's Ambassadors to important countries. Convened for the first time in the history of the People's Republic of China (PRC), the meeting approved far-reaching major changes in China's diplomatic strategy and significantly, also for the first time ever, categorised China's neighbours as "friends" and "enemies." It decided to forge regional, subregional and bilateral "cooperative" security relationships and gave a definite role to the CCP.

Prior to this two-day meeting in October in Beijing, the Politburo convened at least twice over the space of the past year to deliberate the issue. China's new strategic policy towards its neighbours, labelled by Chinese analysts as "Peripheral Diplomacy" (zhoubian), heralds a significant shift in the manner in which Beijing will henceforth conduct relations with its neighbours. Elements of the policy focusing on South Asia were being put in place by Chinese leaders, including Xi Jinping and former PBSC member, Zhou Yongkang, over the past three years.

It is now clear that Beijing's categorisation of nations as "friends" and "enemies" will guide its conduct of bilateral relations. Key features of the new policy aimed at securing global leadership for China will include emphasis on the "China Dream," promotion of bilateral security relationships, and the forging of regional, subregional, or "cooperative" security ties. The new policy strives to strike a balance between the defence of national sovereignty and the maintenance of regional stability. It simultaneously stresses that efforts will be made for better political and economic relations with neighbouring countries, closer security cooperation and people-to-people contact.

Official reporting of Xi Jinping's speech at the two-day conference was predictably guarded. Still, they noted his emphasis that "most of the neighbouring countries have a friendly and mutually beneficial relationship with China" and, importantly, that the strategic goal of China's diplomacy with neighbouring countries is to serve the cause of "national rejuvenation." This was clarified to mean consolidation of friendly relations with neighbours and making the best use of current strategic opportunities. Emphasising that "peripheral diplomacy" is intended to make neighbouring countries "feel safe," Xi Jinping said China's interests must be better integrated with theirs. Regional economic cooperation, establishment of a "Silk Road economic belt," "a maritime silk road for the twenty-first century" and an economic corridor through India, Myanmar, and Bangladesh (BCIM) were listed as among the key objectives. Other features include accelerating the opening up of border areas, deepening reciprocal cooperation between China's border areas and neighbouring countries, and promoting regional and subregional security cooperation.

Xi Jinping specifically highlighted a role for the CCP in safeguarding peace and stability in the region. This points to the CCP, and particularly the CCP CC's International Department and United Front Work Department (UFWD), playing a more proactive role in bilateral relationships including establishing and enhancing party-to-party ties. An example is the UFWD's growing profile in Nepal and direct involvement in Buddha's birthplace of Lumbini. The main objective, Xi Jinping stressed, is to ensure favourable external conditions for China's reform, which includes development and stability, safeguarding national sovereignty, security and development, maintaining world peace and stability and promoting common development. He said "common ground and converging interests" should be emphasised to achieve these objectives.

Salient elements of the new strategy of "Peripheral Diplomacy" have filtered out through commentaries and clarifications offered by senior CCP cadres. China's strategic analysts and academics are unanimous that relations with the US are crucial to China.

Reputed Tsinghua University Professor Yan Xuetong, who is Dean of the Institute of Modern International Relations and Chief Editor of the Chinese *Journal of International Politics*, recently underscored this while explaining the "new type of big power relations" proposed by China's President Xi Jinping to Obama while on a "working" visit to the US. Yan Xuetong's proximity to Xi Jinping adds considerable importance to his observations and analyses. Yan Xuetong said that far from denoting an alliance, this new type of relationship is intended to prevent Sino-US relations deteriorating from one of "competition" to "confrontation." He specifically acknowledged the "complete lack of trust," but suggested this is "not a prerequisite to a relatively peaceful accommodation." He candidly stated that "China and the US have not trusted each other since 1989 and are not likely to in the future. But interests will form the cornerstone of this relationship ... although China and the US are strategic competitors." He said the most desired relationship would be termed "cooperative," like that between China and Russia. The other two categories of relations are "competitive" as with the US and "confrontational" as in the case of Sino-Japan relations.

China's Ambassador to the US, Cui Tiankai, conveyed the same idea more diplomatically in context of the new policy of "Peripheral Diplomacy" to a US audience on February 20, 2014. He underlined the need to shift the orientation of Sino-US relations from one of "crisis management to opportunity management" adding that using coercive language is not constructive. He also cautioned against "unilateral interpretations of some international legal instruments, and attempts to impose these interpretations on others." Cui Tiankai acknowledged that "the United States is a powerful and very strong country ... the most powerful and strongest country in the world, and will remain so for many years to come" and that China's effort to build the "new model of relationship," is based on full recognition of this fact.

In an article in Chinese posted on January 28, 2014, Yan Xuetong said the conference on "Peripheral Diplomacy" signalled China's strategic shift in its foreign policy outlook. He said that unlike the US or West, China will use alternative strategies "to achieve global leadership" and attributed this to the compulsions of nuclear weapons and globalisation. Of the two core principles that have guided

Chinese foreign policy since the early 1990s, Deng Xiaoping's famous dictum of "lie low, bide your time" (taoguang yanghui) has been discarded while the other, of according first priority to relations with the US, has been modified. The new dictum allows that although China and the US are "strategic competitors," they "have common interests, complementary interests and conflicting interests." This provides both countries room for active cooperation when interests converge and a degree of preventive cooperation where interests conflict.

A major change is that while for the past two decades China opted for a neutral stance avoiding confrontation at all costs and never opposing the US, the new policy advocates engaging with neighbouring countries so as to "align their interests with China's rise." Xi Jinping's stress on "friendship and loyalty between China and its neighbours," he said, "is more significant than it sounds."Yan Xuetong clarified that henceforth China's foreign policy will reflect the different treatment for China's "friends" and "enemies." China will find ways to ensure that greater benefits and gains flow from China's development to those willing to play a constructive role in China's rise. In this manner, it hopes to give its neighbours an incentive in China's development. With some select "key" neighbours China will even try to create "communities of shared common destinies." In addition to economic interests the latter will "include a wider range of strategic elements" and a strong political dimension. This could extend to building security relationships, including providing security guarantees as in the case of China's agreement with Ukraine in December 2013.

Referring to the three specific strategic areas of focus identified by China's leadership, namely, the "new silk road" with Central Asia, a maritime silk road with South East Asia, and the economic corridor through India, Myanmar, and Bangladesh, Yan Xuetong said these regions can expect considerably increased willingness by China to underwrite substantive economic, security, and other benefits in exchange for political support for China's regional objectives.

At the same time, Yan Xuetong emphasised that China's new policy of "peripheral diplomacy" means that those who are hostile to China, or oppose it, will be confronted with sustained periods of tough sanctions and isolation. He assessed that China's new foreign policy outlook in the region will provide an expanded set of strategic options and ample chances to avoid using "military conquests" to achieve regional dominance.

China's official news agency Xinhua on February 7, 2014, separately clarified the kind of political support for regional objectives that China seeks as part of "peripheral diplomacy." Describing Russia as a "good example of China's regional diplomacy, the core of which is to treat neighbours as friends and partners and help them to develop," it regretted that,"some countries in the region chose to ignore history and international law inciting territorial disputes with China and disturbing peace and development of the Asia-Pacific region." Referring to Japanese Prime Minister Shinzo Abe's visit to the Yasukuni Shrine, the Xinhua despatch accused Japan of continuously "irritating its neighbours and even US allies by attempting to downplay its fascist history and revise a pacifist constitution to make overseas deployment of soldiers possible." It said Russia and China should both, therefore, commemorate the 70th anniversary of victories in the World Anti-Fascist War and Anti-Japanese War in 2015.

Some features of the new strategy have been clarified by Chen Xulong, Director of the Department for International and Strategic Studies at the China Institute of International Studies (CIIS), a think tank directly subordinate to China's Ministry of Foreign Affairs (MFA). Observing that China's leadership is aware that many of China's neighbours have reservations about the country's rise and that in some cases it has even generated friction, he said handling and readjusting relationships with international institutions and neighbouring countries is one of China's biggest challenges. China's leaders, he said, are conscious that the US pivot had "disturbed" China's strategy in Asia and that Japan and the Philippines had "misinterpreted" its message thereby creating a number of immediate and potential challenges in China's periphery. China can no longer keep a low profile but has to take the initiative and create a favourable periphery. He said the strategy on "peripheral diplomacy" "strikes a balance between the defence of national sovereignty and the maintenance of regional stability." Efforts will be made for better political and economic relations with neighbouring countries, for closer security cooperation and people-to-people contact.

Qin (closeness), cheng (earnestness), hui (benefit) and rong (inclusiveness) were identified as the four basic principles of "peripheral diplomacy." Chen Xulong said with them China will be able to realise "virtuous interaction" with the United States, India and other major countries. He clarified that "closeness" refers to developing close relations through frequent visits; "earnestness" means to show enough sincerity in solving neighbourhood problems; "benefit" refers to the principle of mutual benefit, on which cooperation with neighbouring countries will be strengthened to weave a network of common prosperity thus bringing them benefits from China's development; and "inclusiveness" means that the Asia and Pacific regions are big enough to include all parties for common development.

Problematic in China's efforts to implement the strategy of "peripheral diplomacy" will, however, be its insistence on achieving its sovereignty and territorial claims and desire to project power. Reiterating the explicit assertions made on two separate occasions in 2011 by the official Xinhua news agency, the CCP's *People's Daily* (Renmin Ribao) on November 4, 2013, declared that "China pursues an open strategy of a win-win situation through beneficial cooperation, but will absolutely not trade the nation's core interests away, and definitely will not brook other countries' wilful hurting of China's legitimate rights and interests." Severe complicating factors that could be introduced by the beginning of the next decade will be the survival and livelihood issues of acute water and food scarcities.

A change is discernible in Beijing's posture from the time in 2010, when during Hu Jintao's visit to the US it opted to drop its description of the South China Sea as an "issue of core national interest," to the present when it has clarified that it will not back off from its maritime territorial claims. Beijing's unrelenting insistence on its maritime territorial claims in the South China Sea and East Sea, together with its assertive posture, underscores its ambition for dominance over the entire region.

This ambition is evident in China's occupation of the Mischief Reef and Scarborough Shoal and latest bid to gain control over the Second Thomas Shoal, all claimed by the Philippines; repeated encounters with Vietnamese and Philippines vessels; renewed claims over St. James' Shoal claimed by Malaysia and the Ieodo Rock of South Korea; unilateral declaration by Beijing that non-Chinese citizens and vessels must obtain prior permission to enter or fish in a maritime territorial zone that covers virtually half the South China Sea and which directive is being enforced by China's maritime agencies and Hainan Island authorities who, according to the Hainan Party Secretary, push back fishing vessels each week; refusal to clarify the U-shaped line on maps on which basis Beijing claims sovereignty over territories in these waters; and Djakarta on March 12, 2014, designating as a "dispute" the doubts raised by the U-shaped line on Chinese maps over Indonesia's Exclusive Economic Zone.

Beijing's handling of its disputes with rival claimants has varied, but the end objective of securing control over the territories, preferably without conflict, is unchanged. Chinese officials have, for example, warned the Philippines to be prepared for a tough four years for taking the contested claim over the Scarborough Reef to international arbitration while its patrol vessels continue to muscle Philippines Navy ships out of waters claimed by China. With Vietnam, the communist parties of both countries have been active in trying to keep ties friendly. The situation is more complex with Japan, which has been singled out as a major potential threat. In the dispute over the Senkakus, called Diaoyu in Chinese, China is trying to isolate Japan and has adopted a tough military stance with its aircraft, ships and submarines going up to the Senkaku Islands and beyond Okinawa. It has ceased all official contacts, but at the same time allowed tourism and economic ties to remain unimpeded.

The current tensions in the Asia-Pacific and their effect on Sino-US relations were present in the remarks Cui Tiankai made on US soil on February 20, 2014 when, referring to the interests of both countries in the Asia-Pacific, he clarified that Beijing is not about to resile from its maritime territorial claims. He said the "United States presence, interests, and influential role in the Asia-Pacific is fully and widely recognised" and that China welcomes a "constructive role by the United States in the region." Equally important was his observation that "China is also a Pacific country, and China is also an Asian country. Geographically, China is just situated in the centre of the Asian continent. And we have been here for centuries, perhaps a little bit longer than the whole history of the United States. So I think it may be fair to say that neither Chinese nor Americans are aliens from Mars in the Asia-Pacific, but we are somehow more indigenous than you are." Warning that "any attempt to manage or manipulate the regional affairs at the expense of China's legitimate interests in the region, cannot be justified, and would indeed be detrimental to the stability and prosperity of the entire region, and eventually will serve nobody's interests," he implied that the new model of big power relations was intended to address such issues.

Shanghai-based Chinese venture capitalist and commentator, Eric X Li, more bluntly echoed similar thinking at a conference in Seoul around the same time. He argued that there had been no missteps by China in the territorial disputes in the South China Sea and East China Sea and that history will "probably prove" that China had dealt with these situations with unmatched agility. China's strategic objective in the region, he said, is to change the status quo—the establishment of which it did not have enough power to participate in or influence—to its advantage while avoiding military conflict. He described China's most important achievement in the past thirty years as its mastering of the international economic system, established by the US, without being absorbed by it. He concluded by saying that China has, and always will, act in its own best national interests. He emphasised that consistent with the cultural roots of the Middle Kingdom, China's "world view is to keep out barbarians and not invade them."

Soon after the policy of "Peripheral Diplomacy" was approved, the China Institutes of Contemporary International Relations (CICIR), subordinate to China's Ministry of State Security (MoSS), convened a RoundTable the same month. Entitled, "Current situation in China's surrounding areas and its Strategy," its proceedings were published in CICIR's "Xiandai Guoji Guanxi" (*Contemporary International Relations*). The summary of this RoundTable prepared by the European Council on Foreign Relations observed that its focus was on China's relations with the US, India, Mongolia and Central Asia. It said, "while participants differed in their views, they were unanimous about the role of the US."

Lin Hongyu of Peking University made the interesting disclosure that the Boeing XB-37, the new US space orbiter, overflew Beijing at the beginning of the crisis over the Air Defence Identification Zone (ADIZ) set up by China in the East China Sea in November 2013. Discussants at the CICIR meeting all anticipated there would be an escalation of global competition among the major powers: China, Russia, India, and the US. Almost all speakers took serious note of the TPP, even though they thought its goals very ambitious, and with the discovery of new energy resources such as shale oil and gas and Japan's invention of a process that can tap methane from underwater ice blocks, viewed it as signalling a "third Industrial Revolution." The Regional Comprehensive

Economic Partnership (RCEP) was viewed as China's counter-strategy and some suggested that China and RCEP should join with the TPP. Lin Limin, Editor-in-Chief of the CICIR journal, "Xiandai Guoji Guanxi" (*Contemporary International Relations*) acknowledged these differences and warned that China's "aspirations" should not exceed its "capabilities," because this has in the past spelt disaster for powers such as Russia, Germany, and Japan.

Discussions on India at the CICIR RoundTable were interesting with general agreement that there has been a "gradual maturing process" (zou xiang chengshu de guocheng) in China-India relations since 1988 as evidenced by the lack of open conflict over the border dispute. Li Li, Associate Professor at CICIR who has studied at a university in India, took a generally benign view of the relationship though she blamed lack of trust and mutual understanding for the failure to arrive at any agreement. She said this had been exacerbated by the "malicious" assertions made by Western researchers and part of the Indian media who were creating a "confrontational point of view" and presenting relations between China and India as antagonistic.To deal with this, political leaders of the two countries have increased the number of high-level meetings and set up a formal exchange mechanism. Indo-US relations figured prominently in discussions, with a consensus that these would harm China's security and national interests and had already generated challenges in the maritime arena. It was apprehended that India will obtain technologically advanced long-range weapons from the US to extend its reach deep into China and acquire leverage over China in negotiations. On land, India-US security cooperation was said to be already causing friction on China's western borders. The need for China to take precautions was stressed.

India-China relations are a key component of China's new strategy of "Peripheral Diplomacy," which has obvious implications for India and Japan. The new policy signals that Beijing will intensify efforts for economic engagement with India, including making investments, and accompany this with high-level visits. The visit proposed by Chinese President Xi Jinping for October-November 2014 is a good example as he is likely to be accompanied by more than 150 Chinese Chief Executives (CEO). Beijing will try to focus on the development of economic ties while setting aside resolution of the contentious border dispute till what it deems a more opportune time. Repeated assertions that China will not barter away its "core national interests" substantiate this.

During the premeditated intrusions in the Depsang Plains in Ladakh too, China's media and officials in India and Beijing were insistent that the PLA personnel were well inside Chinese territory. The influential "Zhongguo Qingnian Bao" (*China Youth Daily*) on May 14, 2013 accused India of triggering tensions by adopting a "forward policy" and stressed that "Ladakh was unified with China's Yuan Dynasty as part of Tibet in the thirteenth century" and was "under the jurisdiction of the central government of China's Qing Dynasty until the 1830s." Stating that it was important for access to Central Asia, it added that "although it is under Kashmir, Ladakh shares similarities with Tibet in terms of culture, religion, customs, and language, and it has long been dubbed 'Little Tibet'. The objective will be to maintain India-China relations at a "competitive" level while trying to prevent emergence of uncomfortable warmth in Indo-US relations.

India will have to contend with the policy's likely fallout on its neighbours. Beijing's initiatives in Myanmar and Nepal reflect its new approach. Qiu Guoheng, China's former Ambassador to Nepal and presently Director General of External Security in China's Ministry of Foreign Affairs (MFA) visited Kathmandu in early December 2013. While there he conveyed that, as part of "peripheral diplomacy," Beijing had decided to revise upward the quantum of foreign assistance to developing countries in its neighbourhood and that Nepal and Pakistan will particularly be beneficiaries. He said development of the "new Silk Road economic belt" would benefit Nepal. Talks are separately underway for extending the 1,200-kilometre Qinghai-Lhasa-Shigatse railway to Kathmandu, agreed to by Chinese Premier Wen Jiabao during his unannounced visit to Nepal in 2012 and which, once completed, will alter the geostrategic balance in the region. The CCP CC's International Department and UFWD have both stepped up activities in Nepal, where suppressing pro-Dalai Lama Tibetan activists is not China's sole interest.

China initiated steps to safeguard its interests in Myanmar in early 2013. It replaced its Ambassador in Yangon and, quite unusually, appointed 74-year-old Wang Yingfan, a retired diplomat related to former PBSC member Qiao Shi, as Special Envoy for Asian Affairs. Beijing also, for the first time since the

Mao era, interfered in the internal affairs of a country—albeit at its request—and brokered at least three rounds of meetings between the rebel groups in north Myanmar and Myanmar's army.

Reliable reports from Beijing state that Xi Jinping has taken personal charge of the "Silk Road economic belt" project. This project envisages an outward westward push from Yunnan towards Bhutan, Nepal, Pakistan and Central Asian countries up to and possibly beyond Turkey. India's northeast is part of this as well as the Bangladesh-China-India-Myanmar (BCIM) corridor. The economies of India's northeastern states are very fragile and connectivity is extremely poor. Acquiescing to both these proposals, which will certainly be accompanied by enormous pressure, by India would be premature. It would mean allowing the free influx of Chinese goods and nationals with the attendant danger of the latter settling down in these areas.

"Peripheral Diplomacy" envisages subregional, regional and "cooperative" security relationships. China already has an all-encompassing military relationship with Pakistan. The People's Liberation Army (PLA) has been steadily upgrading ties with the Nepal Army and Beijing recently secured a maritime cooperation agreement with Sri Lanka. A serious precedent is that set by the security agreement signed between China and Ukraine on December 4, 2013. It states that,"China promises … to provide security guarantees to Ukraine if Ukraine is attacked by nuclear weapons or threatened by such aggression." China and Bangladesh signed a civil nuclear cooperation agreement, which has remained inactivated. Enticed by economic largesse these countries could in future be drawn into a subregional, regional or "cooperative" security relationship with China. The end objective of China's "peripheral diplomacy" is to use alternative strategies "to achieve global leadership."

(The article was published in Centre for China Analysis and Strategy, New Delhi, May 2014).

26

Geopolitical Developments and India-China Relations

The world is in a state of continuing flux. The economies of the major powers are still fragile and vulnerabilities exist in those of the bigger emerging powers in the Asia-Pacific like China and India. The balance of power is concurrently undergoing a shift with competing focal points of power surfacing in the East. The fragile nature has been accentuated in the past few years with Beijing's accelerated push for recognition as the dominant power in the Asia-Pacific. This is resisted by the US, Japan and India and has made South East Asian countries nervous.

China's sudden assertiveness since the end of 2007 was prompted by a combination of factors, but mainly by: the global economic downturn; China's considerably enhanced economic and military strength; and Beijing's perception that the US as a global power is on the decline and this is now the opportune moment for China to regain its self-perceived rightful position on the world stage and alter the status quo in Asia. The Chinese Communist Party (CCP) leadership is divided on the issue of whether to write off the US as the sole world power. One view is that the US is a power irreparably on the decline while the other, which seems to be gaining ground, argues that the intrinsic strength and resilience of the US will ensure its return on to the world stage as a stronger, more effective power. There is consensus, however, that the USA's ability to project power simultaneously in different theatres is presently constrained, thus offering China a window of opportunity that would last at most between 5 and 10 years.

China's impetuousness and decision to "take on" the US anticipatedly triggered a response signalling quite clearly that the US is not about to cede either power or influence in the Asia-Pacific. The US encouraged particularly Japan and the Philippines to react to China's aggressiveness. It additionally unveiled the seemingly short-lived "Asian Pivot" with its definite military content. The US has now shifted emphasis, though, to the Trans-Pacific Partnership (TPP) and Trans-Pacific Intellectual Property Provisions (TPIP), which are economic equivalents of the "Asian Pivot." China is now leaning towards joining the TPP/TPIP.

China, however, has not been deterred and continues to press ahead with achieving its global and regional ambitions. The continuing tense stand-off with US ally and East Asia's strongest power, namely, Japan, amidst steady escalation in tensions in the South China Sea, underlines Beijing's willingness to push the envelope in the apparent confidence that the US will stop shy of confronting it and so will Japan and Vietnam. China reasserted the role it desires in the Asia-Pacific in a statement in Washington DC by its Ambassador to the US, Cui Tiankai, in February 2014. There is little doubt that US credibility as a reliable ally willing to back its partners in the region has been dented in the past five-odd years.

In the South China Sea, after a series of confrontations with Vietnam and the Philippines where China seized some maritime territories, Beijing has begun to assert its claims over a larger area. It has revived its claims on St. James' Shoal off Thailand and South Korea's Ieodo Rock and recently began building airports on some islands and extending others. On May 24, 2014, China's largest US$ 1 billion oil rig, the "Haiyang Shi You 981," sailed into Vietnamese-claimed waters escorted by 86 armed ships and Beijing has now sent four more rigs. Simultaneously, tension with Japan over the Senkaku Islands (called Diaoyu in Chinese) rose in recent weeks with the increased frequency of patrols by Chinese Navy ships and People's Liberation Army Air Force (PLAAF) aircraft flying very close to Japanese Self-Defence Force (SDF) aircraft and at times coming near collision range.

Meanwhile, modernisation of the 2.3-million-strong People's Liberation Army (PLA), which coincides with China's continuing assertiveness that has unsettled its neighbours, has entered the final stage of its current phase. The Chinese Communist Party's (CCP) Third Plenum, which was held in November 2013, provided it a substantive push. On January 18, 2014, the

Party Secretary of Liaoning province disclosed that the second domestically-produced aircraft carrier being built at Dalian would be ready in six years. China also allocated US$ 1.6 billion for the first phase of indigenous design, development and production of jet engines.

The Third Plenum approved organisational reforms in the PLA's command structure and the PLA Navy (PLAN), PLAAF and China's strategic missile strike force, namely, the Second Artillery, have been allotted enhanced operational roles and will receive priority in allocation of budgets and manpower. The PLA is to be downsized by 800,000 personnel, including a large number of non-combatants. Reports filtering out of Beijing disclose that plans have been finalised to merge the seven military regions into five "combat zones." This reorganisation will give the PLA a definite "outward orientation" and implies that "recovery" of territories claimed by Beijing will be a central feature of China's strategic agenda and the PLA will reinforce diplomacy aimed at realising "China's Dream."

All this is relevant to India-China relations as is Beijing's stance on "core national issues" in bilateral relations. Beijing has made it explicitly clear in two despatches of China's official news agency Xinhua in August 2011, addressed to Japan and the Philippines, that "burgeoning economic ties do not mean good bilateral relations" which depend entirely on the recognition and acceptance of China's "core national interests." The despatches are important because Xinhua is China's authoritative official news agency and even the CCP Central Committee's (CC) powerful Propaganda Department instructs all Chinese journalists reporting on sensitive topics to adhere strictly to the text of Xinhua reports.

To digress slightly, Chinese Premier Li Keqiang's two-day visit (June 17-18, 2014) to the UK is pertinent. Apart from the fact that Beijing was particular about the minutiae of protocol, the 30-Article Joint Statement issued after the visit revealed UK's capitulation to China. Article 23 stated that Britain recognises Tibet as an integral part of China and does not recognise Tibetan independence. The English-language *Global Times*, a subsidiary of the CCP's official newspaper *People's Daily*, gloated over Britain's difficulty in accepting that it was now a "poor power compared to China." The major inducements were the over US$ 40 billion trade deals signed during the visit and establishment last year of a Yuan swap centre in London.

While assessing a country's foreign and strategic policies, and particularly in the context of India-China relations where there are major stakes and we are directly affected, it is important to understand the nature of the State and its internal leadership dynamics.

There has been a major change in China's politics and leadership style since 2011 and particularly with the ouster of former Politburo (PB) member Bo Xilai in 2012. That was a major event in China's politics, perhaps the first major political upheaval since the Tiananmen Event of 1989, and has seen a visible "hardening" of the Chinese State. Details revealed during the events leading to Bo Xilai's ouster reinforced the conviction of the CCP's nomenklatura that the US remains intent on its strategy of "peaceful evolution"—China's shorthand for US efforts to dismantle the CCP; deprive the CCP of its monopoly rule and introduce multiparty democracy; and replace the "socialist economy" with a "free-market capitalist economy." Factional differences were subordinated to protecting the Party Centre and ensuring the CCP's monopoly on power. All senior veteran cadres backed Xi Jinping and supported him as "leader" of the Politburo Standing Committee (PBSC). As a consequence, in addition to all the three important posts of CCP CC General Secretary, Chairman of the CMC and President of China, Xi Jinping now additionally heads seven of the Party's Central Leading Small Groups, which are the most important and highest decision making bodies. The Party has, in effect, asserted itself and further tightened its grip over key levers of the State.

Doctrinaire policies have also gained ascendance in the Party in the past few years with renewed emphasis on Marxist and Maoist ideology and Party discipline. The Party's guiding narrative is being enforced by the CCP CC's powerful Propaganda Department which has been steadily tightening restrictions on the media, social media and journalists (including most recently last week), since Xi Jinping took over. The elevation of Liu Yunshan, former Director of the CCP CC Propaganda Department, as Member of the PBSC and the country's Propaganda and Ideology Czar is demonstration that the "hardening" of the State is the decision of the Party Centre.

Particularly relevant in this context is Xi Jinping's "China Dream" which envisages: making the Chinese people wealthy; making China a strong nation; and the rejuvenation of China. This muscular aspiration for China spelt out by Xi Jinping at the 18th Party Congress has been adopted by the entire Party and has already entered the lexicon of the CCP. It is particularly pertinent to India-China relations as "rejuvenation" implies the restoration of China to its self-perceived rightful international status and recovery of all its territories. The new passports published by China depict its claimed territories, as do its actions in the South China Sea and East China Sea and the increased assertiveness and expanding claims over Arunachal Pradesh and Jammu and Kashmir.

The Party has concretised Xi Jinping's status in the CCP hierarchy, thus legitimising his status in China. The Party theoretical fortnightly journal Qiushi in its latest issue (June 2014) described Xi Jinping as "one of China's greatest Communist leaders." Xi Jinping is today China's most powerful leader since Mao Zedong.

In India, too, there has been a radical change with a new leader emerging after a resounding democratic electoral victory. Prime Minister Narendra Modi has a reputation as a strong, decisive leader and the BJP as a "right-wing" Party and they have a majority in Parliament unprecedented for thirty years. Modi very quickly used his swearing-in ceremony as an opportunity to outline India's view of its strategic neighbourhood and where Indian interest will focus. The visit to Bhutan and planned visit to Japan reinforces this. The current government can shape and implement medium to long-term policies. In other words, India and China both have strong leaders and this itself offers an opportunity for engagement on fresh and revised terms.

Chinese Foreign Minister Wang Yi's visit was intended to show China's eagerness in engaging with India's new right-wing Government and is part of its strategy of "Peripheral Diplomacy." It sought to project that China desires good relations with India and prevent India from moving close to Japan or towards a US-led anti-China grouping. A Chinese-language official Xinhua despatch of May 29, 2014, is, however, pertinent. Its tone differed noticeably from that of other Chinese media reports which assessed that India's policies towards China would not change and that economic relations would receive a boost. This Xinhua despatch asserted that Modi has no option other than economic cooperation with China as India perforce has to recognise China's economic and military superiority in Asia. It stressed that

Modi would have to accommodate China, not out of choice or inclination, but out of necessity. While this is arguable, the Xinhua despatch exhibits China's self-confidence and at the same time implies there is potential for cooperation.

China's focus is on economic cooperation with India: Xi Jinping and PM Modi's meeting on the sidelines of BRICS Summit also pointed towards the same, though differences on some of the strategic issues remained. Chinese President Xi Jinping's forthcoming visit to India has the economy as its focus and he is reportedly being accompanied by 350 Chinese Chief Executives (CEO) amidst much talk of investing in India's infrastructure, high-speed railways and the Bullet Train. Chinese diplomatic missions in India have already begun selecting locations for the "Special Industrial Parks" and, at least in Maharashtra, Rajasthan and Bengal, have identified middlemen for "benami" purchases of land. China is anxious to find a new market for its huge reserves of surplus cash and as another avenue for investment, and India is an attractive vast market. Undoubtedly it will benefit if China invests in India's infrastructure, but India will need to carefully decide the direction in which to steer Chinese business as otherwise, in a democratic set-up such as India's, China will soon acquire a powerful business lobby capable of adversely influencing national strategic decisions. Roads, flyovers, railways, hydroelectric projects, multi-storey office and residential buildings, are sectors that can benefit from Chinese investment. In order to ensure strategic flexibility and increased investment, however, these must be balanced by offering similar competitive opportunities to other countries like Japan, Taiwan and Singapore. India can particularly benefit in the high-tech, advanced electronics and defence sectors by encouraging investments from Japan and Taiwan on very preferential terms.

Nevertheless, two events are worthy of note in this context. First is the protracted 20-day incursion by Chinese troops in April-May 2013 in the Depsang Plains of Ladakh that cast a cloud over the bilateral relationship and Chinese Premier Li Keqiang's visit. The intrusion was apparently planned and deliberate. It was proposed by the PLA and approved by the Politburo which, after discussions, assessed that India would not cancel Li Keqiang's visit for fear of offending China. It was certainly not, as sought to be made out, a local action by a local PLA Commander. On May 14, 2013, the influential, official "Zhongguo Qingnian Bao" (*China Youth Daily*) published an article implicitly laying claim to Ladakh and describing it as part of Tibet.

Second is the visit (June 8-9, 2014) of Chinese Foreign Minister Wang Yi to New Delhi. In keeping with past practice, just two days before Wang Yi's arrival China alluded to the outstanding border issue and the Dalai Lama's presence by officially protesting the presence of Lobsang Sangay, head of the Central Tibetan Administration, at Prime Minister Modi's swearing-in ceremony. Wang Yi too, at his press conference in New Delhi, asserted China's territorial claims by brushing aside questions on border intrusions and made a carefully worded remark that the issue of stapled visas by China were a "unilateral" "flexible" "goodwill gesture" or, in other words, that the status of Arunachal Pradesh and Jammu and Kashmir remain disputed.

On the vexed border issue, little progress can be anticipated unless both leaders and, especially, Xi Jinping, decide to use their strength and push for a mutually acceptable settlement. China's recent utterances on issues of sovereignty and territorial integrity, however, make this a distant possibility. China can, in fact, be expected to be insistent and expand its claims on Arunachal Pradesh and J&K and may test the resolve of the BJP government on the territorial issue. The status quo in negotiations will not change till India acquires the capability, through asymmetrical power, to impose unacceptable costs on China's "Han heartland," including Beijing and Shanghai. This will take a couple of years as the Agni V series of missiles become operational and are deployed.

China will continue to deepen relations with Pakistan, Nepal and Sri Lanka and exert to establish a formal diplomatic presence in Thimphu, which is only a matter of time. A new and worrying feature is China's focus on Lumbini in Nepal. Not only will construction of a modern airport in Lumbini built by the PLA pose a proximate military threat to India, but more insidious is Beijing's effort to undermine the influence and the authority of the Dalai Lama amongst Tibetan Buddhist monks and lay the groundwork for potentially triggering instability and secessionism across the vulnerable Indo-Tibetan

Himalayan border belt. Plans of China's so-called NGOs to build and operate a monastery-cum-seminary point to this.

Finally, it is pertinent to briefly mention China's strategy of "Peripheral Diplomacy" formulated in October last year. The "Peripheral Diplomacy" strategy for the first time in the history of communist China designates neighbouring countries as "friend" and "enemy" and promises huge benefits and economic largesse for countries that accept and assist China's regional ambitions. These three initiatives aim at obtaining new sources of natural resources and new markets for China and will be secured by China's expanding military might and strategic reach, including in the Indian Ocean.

(The article was published in Centre for China Analysis and Strategy (CCAS) and Vivekananda International Foundation (VIF), New Delhi, July 2014).

27

Q&A-Wall Street Journal

Reproduced below are the Q&A published by the *Wall Street Journal* on the October 30, 2014 on Sino-India relations. The questions were put to Ma Jiali of the China Reform Forum and Mr. Jayadeva Ranade, President of the Centre for China Analysis and Strategy.

The *Wall Street Journal* asked two experienced foreign-policy analysts—one in India and one in China—for their thoughts on the recent military stand-off on the two countries' disputed border. Here is what Ma Jiali, an India watcher at the China Reform Forum, a thinktank affiliated with the Communist Party's Central Party School, and Jayadeva Ranade, President of the Centre for China Analysis and Strategy in New Delhi and a member of the Indian government's National Security Advisory Board, had to say:

WSJ **What are the historical roots of the dispute? What role did the 1962 war play?**

Jiali The roots of the China-India border dispute stem from Britain's expansion policies during its colonial rule over India. The 1962 Sino-Indian war cast a pall over bilateral ties, especially from India's perspective, because as the defeated side, the Indian public came to bear an enduring grudge.

Ranade If one were to put a date on when the border dispute became "active," it would be in 1950 with the occupation of Tibet by Chinese troops. China thereafter began pushing the limits of the frontier beyond what the former Tibet regime had agreed to with the British. In my view, though, there were two other equally important factors. First, that [former Chinese Premier]

Zhou Enlai had formed a very negative opinion about Indian Prime Minister Jawaharlal Nehru, which was reinforced at the Bandung Conference and which he conveyed to Mao Zedong. Mao mentioned this in a telegram to Stalin with the observation that this would limit China's relations with India.

Second, was the deterioration in Sino-Soviet relations and the impending split between the two communist parties, at which stage China felt the Soviet Union was "closer" to India than to its "fraternal" partner China. Deng Xiaoping, incidentally, is reported to have said in early 1979, at the time of the Chinese attack on Vietnam to "teach it a lesson," that Mao's decision to attack India had kept the border tranquil for almost 20 years. The 1962 war has certainly aggravated suspicions and left a lasting mark on the relationship. On the other hand, it galvanised India to modernise and equip its armed forces.

WSJ **What messages were India and China trying to send each other during the recent troop movements around Chumar? Was one side or the other to blame?**

Ma The Sino-Indian border has never been formally demarcated, and both sides have differing interpretations of the Line of Actual Control. India's move to build fixed outposts in the disputed area therefore prompted a strong Chinese response.

Ranade The intrusions at Chumar in Ladakh were undoubtedly deliberate and carefully calibrated. The trigger was China attempting to build a road into the Chumar area. The intrusion's message was reinforced by the visit to Colombo—for the first time ever in such distant waters—by a Chinese Song-class attack submarine. Both overlapped with Xi Jinping 's first visit to India as China's president. The intrusion at Chumar needs to be viewed in the backdrop of the visit two months earlier by China's Foreign Minister Wang Yi, who categorically ruled out that China would yield its current position regarding the border issue, and the earlier intrusion in the Depsang Plains in Ladakh in April

2013 immediately preceding the first visit to India of Chinese Premier Li Keqiang. The latter was followed up by an article in the official Chinese media laying claim to entire Ladakh. In terms of the military stand-off at Chumar, both sides showed restraint, but India sent a clear message that such actions would henceforth meet with a response. It was publicly raised by India's Prime Minister as the first point in his statement and in the press statement issued later by India.

As far as China is concerned, it has used both these intrusions to send a multiplicity of clear messages. These are: to assert its perceived sovereignty and territorial claims; caution India against drawing closer to the US, Japan or Vietnam as China could exert military pressure on India at a place and time of its choosing anywhere, including along the countries' long border, which India would have to defend on its own; and to subordinate its interests to China's economic aspirations. The last was, in fact, spelled out by Xi Jinping in his speech in New Delhi on September 18.

WSJ **What are the strategic interests of China and India in these areas—all of which are remote, inhospitable and sparsely inhabited?**

Ma The border dispute involves territorial and sovereignty issues for each country, as well as sensitive nationalistic sentiments, and therefore bears great significance. Especially during British colonial rule, India seized territory by piecemeal encroachment and wholesale annexation of parts of China's Tibetan region and imposed the illegal McMahon line on China. Therefore, whether viewed from a political or territorial standpoint, [the disputed area] is of strategic interest to China.

Ranade China views the Ladakh region and the adjoining area of Pakistan Occupied Kashmir as important for its security interests and the safety of its strategic investments. These are the Karakoram Highway and projects under construction, or planned, in Pakistan Occupied Kashmir to link up eventually to Gwadar port near Karachi.

This was evidenced way back in 1963 when China concluded an agreement with Pakistan by which Pakistan illegally ceded over 5,000 square kilometres of territory in the Shaksgam Valley to China. That China recognised the territory's disputed status and had no claim of its own at that time is clear from the undertaking included in the agreement to re-negotiate the arrangement with the sovereign entity whose claim is finally recognised.

As far as India is concerned, the region of Ladakh is inhabited and has been under Indian administration since independence. It is of military and strategic importance in the event of conflict with Pakistan or China and is an issue of national sovereignty. Legally, the region of Ladakh was part of the princely state of Jammu and Kashmir, which formally and legally acceded to the Indian Union in 1950.

WSJ **Is a border deal between India and China likely in the foreseeable future? Does either side have incentive to compromise?**

Ma The China-India border dispute involves a very large swath of territory, so the differences aren't easy to resolve. At the moment, both sides have agreed on the political guiding principles for resolving the dispute, and the next step would be talks on the resolution framework. Both sides need to adhere to a spirit of mutual accommodation and accord due respect to history, present circumstances and public sentiment within both countries, and seriously explore a pathway for resolving the dispute. Whether this can be resolved within the foreseeable future, depends on whether both sides can bring strong political will to bear, whether both sides possess strong and powerful leadership, and whether public sentiment on both sides is mutually accommodative.

Ranade A peacefully negotiated, reasonable border agreement would certainly be beneficial to both countries and remove a major obstacle impeding the development of bilateral relations. At the same time, despite decades of negotiations, there has been negligible tangible progress, with China declining to exchange maps which could be the basis for discussions and negotiations. There has also been no indication either of any willingness by Chinese leaders to settle the dispute. On the contrary, the appearance in Chinese media of articles like "Six Wars that China must Fight in the Next Five Decades" and assertions that China will ultimately have to resort to war to settle outstanding border and territorial disputes, suggest that China's leadership is in no hurry to settle.

WSJ **What kind of deal would be acceptable to China? What for India? Would China be willing to relinquish claims to Arunachal if India were to abandon its claim to Aksai Chin?**

Ma China believes that the crux of the Sino-Indian border dispute lies in the eastern segment [areas now in the Indian state of Arunachal Pradesh]. The Chinese hope that the Indians can make meaningful concessions on the eastern segment, while the Chinese make necessary adjustments on the western segment [Ladakh].

Ranade There was a "package deal" proposed by Deng Xiaoping through an Indian journalist in the late 1970s, which envisaged China allowing India to retain Arunachal Pradesh in exchange for Aksai Chin in Ladakh. While this "deal" now appears to be off, a change in the geopolitical situation or in the subcontinent, could see its revival. The emergence of the present strong leadership and government in India and India's growth might prompt Beijing to rethink the earlier proposal in due course. In any case, China has larger interests in the form of substantial investments in the general Aksai Chin area.

WSJ **Can economic relations between India and China really flourish if the boundary issue remains unresolved and the border situation is tense?**

Ma Any impediments to China-India trade ties are mainly due to structural issues. Generally speaking, the border dispute doesn't have much impact on trade.

Ranade Until the border issue is resolved or China meticulously refrains from intrusions and aggressive actions along the border, suspicion in India about China's intentions will remain high. This will place limits on the extent to which China-India economic ties can develop. In any case, India is looking for high-value advanced technological investment and considerable infusions of capital, both of which would probably come from countries like the US, Japan, Germany, France, Taiwan and South Korea. China can invest in the infrastructure sector, but has shown no signs so far of doing so in a substantive manner. It is probably waiting for India to endorse its three major economic initiatives which, if signed, will currently be to India's detriment.

28

Nathu La and the Sino-Indian Trade: Understanding the Sensitivities in Sikkim

As India and China began normalising relations in the mid-1970s they also initiated a process of dialogue. This enabled both countries to explore the feasibility of trade ties and identify areas of common economic interest. At Beijing's persistent initiative, which proposed all-round improvement of ties while setting aside resolution of the border dispute to a later date, moves were gradually started to build economic and trade ties to develop improved bilateral relations. This coincided with the launch of China's Four Modernisations Programme and enunciation of its policy of ensuring a "peaceful neighbourhood environment." The driver for improved economic relations with India, including through various mechanisms like the "Bay of Bengal Initiative for Multi-Sectoral Technical and Economic Cooperation" (BIMSTEC) and the trans-national rail and (Stilwell, or Ledo) road transportation, was the imperative to promote the lagging economies of China's hinterland southwestern provinces and secure for them easily accessible export markets in South and South East Asia. These imperatives remain.

In 1984, India and China concluded a Trade Agreement which accorded both countries Most Favoured Nation (MFN) status. An active bilateral relationship began developing in 1992 and it had made satisfactory progress by 1994. That year the two countries signed a Double Taxation Avoidance Agreement. A fillip was given to the process when both India and China became Dialogue Partners in the Association of South East Asian Nations (ASEAN). The trend continued with both countries signing the Bangkok Agreement in 2003 and deciding to offer some trade preferences to each other. According to the Agreement, China extended concessions on 217 products exported from India while India reciprocated by offering concessions on 188 products exported by China. They also agreed to initiate open border trade along the Silk Route and expressed interest in participating in a multilateral trade system as per WTO commitments.

Sino-Indian Trade: Benefits from Engagement

The economic relationship took off after 2003 and by 2008-9 at least 90 Indian companies had established offices in China. The lead was taken by the IT sector, which saw business opportunities, with some representation from the pharmaceuticals and automotive sectors. Initial trade targets were set at US$ 20 billion by 2008 and US$ 30 billion by 2010. But these were quickly exceeded as bilateral trade grew exponentially, reaching US$ 61.76 billion by 2010, or an increase of 42.4 per cent over 2009. By last year China was India's leading trade partner while India ranked as China's ninth trading partner. During Chinese Premier Wen Jiabao's visit in December 2010, the Chinese visitor's focus remained on bilateral economic ties and both countries agreed to further boost trade and set US$ 100 billion as the target for 2015. A boost to bilateral trade, and especially Chinese exports, was given by the agreement reached to open a branch in India of China's Exim Bank and another to permit settlements in Yuan. A substantive effect of the two agreements, which requires to be underscored, will be the development of business interests vested in stable and growing India-China ties regardless of trade imbalances or problems concerning sovereignty or the border. This could be a poisoned chalice.

Bilateral trade is set to develop rapidly as India continues to invest heavily in infrastructure and power generation. China, in turn, is looking at securing subcontracts for the infrastructure sector and expanding its already substantial profile in the telecommunications sector. Its huge foreign exchange reserves give it the capacity to invest in these sectors. It has also been proposing the establishment of Free Trade Zones and High-Tech Parks and increased access for its civil aviaton industry. While bilateral trade is very unbalanced in China's favour, Indian IT and pharmaceutical companies have been encouraged by Beijing and are active in China. Both these sectors have been identified by China as ones where India leads and China needs to catch up. Efforts are being made to woo India's biotech sector. China is also looking for expertise and participation by Indian entities in the banking, outsourcing and legal sectors. Regrettably, bilateral trade primarily comprises the export of raw natural resources like iron ore. India has also opened other resources like potassium, bauxite and rare earths for export without assessing the utility of these scarce resources for India's future needs. A review is essential on which items need to be controlled, where exports need to be capped, and which require regulation.

Sovereignty and Assertiveness: Issues of Concern

Some caution is essential when the burgeoning India-China economic and trade ties are assessed. Without seeking to underestimate the mutual benefits that accrue from active trade interaction, it is important that Delhi factors in the growing unease in India-China bilateral relations and China's assertiveness. Beijing has shown no signs of changing its policy of trying to legitimise its claims on territories over which India exercises sovereignty, or trying to prevent India from achieving its position in the world that it aspires to. Some recent examples are: the efforts to deny India a waiver by the NSG; sustained opposition to India's bid for a Permanent seat in the UNSC; Beijing's position with regard to issue of visas to Indian citizens who are residents of J&K or Arunachal Pradesh; preventing the Asian Development Bank (ADB) from granting development aid to a poverty alleviation project in Arunachal Pradesh; and vehement opposition to the recent US suggestion for a trilateral US-China-India dialogue on the ground that India cannot be placed on par with China. Official Chinese media articles have also warned, particularly since mid-2010, that China might "teach" India a lesson.

In this backdrop, of which serious note needs to be taken, the efforts of Chinese telecommunications companies Huawei and ZTE need to be scrutinised. Both companies are closely associated with China's Military and Security establishment and neither has made public its accounts or assets. Both receive preferential business consideration and contracts from the People' Liberation Army (PLA). They further China's strategic interests. Huawei and ZTE are maintaining, or setting up, country-wide landline and/or mobile telephone networks in the countries surrounding India, namely, Afghanistan, Pakistan,

Nepal, Bangladesh and Sri Lanka. They are well established in Myanmar. Both Huawei and ZTE have, surprisingly, been able to develop major interests in the Indian telecommunications market despite the obvious implications for the country's security. Both companies have large offices in Bengaluru and Delhi. Huawei has a major software research centre in Bengaluru—an area in which India is a leader. It also claims to have provided "cutting-edge technology to all the telecom operators" in India. ZTE registered a sales volume of US$ 1 billion in India in 2009. It has tied up with the Russian telecom company Sistema, which recently launched operations in India. To boost acceptability both companies have launched scholarship programmes for Indian students.

China's emphasis on cyberwarfare and repetitive targeting of select Indian cyber networks necessitates heightened concern of the access allowed to these firms. Huawei and ZTE are together the "Main Service Providers" (MSP) for the majority of Indian mobile telephone networks and in most cases also maintain the network operations. The vulnerabilities are obvious. Mobile telephones are used by all levels of politicians, bureaucrats, armed forces and security officials. Corporate and industrial tycoons use them too. Confidential subjects are routinely discussed on these lines. Both Huawei and ZTE have the access to eavesdrop and monitor conversations of persons of interest. If considered necessary they are in a position to selectively disrupt, or terminate, communications of certain phones. In times of crisis or hostility these companies could suspend the country's entire mobile telephone network operated or maintained by them causing widespread confusion, systems breakdowns, damage and financial and material loss. Similar concerns prompted UK's Joint Intelligence Committee to issue a warning about Huawei. Other areas vulnerable to attack include those entities—including public utilities—using Chinese computer software and hardware. India is undoubtedly a prime target of Chinese cyberattacks and such attacks could be launched by Chinese IT companies from within India.

It is evident that China's leadership has focused on development of an overarching architecture for cyberwarfare and network operations. This combines the capability for attacking cyber-based communications and information systems as well as space-based communications like mobile and satellite telephone networks. The inclusion of Lanzhou, Chengdu and Guangzhou among the five Military Regions selected for enhanced Information Warfare capability is noteworthy. Significant also are the efforts of the Chinese commercial telecommunications companies, all of whom are linked to the People's Liberation Army (PLA), to penetrate and dominate the communications infrastructure of countries which are of strategic interest to China. The continuous cyberattacks on targets in various countries similarly point to China's efforts to upgrade its capability.

There are two other areas of serious concern that impinge directly on national security. The first relates to the manufacture and supply of turbines for power generation. Presently there are a couple of companies in India that have the capability to manufacture and supply these turbines. High-quality precision engineering is required for the manufacture of these turbines. Chinese companies are able to manufacture and supply these power generation turbines at a lower cost. As a result, Indian power companies buy Chinese manufactured turbines. While this makes abundant commercial sense, India cannot really afford to allow its companies to shut down due to paucity of orders as that would deprive the country of high-quality precision engineering capability. As such, India needs to explore ways to develop and encourage high-precision manufacturing, if necessary by ensuring steady orders and finding ways to accelerate production and bring costs down.

Illegal Chinese settlements are the other concern. An estimated 20,000 Chinese workers are presently housed in temporary facilities at work sites of Chinese subcontractors across India. There is negligible check on their movements or whether they return to China after completion of their contract. Surprisingly a large number have unauthorisedly stayed on and even forged human relationships. In course of time, unless this tendency is checked, India could well have a large illegally settled Chinese population such as in Africa.

Revival of Border Trade: Prospects and Implications

Strategy, sovereignty and territory are inextricably intertwined in deliberations relating especially to national borders. The case of Sikkim and Nathu La are no different. It is these considerations that have also been responsible for the glacial progress with regard to the reopening of the erstwhile traditional trade-marts between India, Tibet and China. The issue became more complicated with the disappearance of one party, namely, Tibet, which had long served as a buffer, and the Chinese aggression in 1962. The gradual improvement in relations between India and China, however, additionally prompted realisation that the revival of border trade would be of mutual benefit particularly to the inhabitants of the border regions.

The region's sensitivity has been heightened by China's claims on Sikkim. It was only after almost sixty years in 2003, during Indian Prime Minister Vajpayee's visit, that Beijing implicitly agreed that Sikkim was a part of India and agreed not to depict Sikkim in its official maps as an independent entity, but as a part of India. This was done in the first set of official maps published by China in 2006-7. But Beijing has retained the potential for introducing ambiguity into the issue at a later stage and has, till date, declined to issue a formal statement recognising Sikkim as part of India. In 2000, for example, Ughyen Thinley Dorjee, who had been confirmed by both Beijing and the Dalai Lama as the XVIIth Gyalwa Karmapa, escaped from Tibet into India with the objective of returning to the Gyalwa Karmapa's spiritual seat in Rumtek Monastery in Sikkim. Chinese officials have maintained a stoic silence on the matter, including because any protest about Ughyen Thinley Dorje assuming residence in Rumtek would imply explicit endorsement of India's sovereignty over Sikkim. There has also not yet been a Chinese reaction to the unusual criticism by Ughyen Thinley Dorjee, recognised by Beijing and the Dalai Lama as the XVIIth Gyalwa Karmapa, of the repression of Tibetans inside China by Chinese authorities, made just a few weeks ago.

Sikkim is especially sensitive politically and militarily for India. Intrusions into Sikkim are particularly worrisome as they additionally cast serious doubt on China's credibility to abide by bilateral agreements. After armed Chinese troops intruded on over 75 occasions in northern Sikkim during 2007, possibly to assess India's vulnerabilities, China raised it as a dispute during India's External Affairs Minister's visit to Beijing in May 2008. China's attention significantly appears focused on the "Finger Area," or area north of Guangyong. At its closest point this area is barely 30 miles north of the "Chicken's Neck," or Siliguri corridor. A sudden military move across this belt, combined with a pincer move down from the Chumbi Valley, would completely cut India off from the northeast. China's objective would be its claimed approximately 90,000 square kilometres of territory comprising Arunachal Pradesh, or what China calls "southern Tibet." China's insistence on opening new areas of territorial dispute such as J&K also cast doubt on its credibility as a partner to an agreement. Factors contributing to the need for serious concern are the all-weather expressway that China has built right up to the border at Nathu La and its plans to extend the Golmud-Lhasa Railway to Yadong, across Nathu La. This will at once facilitate movement of military goods and personnel as also rail-mobile missiles.

Strategic considerations today, in fact, perforce have also to take note of the religious factor and dominant presence in Sikkim of the Karma Kagyu School of Tibetan Buddhism. An incipient non-traditional threat centres around the religious dispute for the throne of the XVIIth Gyalwa Karmapa of the Karma Kargyu sect and Rumtek Monastery, especially in view of Beijing's efforts to woo the Tibetan Buddhists and particularly influential personages among them.

Once the agreement on Sikkim had been reached in 2003, Beijing also agreed to India's suggestion about opening trading posts in Yadong/Nathu La. India had first proposed opening of a border trading post at Yadong during the seventh Joint Working Group meeting held in Beijing in July 1994. Yadong/Nathu La were finally opened on July 6, 2006. It is interesting though that while China opened Yadong/Nathu La only in 2006, they had years earlier constructed an all-weather two-lane highway up to Yadong as well as permanent trading huts, customs buildings and checkposts. There are plans to extend the railway from Lhasa to Yadong by 2015. This will facilitate transportation of goods and passengers. China's construction activity suggests that Beijing has planned to develop Yadong as a major trade port through which it can supply goods to Sikkim, Bhutan, and India's northeast as well as onwards via sea to Bangladesh and Myanmar. Yadong is apparently poised to become a container port. In case India opens Nathu La to large-scale trade, there will be an influx of Chinese goods. Cheap consumer items will flood local markets and heavy items and goods will be shipped in for transport to other destinations in India or for re-export. Indian traders and companies will suffer. The low prices of Chinese goods mean there will be low margins for intermediaries. Indian companies and traders will also be unable to sell their products to China.

Border trade has been slow in this sector due to the meagre facilities provided on our side of the border. Slow growth of trade has, in fact, provided an opportunity for development of infrastructure on the Indian side and this must be taken advantage of. The road linking Gangtok with Nathu La is a narrow two-lane metalled road which is prone to frequent disruption due to weather and other events. This needs to upgraded and another road link added. Gangtok itself is poorly connected with the rest of the country. It is consequently losing out on the immense tourism potential of its scenic and natural beauty. Properly connected, Sikkim and Nathu La can be developed as high-end tourism and adventure destinations. Before opening Nathu La to Chinese trade, it is essential that the transport infrasructure of Sikkim be developed. It should have air and multiple all-weather road connections. Roads should link Sikkim's western and northwestern regions with Gangtok and there should be an adequate number of hotels. Encouragement of and enhanced tourism will automatically grant increased legitimacy to Indian sovereignty over this and adjoining regions. Tourism can be extended to other parts of India's northeast and, for this, a policy should be adopted of aggressively reducing the number of areas requiring inner-line permits. It is only when India has such appropriate infrastructure in place that its businessmen, traders and commercial enterprises can compete effectively with their Chinese counterparts, that border trade should be broadened and deregulated.

(The article was published in Institute of Peace and Conflict Studies, New Delhi, February 2011).

29

Looking Beyond Border Incursions & Li Keqiang's Visit

As the dust settles after Chinese Premier Li Keqiang's visit to India and accompanying intrusions, it will be prudent to objectively assess the nature of the China-India relationship over the long term. An episodic evaluation will be misleading, particularly as the timing of these intrusions marks them out as of significance. They are also an escalation of the unfriendly Chinese behaviour demonstrated shortly before the visits of Chinese President Hu Jintao in November 2006 and Chinese Premier Wen Jiabao in December 2010. Just prior to Hu Jintao's visit to India in 2006, China's Ambassador in New Delhi, Sun Yuxi, publicly declared: "In our position, the whole of the state of Arunachal Pradesh is Chinese territory. And Tawang is only one of the places in it. We are claiming all of that." Later, in the months prior to Chinese Premier Wen Jiabao's visit in December 2010, Beijing denied a visa to India's Northern Army Commander and began issuing stapled visas to residents of J&K thereby implicitly designating the entire state as "disputed," a stand from which it has not backed off. Barely a month earlier, around the visit of Politburo Standing Committee (PBSC) member Zhou Yongkang in November, an article by a senior commentator in the Party mouthpiece, *People's Daily*, had warned India against drawing closer to Japan in pursuit of its "Look East" policy.

Contextualising Li Keqiang's India Visit

The circumstances surrounding Chinese Premier Li Keqiang's visit are relevant as are Beijing's other actions and pronouncements. These need to be viewed in the larger perspective of the new Chinese leadership's strategic foreign policy. Chinese President Xi Jinping's "China's Dream," in fact, promises to wipe out past humiliations and lays bold emphasis on a strong and wealthy China.

There are adequate indications that Beijing assesses that the time is now opportune for it to push for international acceptance of what it perceives is its pre-eminent position in the region, including the Asia-Pacific. It considers that it has adequate stature and strength for it to partner the US in the resolution of international and regional issues. The recent (June 7-8, 2013) Sino-US Summit publicly stated that a start had been made in building a "new type of major power relationship," a point which was often reiterated by the two senior Chinese interlocutors, Vice Premier Wang Yang and State Councillor Yang Jiechi, at the US-China Strategic and Economic Dialogue (SED) held soon after on July 10-11, in Washington DC.

Tacit US acceptance, at least for the short-to-medium term, seemed apparent in US National Security Adviser Tom Donilon's disclosure that the Summit had taken place at a time when the US faces "an intense range of bilateral, regional and global challenges on which US-China cooperation is critical." Describing discussions as "quite unique and important," he added that the Summit aimed to start building a "new model of relations between great powers."

Relevant in this context are the lessening references to the "Asian pivot," for which the preferred term is now "rebalancing." The emphasis seems also to have shifted from the military to the economic sphere with focus on the Trans-Pacific Partnership (TPP), which envisages a whole new set of rules for the international economy and trade. The US and West possibly expect to retard China's economic growth and rise by these new rules, which will also adversely affect a number of other countries.

Shortly prior to the Summit, China's self-image was clearly outlined in two articles by senior commentators which were published in the Party's official mouthpiece, *People's Daily*. On May 28, 2013, Jiemian Yang, Dean of the Shanghai Institute of International Studies (SIIS) and younger brother of Chinese State Councillor and former Foreign Minister Yang Jiechi, candidly declared that the increase in China's comprehensive national strength had given its new leaders more confidence in dealing with the international community. Stressing that China will adhere to its own theories, systems and path of development, he emphasised that this "self-confidence" has enabled China's leaders to be "very firm" in safeguarding sovereignty and territorial integrity while simultaneously being flexible in dealings with smaller countries. He revealed that they will focus more on the neighbourhood and travel oftener in the region.

Conceding that China needs to "normalise relations with Japan" and that the "many maritime disputes" are major challenges, he concluded that so long as "the United States, other major powers, neighbouring countries and other members of the international community" cooperate and support China, "it will eventually emerge as a very peace-loving, powerful and prosperous nation."

The second article was published on June 4, 2013, and written by Li Wen, a scholar from the "Centre for Research on the Theory of Socialism with Chinese Characteristics" of the Chinese Academy of Social Sciences (CASS). Stating that Beijing wanted cooperative relations with major powers, it advised major powers to discard "Cold-War" ideas and hegemonic policies. It urged major countries not to depict a country as a "strategic competitor" and seek to "contain it," but to "show more kindness and less hostility, and respect each other's core interests."

The reference to "core interests," which is China's shorthand for territories claimed by it, is pertinent. While these "core interests" currently include Taiwan, Tibet and Xinjiang, some months ago a Chinese Foreign Ministry spokesperson repeatedly referred to the Senkaku islands, called Diaoyu in Chinese, as China's "core interest." In 2011 and 2012 there were numerous references to the South China Sea as China's "core interest," though these have since tapered off.

This increased self-confidence of China's leadership is visible in its more activist and muscular foreign and strategic policy of the past few months, particularly in its strategic periphery. Beijing has continued to consolidate and expand its strategic investments in Pakistan notwithstanding India's objections or the disturbed conditions there. A slew of new agreements were signed during Chinese Premier Li Keqiang's visit to Islamabad in May this year, and newly-elected Pakistan Prime Minister Nawaz Sharif broke with past practice and travelled to Beijing on his first visit abroad during this tenure.

While he has not returned with financial assistance, there is renewed talk in Pakistan of a Chinese-built railway line linking the Chinese province of Xinjiang with Pakistan's port city of Gwadar. Similarly, the Chinese Embassy and its diplomats are noticeably more active in Nepal. Their primary objectives are to monitor and curb the activities of the Tibetans residing in Nepal and to prevent Tibetans from escaping into Nepal. In Myanmar, too, Beijing has moved to safeguard its strategic investments. It has, for the first time in decades, overtly engaged in the internal affairs of another sovereign nation—albeit at its request—and brokered at least six rounds of "peace talks" between the Kachin Independence Army and Myanmar's military.

Significantly, senior officials of China's Ministry of Foreign Affairs attended the talks where China flaunted its influence by guaranteeing the security of all participants. This has been buttressed by increased, though quiet, contacts between the Chinese and Myanmar's military and Intelligence establishments.

The Chinese Premier's visit to India and the premeditated military intrusion that preceded it had multiple objectives. They brought into sharp definition China's new policy towards its neighbours and countries in the region with which it has unresolved sovereignty and territorial disputes. As evidenced by its policies towards Vietnam, the Philippines and Japan, Beijing is uncompromising on the issues of sovereignty and territorial integrity. China's official news agency, Xinhua, has earlier publicised that growing economic and trade ties will not translate into good bilateral relations unless China's "core interests" are acknowledged. For the first time, it used the economy as a lever against Japan when it banned the export of rare earths to Japan. It repeated this a month later against the Philippines over the Scarborough Reef issue, thus making it amply clear that regardless of international trade laws and practices, Beijing will not hesitate to use economic pressure to achieve its objectives.

The texture of all these relationships is assertive and differs from China's pragmatic, conciliatory, non-confrontational stance with the US. They make clear that while China's new leaders could show flexibility in formulating the framework for a bilateral relationship, there will be no willingness, or concession, on matters perceived as impinging on China's sovereignty or territorial integrity. They also reinforce the assessment that on issues concerning sovereignty and territorial integrity, China's People's Liberation Army (PLA) and the security establishment continue to exercise a prominent role as they have for the past some years.

Some reports circulating in April-May 2013 wildly speculated that a group of Chinese Generals not amenable to control by Central Military Commission (CMC) Chairman, Xi Jinping, were responsible for the "action," or that it was an isolated action by a local commander. The number of such so-called rogue Generals was even mentioned as 45! There is not a shred of evidence to support such speculation.

On the contrary, since at least 2002 the Chinese Communist Party (CCP) has steadily and inexorably tightened its grip on the PLA. Political Commissars, who monitor the political reliability of all personnel, have been granted the power of veto over promotions and three successive year-long campaigns were carried out throughout the PLA to ensure political reliability and loyalty to the CCP. One such campaign is presently underway. Political reliability and loyalty to the CCP has, for at least the past year and a half, been listed as the most important criterion for promotions and was reiterated by Xi Jinping promptly on taking over as CMC Chairman. Additionally, thorough background checks to ascertain the political reliability of officers were conducted last year in the wake of the Bo Xilai affair.

Xi Jinping, who succeeded Hu Jintao as CMC Chairman at the 18th Party Congress in November last year, exercises firm control over the PLA. The new members of the CMC, Commanders of the ground forces, Air Force, Navy and Second Artillery, Military Region Commanders and Generals appointed to key positions have all been selected by Hu Jintao and Xi Jinping. Since his elevation as CMC Chairman, Xi Jinping has paid a lot of attention to the PLA and been continuously visiting military establishments. He also has considerable personal influence in the PLA and knows a number of high-ranking PLA officers, especially the "princelings." The current Director of the important General Political Department (GPD), General Zhang Yang, is also a close long-time associate of the PLA Chief, General Fang Fenghui. These factors preclude the possibility of any local commander attempting such an adventure. Furthermore, there have been no such behavioural aberrations by local Chinese troops over the past so many years. Importantly, Xi Jinping presides over the powerful Foreign Affairs Small Leading Group. The action was undoubtedly approved by the top CCP leadership in Beijing.

The India-China Military Stand-Off (April-May 2013): A Post Mortem

An important attribute of the stand-off that stretched over twelve days in April-May 2013, was that Beijing remained transparently impervious to the three flag meetings at the level of local army commanders, communications from New Delhi, and to the prolonged and adverse media publicity which was embarrassing to the Indian government and damage it caused to India-China relations. The clear message was that for Beijing's leadership the issues of sovereignty and territorial integrity trump all other considerations. This stance is additional confirmation that the stand-off was not a local incident provoked by the action of a local commander, but one initiated with the full knowledge of China's senior leadership.

At the tactical level the prolonged military intrusion by Chinese forces near Daulet Beg Oldi in the Aksai Chin area was intended to send three clear signals. Very pertinently the equipment carried by the PLA troops involved in this act did not point to any military intent. The objectives were to:

- Continue the practice of marking out the increasing extent of Chinese claimed territory along the entire length of the border with India and inhibit India from activities, including civil construction, near the border on its own side;
- Test the rapid reaction capability of Indian forces to deploy to counter a threat, and to test the time it takes for India's military command and political leadership to respond to a threat; and
- Signal that the border can be activated militarily at any time of Beijing's choosing.

In addition to demonstrating the extent of China's territorial claims and attempting to capture areas of importance along the border, of particular importance to PLA Commanders is ascertaining the readiness and response capability of the Indian forces deployed along the border and that of the Indian military and political commands.

This has become important as preparations by PLA Commanders are for a quick, decisive local war. Current Chinese military literature makes amply clear that China's leadership and the PLA envisage a decisive short-duration conflict using overwhelming firepower that concludes with a Chinese victory within a few days and certainly before it can enlarge and involve other powers. In fact, China is preparing for a local war where the initial first phase opens with a cyber-offensive targeted at military and civilian public utilities. The next stage involves the use of missiles and that is followed by use of the PLA Air Force. Ground troops would be used only in the final mopping up stage, if required. This doctrine is a major factor prompting Beijing's recent proposal to Delhi on border management. Realities of capability and terrain would place India at a severe disadvantage in case this is accepted.

Interesting is that during the period of the intrusion, senior Chinese diplomats based in Delhi dissimulated to some foreign diplomats that approval for the action near Daulet Beg Oldi in Aksai Chin by People's Liberation Army (PLA) troops had been granted by China's top leadership in Beijing. The decision regarding timing of the action was left to the local Commander. This green light was given prior to the leadership's final approval for Chinese Premier Li Keqiang's four-nation tour abroad. Significantly, they added that it was Beijing's assessment that India would not cancel the Chinese Premier's visit to avoid damaging relations with China.

These Chinese officials also predictably dismissed description of the PLA's action as "intrusion" or "incursion" and asserted that the troops were within Chinese territory. They added that Chinese Premier Li Keqiang would reiterate China's position in his meetings and not yield ground. At least one Beijing-based foreign diplomat was told by an official in Beijing that there had been no intrusion and that the Chinese troops were inside their territory.

Intrusions by Chinese forces are not a new feature. They have been occurring with increasing frequency since 2008 along the length of the entire 4,057-kilometre border, and in each case are intended to test Indian responses and preparedness in addition to keeping India under pressure. China has, in the past few years, actually sought to increase pressure by expanding its territorial claims.

Examples of the above include the expansion a couple of years ago of the policy of issuing "stapled visas"—followed in the case of residents of Arunachal Pradesh—to residents of Jammu and Kashmir thereby depicting the entire state as "disputed"; reinforcing their territorial claims by successfully preventing international financial organisations from extending developmental aid to projects in Arunachal Pradesh; officially declaring a considerably reduced length of the border with India; reopening the settled issue of Sikkim; and forcibly seizing, or nibbling away, the traditional grazing grounds of Indian herders in areas of Ladakh and Barahoti-Kaurik in Himachal Pradesh and denying them their use.

China has also been steadfast in its opposition to the India-US Civil Nuclear Agreement when it coordinated actions with Pakistan and warned the US that it would assist Pakistan in like manner. When Beijing did make good on its threat and agreed to add to Pakistan's nuclear reactors there was no reaction from the US.

The intrusion of this April and the subsequent ones are assessed to have had at least two major objectives. A major military objective concerns border defences. The PLA has completed construction and refurbishing of border defences along the entire length of its border, including construction of adequate accommodation for additional troops that may be inducted, ammunition and storage dumps and secure fibre-optic communications linking each border and command post. This is a major factor prompting Beijing's proposal to Delhi on border management made late last year at the time of then Chinese Defence Minister Liang Guanglie's visit. The proposal, in effect, suggests that neither side should patrol the LAC up to a specified depth on their own side or augment existing border defences or build new ones. Realities of capability and terrain will place India at a severe disadvantage in case this is accepted.

The larger objective was to warn India against expressing support to Japan during the scheduled visit of the Indian Prime Minister to Tokyo. The CCP leadership at the highest levels continues to be very suspicious of US designs and apprehensive that the US is intent on putting together an anti-China coalition aimed at "containing" China. It sees this US-sponsored coalition as comprising Japan, Australia, India, Vietnam and the Philippines. Pertinent was the observation in the context of the South China Sea dispute as far back as July 2010, in a Hong Kong-based pro-Beijing newspaper, that: "the issue of China's territorial disputes with neighbouring countries will ignite the flames of war sooner or later. If a country must be chosen for sacrifice, India will be the first choice … India's long-term occupation of southern Tibet is indeed worrying … If armed force is used to resolve border disputes, China must pick a country to target first, and it will definitely pick a big country, which means choosing between Japan and India. …" Other references stated that China's relationship with India and Japan had limits imposed by history. The references unmistakably draw India into the ongoing confrontation in the South China Sea.

China's deliberate and prolonged military intrusion near Daulet Beg Oldi in the Depsang Plains in Aksai Chin did cast a perceptible shadow over Chinese Premier Li Keqiang's first visit (May 19-22, 2013) to India as Premier, despite the overt display of courtesy. It embarrassed the government and starkly outlined China's policy towards India and has had an impact on India's relations with China. Indications were immediately available in the 35-paragraph joint statement issued at the end of Li Keqiang's stay in Delhi on May 20, which revealed little forward movement on substantive issues. There was negligible progress on economic issues which mainly comprised Li Keqiang's agenda. India raised the issue of the border incursion and incident in Ladakh, making it clear that such incidents could not form the basis for trying to build friendship. Beijing would have also noted India's departure from usual practice and refusal to reiterate that Tibet was an integral part of China in the joint statement. The last occasion such a stand was taken was during Chinese Premier Wen Jiabao's visit in 2010. China also did not have its way in the references to the Asia-Pacific and South China Sea in the joint statement and received, instead, an ambiguous comment on international cooperation and freedom of navigation. Importantly, it ensured a more fruitful and positive visit by the Indian Prime Minister to Japan. China's deliberate and prolonged military intrusion could well have been prompted by the rapid progress by India in the past few years in building forward border defences and intended to slow it down. Instead, China's action cast a perceptible shadow over Chinese Premier Li Keqiang's visit and brought China's policy towards India into bold relief. This and similar intrusions along with Beijing's other actions that impinge on India's sovereignty, make it imperative that there should be no easing in the construction and augmentation of India's defence build-up. Construction of border defences, including of border roads and ALGs in forward areas, should continue apace as also the acquisition of modern military hardware, equipment and effective strategic deterrent capability.

Conclusion

Any evaluation of India-China relations over the long term needs to factor in Beijing's views. In this context, worth recall is Mao Zedong's telegram to Stalin around 1950 when he conveyed Zhou Enlai's very unfavourable opinion of Indian Prime Minister Jawaharlal Nehru and observed implicitly that this would guide the tenor of the relationship for a very long time.

In recent conversations with foreign diplomats and analysts their Chinese interlocutors list three main issues as responsible for the strain in India-China bilateral relations. These are: the Dalai Lama's presence and activities in India; the unresolved border dispute; and India's international aspirations. Viewed along with the statements publicised by China's official media that "limits have been imposed by history on the extent to which China can develop relations with India," it is clear that tensions will exist in India-China relations for the foreseeable future.

Two other major issues, in addition to the unresolved border or shrinking export markets sought by both countries and competition for scarce energy, natural and mineral resources, have a real potential to erupt into serious confrontation between India and China. Water is the most important. Much of north China faces severe water shortages and as this gets increasingly accentuated it will probably accelerate Beijing's ambitious plans to divert waters from the south to the north. Diversion of the Brahmaputra River to the north at a currently estimated cost of US$ 66 billion is a major part of these plans. Chinese engineers are going ahead with the construction of a series of dams along the course of the Tsangpo (Brahmaputra) and the project is presently under the direct supervision of Chinese Premier Li Keqiang.

Thus far Beijing has exhibited marked insensitivity to either India's concerns or those of other lower riparian nations as in the case of the Mekong River. The deleterious effects of diversion of the river will be heightened by the quickening retreat of the snow-fed glaciers in Tibet caused by warming and the rise in temperatures because of the new dams and development projects undertaken by China in Tibet. Together this will affect the 40 crore people residing in the Indus, Ganges and Brahmaputra river basins.

The other area of likely competition is food. At a time when global population is rising, both China and India, according to analysts, will move from their current self-sufficiency in food to become foodgrain deficient nations between 2045 and 2050. Global warming has an adverse impact on food production which registers a decline for each degree Celsius rise in temperature above the norm. During the growing season, farmers can expect a 10 per cent decline in wheat, rice, and corn yields.

Four countries, namely, the US, Canada, Russia and Australia will remain the main sources of foodgrain supply for the world. China and India will compete for the limited supplies and grain prices will soar. China will also try and enhance food production by using the large tracts of arable land in its water starved north, thus accelerating implementation of the south-north water diversion project.

If India is to persuade China to cooperate, it must accelerate efforts to, at least in asymmetric terms, acquire the ability to impose costs and deter China. The growing restiveness among China's minorities and increasing societal discontent are vulnerabilities that will potentially constrain Chinese leaders in the not too distant future.

Meanwhile, India should build the capacity to frustrate Chinese ambitions and ensure a calibrated enhancement of resistance to Chinese pressure. For this India will need to recast its strategic foreign policy objectives to enable it to urgently find and attract good sources of large-scale capital investments, advanced technology and high-tech joint manufacturing ventures. India will simultaneously have to upgrade the skills of its workers; favour establishment and growth of a manufacturing industry especially in the high-precision and advanced technology sectors; and put in place the backbone for a secure, modern telecommunications and global navigation systems. China's entry into the Indian economy will require to be controlled and India's indigenous critical industries safeguarded.

(The article was published in Institute of Peace and Conflict Studies, New Delhi, August 2013).

30

India and China: An Assessment of October 2013 Agreements—No Tangibles

Indian Prime Minister Manmohan Singh's three-day (October 21-23, 2013) tour to Beijing marked the first time in sixty years that the Indian and Chinese Prime Ministers exchanged visits within a year. As seasoning for the event the Chinese threw in invitations to meals by Xi Jinping and former Chinese Premier Wen Jiabao, the importance of which was sought to be exaggerated by diplomats. These could not, however, dispel the shadow cast on bilateral relations by China's unusually protracted intrusions across the Line of Actual Control (LAC) in the Ladakh and Arunachal Pradesh sectors just months earlier. As anticipated, the visit was high on hospitality but short on tangibles.

During his sojourn in Beijing, Prime Minister Manmohan Singh met Chinese President Xi Jinping, Premier Li Keqiang, former Chinese Premier Wen Jiabao and the Chairman of the National People's Congress (NPC), Zhang Dejiang. He also addressed the Central Party School in Beijing, which is the crucible for training select upwardly-mobile Party cadres.

Prime Minister Manmohan Singh's trip to the US earlier this September, when an important agreement on co-production of defence equipment and transfer of defence technology was signed, was one backdrop for the visit. Officers of China's People's Liberation Army (PLA) had specifically taken note of the India-US Joint Declaration on Defence and identified use of the term "closest partners" to describe the India-US bilateral relationship as indicative of the growing India-US ties. They particularly observed that it provided for technology transfer, co-development and co-production of defence equipment. Note was taken of India's decision to participate for the first time in the world's largest US-led multilateral military exercises, the "2014 Rim of the Pacific Exercise," in Hawaii.

Beijing's continuing suspicion and critical view of the US was separately revealed in a commentary published in the official news agency Xinhua, on October 13, 2013. The Xinhua commentary called for a "befuddled world to start considering building a de-Americanised world." Interestingly, it was published only in English and only in Xinhua.

In an apparent bid to build a positive atmosphere for the visit, the *Liberation Army Daily* published an interestingly worded article by Sun Peisong, President of the Jiangsu Lianyungang Institute of Development. Published on October 22, the article said China and India are trying to restore bilateral relations to a "long-standing condition of stability." It accused the Indian media of always regarding China as India's "regional opponent." Dismissing this description, the author said, "China has been taking care of India's concerns: even though the Western countries have multiple times reminded China to take part in the NATO's military operations in Afghanistan, China didn't do that. One of the major reasons is that Afghanistan is located in the flank of India. Once China sends troops there, it'll make India feel contained. China's military deployment in Tibet Autonomous Region is to a large degree out of an overall consideration instead of being levelled against India. That is the reason why China's heavy artillery, tanks, mid- and short-range tactical missiles are not forwardly deployed. When China launched the great-scale project of diverting water from the south to the north, China didn't use the abundant water resources of the Yarlung Zangbo River to supply the north. Besides, China was the last among the permanent members of the United Nations Security Council to dispatch naval taskforce to the India Ocean to fight against piracy." Describing the border conflict in 1962 as "just a little 'episode' in the China-India friendship for thousands of years," it added that "both parties have no reason to let the past history obstruct the future path." It concluded that, "as long as China and India are not enemies to each other, Asia is safe from big turbulence. China-India friendship is the basis for the new order in the future of Asia."

The Tibet issue, according to one official, was not raised during the three days of meetings at the Diaoyutai State Guest House in Beijing; however,

China's State Council timed the release of its eleventh White Paper on Tibet for barely a few hours before the Indian Prime Minister's arrival in Beijing on October 21, 2013.

The six-chapter White Paper, which is a meticulous compilation of the economic development in Tibet since its takeover by Communist Chinese troops, devoted an entire, albeit brief, paragraph to castigating the Dalai Lama and implied that he was engaged in activities aimed at China while in India. The White Paper charged that "the 14th Dalai Lama and his clique in exile are conducting separatist activities for a long time to sabotage the development and stability of Tibet. After the failure of their armed rebellion in 1959, they fled abroad and began to harass China's borders for years." It asserted that the "so-called" concepts of "Greater Tibet" and "a high degree of autonomy" are against China's actual conditions and violate its Constitution and laws. It said, "their true aim is to overthrow the socialist system and system of regional ethnic autonomy that have ensured the development and progress of Tibet."

The White Paper added that there "are some others in the world who intentionally distort the past and present of Tibet due to their ideological bias or out of consideration for their self-interests. They created a Shangri-La myth, wishing to keep Tibet in a backward primitive state forever."

For the third consecutive time, in joint statements issued after meetings between Chinese Premiers and their Indian counterparts, the routine ritual statement recognising Tibet as an inalienable part of China was not included. Such mention was omitted during the visits to India of Chinese Premiers Wen Jiabao (2011) and Li Keqiang (2013).

There was limited, but apparent, forward movement on the border issue evidenced by inclusion in the Joint Statement of the observation that: "peace and tranquillity on the India-China border was recognised as an important guarantor for the development and continued growth of bilateral relations." The statement indirectly pointed to the growing incidence of border intrusions by China and negative reactions it was provoking.

The Border Defence Cooperation Agreement (BDCA) was described in paragraph 5 of the Joint Statement as intended to "strengthen maintenance of stability on the border." It was clubbed with the agreements signed earlier in 1993, 1996 and 2005 and portrayed as merely another confidence-building measure. There was no reference to ensuring the current status quo of border defences and neither was there mention of any limits on patrolling by either side.

However, Article II (i) of the BDCA, which provides for the exchange of information, "including information about military exercises, aircrafts, demolition operations and unmarked mines—and take consequent measures conducive to the maintenance of peace, stability and tranquillity along the line of actual control in the India-China border areas," raises some concerns. The wording suggests that advance intimation would require to be given of construction activity as well as aircraft operations near the LAC, which could open the window for objections that such activity was occurring in territory the ownership of which was under dispute. Recent occurrences in Ladakh substantiate such concern.

Another new feature was in Article VI, which provided that "the two sides agree that they shall not follow or tail patrols of the other side in areas where there is no common understanding of the line of actual control in the India-China border areas." The wording in this Article leaves ambiguous the manner of responding to an intruding patrol.

Indications were available earlier that the PLA appeared to have distanced itself from the BDCA, with its officers saying that its signing was a "political" decision based on the briefing given to the Politburo by State Councillor Yang Jiechi. The PLA's stance could have implications.

Article VII of the Joint Statement, which dealt with river management issues, made no mention of the Brahmaputra (YarlungTsangpo) giving little cause for comfort on the issue of the river's diversion. Mentioning strengthened cooperation, it said there could be an "exchange of views on other issues of mutual interest." China had earlier hinted at its position on diversion of the Brahmaputra through an article by a researcher in the government-owned think tank Chinese Academy of Social Sciences (CASS), which recommended that China ignore India's protests and go ahead with the project to divert the river.

The economic agenda saw mixed results. While there was no progress on the issue of a Free Trade Agreement or, as the Chinese refer to it, the Regional Trade Agreement, there seemed to have been some progress regarding the Special Economic Zones and some incremental progress on the so-called

Southern Silk Route, or BCIM Economic Corridor. The latter proposal, which is being ardently pursued by China and its supporters in India, especially needs to be carefully studied. Its implementation without adequate preparation will threaten the fragile economy of India's northeastern states and at once cause India's approximately US$ 39 billion trade deficit with China to burgeon while simultaneously opening the way for hundreds of Chinese workers to enter the country.

The Indian Prime Minister's visit was essentially a diplomatic overture to signal that India was keen on peace and tranquillity along the borders and was not teaming up with the US against China. It also sought to convey that border intrusions would undercut the basis for building relations and a hint of India's ire was its failure to reiterate that Tibet is a part of China. China's leaders sought to similarly convey a message of their interest in peaceful borders, accompanied by interest in economic interaction. There was, however, little forward movement on key, substantive issues.

(The article was published in Institute of Peace and Conflict Studies, New Delhi, October 2013).

31

The Second Modi-Xi Jinping Summit

In mid-May this year Prime Minister Narendra Modi will travel to Beijing to meet Chinese President Xi Jinping for their second summit within a year. With this Modi has clearly indicated a desire to improve ties with China. Countries around the world will closely watch this meeting between a decisive, nationalist and pragmatic Modi and Xi Jinping, China's most powerful leader since Mao Zedong whose vision for China is encapsulated in the muscular "China Dream."

Modi goes to China after enhancing border patrols and initiating steps to strengthen India's border defence infrastructure. He has given Indo-US relations an unambiguous orientation and potentially more enduring footing. He has consolidated links with Japan and Vietnam and will have concluded successful engagements with France, Germany and Canada, all of which include economic, high-tech or defence-related agreements.

Receiving Modi will be a self-confident Chinese leadership buoyed by the successful launch of the New Development Bank (formerly the BRICS Development Bank), the Contingency Reserve Arrangement and the Asian Infrastructure Investment Bank (AIIB). Particularly gladdening for Beijing has been that so far 46 countries, including advanced nations and close allies of the US like the UK, Australia and potentially Japan, have disregarded US advice and queued to join the AIIB. The financial institutions complement Xi Jinping's twin economic initiatives of the New Silk Road Economic Belt and the Maritime Silk Route—popularly referred to as the "One Road, One Belt"—that the Chinese President has elevated to national strategy.

Preparatory groundwork for the "One Road, One Belt" was laid with the "Conference on Peripheral Diplomacy" held in Beijing in late October 2013, which hinted that China would attempt to alter existing power relationships that have defined the Asia-Pacific region's geostrategic environment. For the first time in the history of the People's Republic of China (PRC), Beijing designated neighbours as "friends" and "enemy," promised huge fiscal and other benefits to "friends" and articulated the concept of Beijing-led security alliances. This was reiterated by Xi Jinping, albeit less directly, at the "Central Conference on Work Relating to Foreign Affairs" in Beijing in November 2014. Relevant for India is Beijing's identification so far of Myanmar, Bangladesh, Nepal, Pakistan, Sri Lanka, Maldives and Turkey as "friends."

As on the occasion of his visit last September, India should anticipate another definite push for endorsement of these twin economic initiatives being steered personally by Xi Jinping. Their acceptance would put at serious risk the fragile economies of India's vulnerable northeastern states.

Pertinent too is Beijing's bid to upgrade its international standing by getting Washington to accept its formulation of a "New Type of Great Power Relations." Raised by Chinese President Xi Jinping in meetings with US President Barack Obama first in June 2013, and later in July and November 2014, the formula states: (i) major powers should have no conflict or confrontation, should emphasise dialogue and should treat each other's strategic intentions objectively; (ii) they should have mutual respect, including for each other's core interests and major concerns; and (iii) they should conduct mutually beneficial cooperation, abandon the zero-sum game mentality and advance areas of mutual interest. Significant is the consistent emphasis on respect for "each other's core interests," which points to China's abiding ambition to dominate the South China Sea and Asia-Pacific region.

Xi Jinping's focus on China's "rejuvenation" and emphasis on "core interest" rules out any compromises on issues concerning the country's sovereignty and territorial integrity and has contributed to a decisively assertive foreign policy. Relevant is Xi Jinping's speech at a Politburo "study" session on January 28, 2013, where he asserted: "China will never … give up our legitimate rights and will never sacrifice our national core interests. No country should presume that we will engage in trade involving our core interests or that we will swallow the 'bitter fruit' of harming our sovereignty, security or development interests." The 18th Party Congress document adopted in November 2012 also, for the first time, emphasised that there will be "no compromises" on issues concerning "national sovereignty and security of core interests." This has been reiterated at regular intervals by senior Chinese Party and military officials.

Leading Chinese strategists close to Xi Jinping endorse this while advocating a tougher, more direct stance on settling outstanding issues with neighbours. They insist these should not be temporarily set aside on the ground that they could strain relations. These views were reflected in at least two high-level, closed-door conferences chaired by Dai Bingguo, till recently State Councillor and China's Special Representative for talks with India, in Beijing late last year.

For there to be meaningful forward movement in the India-China relationship, five main issues require to be addressed during Prime Minister Modi's upcoming visit to China. These are: (i) the disputed border; (ii) the unprovoked intrusions, including road construction inside Indian territory, by Chinese troops; (iii) plans for diversion of the Brahmaputra River to the north; (iv) Chinese activities in POK and the close Sino-Pakistan relationship which is essentially strategic and defence-related and impinges directly on India's sovereignty, security and territorial integrity; and (v) the immense trade deficit disadvantageous to India.

The first three are particularly emotionally-charged issues as they impact on the country's sovereignty, national pride and future. Another is China's aggressiveness in the South China Sea. Any attempt to gloss over these would have consequences.

Beijing has already, prior to the visit, through an unusual number of articles in its official media and comments by officials—including diplomats in the Chinese Embassy in New Delhi—stated its position on the border issue. These statements reveal no hint of flexibility in China's position, with China putting the onus on coming up with "innovative" and "out-of-the-box" thinking on India. Since September 2014, China has sought to keep the focus on the eastern sector—comprising the entire state of Arunachal Pradesh—highlighting that this is the biggest problem. This was repeated on April 9, 2015, by Chinese Foreign Ministry spokesperson Hu Chunying who said: "There is a huge dispute in the eastern border of China-India border. This is undeniable fact."

Beijing has also deftly avoided mention of the 14,380 square miles (approx. 37,244 sq. km) of territory under its forcible occupation in the Aksai Chin area of Ladakh in an attempt to place it outside the scope of discussion. This was indirectly indicated in the composition of the delegation led (February 27-March 2, 2015) by General Zhang Youxia, Director of the People's Liberation Army's (PLA) General Armaments Department (GAD) and one of the few at this level with actual battle experience. He has publicly favoured a tough stance by China on territorial issues, though in the context of the maritime disputes in the South China Sea. The delegation included Lt. General Zhang Hongzhe, Deputy Commander of the PLA Air Force (PLAAF), Lt. General Zhou Yaning, Deputy Commander Second Artillery (or China's strategic missile force) and, pertinently, Lt. General Shi Xiangyuan, Deputy Commander of the Chengdu Military Region which exercises direct operational control over a major portion of the India-China border except for the western, or Ladakh, sector. This latter is under the operational jurisdiction of the Lanzhou Military Region.

Articles in the official Chinese media simultaneously injected a note of realism and said that resolution of the border issue may not be possible during Modi's visit in May. On February 26, 2015, China's official media instead suggested that "identifying the lines of control on each side will be a key step to facilitating the long-stalled process of bringing the disputes to a peaceful resolution. In that case, border stand-offs between India and China, such as the one in September last year which started before Chinese President Xi Jinping's trip to India, should be avoided, helping create a friendly atmosphere to further deepen bilateral ties."

This was endorsed by Prime Minister Modi in his interview with the *Hindustan Times* on April 9, 2015, when he said: "In so far as the border is concerned, the most important point right now is that peace and tranquillity must not be disturbed. That would create conditions for us to arrive at a mutually-acceptable solution. This is a complicated and old problem and needs to be addressed with care and with deliberation."

Obviating intrusions by Chinese troops would certainly be a major first step towards addressing the issue of absent trust and improving India-

China relations. As negotiators settle down to discuss the proposed "lines of control," however, it would be prudent to keep in mind that in the context of the western sector, i.e., Ladakh, where the maximum number of intrusions have been taking place, Beijing is likely to approach it as a potential basis for a future settlement.

The eastern sector where China claims the entire state of Arunachal Pradesh, and particularly Tawang, will be a difficult sticking point. When the Chinese for the first time officially raised their claim on Tawang in September 2005, they had cited the sentiments of the Tibetan people as a principal reason for raising the claim. This will be reiterated especially at this juncture when China is giving high priority to avoiding a situation of "twin Dalai Lamas" and is insistent that he reincarnates inside China. The prospect that the Dalai Lama's reincarnation could potentially be "discovered" at Tawang is unnerving for Beijing. China can be expected to subject India to severe pressure on the issue of the Dalai Lama's reincarnation and presence of the Tibetan administration.

For India it will be essential to discuss the issues of China's expanded territorial claims on Arunachal Pradesh and Jammu and Kashmir, reiterated unequivocally in the context of stapled visas by Chinese Foreign Minister Wang Yi in June 2014. Discussions should include Beijing's unwavering pressure on international financial institutions, like the ADB, compelling them not to give financial assistance to development projects in Arunachal Pradesh and not even referring to these states by name in their reports. If such a line to limit patrolling is to be discussed then China will need to give up this stance as otherwise it will cite this as evidence to further bolster its claim in future.

The ambit and independence of the AIIB, which India joined in October 2014, could well figure in these discussions.

The Shaksgam Valley, which is almost 5,180 sq. km, or 1,930 square miles, of territory ceded illegally and unilaterally by Pakistan to China in 1963 is another issue that needs to be discussed in the context of the border negotiations and the Sino-Pak relationship. The presence of Chinese military and civil personnel and defence-related infrastructure construction activities in Pakistan's northern areas as well as the Gilgit-Baltistan region, impinge directly on India's security and sovereignty. In event of future conflict, Chinese presence could hamper India's military planning and actions.

Selective encouragement of Chinese participation in identified, non-sensitive sectors would be of mutual advantage. These will, of course, be on the agenda and include a range of issues such as Chinese investments in India, investment in Indian infrastructure and the manufacturing sector, cooperation in "green" energy and the climate sector, etc.

A high priority on China's agenda would be to prevent India from drawing too close to the US and Japan. An early indicator are the remarks recently of China's Ambassador to India, who said the Chinese people are courteous and would give a warm welcome to India's Prime Minister. This could have also been intended to partially address lingering apprehension in New Delhi that Beijing may plan some action to embarrass the visiting Indian dignitary.

While Beijing will undoubtedly highlight all agreements, it can be anticipated that it would try and portray Beijing's "flexibility." Beijing can be anticipated to push for an agreement, or positive statement, on discussions on the proposed "line of control." China might also express support for India's bid for a seat in the UNSC—thus further isolating Japan while secure in the knowledge that none of the UNSC's permanent members really want reform! Both will be held up as achievements for Prime Minister Modi and Beijing's "accommodative" policy.

(The article was published in Centre for China Analysis and Strategy, New Delhi, April 2015).

32

Brief Analysis of Chinese Official Media Reporting on Prime Minister Modi's Visit to China

Beijing pays especially close attention to border issues and bilateral ties, both of which it regards as sensitive. The Chinese realise that settlement of the border issue is central to any improvement in India-China relations, but have kept it unsettled over the decades to pressure India. China has simultaneously sought to weaken India's stand in the border negotiations by promoting doubts regarding the actual alignment and even legitimacy of the McMahon Line.

The Chinese are meticulous record keepers and the Chinese Communist Party's (CCP) increasingly powerful Propaganda Department keeps tight control to ensure a narrative approved by the Party. It controls appointments and removals of senior editorial personnel in the state-owned audio-visual and print media nationwide. It additionally approves and closely supervises content by issuing instructions thrice a day detailing which topics should be covered, ignored or downplayed, and the prominence that each should be given. China's communist regime is adept at harmonising records with the Party's approved narrative, and the predictably selective reporting by China's official media, including Xinhua, of important bilateral events and discussions is, therefore, important.

In the context of Prime Minister Modi's visit (May 14-16, 2015) to China, there have been an unusual number of comments and articles by China's normally reticent officials and media, including on the disputed India-China border. Bilateral relations and border issues are subjects that are usually off limits for the Chinese media where only authorised officials are permitted to voice "views." Illuminative were at least fifteen articles noticed in the official Chinese mainstream media in the fortnight surrounding the visit. Though they were a mixed bag of some critical articles and others that were pessimistic regarding the outcome of the visit, a few sought to strike a positive note. China's assertive self-confidence, with possibly a touch of arrogance, was visible in almost all articles.

On April 18, 2015, China's authoritative official news agency Xinhua reported the arrival in India on a four-day (April 15-18, 2015) visit of a CCP delegation led by Politburo Member and Party Secretary of Shaanxi, Zhao Zhengyong. Zhao Zhengyong was quoted as saying that India and China were both "implementing the outcomes of Xi Jinping's visit to India, the momentum in development of China-India relations is good, and that there is positive progress in inter-party exchanges and regional cooperation." He said,"China expects that Indian PM Modi's visit to China will give a new impetus to China-India relations." Hinting at the inequality in the two economies, Xinhua observed that the "Indian side admired the leadership of the CCP and China's economic and social achievements, and said that India is willing to learn from China's successful experiences and further deepen China-India pragmatic cooperation. Both sides hope that the Indian PM Modi's visit to China is an opportunity for both the countries and it will take bilateral relations to a new height."

A week later, the Chinese-language Meijiang Network, an economic news service established in December 2004 and owned by the State Financial Daily Press and Publication Administration, commented on the upcoming visit. It quoted China's Ambassador to India as remarking that in case ongoing discussions concluded successfully then agreements totalling US$ 10 billion could be signed during Prime Minister Modi's visit. The article included explicit references to the New Silk Economic Road and, referring to Modi's itinerary, said his "first stop in China will be Xian, the historical city from where the Silk route begins." It sought to lure India into supporting the "One Belt, One Road" by hinting at the potential for Chincsc invcstmcnts and pointing to the investments worth US$ 46 billion announced by Xi Jinping while on his recent state visit to Pakistan. It added that as "China-India are the two large developing countries in Asia, so trade and economic cooperation will be the main agenda of Modi's visit to China."

Wu Tiaoli, an Assistant Researcher at the Institute of Asia-Pacific and Global Strategy in the Chinese Academy of Social Sciences (CASS), described the Modi government's policy towards China as "reflecting a "double track policy." He said, "India wants to expand economic, trade and investment cooperation with China and wants to decrease the balance of trade gap with China and, therefore, the deepening of China-India Trade will create new opportunities." Trying to put the gloss of economic development on China's relations with Pakistan, he reasoned that, "construction of the China-Pakistan Economic Belt will eliminate the Indian doubts, moreover, it will help India to understand the project." He added that "China is also promoting the BCIM Economic corridor as part of the 21st Century Maritime Silk Route Project, which also requires India's support and participation." Wu Tiaoli assessed that as the world's two largest developing nations, "China-India relations have gone beyond the bilateral context, and now have global and strategic significance." He described the bilateral trade volume of almost US$ 70 billion in 2014, as "modest."

The Deputy Director of the South Asia Research Institute of the Yunnan Academy of Social Sciences, Yang Siling, recalled Chinese President Xi Jinping's suggestion in New Delhi in September 2014, that India "converge" its "Mausam Project" with the "One Belt, One Road" and the observation of Chinese Ambassador Le Yucheng that this would "make India a natural and significant cooperative partner of China." He conceded that, "in comparison to China's enthusiastic attitude, India seems to be ambiguous about the initiatives of China's 'One Belt, One Road' and attributed this to its feeling 'limited by the geopolitical competition.'"

Four questions relating to Prime Minister Modi's visit to China were raised in Chinese at the regular weekly briefing by China's Ministry of National Defence (MND) held on April 30, 2015. The fourth and last question sought clarification whether China's decision to invite India's Northern Army Commander indicated a change in its position on Kashmir. The MND spokesman's reply was categoric. Reiterating China's claim on J&K, the spokesman stated: "China has a consistent and clear stance on the issue of Kashmir. And on the specific arrangements of border defence exchanges, discussions between the two sides are still going on."

The reply to the second question was also interesting. Asserting that, "the China-Indian boundary issue is a problem left over from history," the spokesperson added, "joining hands to maintain peace and tranquillity in areas along the China-Indian border is the important consensus reached by both sides. The Chinese defence troops have always been strictly abiding by the agreements reached by the two governments, and we hope the Indian side can meet China halfway."

A Chinese-language Xinhua despatch of May 7, 2015, which officially announced Modi's visit to China from May 14-16, went viral on China's social media. The despatch listed Modi's itinerary and said, "China has done its homework for the visit of powerful and popular Modi. Ten days before his visit, he opened Chinese Weibo to play the emotional card, and the blog posts are full of 'friendship,' 'blessing' and other words. He is ready to embark on the road to the East. Modi expects a lot from China, and in the economic aspect his main focus is investment and the projects under negotiations, and political dialogue involving the Sino-Indian border dispute." Saying, "It is foreseeable that Modi's pragmatic China policy will continue—cooperation on economic and trade and balance in diplomacy," it pointedly asked whether "Modi can have both—the fish and bear's paw?"

Comments of the spokesperson of the Chinese Ministry of Foreign Affairs (MFA) at the regular briefing a day earlier (May 6) were carefully worded. Important was the Chinese Foreign Ministry spokesperson's statement that, "The bilateral relationship boasts strategic significance and global influence. Over the past years, China and India have kept their relationship developing in a sound and steady manner and figured out a way to get along with each other that focuses on mutual benefit and cooperative development, accommodates each other's concerns and properly handles differences." The spokesperson added, "President Xi Jinping paid a successful state visit to India last September when he mapped out the development of China-India strategic cooperative partnership for the next five to ten years together with Indian leaders." Stating that both sides are closely coordinating the visit, and "It is believed that efforts by the two sides will ensure the success of Prime Minister Modi's visit and showcase the importance attached by the Chinese side to China-India relations and to the visit," the spokesperson said in conclusion that, "We expect and believe that the visit will help enhance mutual understanding and mutual trust between the two countries, step up bilateral cooperation across the board and enable the bilateral relations to make bigger strides at a faster pace and in a more stable manner."

In the span of a week till May 15, 2015, the state-run *Global Times*, a subsidiary owned by the CCP's official newspaper *People's Daily*, published at least six articles on the visit. All the articles underlined the mutual lack of trust and emphasised that China was far ahead of India in economic terms.

Particularly acerbic and critical was the article on May 11, 2015, by Hu Zhiyong, a research fellow with the Institute of International Relations at the Shanghai Academy of Social Sciences. Hu Zhiyong is reputedly close to the CCP leadership and articulates their views. Describing Modi as a "pragmatist, rather than a visionary," he said Modi had "been busy strengthening India's ties with neighbouring countries to compete with China, while trying to take advantage of the tremendous opportunities for economic development created by China." It accused him of "also playing little tricks over border disputes and security issues, hoping to boost his domestic prestige while increasing his leverage in negotiations with China." Saying that, "the ball is in India's court to deepen the bilateral relations," he added that, "for China, developing friendly cooperation with surrounding countries has always been the foothold of its diplomacy" and that "close ties with India, China's largest neighbour in South Asia, is of great importance to China's perimeter security and stability." He added that improvement in Sino-Indian relations are "severely constrained" by the views of a number of Indian elites who "deem the rise of Beijing as a threat to New Delhi's development."

Asserting that the "two sides have never established real strategic trust," he listed steps that Modi should take, namely (i) "he should no longer visit the disputed border region in pursuit of his own political interests"; (ii) he should "not deliver any remarks that infringe on the consensus on bilateral ties"; and (iii) "the Indian government should completely stop supporting the Dalai Lama, and stop making the Tibetan issue a stumbling block to the Sino-Indian relationship."

Hu Zhiyong was equally uncompromising on issues of economy and trade, saying that, "New Delhi is reluctant to admit the widening trade gap is its own fault, nor is it willing to examine its own economic structure and the quality of its exports to China," but instead repeatedly accuses or directs its anger at China. Scathing was the observation that, "due to the Indian elites blind arrogance and confidence in their democracy, and the inferiority of its ordinary people, very few Indians are able to treat Sino-Indian relations accurately, objectively and rationally." He accused some Indian media of "irresponsibly exaggerating the conflicts between the two sides, adding fuel to the hostility among the public." Hu Zhiyong concluded with the comment that, "Modi should seize the chance of his China visit to enhance bilateral cooperation" and "political mutual trust between leaders."

Ding Gang, a Senior Editor of the CCP's authoritative mouthpiece *People's Daily*, apparently voiced the Party's views on May 13, 2015, in a column in the *Global Times*. He wrote that if India and China join hands they could change Asia's geopolitical and economic landscape, but "there seems always to be a lack of mutual trust between the dragon and the elephant." He added that, "there is more competition than complementarity" between India and China leading directly "to a zero-sum game. In other words, one side moving up on the supply chain will likely squeeze the domain of the other."

Stating that there are many "unsustainable factors in the trade structure of China and India," he said if China invests more in India's infrastructure this may prove counterproductive as it could "cause more concerns for India about the flooding of Chinese commodities," and that involvement of Chinese enterprises could entangle them in "India's perplexing land system." He recommended that China "make well-planned and targeted industrial transfers in accordance with the development and investment ability of its enterprises and set up production bases in India to make use of its cheaper labour force and invest in training selected Indian workers through the Asian Infrastructure Investment Bank. He asked India to draw upon China's strength in technology and funding. He urged more access to local markets for Chinese telecommunications enterprises, saying China could do likewise for India's pharmaceutical companies and forecast that the two countries could "ultimately create a common market of 2.6 billion people."

Global Times on May 13, 2015 published an article by Swaran Singh, an Indian scholar in JNU, Delhi, which said that the PMO's last-minute decision to cancel BJP President Amit Shah's meeting with the Dalai Lama at Dharamsala on May 2, 2015, "showed the cost that the Modi government was willing to take to please Chinese leaders." Stating that the RSS has had a negative view on China since 1962, it referred to an article in the RSS's official paper *Organiser*, which said that "the well-calibrated symbolism of Modi and Chinese President Xi Jinping shows the duo has a better chance in achieving breakthroughs and bringing down negativity over political questions." The author said, "the story compares Modi to the Buddha and the poet Tagore in having left a deep impression on China's popular consciousness." Stating that the "ruling establishment of India does not wish to leave any stone unturned to ensure the positive environment for the Xi-Modi summit, which is expected to usher in a subtle 'reset' in China-India relations," it commented that "their summit should mark an important but first step in their long journey together into building, not just theirs, but Asia's future."

The article in the *Global Times* on May 14, 2015, by Liu Zongyi, an assistant research fellow of the Shanghai Institutes for International Studies (SIIS) and a visiting fellow of the Chongyang Institute for Financial Studies, Renmin University of China, was interesting. It blended veiled warnings with the potential promise of improved ties. Pertinent were the statements that "realising regional security, including the stability in Afghanistan and the security in the Indian Ocean, requires concerted efforts from both China and India," and that "at present Washington is the major provider of security in the vast Indian Ocean, so if it exits, India will need the cooperation of other countries."

It candidly stated that, "the boundary disputes are a conundrum in the bilateral relationship. If they can't be solved at an earlier date, the two sides should more closely stick to the code of conduct they reached before." It recalled the proposal by Xi Jinping made last September that "China and India should work together to establish a closer partnership of development rather than becoming rivals in competition," and said, "Modi is considered as a state leader with strategic insights. He may become a Nixon-style statesman because of his pragmatism and capacity to resolve major contradictions between China and India and to tackle the common challenges of development."

Acknowledging that "there is indeed competition and a lack of mutual strategic trust between the two rapidly emerging Asian powers," it said, "over the past year, India, under the Modi administration, has become a star on the world stage." It cautioned, however, that "Modi's victory in the country's general elections last May has injected enormous confidence into India's economic development," but "had also offered hope to the US, Japan and other nations attempting to take advantage of New Delhi to contain China." It took note of India's ambiguous attitude towards China's "One Belt, One Road," the 21st Century Maritime Silk Road initiatives, and the Asian Infrastructure Investment Bank (AIIB). In conclusion, the article observed that, "India longs for economic integration in Asia. However, it is reluctant to see China acting as the single leader in the region but expects to share the role."

A Xinhua editorial of May 14, 2015, was more balanced. It described the "exchange of visits by the leaders from the world's two largest emerging economies" as signalling "warming relations between the two oriental giants." The report played up the fact that Xi Jinping had travelled outside Beijing to receive Modi and said, "Sino-Indian ties could be among the most important bilateral relationships." It said, "if the 'Chinese Dragon' and the 'Indian Elephant' coexist harmoniously and realise peaceful, cooperative development, it will bring benefit to not only their combined 2.5 billion people, but also those living beyond their borders." Emphasising that "China is an infrastructure powerhouse, while India has infrastructure deficits," it said, "China can help India upgrade its railway stations and overhaul its high-speed rail networks," thereby giving both economies a big boost. It noted that India has created world-class software and competitive pharmaceutical industries.

Another *Global Times* editorial on May 15, 2015, captioned "Sino-Indian ties can conquer West's doubts," focused on the so-called attempts by the West to sow discord between India and China. It said, "The dragon-elephant pas-de-deux has made headlines once again, but suspicions from the Western world soon poured in, saying the surface friendliness cannot cover the fact that Sino-Indian relations have irreconcilable maladies. No matter how much cooperation they can establish, border disputes will offset all progress." Asserting, "it is obvious that the Western elite doesn't want to see India and China drawing closer to each other," the editorial said, "it will be a long-term test for China and India to get rid of distractions imposed by the West and stick to a path which can benefit the national interest of both countries." Admitting that, "the bilateral relationship is still vulnerable to many sensitive issues," it said, "although no bullets have been fired along the border for decades, tensions still remain." The editorial conceded that, "lack of mutual trust still disturbs both sides," and "media reports raise concerns about each other from time to time," but stressed that, "China and India should think out of the box where delusions of persecution prevail," otherwise cooperation will not be possible when "only distrust and hostility are rife." It underlined this theme saying that it "is hard for China and India to develop a strategic partnership, but it will be dreadful for both sides to vie with each other," and that mutual fundamental interests demand that "no side should look at the other with contempt or arrogance, and their problems should be addressed between the two with no need to introduce a third party."

China's authoritative official news agency Xinhua on May 15, 2015, reported on the meeting between India's Prime Minister Modi and Chinese Premier Li Keqiang. Stating that the two met in the Great Hall of the People on May 15 morning, Xinhua quoted Li Keqiang as saying, based on the statement issued by the Chinese Ministry of Foreign Affairs (MFA), that, "Last year, the Chairman Xi Jinping successfully visited India. Yesterday, Chairman Xi Jinping carried out a fruitful meeting with you at Xian. My first state visit as the Chinese Premier was India. China and India are not rivals and should become an important partner." Stating that, "Both sides need to expand their relation from Asia to the world, and promote strategic mutual trust, economic cooperation ... and promote the common development of China and India," it said, "Li Keqiang pointed out that China is willing to join hands with India to build a closer partnership for development."

Li Keqiang was reported as saying that the leaders of both countries should "make full use of wisdom to deal with sensitive issues such as borders, maintaining momentum in the negotiations to establish cooperation framework mechanism to ensure peace and tranquillity in the border area, while focusing on promoting the bilateral strategic cooperation and common development, and promote the formation of a true 'Asian Century'". To complement their economic advantages and in a veiled reference to the "One Belt, One Road," he said they should be "docking development strategies" and "pushing ahead BCIM Economic Corridor," etc. He pointed out that China is willing to participate in India's Industrial Corridor. The Xinhua report included no reference to Prime Minister Modi's comments on the need for China to reconsider its approach on the border and other issues which would otherwise restrict development of bilateral ties.

The focus of China's official media in the days around Prime Minister Modi's visit to China was clearly on the promotion of bilateral economic ties. There was a definite effort to push China's major economic initiative of "One Belt, One Road" together with calls for enhanced access for Chinese companies. While authoritative articles and comments by senior CCP officials in the months leading up to the visit had emphasised China's unchanged stance on the issue of the border, in the days proximate to the visit the border issue found very brief mention. Where it did, like in the Chinese Defence Ministry briefing, India was urged to meet China at least halfway. Hu Zhiyong's article in *Global Times* on May 11, 2015, was rather blunt in listing the steps that India needs to take to improve bilateral ties. All articles underscored the distrust in the relationship. Pertinently, Xinhua and China's official media blanked out Modi's remarks urging China to "reconsider its approach" on the border and other outstanding issues, made during meetings with Chinese President Xi Jinping, Premier Li Keqiang and in his address to students in Tsinghua University in Beijing.

(The article was published by the Centre for China Analysis and Strategy (CCAS) and Vivekananda International Foundation (VIF), New Delhi, June 4, 2015).

33

China's Belt and Road Initiative: Indian Perspective

China's "One Belt, One Road," which was first proposed in September 2013 and combines the twin initiatives of the Silk Road Economic Belt and Twenty-first Century Maritime Silk Road, is a grand concept that envisions China girdling the globe. Potentially covering 55 per cent of the world GNP, 70 per cent of the global population, and 75 per cent of known energy reserves, it is essentially a plan for a China-built land and sea transportation artery to link China's production centres with markets and natural resource centres around the world. At the same time, it will harness much of China's hitherto idle economy, manpower and infrastructure-technology reserves to get much needed returns. It has the potential to bend borders and alter the status quo in China's neighbourhood—as it already has begun to do in South Asia—and adversely impacts India directly. The initiative blends geopolitical and diplomatic objectives and has a strong domestic agenda.

The proposed "One Belt, One Road" (OBOR) is an approximately US$ 1.4 trillion project. China claims to be willing to make a huge financial commitment upwards of US$ 300 billion in infrastructure financing for the project in the coming years, though some multilateral and bilateral pledges may overlap. Underscoring China's commitment, the official *China Daily* reported on May 28, 2015 that Beijing plans to invest US$ 900 billion. The OBOR is planned to be completed over 35 years, in time for the 100th anniversary of the People's Republic of China in 2049!

The "Belt Corridors" run along the major Eurasian Land Bridges, through China-Mongolia-Russia, China-Central and West Asia, China-Indochina Peninsula, China-Pakistan, Bangladesh-China-India-Myanmar. The Maritime

Silk Route or "Road" is the maritime equivalent of the "Belt Corridors" and comprises a network of planned ports and other coastal infrastructure projects that dot the map from South and Southeast Asia to East Africa and the northern Mediterranean Sea.

The most publicised recent bilateral commitment to OBOR was the investment pledged for the China-Pakistan Economic Corridor (CPEC) by Xi Jinping during his two-day visit to Pakistan in April 2015. Pakistani analysts have valued it at US$46 billion. Deals valued at a further US$ 15.7 billion were subsequently signed in Belarus that May. More might have been signed during Xi Jinping's visits to Kazakhstan and Russia on the same trip. Discussions are known to be underway with Russia on overland transport, energy, and cyber-connectivity. Concrete data in respect of OBOR-related agreements is, however, not easily available in published Chinese sources.

International financial institutions, some of them new, are getting involved with OBOR like the Asian Infrastructure Investment Bank (AIIB), BRICS' New Development Bank, Silk Road Fund, a CIC-backed fund (announced recently, during Li Keqiang's visit to Brazil), and, possibly, an SCO Development Bank. This has had an effect on private investors, lenders and countries in the region. Japan, for example, announced a US$ 110 billion infrastructure fund for Asia and the Asian Development Bank (ADB) revised its disbursement rules to increase lending capacity. The AIIB is to serve as the financing arm of OBOR.

An effort by China to use these banks, especially the AIIB, to extend fiscal assistance to Pakistan for projects in the CPEC in furtherance of its strategic objectives immediately puts India to the test. On May 9, 2016, the official English-language *China Daily* reported that the AIIB announced it would co-finance a US$ 300 million motorway project in Pakistan with the Asian Development Bank. Asserting that "Pakistan is a strong ally of China," the report indicated there would be more such projects. To advance its national interest, China had used its economic clout with the ADB to block developmental assistance for poverty alleviation projects in India's northeastern state of Arunachal Pradesh on the ground that it was disputed. Identically, the CPEC goes through India-claimed and disputed territory.

While Chinese officials and academics emphasise the economic aspects and commercial advantages of OBOR, it is definitely a geopolitical and diplomatic offensive. Chinese President Xi Jinping's articulation of a "community of destiny" among Asians is relevant. Despite Chinese interlocutors insisting that China seeks to "supplement" the existing international order rather than revise it, the numerous statements by influential Chinese strategists asserting that the time is now opportune for China to alter the status quo, are strong in the background. Implementation of OBOR will also augment China's economic influence in the participating countries. The strategy of disbursing them large sums as loans and aid will enhance the financial power that China already exercises through its trading relationship.

Huang Yiping, a Professor of Economics at Peking University's National School of Development, assessed in February 2015, that OBOR represents a sea change in China's international profile. According to him, OBOR has ended the phase of low-profile diplomacy based on Deng Xiaoping's advice to "hide your capabilities and bide your time" and transformed China into "a new great power" which "is trying to supplement the international economic order." Huang Yiping sought to justify China's more active role as an attempt to redress the limited role given to developing countries in international institutions and in line with US President Barack Obama's demand that China take on more responsibility for providing international public goods. A Renmin University report similarly asserted the need to "supplement, not challenge" the existing order because of the "zero-sum thinking" which ensured that OBOR projects were greeted with scepticism including in China's immediate neighbourhood. Taking note of the challenges ahead, Huang Yiping conceded that: "One Belt, One Road is a good international economic strategy, but for now it is certainly not an easy one."

A report in 2014 from Renmin University, described by the official Xinhua news agency as the first think-tank report on the projects, clearly outlined the scale of the project's ambition and limits of current planning. It revealed that China will commence strategic planning in 2016 and this would take five years. The report estimates that the Silk Road (OBOR) projects will be fully realised in about 35 years by 2049, the 100th anniversary of the foundation of the People's Republic of China! Chinese President Xi Jinping was quoted by Xinhua on December 6, 2014, as describing the OBOR at a Politburo session as a "new round of opening to the world." This was echoed by a Ministry of Commerce official who implicitly underscored the domestic political agenda by telling *Caijing* magazine that the "new 30 years" will put today's China on the threshold of a third era comparable to those begun by Mao Zedong and Deng Xiaoping!

While the basis for OBOR appears to be geopolitics and export of its huge infrastructure-building capacities, there are foreseeable difficulties. Geographical and geopolitical conditions differ widely outside China and the investment climates are uncertain in many of the countries which can be categorised as low-return and high-risk countries. This has triggered debate among government academics and strategists as to the advisability of making massive investments in such countries. There is, additionally, concern about overreliance on public financing and State-owned Enterprises. There is also concern about the reactions from China's neighbours.

Acknowledging the "great potential" of OBOR, Jia Qingguo, a member of the Standing Committee of the Chinese People's Political Consultative Conference (CPPCC) and Dean of the University of International relations at Beijing University, highlighted the need for caution and said China should not succumb to "wishful thinking." Confirming the differences between academics and government officials about the goal and scope of the project, he said for OBOR to succeed it will need a clear plan and solutions will have to be found to the problems of harsh terrain, political instability, and geopolitical threats. Stating that regional powers like Russia are wary of China's rise, he said China must avoid giving rise to the perception that it is challenging Russia's position in Central Asia. Interestingly, linking with Russia was an afterthought and not in the original OBOR plan. Russia was included only after Putin called Xi Jinping in the Spring of 2015 and Moscow dispatched an emissary to Beijing after which the Russian "loop" was included. Problems, however, remain regarding routing of the railway. Jia Qingguo pointed out that many of the target countries for the Maritime Silk Road project are currently involved in territorial disputes with China, which may make them reluctant to cooperate. To overcome their scepticism, China should use its growing strength to persuade its neighbours to "shelve disputes and pursue joint development."

In similar vein Chu Yin, an Associate Professor of International Relations at the prestigious Tsinghua University in Beijing, in an article in January 2015 focused on political risk and warned China not to take smaller countries for granted. He said: "Although we are a righteous country, free of Western imperialism, colonialism, and racism, we and the OBOR countries are absolutely not equals." He pointed out that Chinese planners had frequently failed to consider local and regional politics, which exposed projects to political risk both from local opposition parties and from competing regional powers. He said recent events in Thailand and Myanmar showed that political instability is a major risk. In an interesting observation, he said the defeat of a Beijing-friendly government during the elections in Sri Lanka could disrupt the construction of a key port there since, in contrast to the US during the Marshall Plan, China does not have the luxury of militarily occupying the countries in which it invests. He said on a regional level, India, the US, Russia, and Japan are all important players in OBOR countries and could use their power to block China's plans.

Security is obviously a major challenge. For example, protection of the 81,000 kilometres (about 50,000 miles) of high-speed railway that China proposes to build through 65 countries, will be a major task. Similar will be the case with the 51 planned projects in the CPEC, which passes through Balochistan—among the world's most vulnerable and domestic insurgency-ridden territories.

As reflected by the ongoing military reforms, China has begun to address some of these issues. The Conference on Peripheral Diplomacy held in Beijing on October 24-25, 2013, prepared the ground for the OBOR. Identifying countries for the first time ever as "friend" and "enemy," it decided that "friends" would receive "untold benefits," including those flowing from China's international standing and diplomatic clout. It promised that China could even offer "security alliances." The China-Pakistan Economic Corridor (CPEC), which is part of OBOR and envisages road links, pipelines, energy centres and ports, is a good example. It combines financial assistance with diplomatic support reinforced by military muscle.

By announcing the CPEC, Beijing dispelled the ambiguity maintained by China thus far on the issue of Kashmir. It is also preparing to protect the CPEC inside Pakistan. A secure fibre-optic link has been laid connecting Kashgar with Rawalpindi, highlighting the close military coordination between Pakistan and China. The establishment early this year of the People's Liberation Army's (PLA) West Zone is intended to safeguard Chinese investments and projects in the CPEC in addition to protecting China's land frontiers. China has at the same time informed Islamabad that it is creating a Division-strength "private army" for deployment in the areas covered by the CPEC. The West Zone's operational jurisdiction is anticipated, in course of time, to include eastern Africa where China has considerable economic interests and where it has very recently signed an agreement for a base at Djibouti. China has already put in place a domestic legal basis for the deployment of Chinese troops and security personnel to protect Chinese investments and workers abroad. The operational tasks assigned to the PLA's West Zone represent the first of more such arrangements.

For India, the Bangladesh-China-India-Myanmar (BCIM) corridor, which is part of OBOR and which Beijing is pressurising India to sign on to, is not feasible. Opening the BCIM would mean that Chinese goods—neither Myanmar nor Bangladesh produce goods in demand in India—will flood India's northeast where poor connectivity presently makes access difficult for Indian products and people. There is the additional risk of thousands of Chinese illegally settling in India's sparsely populated northeastern states, as they have in other countries. A detailed posting on a PLA-maintained website had, in fact, a few years earlier enumerated the advantages of "recovering" Arunachal Pradesh, including to settle China's growing population.

The economic import of the OBOR has correctly been emphasised by Chinese academics and officials. Jia Qingguo observed that OBOR is an international strategy, but its success will be measured by its effects on China's domestic economic rebalancing. While China will send out its own capital, technology, and management experience and promote the development and prosperity of neighbouring countries, he was emphatic that the yardstick for gauging OBOR's success would be whether it encourages China's own economic transformation and makes it the centre of the regional economy. He recommended that to ensure that investment is allocated efficiently and state assets are protected, private capital should take the lead. Jia Qingguo recommended making private enterprises the "backbone" of the project—to leverage their energy, flexibility, and sensitivity to investment efficiency, and avoid the "drainage" effect of SoEs.

Caution has been expressed also by Chen Gong, Chief Researcher at Anbound, a Chinese consulting firm and think tank of the PRC State Council. He suggested that OBOR projects are a large-scale reproduction of China's unbalanced model of development over the last ten years: based on public actors and infrastructure spending, and excessively supply-based. He said this goes against the government's desire to put these stimulus-based growth levers aside—but agreed that perhaps using them outside China is more acceptable and less contentious. Chen Gong particularly questioned the advantage of the Maritime Silk Route, saying: "What China produces, ASEAN countries also produce, and what China thinks about developing, ASEAN also wants to develop." Therefore, the two regions are bound to compete more intensively, and China will face much greater difficulties along the Maritime Silk Road than it would have if it had focused only on the western route.

The main players in OBOR projects will, however, be China's State-owned Enterprises (SoE). According to Xu Gao, Chief Economist at Guangda Securities and former economist for the IMF and the World Bank, this implies that the opportunity cost would actually be negative for China. He has assessed that because China's economic structure is dominated by SoEs, further investment should actually reduce waste in the public sector and help to stabilise employment as well as the economy. It will offer a new investment opportunity for China's huge foreign exchange reserves, which have so far been heavily invested in low-return US bonds.

Meanwhile, data released at the end of 2014 by the State-owned Assets Supervision and Administration Commission of the State Council (SASAC) gives an overview of the preparedness of Chinese SoEs for participating in "OBOR." The report shows that 107 SoEs out of 110 had set up 8,515 branches overseas by the end of 2014, and among them over 80 Chinese SoEs had established branches in countries and regions along the "Belt and Road." Statistics show that the total overseas assets of Chinese SoEs had risen from 2.7 trillion yuan to 4.6 trillion yuan since the implementation of the 12th Five-Year Plan. Chinese SoEs have undertaken major projects like crude-oil pipelines of China-Russia, China-Kazakhstan, and China-Myanmar, natural gas pipelines of China-Russia, China-Central Asia, and China-Myanmar, and railway construction with Myanmar, Thailand, Laos, etc. The SASAC report added that over 40 SoEs have set up International Business Management Departments and over 30 have drawn up overseas legal risk prevention plans.

Separately, Xinhua quoted China's State Administration of Taxation as announcing on March 14, 2016, that Tax treaties with countries along the "Belt and Road" will save financial institutions in China 9.6 billion yuan (about US$ 1.5 billion) in taxes.

While for the present countries cannot ignore China's economic strength or track record in building massive infrastructure, serious doubts remain as to Beijing's real objectives. That Beijing is aware of these concerns is evident in Chinese Foreign Minister Wang Yi's annual address to the press on the sidelines of the CPPCC-NPC sessions in March 2015 and 2016. He asserted that the OBOR was not a "tool of geopolitics" and should not be viewed through an "outdated Cold War mentality." This March, Wang Yi again emphasised that China is a responsible emerging country and promotes periphery diplomacy with reciprocal benefits. He said the "Belt and Road" initiative has made significant progress, including establishment of the Asia Infrastructure Investment Bank (AIIB) and launch of the New Silk Road Fund, and enhanced connectivity with participating countries in economic and trade cooperation, cultural and educational exchanges. China's Vice Foreign Minister, Zhang Yesui, echoed this message of reassurance at the China Development Forum in March 2015. Later the same month he described China as fully integrated into the international system and reiterated that OBOR is "not directed against any specific country or organisation" but intended to "complement" existing international and regional institutions.

Nevertheless, major difficulties confront the OBOR. The slowing domestic economy is one. Chinese economists have warned the Chinese government against taking on too much of the project, saying this would risk repeating the errors made in the development of China's west, but this time on an international scale. The problem is compounded by the desire of many local and provincial governments in more than 22 provinces to participate in

OBOR. An article in February 2015 in the "Guoji Jinrong Bao" cautioned that this could lead to wastage. It pointed out that many international railway projects are coming up on expensive and often underused routes and that a number of provinces have poured subsidies into projects that are not economically viable. Another future complication affecting social stability could stem from plans for cooperation with Central Asian countries developed by local officials and focused on narrow regional interests.

Though 20 European countries are engaged in talks with China on the OBOR and despite China's offers of economic assistance, the EU in May 2016 declined to give China "Market Economy" Status (MES) based on the 2001 terms of China's accession to the World Trade Organisation (WTO). Differences over interest rates, with Thailand complaining in March 2016 that they are too high, now threaten the Chinese-Thai Rail project.

Problems of harsh terrain, political instability, and geopolitical threats, are likely to get accentuated by the inherent political turbulence in many of the regions that the OBOR traverses. The rising tide of Islamic extremism in Pakistan, Afghanistan and potentially soon in the Central Asian Republics, will threaten stability in the Xinjiang-Uyghur Autonomous Region and other Muslim areas in China. Safeguarding the CPEC's 51 projects in Balochistan—among the world's most vulnerable and domestic insurgency-ridden territories—will also be difficult. Together, these cast serious doubts about the viability of the OBOR.

(The article was published in Centre for China Analysis and Strategy (CCAS) and Vivekananda International Foundation (VIF), New Delhi, May 2016).

34

The Future of China-Pakistan Relations

The dropping of Pakistan from Chinese President Xi Jinping's travel itinerary for South Asia in mid-September 2014 prompted speculation in some quarters that it was indicative of a dilution in China's "all-weather" relationship with Pakistan, described by leaders of both countries as "higher than the highest mountain, deeper than the deepest ocean and sweeter than honey." While there are undoubtedly some difficulties in the Sino-Pakistan bilateral relationship, such speculation is presently unrealistic. A scenario depicting rapid deterioration in Pakistan's political stability and security, where Islamist extremists acquire increased salience, however, could cause Beijing to pause and rethink its policy toward Pakistan and South Asia.

Facts are that even a week before Xi Jinping's visit (September 17-19, 2014) was officially announced, the visit to Pakistan had been confirmed and was very much on the agenda. The domestic political scene in Pakistan, however, witnessed dramatic changes and heightened political uncertainty, which raised doubts about the continuance of Prime Minister Nawaz Sharif and the possibility of violence, prompting China to reassess the feasibility of a visit by its President, Xi Jinping. Beijing is usually loath to alter programmes once they are finalised and, particularly, to give the impression that it does not stand beside a friend going through troubled times.

A high-level delegation of China's Ministry of State Security (MoSS) headed by its Minister, 63-year-old Geng Huichang, therefore, travelled to Islamabad to assess the situation first-hand. The Pakistani authorities, and especially Pakistan Prime Minister Nawaz Sharif who was keen on the visit and later expressed disappointment at its cancellation, also offered Lahore and Karachi as alternate venues to China's MoSS Minister, but the Chinese were not satisfied about the security situation at any of these places. The visit was consequently, and rather unusually, deferred reflecting the serious doubts that exist in Beijing about the instability in Pakistan.

Within days of Chinese President Xi Jinping's visit to the Maldives, Sri Lanka and India, however, there was visible demonstration that relations between the two nations remain strong. A flotilla of Chinese People's Liberation Army Navy (PLAN) ships, which included the guided missile destroyer Changchun and guided missile frigate Changzhou, paid a five-day visit to Karachi from September 27, 2014. Earlier, a Chinese Song-class diesel-powered attack submarine for the first time ever sailed to Colombo port, where it stayed for five days, overlapping with Xi Jinping's visit to Sri Lanka and India. In early October 2014, the Chinese Navy announced that it would deploy Type 093 Shang-class nuclear-powered attack submarines for anti-piracy operations off Somalia, thereby raising the real prospect that PLAN's Type 093 Shang-class nuclear-powered attack submarines could regularly begin visiting Karachi in the very near future. This will expand the scope of extant military contacts between the two countries.

Significant in the context of Sino-Pak military ties is China's growing influence on Pakistan's military establishment, indicated by the number of Pakistan military personnel going for training to PLA establishments. Their number, at least since 2010, already exceeds those going to the US, which for many years was the traditional source for training of Pakistan military officers. Similarly, weapons sales have steadily increased and between 1978 and 2008, China sold almost US$ 7 billion in military equipment to Pakistan. As China emerged as the world's largest arms seller with global sales estimated at approximately US$ 2 billion, Pakistan had by 2013 become the largest purchaser of Chinese weaponry accounting for nearly 47 per cent of China's total arms sales.

Sino-Pak diplomatic relations can be traced back to the early 1950s with Pakistan's recognition on January 9, 1950 of the newly established People's Republic of China (PRC). Diplomatic ties between Pakistan and China were formalised in 1951 when Pakistan opened its mission in Beijing. The China-Pakistan bilateral relationship has endured to become one of the most comprehensive that Beijing has with any country. It has stood the test of time, prompted to a large extent by the strategic imperatives of developing Pakistan as a bulwark against India; using Pakistan as an access point into the larger Islamic world; as another option to gain access to the Arabian Sea and Indian Ocean; and as an ally in securing its interests in Afghanistan.

This relationship, nurtured by successive Chinese and Pakistani leaders, soon yielded benefits for Beijing with Pakistan lobbying for China's entry on to the world stage and the UNSC instead of Taiwan. Pakistan also brokered the meeting in July 1971 between China's Mao Zedong and US President Nixon, which led to the normalisation of US-China relations. In the process, it solidified ties with the US and Chinese leaderships. Pakistan, for its part, has stayed steadfastly by China's side and been a good client state, eager to stand up for China wherever the need arose. Over the years, China successfully and effectively built influence in Pakistan and ingressed Pakistani society. The effectiveness of its lobbying with Pakistan's military, diplomatic and scientific elite was exhibited in 2013 when a number of former Pakistani diplomats and others wrote in Pakistan's media and successfully urged that Gwadar Port be handed over to China as the experience with the Singapore Port Authority had been unsatisfactory.

The Sino-Pak strategic partnership and cooperation is mainly manifested in four aspects, namely, economic and trade cooperation; people-to-people contacts; defence and security cooperation; and cooperation and coordination in international and regional affairs. The five main drivers of China's "multidimensional" relationship with Pakistan were best identified by former Chinese President Hu Jintao during a visit to Pakistan in 2006. He listed these as: (i) deepening strategic cooperation and consolidating traditional friendship; (ii) expanding "win-win" business ties; (iii) expanding cultural and social exchanges and strengthening the basis of friendship; (iv) strengthening cooperation in international affairs and upholding common interests; and (v) promoting exchanges among civilisations to enhance world harmony.

India is an important factor that ensured development of Sino-Pakistan relations. After the India-China border war in 1962, where deteriorating Sino-Soviet relations were also a factor, India looked towards the Soviet Union while China accelerated the strengthening of its relationship with Pakistan. Pakistan, which has viewed India as a threat and "enemy" and has traditionally sought to preserve a solid relationship with the US, now assiduously began building relations with China. China, in turn, with an eye to enforcing its territorial claims and perceiving shared interests, helped Pakistan enhance its military and nuclear capabilities with the objective of keeping India engaged and focused on threats emanating from Pakistan, thus practically freeing itself of any military threat from India.

A major step in China-Pakistan relations was taken in 1963, when the two countries signed a border agreement transferring 2,000 square miles (5,180 sq. km) of territory in Pakistan Occupied Kashmir to China. This agreement (also known as the Sino-Pakistan Frontier Agreement and Sino-Pak Boundary Agreement) claimed to establish the border between the two countries and effectively paved the way for China's claims of sovereignty over hundreds of square kilometres of land in northern Kashmir and Ladakh. The transfer facilitated building of the high-altitude 1,280 km Karakoram Highway, which traverses the 19,000 feet high Khunjerab Pass north of the Siachin glacier, and connects China's Xinjiang-Uyghur Autonomous Region with Pakistan's Northern Areas (NA). It has been developed into an all-weather road with substantive Chinese assistance.

The Sino-Pak relationship is reinforced by strong mutual geostrategic interests as well as perceived national security interests. Of particular relevance to India and the region are the agreements between China and Pakistan to upgrade the "all-weather" Karakoram Highway, establish a Defence Electronics Complex in Pakistan, develop Gwadar Port as an energy hub and probably a naval base, lay a pipeline as proposed by Pakistan from Balochistan to Xinjiang, and a slew of other defence cooperation agreements.

Illustrative of the seeming "permanence" with which China views its relationship with Pakistan is the construction of Gwadar Port, viewed by China as an energy hub, strategically located just 250 miles from the Straits of Hormuz and through which nearly 40 per cent of the world's oil supplies flow. The port is well placed to serve as a key shipping point in the region. China agreed to fund the port after Pakistan agreed to give it "sovereign guarantees to the port facilities." In the formal inauguration on March 20, 2007, Pakistan President Pervez Musharraf said that friendly Pak-China relations had "made the dream of Gwadar Port a reality."

Gwadar Port is a major initiative intended to help China project its strategic presence and military power across the subcontinent and diversify and secure its crude oil import routes and gain access to the Persian Gulf, Arabian Sea and Indian Ocean. Chinese officials have stated that they will use this as part of the "Maritime Silk Route" to enhance trade and commerce. It has the potential to facilitate PLAN's operations in the Arabian Sea and Indian Ocean. Reports of China setting up electronic eavesdropping posts at Gwadar to monitor US and Indian naval activity and shipping traffic through the Straits of Hormuz and the Arabian Sea lend credence to this. It also augments the Pakistan Navy's capabilities and enhances Pakistan's importance in the region as a commercial and trade-transit point.

China's huge plans for the development of Gwadar suggest long-term involvement. The China-Pakistan Economic Corridor envisages construction of a 2,870-mile road connecting Kashgar in China's Xinjiang-Uyghur Autonomous Region with Gwadar at an estimated cost of US$ 18 billion. An international airport is under construction at Gwadar as are six coal-fired power plants. The China-Pakistan Economic Corridor, for which an MoU was signed in Islamabad on August 27, 2013, will entail massive capital investment. It provides that China will build a highway connecting the Karakoram Highway (KKH) to Gwadar. Beijing has completed surveys and is preparing to extend the Karakoram Highway down to Gwadar. Plans provide for a railway line, stretching from Xinjiang through Kyrgyzstan and Afghanistan to Gwadar, alongside the extended Karakoram Highway.

The support infrastructure built around the port will help integrate Pakistan into the Chinese economy by outsourcing low-tech basic production and manufacturing jobs. For China, this is an important strategic venture as it will be the only rail link affording landlocked Afghanistan access to a warm water port and will offer Kyrgyzstan an alternative to the existing solitary transport route controlled by Russia. That China was determined to push ahead with the China-Pakistan Economic Corridor became evident when China ignored India's objections raised during the visit of Chinese Premier Li Keqiang in May 2013.

Another pointer to China's plans for long-term involvement with Pakistan are the almost 35 projects that China has been engaged in at least since 2009 in the POK and Pakistan's Northern Areas, or the Gilgit-Baltistan belt in POK. These include hydel projects, roads and the construction of helipads. PLA engineers are mainly known to be involved in many of these projects, especially the construction of a 200-km long tunnel at a cost of US$ 18 billion to facilitate the transportation of goods, military materials and personnel from Xinjiang to Gwadar. Meanwhile, one informed US-based source claimed that up to 10,000 PLA troops were present in the area. The Indian Army's Chief of Staff, General V. K. Singh, in 2011 referred to the presence of nearly 3,500 PLA personnel in Pakistan Occupied Kashmir (POK) and the same year the Northern Army Commander Lt. Gen. K. T. Parnaik, warned that, "The Chinese presence in Gilgit-Baltistan and the Northern Areas is increasing steadily."

At the same time, Hong Kong-based Chinese controlled media reports in 2010 revealed that China's leadership is considering the possibility of deployment in the future of Chinese Special Forces in these areas to safeguard Chinese assets. Some official Chinese media reports questioned whether Chinese strategic investments in Pakistan's Northern Areas and, in fact Pakistan itself, are safe. They pointed to the new upgraded Karakoram Highway, plans for a railway line running down to Gwadar Port and for which surveys had been completed, and an oil pipeline from Gwadar to Xinjiang.

Similarly, there has been no let-up in China-Pakistan cooperation in the nuclear and space fields, which has actually expanded. China is the single major partner in the development of Pakistan's nuclear weapons and missile programmes. Details of Chinese assistance to Pakistan, initially with the sale of M-9 and M-11 missiles in violation of the Missile Technology Control Regime (MTCR) in the mid-1980s, and later the development of enhanced range and capability missiles are well known. In fact, when leaned upon by the US, Beijing continued to assist Pakistan and brokered and facilitated a missiles-for-nuclear technology deal between Pakistan and North Korea.

China has helped Pakistan with research in space technology in Ormara, Balochistan, under the supervision of SUPARCO (Space and Upper Atmospheric Research Commission) in Karachi and in the development of Pakistan's space launch vehicle. Beijing collaborated, albeit unsuccessfully, to frustrate the Indo-US Civil Nuclear Cooperation Agreement and warned the US that another country could similarly violate the international non-proliferation regime. China soon after contracted to supply two nuclear reactors to Pakistan. Most recent reports state that China is building three 1 GW nuclear power plants at Karachi and another three elsewhere in Pakistan.

Nonetheless, despite these close ties, serious tensions exist in the China-Pakistan relationship with Beijing particularly concerned about Pakistan's internal stability. Attacks on Chinese individuals inside Pakistan, training of Uyghurs in extremist Islamic organisational facilities and the suspected assistance by Pakistan-based religious tanzeems to fundamentalist elements in Xinjiang province are the thorny issues in Sino-Pak relations.

But these tensions have existed for a while. As far back as in the 1990s, Pakistan Prime Minister Benazir Bhutto was "advised" to tighten controls on Pakistani "preachers" travelling to Xinjiang and China re-routed Hajj flights to avoid stopovers in Pakistan. More recently, tension surfaced between Islamabad and Beijing over attacks by Islamist extremists on Chinese workers, who number about 10,000 in Pakistan. China was incensed in Summer 2007 when Islamist militants kidnapped several Chinese citizens whom they accused of running a brothel in Islamabad. Around the same time, three Chinese officials were killed in Peshawar. Several days later, a suicide bomber attacked a group of Chinese engineers in Balochistan. Then Chinese President Hu Jintao called on Pakistani leaders to increase protection for Chinese workers in Pakistan and threatened to stop funding for projects where Chinese workers were under threat.

Pakistan sought to limit damage by intensifying cooperation between Chinese and Pakistan Intelligence agencies to apprehend Uyghurs residing in Pakistan and promising to help China curtail violence in Xinjiang. Chinese leaders used their relationships with Pakistani military officials and Islamist political parties to persuade them to discourage attacks on Chinese interests. China also reached agreements with the Taliban to prevent Uyghur separatists from using Afghanistan as a training ground for militant activities. In late September 2011, China's Vice Premier in charge of Public Security, Meng Jianzhu, visited Pakistan to strengthen cooperation with Islamabad in dealing with the challenge of militancy in Xinjiang. China's interest in supporting counterterrorism initiatives in Pakistan is aimed at containing threats to the internal stability of Xinjiang and safeguarding Chinese investments and personnel in Pakistan.

As ethnic unrest and violence in Xinjiang increases, there are signals that the Chinese government's frustration over Pakistan's inability to check cross-border militancy is increasing. Delegates to the Eleventh and Twelfth National People's Congress (NPC) and senior officials from the Xinjiang Uyghur Autonomous Region pointed to Pakistan as a source for the unrest and went to the unusual extent of naming Pakistan. Local Chinese authorities in Xinjiang charged that the person who mounted the attacks in Kashgar this July had received training in Pakistan, the first time China had publicly pointed a finger at Pakistan. The accusations were repeated in the official English language newspaper, *China Daily*. Similar charges were levelled after the knife attack in Kunming in mid-2014.

Notable, though, is that following the 2008 Mumbai attacks, Beijing did not condemn the Lashkar-e-Taiba (LeT) or criticise the alleged responsibility of Pakistan Inter-Services Intelligence (ISI). There was also an intrusion by Chinese troops in the Ladakh sector during this period. China did, however, eventually vote for sanctions against the Jamaat-ud-Dawa (JuD), the political wing of LeT, at the UN Security Council after having opposed this on three previous occasions.

A factor that will contribute to keeping Sino-Pakistan relations strong is Afghanistan. Apprehending political uncertainty consequent to the impending US withdrawal puts at risk Chinese investments in Afghanistan. Beijing's interest in resource-rich Afghanistan has been evident in the number of MoUs it has signed, though these have not yet materialised into tangible investments. The sanctuary that Islamist extremist elements have enjoyed in Afghanistan poses a serious threat to China's effort to maintain stability in its restive border Xinjiang-Uyghur Autonomous Region, and the prospect of trained Uyghur militants indulging in terrorist acts across China is very troubling. Here, Beijing will seek to secure more direct assistance from Pakistan as well as the Central Asian Republics and possibly utilise the Shanghai Cooperation Organisation.

China's strategic and substantial financial investments in Pakistan, including since 2010 despite the troubled conditions, clearly reveal its long-term stake in Pakistan. These reinforce its interest in ensuring a stable Pakistan. On the question of Pakistan, US and Chinese interests would seem to converge. China's commitment is evidenced by official Chinese media reports that promote favourable rhetoric and project the image of their strong partnership. Chinese Premier Li Keqiang too, during his visit to Pakistan in May 2013, asserted that, "China will give Pakistan every support and assistance and by helping you, we have to help ourselves." The assertion underscores the interdependency in the relationship and highlights that unless there is a drastic deterioration in its internal stability, Pakistan's importance for China under Xi Jinping will remain unchanged.

(The article was published in Seminar Magazine, New Delhi, December 2014).

35

Upgraded Sino-Pak Relationship Increases Pressure on India

At times individual events irreversibly change the dynamics of regional geopolitics and texture of bilateral relations. Xi Jinping's well publicised two-day (April 20-21, 2015) visit to Pakistan, barely three weeks prior to Indian Prime Minister Narendra Modi arriving in China, is one such.

During his visit, Chinese President Xi Jinping announced plans for the China-Pakistan Economic Corridor (CPEC), including construction of a slew of infrastructure projects valued by Pakistani officials at an estimated US$ 46 billion! The visit is the first step towards implementing the recommendation of Chinese strategists that, "China should begin to shape, rather than just integrate into, the regional and international environment because China now has the capacity to do so," and thereby alter the status quo. The visit has decisively altered the strategic environment in the region.

With his decision to visit Pakistan, Xi Jinping became only the second Chinese leader to travel to Pakistan after Hu Jintao (November 23-26, 2006) nine years earlier. Unmistakably deliberate in its timing, the visit was important and marked the initiation of a bold new policy which signalled that in the pursuit of national interest Beijing would ignore diplomatic niceties or the sovereignty concerns and sensitivities of other nations, including its neighbours. This visit has far-reaching implications as well as the potential to alter the geostrategic landscape in South Asia.

Chinese President Xi Jinping's decision to visit Islamabad barely three weeks before Indian Prime Minister Modi's visit to China clearly showed that Beijing no longer feels the need to retain even the diplomatic façade of exhibiting sensitivity to India's concerns and that, in the backdrop of warming

Indo-US relations, will use Pakistan to exert greater pressure on India. Equally clear is that China's leadership has determined that elevating its comprehensive relationship with Pakistan would best serve its strategic interests and that this objective will overshadow any other foreign policy considerations including that of a benign, peaceful neighbourhood. By announcing construction of several major civil and military infrastructure projects as part of the CPEC in Pakistan Occupied Kashmir (POK) and the areas of Gilgit and Baltistan, China has accorded de facto "legitimacy" to Pakistan's illegal occupation of Kashmir, Gilgit and Baltistan as well as Pakistan's illegal cessation in 1963 of the Shaksgam Valley in Pakistan Occupied Kashmir (POK) to China. Beijing has thus chosen—after decades of ambiguity—to side with Pakistan on the Kashmir issue and ignore India's concerns regarding its sovereignty and territorial integrity.

Reflective of China's attitude was Chinese Assistant Foreign Minister Liu Jianchao's remark in mid-April 2015, that "the project between China and Pakistan does not concern the relevant dispute between India and Pakistan. I do not think the Indian side should be over-concerned about that." The comment is at obvious odds with Beijing's prickly reaction to India's offshore exploration efforts in Vietnamese waters and stand on the South China Sea dispute. Equally insensitive were suggestions by senior Chinese Communist Party (CCP) officials and influential Chinese academics, just weeks after Prime Minister Modi's visit to Beijing, that India could even join the CPEC to benefit!

The CPEC sets the stage for China to wield pre-eminent economic, military and diplomatic influence in Pakistan. Chinese President Xi Jinping's decision to construct 51 Chinese-aided infrastructure, energy and military projects reveals that Beijing's commitment to Pakistan is for the foreseeable long term. It implies that power generation, transport, commerce, R&D and the defence of Pakistan will all be increasingly tied to Chinese investment and interests.

Independent credible information states that Beijing very recently informed Islamabad that it is "raising" a Division strength "private army" for deployment in the POK, Gilgit and Baltistan areas. China has already put in place the necessary legal framework permitting deployment of troops and security personnel for safeguarding Chinese national interests abroad.

Pakistan has separately established a 10,000-strong Division comprising elements of the Frontier Corps, Police and Levies under Major General Abdul Rafique to protect Chinese personnel and Chinese-aided projects in Balochistan. Pakistan's newspaper *Dawn* reported that Q.U. Jainging, Deputy Director General of China's Ministry of Public Security (MPS), along with "senior officials" of China's Ministry of Foreign Affairs Ms. Li Li and Zhang Maoming, visited Gwadar in November 2015 to meet Major General Azhar Naveed, Home Secretary of Balochistan, senior Pakistan army and civil officers and assess the security environment.

The report in *Dawn* of January 7, 2016, that Pakistan plans to upgrade the constitutional status of the disputed Gilgit-Baltistan region, is a corollary to Chinese President Xi Jinping's visit to Islamabad. Described by a senior "government" official from Gilgit-Baltistan as intended to give "legal" cover to proposed Chinese investments, since "China cannot afford to invest billions of dollars on a road that passes through a disputed territory claimed both by India and Pakistan," such a move has other major implications. It will integrate this portion of Kashmir with Pakistan by giving it considerably enhanced legislative powers, control of its revenue and allowing it to be represented in Pakistan's federal parliament by two members for the first time—albeit as observers. Pakistani strategic analyst, Ayesha Siddiqa, interpreted the move as possibly demonstrating "Islamabad's desire to end the Kashmir conflict by formally absorbing the territory it controls—and, by extension, recognising New Delhi's claims to parts of the region it controls, such as the Kashmir Valley." She said: "If we begin to absorb it so can India. It legitimises their absorption of the valley."

This could, however, well be the thin end of the wedge. China had indicated its position on Gilgit-Baltistan as early as in the 1980s when its official media referred to this as Pakistani territory. China's official and authoritative news agency Xinhua on March 2, 1984, for example, referred to trade between China's Xinjiang-Uyghur Autonomous Region and "Pakistan's Northern Areas." Two days later on March 4, 1984, another Xinhua despatch mentioned the increased "traditional border trade" between a prefecture of the Xinjiang-Uyghur Autonomous Region and Gilgit in "Northern Pakistan."

China has on separate occasions also laid claim to Kashmir. An official Chinese map published in 1954—still used in Chinese school textbooks—depicts territories taken by "imperialist" powers and which China has said it would "recover." Ladakh is part of these territories along with Arunachal Pradesh and the Andaman Islands. On March 1, 1992, "Shijie Zhishi" (*World Affairs*) published a map showing India without the state of J&K and depicting Kashmir as part of China. Again, in January 1993, the restricted-circulation "internal" version of "Ban Yue Tan" depicted portions of Kashmir and Arunachal Pradesh as part of China. This was repeated on June 16, 1993 in a map published by "Shijie Zhishi" (*World Affairs*) which showed areas of Kashmir and Arunachal Pradesh as parts of China. From August 2010, China designated the entire state of Jammu and Kashmir as "disputed" and began to issue "stapled visas" to residents of the state. More recently, Chinese Foreign Minister Wang Yi, at his press conference in New Delhi in August 2014, reiterated Beijing's stand by making a carefully worded remark that the issue of stapled visas by China were a "unilateral," "flexible" "goodwill gesture" or, in other words, that the status of Arunachal Pradesh and Jammu and Kashmir remains disputed.

Pertinent is that soon after China's intrusion in the Depsang Plains in Ladakh immediately prior to Chinese Premier Li Keqiang's first visit to India as Premier in April 2013, Beijing reiterated its claim over Ladakh. On May 14, 2013, Zhongguo Qingnian Bao (*China Youth News*), the influential high-circulation official mouthpiece of the Communist Youth League (CYL), published a lengthy article alleging that "since 2008, India has used the so-called 'China threat' to launch the largest border troop build-up programme in the past 30 years, greatly increasing troop deployments to Chinese-Indian border areas." Asserting that India had adopted a more "radical border policy" of stepping up patrols and control of border areas, it described the 20-day "tent confrontation" in the Depsang Plains in April 2013, which ended with the simultaneous withdrawal on May 6, 2013, as "the most serious border friction since the armed confrontation in the Sumdorong Chu Valley on the eastern sector of the Chinese-Indian border in 1987." It cautioned that though the stand-off had been "eventually resolved peacefully, its negative impact offers numerous warnings to the world."

Significantly, the Zhongguo Qingnian Bao article elaborated that the Ladakh region "has been part of Tibet since ancient times ... Ladakh was unified with China's Yuan Dynasty as part of Tibet in the thirteenth century. Ladakh was under the jurisdiction of the central government of China's Qing Dynasty until the 1830s. The archduke of Kashmir, which adjoins Ladakh, launched an armed invasion of the Ladakh region in 1843. Although it is under Kashmir, Ladakh shares similarities with Tibet in terms of culture, religion, customs, and language, and it has long been dubbed 'Little Tibet.'" Observing that the British East India Company transported opium to Xinjiang via Ladakh, it said "Britain's unilateral illegal acts sowed the seeds of future trouble, with Aksai Chin becoming a disputed region ... After gaining independence, India inherited everything from British colonists and actively pursued a 'forward policy' based on the illegal borderline drawn up by them. It constantly crossed the traditional customary line to nibble away at Chinese territory in an attempt to occupy the Aksai Chin region. This ultimately triggered a border war between China and India in 1962. During the war, Chinese troops removed all the outposts set up by India across the traditional customary line, including outposts at Tianwentian in the Chip Chap Valley and at Daulat Beg Oldi (DBO), the site of the current 'tent confrontation.' After the war, Chinese and Indian border troops successively withdrew from the Line of Actual Control pursuant to the agreement reached by the two sides, and calm was restored in the Chip Chap Valley." The article pointedly mentioned that,"India and Pakistan fought fiercely for the Siachen Glacier in the 1980s. The Siachen Glacier, located to the west of the Chip Chap Valley, and the DBO are two corners whose positions are prominent because they are two important points that guard India's northern borderline. For this reason, India resumed patrols of the DBO in the late 1980s, but the situation in the region was generally calm because Indian troops only conducted seasonal patrols." It accused India of having "frequently tried to nibble away at our country's territory, including Aksai Chin and other disputed regions. India's military build-up has not only seriously undermined the agreement reached by the two countries to keep their border areas peaceful and calm and posed a material challenge to China's territorial sovereignty but has also greatly increased the odds of friction and conflict between border troops from the two sides. The high incidence of friction in Chinese-Indian border areas in recent years is proof positive of that. For this reason, the 'tent confrontation' is actually a 'microcosm' of a series of incidents of border friction between China and India in recent years, an inevitable result of India's pursuit of a 'forward policy.' Only that the majority of border friction incidents in the past occurred on the Chinese side as a result of provocation by India, but this time around China hit back. India feels that it has gotten the short end of the stick and has started to play the victim by hyping the incident to gain the sympathy of the world. This is really a case of a thief crying thief." Identifying the border issue as a bottleneck impeding the development of relations between the two countries, the article added, "We can expect that border friction incidents will become normal in the future as China's and India's overall national strength continues to grow." It concluded that, "There is little possibility of peacefully resolving the border issue in the short term given the considerable differences between China and India on the border issue. For this reason, the top priority right now for the two countries is to maintain stability in their border areas. India needs to abandon its Cold War mentality."

Anticipating a long-term commitment in the region and further upgrading of the bilateral Sino-Pakistan defence relationship, the PLA too initiated substantive preparations a few months before Xi Jinping's visit. The erstwhile Lanzhou Military Region (MR)—since January 2016 merged into the West Zone—exercised operational jurisdiction across India's Ladakh region, POK and the northern areas occupied by Pakistan, and was the pivotal Military Region involved. It was headed till January 2016—when the extensive ongoing military reforms began—by General Liu Yuejun, a "princeling" like Xi Jinping, who was the Commander during the intrusions in April 2013 in the Depsang Plains and in September 2014 in Chumar and was promoted to the rank of General in early January 2015. Three months prior to Xi Jinping's visit to Islamabad, the Lanzhou MR in January 2015 received directives to particularly begin to "cultivate joint operational command talent"; train selected operational and border defence officers on "informationisation" and "joint operations command"; and guide border defence colleges to train officers in "border discussions" and the usage of mortars. Specifically, the Lanzhou MR was tasked to commence language training for its "backbone personnel" in Pushto and Urdu.

Commitment in this sector was obviously envisaged by China's leadership when it merged the Lanzhou and Chengdu MRs to create the West Zone. Comprising more than half China's land area, 22 per cent of its population and more than one-third of China's land-based military, the newly constituted West Zone represents a strengthened military formation. Merger of the Lanzhou and Chengdu MRs enhances joint planning, coordination and Integrated Joint Operations (IJO). Incorporation of the Qinghai region in the West Zone facilitates the rapid induction and deployment of high-altitude acclimatised and trained troops into Tibet and across Ladakh. Chinese media reports state the West Zone will also focus on "threats in Xinjiang and Tibet as well as Afghanistan and other states that host training bases for separatists and extremists."

Equally pertinent is the appointment of General Zhao Zongqi as Commander of the new West Zone. His credentials indicate he was hand-picked for this post. General Zhao Zongqi is fluent in Arabic and has experience of Tibet. He has battle experience, having participated in the Sino-Vietnam War in 1979 when he is reported to have often disguised himself as a Vietnamese to gather information. He has served over 20 years in Tibet as Deputy Chief of Staff (1984-99) and Chief of Staff (1999-2004) of the Tibet Military District (TMD). Born in 1955, General Zhao Zongqi additionally has experience of Foreign Service consequent to his posting in Tanzania as a Defence Attaché. Creation of the West Zone and appointment of Zhao Zongqi as its Commander reveals China's enhanced and abiding military interest in the region.

Beijing's commitment to the upgraded relationship with Pakistan was evident during Prime Minister Modi's visit to Beijing in May 2015. During their meeting at Xi'an, when Modi raised the border issue Chinese President Xi Jinping sidestepped any substantive response. Instead, Modi was informed of China's stance on Pakistan and the Chinese raised the issue of the Dalai Lama. A few weeks following Prime Minister Modi's visit an Indian delegation met high-level central Chinese Communist Party (CCP) and military officials in Beijing. The Chinese delegation was led by 1952-born He Yiting, hand-picked by Chinese President Xi Jinping in 2013 for appointment as Executive Vice President of the Central Party School. On this occasion too, the Chinese side avoided any discussion on the issue of the border and intrusions and, instead, insisted that India needs to curb its media and restrain hardliners from writing "unhelpful" articles in the press. China's stand regarding the Dalai Lama was read from a prepared text. Explanations were offered about the CPEC emphasising that it was a "commercial venture" and that even India could join to benefit! It was, however, made clear that Beijing would not dilute the CPEC nor change its stand regarding the territories it claims. Towards the end of the day-long deliberations, a retired but influential General still affiliated with a PLA think tank, interjected and underscored China's close ties with Pakistan. He unequivocally stated that India must ease tensions with Pakistan, that it must resolve the Kashmir dispute and that India's relations with China would improve only thereafter. His remarks were not contradicted.

A 28-member delegation of Indian think tanks that travelled to Beijing and Shanghai in December 2015 had a similar experience. They found that in their interactions with Chinese scholars and analysts in six Chinese think tanks and universities as well as the Ministry of Foreign Affairs (MFA), the boundary dispute and other contentious issues like Jammu and Kashmir, Tibet and transnational rivers were not discussed and found place only as isolated remarks or queries.

Beijing's intentions became clear within weeks of the CPEC being announced. It increased its land holding around Gwadar Port and supported Pakistan in the UN by using its veto to protect Lashkar-e-Taiba (LeT) operational Commander Zakiur Rehman Lakhvi, thus disregarding its assurances to India and the international community of working together to eliminate terrorism. Sino-Pakistan defence cooperation accelerated with the US$ 4-5 billion agreement to jointly produce eight submarines—four each in Karachi (where Pakistan is building a submarine training centre) and China. These Yuan-class submarines will be a variant of China's S-20 Yuan Class Type 039A/Type 041 class diesel-electric submarine with air independent propulsion (AIP) and represent "China's largest ever arms deal." Beijing and Islamabad continue to collude to block India's entry to the UNSC. Other areas of probable heightened Sino-Pakistan cooperation and collaboration are Afghanistan and Balochistan. The latter was suggested in an article contributed by former Pakistan Foreign Secretary Riaz Khokhar to China's state-run *Global Times* on April 19, 2014. Pointing quite obviously to this region through which the CPEC passes, he recommended: "The two should also cooperate to identify hostile foreign elements, which create problems to undermine the solid relations between them."

Beijing is unlikely to waver in its commitment to Pakistan in the near to medium term despite the reservations harboured by Chinese strategists about Pakistan's stability or the differences beginning to appear inside Pakistan between provincial politicians and the military, over the CPEC. Well informed senior Chinese academics specialising on Pakistan-Afghanistan said that Pakistan is China's "only friend" and privately confided that the CPEC is primarily a political decision. Talking to the *New York Times* on February 9, 2016, Prof. Yan Xuetong, Director of the Institute for International Relations at Beijing's Tsinghua University and an influential Chinese strategic analyst close to Xi Jinping, similarly said: "China has only one real ally, Pakistan."

For India, in the near to medium term these developments will imply difficulties in Afghanistan, increased military pressure along its borders, and enhanced Pakistan-instigated activity in Kashmir and on the Kashmir issue. China will fully back Pakistan's efforts to secure predominant influence over any post-US Afghanistan regime, acquire so-called "strategic depth," and exclude or marginalise India in Afghanistan. US, Chinese and Pakistani interests converge on Afghanistan, as evidenced by only the US, China, Pakistan and Afghanistan deciding to hold direct peace talks with insurgent groups in Pakistan next week. Beijing's interest will be in getting India to acquiesce to Pakistan's occupation of Kashmir, Gilgit and Baltistan. It could exploit its contact with the Hurriyat for a role in the Kashmir issue. India should anticipate that Pakistan, emboldened by its relationship with China, will stir up the Kashmir issue, including through supporters in Kashmir and inside India. Reliable reports suggest that Pakistan has established a chain of "madrasas" along the border opposite India's Bikaner District to support the launch into India of cadres of the Lashkar-e-Taiba (LeT), Jaish-e-Mahmud (JeM) and Hizb-ul-Mujahiddin (HuM). It is also setting up a new outfit called the Ahle Summat Wal Jamaat (ASWJ) to especially target India's Sunni Muslim population. It would be prudent for India to craft a definitive long-term policy on Kashmir where "separatist" elements have no place. China and Pakistan will also both keep India under military pressure.

(The article was published in Centre for China Analysis and Strategy, New Delhi, March 2016).

36

Implications of the China-Pakistan Economic Corridor

The China-Pakistan Economic Corridor (CPEC), announced during Chinese President Xi Jinping's well-publicised two-day (April 20-21, 2015) visit to Pakistan and with a value estimated by Pakistanis at US$ 46 billion, is a bold geo-economic initiative which alters the strategic environment in the region. It is the first step towards implementing the recommendation of Chinese strategists that "China should begin to shape, rather than just integrate into, the regional and international environment because China now has the capacity to do so." It has begun to alter the status quo and potentially bend borders in the region.

The CPEC sets the stage for China to wield pre-eminent economic, military and diplomatic influence in Pakistan. The agreement for Chinese companies to construct 51 Chinese-aided infrastructure, energy and military projects shows that Beijing's engagement with Pakistan is for the foreseeable long term. It seeks to bind Pakistan to China as power generation, transport, commerce, R&D and the defence of Pakistan will all be increasingly tied to Chinese investment and interests. Almost six months before Xi Jinping's visit to Islamabad an influential senior Chinese academic, specialising in researching Afghanistan-Pakistan and who is occasionally called to brief the Chinese Communist Party (CCP) Central Committee's (CC) Politburo, said in private conversation that, "while we had earlier purchased the loyalty of the Pakistanis, now we will buy Pakistan!"

With his decision to visit Pakistan, Xi Jinping became only the second Chinese leader to travel to Pakistan after Hu Jintao (November 23-26, 2006) nine years earlier. Unmistakably deliberate in its timing just three weeks prior to Indian Prime Minister Modi's arrival in China, the visit was important and marked the initiation of a bold new policy. It signalled that in the pursuit of national interest Beijing no longer feels the need to retain even the diplomatic façade of showing sensitivity to India's concerns and that, in the backdrop of warming Indo-US relations, will use Pakistan to exert greater pressure on India. Equally clear is that China's leadership has determined that elevating its comprehensive relationship with Pakistan would best serve its strategic interests and that this objective will overshadow any other foreign policy considerations including that of ensuring a friendly, peaceful neighbourhood.

By announcing the construction of several major civil and military infrastructure projects as part of the CPEC in Pakistan Occupied Kashmir (POK) and the areas of Gilgit and Baltistan, China has accorded de facto "legitimacy" to Pakistan's illegal occupation of Kashmir, Gilgit and Baltistan as well as Pakistan's illegal cessation in 1963 of the Shaksgam Valley in Pakistan Occupied Kashmir (POK) to China. Beijing has thus dispelled decades of ambiguity to side with Pakistan on the Kashmir issue ignoring India's concerns regarding its sovereignty and territorial integrity. Within weeks of Xi Jinping's visit, senior Chinese leaders and officials were describing Pakistan as China's "ally" and "only friend." This enhanced relationship was publicised when Prof. Yan Xuetong, Director of the Institute for International Relations at Beijing's Tsinghua University and an influential Chinese strategic analyst close to Xi Jinping, told the *New York Times* on February 9, 2016, that, "China has only one real ally, Pakistan." The CPEC has far-reaching implications.

Reflective of China's attitude was Chinese Assistant Foreign Minister Liu Jianchao's condescending remark in mid-April 2015, that, "the project between China and Pakistan does not concern the relevant dispute between India and Pakistan. I do not think the Indian side should be over-concerned about that." The comment is at obvious odds with Beijing's prickly reaction to India's offshore exploration efforts in Vietnamese waters and stand on the South China Sea dispute. Equally insensitive were suggestions by senior Chinese Communist Party (CCP) officials and influential Chinese academics, just weeks after Prime Minister Modi's visit to Beijing, that India could join the CPEC and benefit!

Over the years, China has built a solid constituency in Pakistan's Army, bureaucracy and diplomatic corps, all of which are strong supporters of close strategic ties with China. They have backed the development and management of Gwadar Port by China and the CPEC. Since 2010, more officers of the Pakistan armed forces undergo training in China than the US. In April 2015, just weeks before Xi Jinping's arrival in Pakistan, former Pakistan Ambassador Riaz Khokar hinted at the need for elevating the existing intelligence cooperation and wrote in China's state-run *Global Times* that the two countries must identify hostile elements operating in Balochistan. Later, in an article in *Dawn* on April 17, 2016, prior to the meeting between the Foreign Secretaries of India and Pakistan, former Pakistan Ambassador Munir Akram said, "So long as India persists in its reported support for the Tehreek-e-Taliban Pakistan, and the Balochi Liberation Army, Pakistan would be unwise to give up the option of supporting the legitimate struggle of the Kashmiri people for freedom and self-determination." Calling for "much closer ties with China," he described strategic cooperation with China as critical. Despite the opposition and reservations expressed by some Pakistani provincial politicians, the Pakistan Army under General Chief Raheel Sharif has staunchly backed the CPEC.

Opposition to the CPEC centres primarily on the terms for loans with quite a few prominent Pakistani journalists and academics pointing out that the interest rates are high and the projects, especially the energy projects, are commercially unviable. Pakistan's provincial and local politicians are objecting to the paths designated for the transportation corridors and the location of projects, with Punjab and Sindh accused of having cornered the majority. There is also widespread dissatisfaction at the employment only of Chinese workers and the project construction sites being isolated inside 10-foot high walled perimeters ostensibly for security. Locals in Balochistan and the Northern Areas also reportedly resent the exploitation of their natural resources and not being employed on these projects. This has prompted critics to question the supposed benefits accruing to Pakistan and Pakistanis and the burden of debt that the CPEC will place on Pakistan. Security is a serious concern after the attacks on Chinese workers in Balochistan, and now visiting Chinese officials and workers move around Gwadar only with heavy security provided by the army and police. The attacks have the potential to spread, though, as indicated by the bombing in Karachi in May 2016, when a Chinese engineer and his driver were injured. Responsibility for the bombing was claimed by Sindhudesh Revolutionary Army, a little-known separatist group advocating the independence of Sindh.

To assuage the concern of Chinese companies and their employees working on Chinese-aided projects in Balochistan and other areas, the Pakistan army has raised a 10,000-strong division comprising elements of the Frontier Corps, police and Levies under Major General Abdul Rafique. In November 2015, Q. U. Jainging, Deputy Director General of China's Ministry of Public Security (MPS), along with "senior officials" of China's Ministry of Foreign Affairs, Ms. Li Li and Zhang Maoming, visited Gwadar to assess the security environment and met Major General Azhar Naveed, Home Secretary of Balochistan and senior Pakistan army and civil officers. Since then there have been a number of senior-level Chinese security and military delegations to Pakistan including to CPEC project sites. The delegations have met local politicians, government officials and interacted closely with Pakistan army and ISI officers in Islamabad, Rawalpindi, Gwadar and Quetta. Pakistan-based Chinese diplomats have also been attending coordination meetings. At least two conferences were held in Gwadar and Quetta in April this year. A two-day (April 11-13, 2016) "national conference" held in Gwadar, for example, was attended by politicians, influential citizens and over 30 Pakistan Army and ISI officials and Chinese diplomats from Islamabad.

While China has appreciated the Pakistan Army's new security force, there is credible information that in early January 2016, Beijing informed Islamabad that it is "raising" a division-strength "private army" in China for deployment to protect the CPEC, including in the POK, Gilgit and Baltistan areas. The Chinese security personnel are to be deployed in addition to the force provided by Pakistan. China already has in place the necessary legal framework permitting deployment of its troops and security personnel abroad for protecting China's national interests.

Other steps are being taken to safeguard China's investments. A report in *Dawn* of January 7, 2016, disclosed that Pakistan plans to upgrade the constitutional status of the disputed Gilgit-Baltistan region as a corollary to the CPEC. A senior "government" official from Gilgit-Baltistan described this as intended to give "legal" cover to proposed Chinese investments since "China cannot afford to invest billions of dollars on a road that passes through a disputed territory claimed both by India and Pakistan." China had indicated its position on Gilgit-Baltistan as early as in the 1980s when its official media referred to this as Pakistani territory.

The move also has other major implications. It will integrate this portion of Kashmir with Pakistan by giving it considerably enhanced legislative powers, control of its revenue and allowing it to be represented in Pakistan's federal parliament by two members for the first time—albeit as observers. Pakistani strategic analyst, Ayesha Siddiqa, interpreted the move as possibly demonstrating "Islamabad's desire to end the Kashmir conflict by formally absorbing the territory it controls—and, by extension, recognising New Delhi's claims to parts of the region it controls, such as the Kashmir Valley." She said: "If we begin to absorb it so can India. It legitimises their absorption of the valley."

This could, however, well be the thin end of the wedge as Pakistan appears to have got emboldened following the upgrading of its relationship with China. Examples are its renewed efforts to raise the Kashmir issue internationally, the uptick of restiveness and violence in Kashmir over the past year, and higher likelihood of further terrorist attacks elsewhere in India. Beijing had, incidentally, earlier hinted at its ability to meddle in India's internal affairs and specifically in J&K, when in 2010 a so-called Chinese NGO invited Hurriyat "leader" Mirwaiz Umar Farooq to China. Mirwaiz Umar Farooq had then stated that China has a role in settlement of the Kashmir issue. More recently on March 14, 2016, the *Deccan Chronicle* quoted the hardline Pakistan-backed Syed Ali Shah Geelani of the Hurriyat Conference as describing "China as a reliable friend of the people of Kashmir" and saying, "it is extremely thankful to Beijing" for its "unconditional support" and for not recognising the Himalayan State's "illegal and forced occupation by India."

China has on separate occasions also laid claim to Kashmir. An official Chinese map published in 1954—still used in Chinese school textbooks—depicts territories taken by "imperialist" powers and which China has said it would "recover." Ladakh is part of these territories along with Arunachal

Pradesh and the Andaman Islands. On March 1, 1992, "Shijie Zhishi" (*World Affairs*) published a map showing India without the state of J&K and depicting Kashmir as part of China. There have been other such claims. From August 2010, China designated the entire state of Jammu and Kashmir as "disputed" and began to issue "stapled visas" to residents of the state. Chinese Foreign Minister, Wang Yi, at his press conference in New Delhi in August 2014, reiterated Beijing's stand in a carefully worded statement asserting that the issue of stapled visas by China were a "unilateral," "flexible," "goodwill gesture" or, in other words, that the status of Arunachal Pradesh and Jammu and Kashmir remains disputed.

Pertinent is that soon after China's intrusion in the Depsang Plains in Ladakh immediately prior to Chinese Premier Li Keqiang's first visit to India as Premier in April 2013, Beijing reiterated its claim over Ladakh. On May 14, 2013, Zhongguo Qingnian Bao (*China Youth News*), the influential high-circulation official mouthpiece of the Communist Youth League (CYL), published a lengthy article claiming that the Ladakh region "has been part of Tibet since ancient times ..." and that "Ladakh was under the jurisdiction of the central government of China's Qing Dynasty until the 1830s." It added, "Although it is under Kashmir, Ladakh shares similarities with Tibet in terms of culture, religion, customs, and language, and it has long been dubbed 'Little Tibet.'"

The CPEC has a definite military component. A secure fibre-optic link connecting Kashgar in the Xinjiang-Uyghur Autonomous Region with the Pakistan Army GHQ in Rawalpindi is being laid at a cost of US$ 44 million, highlighting the close military coordination between Pakistan and China. It goes via Khunjerab, Karimabad, Gilgit, Babusar Top, Naran, Mansehra and Jharikas. Kashgar is the headquarters of the South Xinjiang Military District of the erstwhile Lanzhou Military Region, now called the Xinjiang Military Command. The latter is merged in the People's Liberation Army's (PLA) Western Theatre Command or West Zone. The responsibilities of the PLA's West Zone, established in January 2016, include safeguarding the borders with Afghanistan, Pakistan, protecting Chinese investments and projects in the CPEC, protecting China's land frontiers with India and focusing on "threats in Xinjiang and Tibet as well as Afghanistan and other states that host training bases for separatists and extremists." Instructions received in January 2015 by the erstwhile Lanzhou Military Region confirmed that the West Zone's commitment in Afghanistan, Pakistan and the CPEC are long-term. The instructions directed that selected operational and border defence officers be trained in "informationisation" and "joint operations command," that border defence colleges train officers in "border discussions" and the usage of mortars, and, specifically, that its "backbone personnel" be trained in the Pushto and Urdu languages.

The West Zone's operational jurisdiction is anticipated, in course of time, to expand to include Gwadar port and China's considerable economic interests and investments in eastern Africa where it has very recently signed an agreement for a base at Djibouti. China's interest in Gwadar, where it has "sovereign guarantees to the port facilities" and where reports claim it has set up electronic eavesdropping posts to monitor shipping traffic through the Straits of Hormuz and the Arabian Sea, has been evident since 2002. A total of nine projects valued at approximately US$ 1 billion (or 2% of US$ 46 billion), each intended to augment China's commercial and military capacity, are now planned in and around Gwadar as part of the CPEC. These are a new international airport (US$230 million); a Gwadar Easterly Expressway (US$ 141 million); construction of breakwaters (US$ 123 million); dredging of berthing areas and channels (US$ 27 million); infrastructure for Free Zone and EPZs and port-related industries (US$ 32 million); fresh water treatment and supply plant (US$ 130 million); hospital at Gwadar (US$ 100 million); and a technical and vocational institute (US$ 10 million). China's continuing interest in Gwadar was underscored in April 2016 when, to calm differences over implementation of CPEC projects, it decided to give the estimated US$ 230 million required to construct the new international airport at Gwadar as a grant. Beijing is yet to decide whether interest will be charged on the loans to be given for the other projects in and around Gwadar or whether these will also be grants.

Tensions between China and Pakistan centring on the CPEC were especially high from early this year till at least end April, with Pakistan complaining that it had done all that was asked but China appeared to be dragging its feet. Acknowledging that the CPEC is a "multi-billion-dollar mega project based on the principle of mutual consultation," Pakistani officials complained about undesirable delays caused by differences regarding ease of engineering, economic benefits and calculations of costs of particular projects. Concern was voiced that the situation with the CPEC had almost reached the stage where "mutual consultation turns into mutual accusation." At the end of April 2016, China informed Pakistani officials that it would adopt more flexible financial arrangements favouring Pakistan. Beijing said it would urge Chinese companies to put money into social welfare projects and invest in "needy short-term projects" on the basis of a grant or zero interest loan. Among the social welfare projects identified are a water treatment plant in Gwadar and a hospital at Gwadar. This is in addition to the US$ 230 million, estimated as the cost of construction of the new international airport at Gwadar, that China is giving as a grant.

China has earmarked the financial institutions established by it, like the Asian Infrastructure Investment Bank (AIIB), BRICS New Development Bank, Silk Road Fund and possibly a SCO Development Bank, for aiding the "One Belt, One Road" (OBOR) of which the CPEC is a part. The AIIB is to serve as the financing arm of OBOR. China's decision to use these banks, especially the AIIB and BRICS New Development Bank, to extend fiscal assistance to Pakistan for projects in the CPEC in furtherance of its strategic objectives immediately puts India to the test. On May 9, 2016, the official English-language *China Daily* reported the AIIB's announcement that it would co-finance a US$ 300 million motorway project in Pakistan with the Asian Development Bank (ADB). Asserting that "Pakistan is a strong ally of China," the report indicated there would be more such projects. The case is identical with that when China used its economic clout with the ADB to block developmental assistance for poverty alleviation projects in India's northeastern state of Arunachal Pradesh on the grounds that it was "disputed." The CPEC too goes through India-claimed and disputed territory.

The upgraded relationship with China following the agreement on the CPEC is already yielding Pakistan dividends, despite the reservations harboured by Chinese strategists about Pakistan's stability or differences inside Pakistan between provincial politicians and the military over the CPEC. Beijing's commitment to the upgraded relationship with Pakistan was evident during Prime Minister Modi's visit to Beijing in May 2015. When Modi raised the border issue with Chinese President Xi Jinping at X'ian, the latter sidestepped any substantive response. Instead, Modi was informed of China's stance on Pakistan and the Chinese raised the issue of the Dalai Lama. A few weeks following Prime Minister Modi's visit an Indian delegation met high-level central Chinese Communist Party (CCP) and military officials in Beijing. The Chinese delegation, led by the Executive Vice President of the Central Party School, He Yiting, similarly avoided any discussion on the border issue or border intrusions. Towards the end of the deliberations, however, a retired but influential General still affiliated with a PLA think tank, underscored China's close ties with Pakistan. He unequivocally stated that India "must ease tensions with Pakistan, that it must resolve the Kashmir dispute" and that India's relations with China would improve thereafter. His remarks were not contradicted. The upgraded relationship appears to have emboldened Pakistan. Pakistan Army Chief General Raheel Sharif's warning early this year that "Kashmir is an unfinished agenda of partition. Pakistan and Kashmir are inseparable," is a pointer. Beijing is unlikely to waver in its commitment to Pakistan in the near to mid-term.

There have been additional substantive benefits for Pakistan. During the proposed meeting between Chinese President Xi Jinping and Pakistan Prime Minister Nawaz Sharif on the sidelines of the Nuclear Summit (March 31-April 1, 2016)—which Nawaz Sharif finally did not attend—the two were to discuss China "extending diplomatic or other substantive support" to Pakistan to counter US insistence that Pakistan go slow on the development of its tactical nuclear weapons. Bilateral Intelligence cooperation has also increased and now encompasses sharing of operational information on Afghanistan, developments relating to the Taliban and its leaders, and the tracking of operational activities of Afghanistan's NSD and India's R&AW. Yet another demonstration of Beijing's support to Pakistan is China's stance at the UN Sanctions Committee where it has placed holds on India's request to list Syed Salahuddin of the United Jihad Council; to investigate the source of Lashkar-e-Taiba (LeT) chief Hafiz Saeed's funds despite financial sanctions; to ask Pakistan how LeT commander Zaki-ur Rahman Lakhvi posted bail and Pakistan let its courts set him free; and, most recently, the blocking of India's request in the case of Jaish-e-Mohammed (JeM) chief, Masood Azhar. This has emboldened terrorist leaders in Pakistan. Pakistan and China continue to work in collusion to ensure that India does not enter an expanded UN Security Council as a Permanent Member with full veto rights. A vivid example of such cooperation was their coordinated activity recently during the process of India's admission to the Nuclear Suppliers Group (NSG). This cooperation will extend to the Shanghai Cooperation Organisation (SCO).

Problems and differences between China and Pakistan are likely to surface in the next few years. Beijing, though, will be reluctant to forgo its strategic investments in Pakistan and will try to maintain the relationship but while holding back on further financial investments. Beijing's current track record of fulfilling committed investments is barely 6-12% and this is unlikely to change leading to frustration in Pakistan. The CPEC will directly contribute to this dissatisfaction as, once the thermal power projects in POK, Gilgit, Baltistan and Balochistan are completed, the tariff per unit of electricity will be excessive as coal will be imported from Xinjiang. Further, as Pakistan begins to repay the loans, Islamabad will realise that the interest rates are too high and impose strains on Pakistan's finances. Renegotiating them will be almost impossible as Sri Lankan President, Maithripala Sirisena, discovered during his visit in March 2016 to Beijing, when the Chinese declined to renegotiate terms on the plea that they are part of the "One Belt, One Road" which is Xi Jinping's personal initiative and any amendment would be a "loss of face"! Finally, the CPEC will facilitate the passage of radical Islamist elements, including that of returning battle-hardened Uyghurs, into China's sensitive and restive Xinjiang-Uyghur Autonomous Region. Underscoring the steadily increasing radicalisation of Pakistan, the Chief of the Jamaat-ud-Dawa (JuD) and Lashkar-e-Taiba (LeT), Hafiz Saeed told the Nawaz Sharif government in late May 2016 to, "show some courage and direct China to stay away from hurting Islamic sentiments." A high-powered delegation of Pakistan's Ministry of Religious Affairs subsequently left for China on June 28, 2016 to check the veracity of reports that Chinese authorities have banned fasting in the holy month of Ramadan in the Xinjiang-Uyghur Autonomous Region. Hafiz Saeed is the first Pakistani national to express concern about the plight of Muslims in China. The ISIS has separately earlier targeted the Xinjiang-Uyghur Autonomous Region. These are signs that clearly portend trouble.

Meanwhile, in the near to medium term India can expect to come under increased pressure. China will fully back Pakistan's efforts to secure predominant influence over any post-US Afghanistan regime, acquire so-called "strategic depth," and exclude or marginalise India in Afghanistan. US, Chinese and Pakistani interests converge on Afghanistan, as evidenced by only the US, China, Pakistan and Afghanistan deciding to hold direct peace talks with the insurgent groups in Pakistan. Some academics and officials in the US are additionally recommending that the US should participate in the CPEC. Beijing's interest will be in getting India to acquiesce to Pakistan's occupation of Kashmir, Gilgit and Baltistan. It could exploit its contact with the Hurriyat for a role in the Kashmir issue. China and Pakistan will both keep India under military and diplomatic pressure.

(The article was published by Centre for China Analysis and Strategy (CCAS) and Vivekananda International Foundation (VIF), New Delhi, July 19, 2016).

37

Does the China-Pakistan Economic Corridor Really Help Pakistan?

The China-Pakistan Economic Corridor (CPEC) encapsulates a number of China's strategic objectives and cannot, therefore, be viewed only as a silver bullet that will lift Pakistan out of its economic difficulties or solve the issues afflicting its society. The first unstated but major obstacle is that the objectives of China and Pakistan are quite different—while China has a larger strategic objective and views it as an essential stepping stone towards global leadership, Pakistan sees it as a solution for its economic difficulties. To put it in context, the CPEC is part of the "One Belt, One Road" (OBOR) strategic geo-economic initiative launched by Xi Jinping with the express purpose of making China a global power by 2049, or the hundredth anniversary of the People's Republic of China (PRC)!

Since particularly the 18th Party Congress in November 2012, China has switched to an increasingly assertive and muscular foreign policy focused on China attaining its self-perceived global status as a world power. In an article on January 28, 2014, Prof. Yan Xuetong, a reputed Chinese strategist with proximity to Xi Jinping and Dean of the Institute of International Studies at Tsinghua University, said the new policy decided at the path breaking Conference on Peripheral Diplomacy convened in Beijing in October 2013, aims at "achieving global leadership" for China with emphasis on the "China Dream".

A large part of what drives today's Chinese leaders—and particularly Xi Jinping -- is a strong sense of destiny manifest in the China Dream. The China Dream is the desire to redress the "humiliations" inflicted on China for over 110 years in the Nineteenth Century when it suffered repeated military defeats and "unequal" treaties were imposed. During that period China lost territory, had entire provinces taken over, puppet regimes installed, and was coerced to trade on disadvantageous terms by victorious foreign powers who established "concessions" or enclaves mainly in coastal cities. Official Chinese accounts describe the period as when China's rulers were forced "to surrender sovereign rights and bring humiliation to the country." The need to redress this humiliation is today a recurrent theme in the statements of Chinese leaders and the China Dream.

Cognisant of the growth in China's economic and military might, the Conference on Peripheral Diplomacy decided on a more robust foreign policy reinforced by military muscle. The aim of the new foreign policy is to provide China's leaders an expanded set of strategic options and "ample chances to avoid using 'military conquests' to achieve regional dominance."

It designated countries as "friend" or "enemy", with "friends" benefitting from the gains flowing from China's development and rising global influence. It envisaged regional or subregional "cooperative" security agreements. An objective is to create a "community of common destiny" with select countries. It simultaneously emphasised that those who are hostile to China, or oppose it, will be confronted with sustained periods of tough sanctions and isolation. Chinese strategic analysts have been advocating that China should now, since it has the capacity to do so, change the status quo to its advantage while avoiding military conflict and begin to shape the international and regional environment. They argue that China should take the initiative and create a favourable periphery.

The expectation is that the CPEC, which is a part of the OBOR, will give a much needed fillip to China's economy and stature by putting to use the hitherto idle infrastructure technology capabilities of its State-owned Enterprises (SoE), huge unemployed labour, and unutilised fiscal reserves available with its banks, in revenue-generating ventures abroad. It will facilitate China in its quest to extend economic influence and military power well beyond its borders to dominate the region. China has, therefore, been aggressively pushing the OBOR with, for example, Nepal where 184 of 312 roads connect Tibet with South Asia, Bangladesh, Bhutan and India. Beijing's close ties with Pakistan since 1951 and the anti-India attitude of both facilitated the CPEC. Its operationalisation impacts adversely on India's sovereignty and territorial integrity—as it alters the status quo in the region and begins to bend borders and shape the geopolitical environment—and its military content lends weight to the prospect of a two-front war.

Assessments of the CPEC's benefits to Pakistan vary considerably, but a recent study by Deloitte is interesting. Pointing out that the volume of trade between Pakistan and China had increased to US$ 16 billion by 2014-15, the study alluded to impending benefits. It estimated that if all planned projects are implemented, their value would exceed all foreign direct investment in Pakistan since 1970 and would be equivalent to 17% of Pakistan's gross domestic product in 2015. It further estimated that the CPEC will create some 700,000 direct jobs during 2015–30 adding up to 2.5 percentage points to the country's growth. Importantly, it noted that the Karakoram Highway between Rawalpindi and the Chinese border will be completely reconstructed and overhauled and Pakistan's railway network will be extended to eventually connect to China's Southern Xinjiang Railway in Kashgar. Almost 80% of China's oil is currently transported over 16,000 km from the Strait of Malacca to Shanghai, but once Gwadar becomes operational this distance would reduce to less than 5,000 km. The CPEC will also open immense economic opportunities for Pakistan and physically connect China to its markets in Asia, Europe and beyond. According to *China Daily*, the energy projects would provide up to 16,400 MW of energy altogether with over 10,400 MW of energy generating capacity developed between 2018 and 2020 as part of the corridor's fast-tracked "Early Harvest" project.

The assessment of the Deloitte study is not mirrored in the numerous comments and articles by Pakistani politicians, journalists and academics. While they are appreciative that the CPEC has brought a massive influx of much needed infrastructure aid and investment to Pakistan, they are very apprehensive that Pakistan risks losing sovereignty to China.

The study neither takes into account the high energy production cost of these power plants. With fuel imported from China's Xinjiang Autonomous Region the cost per unit of electricity generated by the new power plants would be double the present, imposing a very high burden on the consumers. Early indicators suggest the time and production estimates are exaggerated.

Politicians in Pakistan's provinces have complained for the past year that locals are not getting employment in CPEC projects and are not even being allowed access as the sites are "protected" by 10-foot high perimeter walls. On the other hand, they say, there has been a huge influx of Chinese labour. Serious concern has been voiced by politicians, academics and journalists about Pakistan's mounting debt and the anticipated high cost of electricity from the new energy projects.

Expressing concern about the viability of the CPEC, Ali Malik, a researcher at the South Asia Programme at Hudson Institute in Washington DC, on January 4, 2017, pointed out that "most of Pakistan's urban centres are located in the east not the west and that inter-provincial resentment and differences have flared, with provinces in the west accusing the centre of favouring the country's eastern portion where the majority of Pakistan's economic bases are located." Contributing to this is the historically poor record of the Pakistan government in fulfilling past guarantees of investment. One article disclosed that because of inadequate investment in infrastructure and chronic electricity shortages, factories in Khyber-Pakhtunkhwa (KP) have been closing down. Mounting criticism has prompted Pakistan Prime Minister Nawaz Sharif to promise that 12 out of 48 special economic zones will be built in Khyber-Pakhtunkhwa (KP) and Balochistan. Nonetheless, doubts persist whether the central government—seen as unstable—will be able to deliver on its promises.

There are other questions about the economic viability of the CPEC, for which the bulk of financing has come as loan-based financing and not unconditional grants by the Chinese government. Though the loans are given to individual construction companies involved with the projects, there are significant risks for the government. Many of the power projects are under sovereign guarantees thus making the Pakistan government responsible if these companies fail to meet their debt obligations. Pakistan's current liabilities (debt), both private and public, have reached a staggering 75 per cent of GDP (Rs. 22.5 trillion). In 2015, the circular debt of Pakistan's energy sector rose 23 per cent to Rs. 633 billion. In November 2016, Pakistan was unable to repay Rs. 136.5 billion in bank loans of the energy sector and it postponed payment for another two years. Many provincial politicians, journalists and academics feel Pakistan is taking a gamble by putting all its eggs in the CPEC "basket" and hoping that the benefits will be able to outweigh the risks. They stress that there is no "Plan B" if things go awry.

In a recent report the State Bank of Pakistan pointed to heavy borrowings from Chinese commercial banks at questionable rates to pay for Chinese machinery imports. Loans to Pakistan from China during the first quarter this financial year jumped to US$ 979 million, compared to US$ 138 million during the comparable period last year. Saying he does not know what the terms of these loans from China are, the Governor of the State Bank of Pakistan Ashraf Wathra in December 2015 said the "CPEC needs to be more transparent." He added that he does not "know out of the US$ 46 billion how much is debt, how much is equity and how much is in kind." The State Bank of Pakistan, meanwhile, recently confirmed that Pakistan's tax collection is unable to pay for debt servicing. The IMF has also urged caution on Pakistan. Some analysts say much of the criticism of the CPEC is possibly based on hypotheticals and "what-ifs," but concede that the lack of a contingency plan is a major source of anxiety. The example is cited of Sri Lanka which, saddled with unpayable Chinese loans, is now set to allow US$ 1.4 billion debt for 80 per cent equity swap that will allow China a 99-year lease on the Hambantota port and 1,500 acres of adjacent land where the Chinese are expected to set up a Special Economic Zone. Similarities between Sri Lanka's Hambantota and Gwadar are unmistakable. In Gwadar, the Chinese have signed a 40-year lease on 2,300 acres of land to develop a Special Economic Zone and an international airport.

Amidst rising criticism in Pakistan about the CPEC, the official *China Daily* on September 14, 2016, reflected Beijing's growing concern and expressed apprehension about the successful implementation of the CPEC. It warned that China and Pakistan should be prepared for "potential setbacks" and that implementation of the CPEC might slow down due to "security reasons" as the project passes through some turbulent areas like Gwadar and Kashmir. Concern was also expressed about the likely poor rate of return of Chinese investments under the CPEC. The *China Daily* article even suggested that instead of relying too much on Pakistan, China should focus on economic cooperation with Southeast Asian countries.

China's Ambassador in Pakistan Sun Weidong met Pakistan Tehreek-e-Insaf (PTI) chief Imran Khan on October 18, 2016 to seek assurances that projects under the CPEC would not be harmed or sabotaged in Khyber Pakhtunkhwa province. Separately, Khyber Pakhtunkhwa took matters concerning the CPEC to court. China retaliated and denied visas in November 2016, to a high level delegation from Khyber Pakhtunkhwa, comprising Ministers and senior bureaucrats, who were to travel to China to study the mass transit transport system. Chinese officials also sought to directly dispel misgivings about the CPEC and Zheng Xiaosong, Vice Minister of the CCP CC's International Department, met representatives of political parties in Islamabad on December 20, 2016, and urged them to unite for the success of the CPEC. Assuring them of China's assistance he said both would jointly work for it. Muhammad Lijian Zhao, a senior Chinese diplomat based in Islamabad, also sought the Pakistani public's support on December 20, 2016, to counter "disinformation" over CPEC. He criticised those maligning the CPEC and claimed the project enjoyed popular public support.

These concerns compelled China to take the unusual step of holding the Joint Cooperation Council (JCC)—the highest decision-making body of CPEC—in Beijing during December 2016, where for the first time the chief ministers of the five constituent units of Pakistan were invited. Beijing calmed the parties with assurances of evenly-distributed industrial estates and mass-transit systems. However, misgivings remain.

Additional worries are that the CPEC's success depends entirely on Pakistan's ability to export its goods and services and show a strong rise in exports. Pakistani analysts warn that these sectors of the economy would have to compete with the influx of cheaper Chinese imports that have the ability to strangle the domestic market. Chinese imports have, incidentally, already grown from 4 per cent in 2010 to 9 per cent in 2015. Economists say that if the downward trend of exports and increase in imports continues, Pakistan will face a serious balance of payments crisis. Others suggest that Pakistan is already on the verge of experiencing a crisis as debt servicing will increase to between 30% and 60% by 2020 because of the CPEC and Pakistan's purchase of Eurobonds. There is a general view that to safeguard its economic future Pakistan must be cautious in how it implements and administers completion of the CPEC. More importantly, they assert that the central government must be honest about the nature of Chinese investment as Pakistan risks losing its sovereignty and being beholden to China and exploited by it for its natural resources and geostrategic location.

For China, however, the centrepieces of the CPEC are the Gwadar Port and area of the Karakoram in the north. It has eyed Gwadar for years and agreed to fund its development only after Pakistan agreed to grant it "sovereign guarantees to the port facilities" in 2007. The importance of Gwadar for China is emphasised by the inclusion of Gwadar International Airport and major development works of Gwadar Port in the CPEC's first phase with completion targeted for 2017. A total of 9 projects valued at approx US$ 1 billion, each intended to augment China's commercial and military capacity, are planned in and around Gwadar. China is reported to have established electronic eavesdropping posts at Gwadar. The CPEC's first phase also includes expansion of the Karakoram Highway, connecting Pakistan's railway network to China's Southern Xinjiang Railway in Kashgar, and placement of a secure fibre-optic line between Kashgar and Rawalpindi, all projects of military significance. Interesting is that when tensions rose early last year because of Pakistani complaints about rising costs and the slow pace of work, China sought to assuage Pakistan and said many of the projects around Gwadar would be grants!

The security of Gwadar is a source of continuing concern for the Chinese and has imposed a heavy financial burden on Pakistan. In January 2016, the Pakistan Navy decided to deploy two additional Marine Battalions to provide around the clock security at Gwadar. On September 21, in the wake of the deterioration in Indo-Pakistan relations over Kashmir, Chinese Premier Li Keqiang publicly expressed reservations and told Pakistan Prime Minister Nawaz Sharif that he "hoped" Pakistan can continue to provide protection to the CPEC and Chinese personnel in Pakistan. The official Chinese newspaper *Global Times* similarly warned that "the increasing cost of security is becoming a big problem in efficiently pushing forward the project." In November 2016, during the inaugural Kashgar-Gwadar cargo run and subsequent transfer of the containers to waiting vessels at Gwadar port, Pakistani officials went to great lengths to allay Chinese concerns and the

Pakistan Navy deployed ships and aircraft to provide security cover to ensure safe and secure transit.

Since Gwadar became operational, the role of Pakistan's maritime forces has increased and the Pakistan Navy has been assigned special responsibility to protect the Gwadar seaport project and the more than 500 Chinese working there from offshore threats. Hussain Sayed, who chairs Pakistan's parliamentary committee on the CPEC, recently said that Pakistan plans to double the size of the Special Security Division (SSD), set up under a Major General solely for protecting CPEC construction sites and the estimated 10,000 Chinese workers, by the end of March 2017. With China refusing to provide any financial assistance towards security expenses of the CPEC, the Pakistan government on September 24, 2016, decided to meet such expenses by adding 1 per cent more to the cost of all central energy projects and recovering it from consumers through the National Electric Power Regulatory Authority. This cess is to help the Pakistan Army meet expenses incurred on the SSD. The Senate Standing Committee on Planning Development and Reform has protested over billing citizens for providing security to Chinese in Pakistan. Pakistani politicians are already complaining about the US$ 12 million a year expenditure on the SSD, which will now double.

Success of the CPEC and Gwadar Port depends on having a safe and secure maritime environment in the Arabian Sea and Indian Ocean region in general. Envisaging attacks by militant groups or insurgents on seaports and vessels, and use of container vessels to smuggle weapons, drugs, etc., Pakistan has strengthened maritime security capabilities. This includes: intensifying security patrols and coastal exercises; creation of Coastal Watch Stations; establishing a Joint Maritime Information Coordination Centre (JMICC); establishment of the Force Protection Battalion of the Pakistan Marines; and more robust maritime security activities jointly by Pakistan and China.

Collaboration in building navy craft has been stepped up. China and Pakistan have agreed to jointly construct the F-22P frigate in addition to the Azmat and Jalalat class fast attack craft and corvettes for the Pakistan Maritime Security Agency. In June 2015, Pakistan's Ministry of Defence Production signed a contract with China Ship Trading Company for construction of seven Maritime Patrol Ships, four of which are being built in China and the others at the Karachi Shipyard and Engineering Works. The China Shipbuilding Industry Corporation (CSIC) is to also provide Pakistan's Navy with eight attack submarines. Pakistan has to pay for these vessels.

Other serious issues threatening the development of Gwadar have surfaced with Pakistani analysts implying that China has undue interest in Gwadar port, described as an "island isolated in an arid landscape with roads and railways linking it to the rest of the nation." The city's water-supply dam has dried up following three years of drought. The existing desalination plant does not work and there is no more water. Unless Gwadar gets its full road and rail connectivity, the port cannot flourish. Gwadar additionally symbolises the sense of alienation felt by many in Balochistan, who suspect that most of the benefits of the CPEC are going to outsiders.

The biggest threat to the CPEC and, potentially Sino-Pak relations in the future, is the unchecked—or uncheckable—rise of radical Islam in Pakistan. The CPEC will facilitate the passage of radical Islamist elements, including that of the returning battle-hardened Uyghurs into China's sensitive and restive Xinjiang-Uyghur Autonomous Region. The announcement on January 11, 2017, that China's restive Xinjiang-Uyghur Autonomous Region has closed its borders with Pakistan is the first visible crack in the gloss of lacquer that the China-Pakistan Economic Corridor (CPEC) seeks to put on the China-Pakistan relationship.

Chinese provincial officials have earlier vented their frustration at the persistent efforts at proselytisation by Pakistani religious tanzeems and named Pakistan during discussions earlier at the National People's Congress sessions. The links to Pakistan of persons involved in terrorist actions in China—like in the knife attacks in Kunming—have, quite unusually, been mentioned in China's official media. Communist Party leaders of Xinjiang have also expressed fears of militants getting training in Pakistan and Afghanistan and returning to the province to carry out terror attacks. The decision of January 11 would have had high-level approval and followed protracted discussions between Chinese and Pakistani officials including between the respective Intelligence and security services. The terrorist attack in Hotan on December 28, 2016, that killed five people was the trigger. Separately, Xinhua quoted the Chairman of the Xinjiang Regional People's Congress, Shohrat Zakir as saying that security along the China-Pakistan border would be further tightened "to prevent terrorists from entering or leaving the region illegally in 2017." Local officials in Kashgar prefecture, that borders Pakistan, specifically stressed the need to check illegal infiltration from Pakistan.

One reason for China's concern about the situation in Afghanistan and its effort to open independent channels of communication with elements of the Taliban is the desire to reduce dependence on Pakistani security forces for preventing extremist elements from crossing into Xinjiang. It is also, of course, to allow Chinese companies to exploit Afghanistan's natural and mineral resources. China's concern is long term and this is clear from the tasking of the PLA's Western Theatre Command which mandates that it focus on "threats in Xinjiang and Tibet as well as Afghanistan and other states that host training bases for separatists and extremists." Troops of the PLA Western Theatre Command can be deployed to protect Chinese workers and projects inside Pakistan and the CPEC. China's National Security Law enacted in 2016 authorises China's armed forces and Intelligence and security personnel to enter foreign countries to apprehend terrorists.

The other potential threat to the Sino-Pakistan bilateral relationship is the growing confidence of the extremist Islamic radical groups in Pakistan. Underscoring the steadily increasing radicalisation of Pakistan, the Chief of the Jamaat-ud-Dawa (JuD) and founder of Lashkar-e-Taiba (LeT), Hafeez Saeed told the Nawaz Sharif government in late May 2016, to "show some courage and direct China to stay away from hurting Islamic sentiments." Hafeez Saeed is the first Pakistani national to express concern about the plight of Muslims in China. Surprisingly, a high-powered delegation of Pakistan's Ministry of Religious Affairs subsequently left for China on June 28, 2016 to check the veracity of reports that Chinese authorities in the Xinjiang-Uyghur Autonomous Region have banned fasting in the holy month of Ramazan. The ISIS has earlier identified the Xinjiang-Uyghur Autonomous Region as a place of its interest. These are signs that clearly portend trouble.

Finally, the opposition in Balochistan where the CPEC is perceived as harming their sense of identity with their historic homeland is serious. Many non-locals, businesses and multinational companies' personnel have recently come under attack in the restive Balochistan region. Local Balochis already debate that the CPEC will benefit only Chinese interests and would convert the local population into a minority. Allah Baloch, leader of the Balochistan Liberation Front, has called the Gwadar project "fake" and a conspiracy against the Baloch people. The Balochistan National Party, Baloch National Front, and the Baloch Republic Party have opposed the project. Adding to the resentment is the estimate that by 2048, the native Baloch population will be outnumbered by an influx of Chinese and migrant workers from Pakistan's other provinces. The Baloch people's sense of marginalisation is further fuelled by governmental actions. The President of the Gwadar Educational Welfare Society recently said that "Gwadar fishermen are not allowed near the port boundaries. Thousands of fishermen have been asked to leave the harbour." These concerns of marginalisation are shared by residents of Gilgit-Baltistan, in Pakistan's north, who fear "we will become a minority and economically subservient." Unless these sentiments are assuaged with investments made for the local people, the ensuing resentment and restiveness cannot be calmed.

While there are serious doubts about the viability of the CPEC and its completion, India must see it as the thin end of the wedge. It represents an enhanced level of Sino-Pak collusion which potentially threatens large portions of Indian territory, including Kashmir. China has already laid claim to Ladakh and is pressuring India to ease tensions with Pakistan and "resolve" the Kashmir dispute. Western and Chinese interests also converge in preventing the collapse of Pakistan. With China rising and getting increasingly aggressive, the CPEC's frailties need to be exploited. Already, Prime Minister Modi's remark last year expressing empathy with the Balochi people has caused disquiet in Islamabad and Beijing and, in China's assessment, put the CPEC at risk.

A Pakistani Major General responded with a superficial "invitation" in December 2016 to India to join the CPEC while Beijing sought to broaden participation in the CPEC by getting Iran, Turkmenistan and Russia to join so as to portray it as an international venture. A section of US academics are also suggesting that US companies be allowed to participate in the CPEC. To safeguard its national interests and given the discomfort with the CPEC in Pakistan, India must insist—as China has done with the Asian Development

Bank and World Bank in the case of funding for poverty alleviation projects in Arunachal Pradesh—that the AIIB and other designated banks for the OBOR and CPEC do not give loans or funds for CPEC projects located in the POK or Gilgit-Baltistan. The Balochis, who are unhappy at being marginalised, must be assisted with the twin objectives of frustrating the CPEC and putting Pakistan under pressure. This will prevent Chinese pressure and influence from gaining ascendance in countries in the region including Nepal and Bhutan, and make India a serious factor in the politics of the region.

(The article was published in the Centre for China Analysis and Strategy, New Delhi, February 2017).

38

China, Tibet and Beijing's New Thinking

As China's new leaders began settling into their jobs soon after the 18th Party Congress held in Beijing in November 2012, indications became available that the Chinese Communist Party's (CCP) senior leadership would focus attention on the Tibet issue. This included making some key personnel appointments, including in the now more powerful CCP Central Committee's (CC) Secretariat. The CCP leadership is also confronted with the growing discontent among Tibetans in China.

Meanwhile there is speculation among sections of the Tibetan community in exile, based mainly on wishful thinking, that Chinese President Xi Jinping would be influenced by his family background and adopt a "softer" policy towards Tibetans and the Tibet issue. While there have been signs that China's leadership is taking some initiatives intended to diffuse the situation, there are no indications whatsoever that the present tough policy on Tibet will mellow. For example, Xiao Wunan, a senior CCP cadre affiliated to the CCP CC's United Front Work Department (UFWD), fronted two overtures, including one made directly to the exiled Tibetan hierarchy in Dharamsala last year. Both were aimed at undermining the Dalai Lama's influence and creating schisms among Tibetan Buddhists. There have very recently been two other events which merit attention.

The first is a curious invitation extended on June 3, 2013, by the little known "Hong Kong Tibetan and Han-Chinese Friendship Organisation." Suspected to be a pro-Beijing "front" organisation, it came to notice when it tried to disrupt pro-democracy protests in Hong Kong on June 1, 2009. It is headed by Philip Li Koi-hop, the bankrupt former head of the "Hong Kong North West Express Shipping Company," who is now reportedly a Marine Inspector.

The other is an interesting, and apparently important, interview by Prof. Jin Wei of the CCP Central Party School which was published on June 6, 2013, by the Chinese-language Hong Kong-based *Asia Weekly*. Captioned, "Reopen Talks and Resolve Tibetan Issues," her interview to *Asia Weekly* reveals important elements of the Chinese leadership's thinking on the Tibet issue and the Dalai Lama. It confirms too that there will be no relaxation in Beijing's increasingly tough policy concerning Tibetans.

The Central Party School is the crucible for training upwardly mobile Party cadres and is presently under the direct control of Liu Yunshun, member of the Politburo Standing Committee overseeing the propaganda apparatus and former Chief of the Party's Central Propaganda Department. Prof. Jin Wei is a senior member of its faculty with a pronounced background in minority issues. She is currently Deputy Director of Minority Issues in the Central Party School and has previously held the post of Director of Ethnic Religious Studies, Institute of Social Development Research at the Central Party School. Central Party School teachers are hand-picked and periodically tested for "political reliability."

Echoing Mao Zedong's observation of 1952 that the Tibet nationality question is "extremely serious" and cannot be handled in a "routine" manner—an assertion reiterated recently by Yu Zhengsheng, the new Chairman of the Chinese People's Political Consultative Conference (CPPCC) which oversees Dalai Lama and Tibet-related issues and the CCP CC's United Front Work Department—in the interview Prof. Jin Wei asserted that the "Dalai Lama Clique" is engaged in "separatism." She noted that the official term "Tibet-related issue" is used to describe "social management and social development of the six million Tibetan people living in the five provinces of the TAR, Qinghai, Sichuan, Gansu, and Yunnan." Blaming "domestic and overseas Tibetan independence extremists" for pursuing the "Tibetan independence" issue and "infiltrators" for "sabotage," she nonetheless conceded that "some of the domestic contradictions and conflicts that occur are mostly due to nationality and religious issues." She was categoric that differences between the Chinese authorities and "the Dalai Lama Clique" are "antagonistic and irreconcilable" because the Dalai Lama had promoted "separatist activities for Tibetan independence" since 1959, and directly challenged China's sovereignty and territorial integrity.

At the same time, Prof. Jin Wei acknowledged that the Dalai Lama is considered a "living god" by six million Tibetan people and is "the object of their spiritual worship, and has considerable appeal." Stating that how China deals with him "affects the feelings of thousands and thousands of Tibetans," she said, "we cannot simply treat him as an enemy." Describing him as a "key figure" in Tibet-related issues, she said the "Dalai Lama issue and the Tibet-related issues" would be best solved with an eye towards the future and recommended restarting the talks with his representatives that had remained suspended since 2010. At the same time, she endorsed that the "Dalai Lama question" should continue to be dealt with "in a hostile way."

Prof. Jin Wei advanced a framework for the new round of discussions. The first step, she said, should be to put aside disputes and break the current impasse. She clarified that this meant tackling easy issues first while setting aside the "Middle Way" and other political issues. Allowing the Dalai Lama to visit Hong Kong or Macau purely in his capacity as a religious leader could be discussed, with the ambit being expanded later to consider allowing him to reside in Hong Kong. Subject to it being proved that his decision in 2011 to completely retire from politics and be solely a religious leader was genuine, he could even perhaps be allowed to visit Tibet.

Secondly, she stressed that it is imperative to ensure that the Dalai Lama, who has reached an advanced age, is reincarnated only inside China. Failure to achieve this would mean "twin Dalai Lamas," with one reincarnation recognised abroad and one domestically. Such an eventuality would have a "great impact on the stability and security of the Tibetan region." She said once talks resumed and the current impasse was broken, China would have to "fight" to ensure the Dalai Lama's reincarnation inside the country. While China could use "Drawing Lots from the Golden Urn" to prevent the Dalai Lama's reincarnation overseas, she pointed out that there is a historical precedent for Living Buddha's designating their own successors and China must "make every possible effort to avoid the embarrassment of the 'twin Panchen Lama' event."

A crucial assessment put forward by Prof. Jin Wei was that after the present Dalai Lama, the obsession of people in Western countries with the Dalai Lama will "gradually fade" and international pressure on Tibet-related issues will "slowly reduce." The anxiety and "violent sentiments of Tibetan groups inside China" will be further calmed if a "believable Dalai Lama is produced by religious rituals" inside China. She anticipated that in the post-Dalai Lama phase, the exiled Tibetan government will probably join other extremist organisations to engage in extreme violence. If China succeeds in resolving the "Dalai Lama Dilemma," however, it will be able to disintegrate overseas Tibetan independence forces.

She emphasised that a couple of things had to be done prior to the Dalai Lama being allowed to return to China. First, it was essential to carefully assess the "trust and feelings of the six million Tibetan people towards the Communist Party." Second was to correctly assess how the Tibetan people worship the Dalai Lama and how they feel about him. Stating that she had made successive trips to Tibet, she disclosed that ordinary people had frequently and "straightforwardly" told her that: "In this life I depend on the Communist Party, in the next life I depend on the Dalai Lama." These few words, she said, provided the key to her evaluation.

She averred that the Chinese Communist Party had every reason to be highly confident as, since the "Peaceful Liberation of Tibet in the fifties, the Communist Party has devoted a great deal of care and love to Tibet and the general population of Tibetans," and has extended massive support and assistance for its economic development. There has been great progress in economic and social development in Tibetan areas over the last 50 years, with huge visible improvements in material life, health, education, and transportation. For this, she said, the Tibetan people are "profoundly grateful to the Communist Party, and fully recognise the People's Republic of China which is under the leadership of the Chinese Communist Party."

Nevertheless, she cautioned that despite all the effort and work by the Communist Party to enhance economic and social development, it is "impossible to deny the Dalai Lama's status in the eyes of the general public." It is similarly impossible to change the way the Tibetan people "worship the Dalai Lama and are dependent on him." She emphasised, however, that, "this worship has no political significance or plans" and that for most people "Tibetan independence" is just an empty phrase. They have no interest in it and do not understand what it means. According to her the Tibetan people are actually full of gratitude for the Communist Party, which is highly recognised. She assessed, therefore, that "our leaders at all levels" and in all relevant departments could very confidently discuss the issue of allowing the Dalai Lama to return to the country.

Prof. Jin Wei discussed the issue of self-immolations and, perhaps for the first time, provided an insight into the CCP leadership's thinking on this phenomenon, which has seriously vexed them. She enumerated the following four attributes:

- The spate of self-immolations has increased and become a kind of "virtual hysteria," or an "infectious disease." It has "become a movement";
- Measures taken to stop them have not yet been significantly effective;
- The self-immolations have the potential to trigger more serious conflicts. Media reports, recordings, prayers for self-immolators, condolences and other acts have progressively widened their impact on the populace. The agitated emotions of Tibetans and actions by local governments to stop confrontations have promoted tensions and transformed the self-immolations from a "religious movement" into a "political movement" and even one spreading "hatred." Disaffection has now spread throughout the Tibetan ethnic group and evolved from being a problem between the central government and the "Dalai Lama separatist clique" into an ethnic conflict between Chinese and Tibetans; and
- Self-immolation is a violent emotional act that is performed after an individual is "instigated." The reason for mainly the youth committing self-immolation, is because their feelings towards the Communist Party are different from that of the older generation of Tibetans. While the latter are deeply grateful and thankful to the CCP for their emancipation and their share of land and livestock, the Tibetan youth are unable to compare the material improvement in their lives or the new and old governments. The younger Tibetans are also very impulsive and give expression to their emotions.

In conclusion, Prof. Jin Wei advised cadres working in the Tibetan regions to be particularly careful while handling religious affairs, and said the anti-religious bias of several former Party Secretaries of the Tibet Autonomous Region (TAR) had contributed to present grievances. Significantly, she urged the separation of religion and politics. Saying that Tibetans have been influenced by religion for thousands of years, she described their philosophy as: "heavily spiritual and light on materialism, heavy on the next life and light on this life." The CCP, as the ruling party, needs to understand this huge difference between the Tibetans and the Han. She stressed that Tibet-related issues are crucial for China and it is essential to promote social stability and prevent long-lasting division between the nationalities. It would also be useful for reunification with Taiwan and improving China's international image.

Prof. Jin Wei's interview suggests that the CCP is probably reviewing its policy on talks with the Dalai Lama's representatives. Her recommendations acknowledge the importance to China of: working towards reincarnation of the Dalai Lama inside China; effectively tackling the issue of self-immolations; diffusing rising tensions between the Han and Tibetan nationalities including by being more tolerant of the latter's religious practices; diluting international pressure on Tibet and Human Rights issues; and facilitating reunification with Taiwan. The objectives of the overtures being made by Xiao Wunan dovetail with these. Notable though is that Prof. Jin Wei, quite pointedly, does not waver in her observation that differences between the CCP and "the Dalai Lama Clique" are "antagonistic and irreconcilable" and nowhere does she recommend an easing in Beijing's steadily increasing stringent policy towards Tibetans.

(The article was published in Institute of Peace and Conflict Studies, New Delhi, June 2013).

39

China's New Initiatives on the Tibet Issue

In the midst of reports of emissaries being exchanged between Beijing and the Dalai Lama's set-up and positive references to Buddhism by Chinese leaders, clearer indications are becoming discernible in recent months to suggest that Beijing is contemplating a new initiative on the Tibet issue. There has, at the same time, been no easing in the policies being enforced in the Tibet Autonomous Region (TAR) or Beijing's efforts to shrink the room for manoeuvre available to the Dalai Lama.

The latter has been highlighted by Beijing's orchestration of protests against the Dalai Lama during his travels abroad by Shugden worshippers and groups of "nationalist" Chinese students. This is reinforced by the steadily increasing diplomatic and economic pressure on foreign governments to refrain from meeting the Dalai Lama. As a result, the number of world leaders who have officially received the Dalai Lama has dwindled appreciably in the past couple of years. Examples are: Denmark shying away from scheduling any official meetings in the second week of February 2015; the Pope declining to meet the Dalai Lama in Rome in mid-December; earlier South Africa refusing him a visa; the Norwegian government refusing to officially receive him in May 2014; and the capitulation of UK on the Tibet issue in the formal Joint Statement issued during Chinese Premier Li Keqiang's visit in April 2014. The US, however, declined to succumb entirely to Chinese pressure and invited the Dalai Lama to the annual breakfast prayer meeting in Washington on February 5, 2015, although US President Obama avoided any direct interaction with him.

All this has been accompanied by an apparent mellowing in references by senior Chinese leaders to the 79-year-old Dalai Lama, prompting him to describe Chinese President Xi Jinping as "more realistic" and his government as "softer" during an interview to the *Nikkei Asian Review* on November 25, 2014. Interesting is the Dalai Lama's remark of October 8, when he said, "some Chinese officials, for example the Deputy Party Secretary in the autonomous region of Tibet, he also mentioned the possibility of my visit." Though reports of any formal contacts have been denied by the Dalai Lama's set-up, fresh speculation was sparked by the Dalai Lama's interview on BBC's "Newsnight" programme on December 17, 2014, where he commented that he may not have a successor. He was quoted by BBC as saying, "The Dalai Lama institution will cease one day. These man-made institutions will cease. There is no guarantee that some stupid Dalai Lama won't come next, who will disgrace himself or herself. That would be very sad. So, much better that a centuries-old tradition should cease at the time of a quite popular Dalai Lama."

Of particular interest are the activities of Prof. Jin Wei, a senior member of the faculty of the Central Party School in Beijing, which she joined in 1985. Jin Wei has a pronounced background in minority issues and is Deputy Director of Minority Issues in the Central Party School. The Central Party School is the crucible for training senior cadres of the Chinese Communist Party (CCP) earmarked for upward progression and its faculty comprises CCP members hand-picked for their reliability. An "insider" joke in the Central Party School at one time said that everyone drove carefully within its precincts as no one knew who would rise to become the CCP Central Committee's (CC) General Secretary!

An important interview by Prof. Jin Wei, which was published on June 6, 2013, by the Hong Kong-based Chinese-language magazine "Yazhou Zhoukan" (*Asia Weekly*), appeared to reveal important elements of the Chinese leadership's new thinking on the Tibet issue and the Dalai Lama. Pertinent is that Simon Kei Shek Ming, the journalist who interviewed Prof. Jin Wei, used to be noticed accompanying Xiao Wunan, a former provincial level cadre of the CCP Central Committee's (CC) United Front Work Department (UFWD), on his travels. Xiao Wunan is Executive Director of the Chinese government-sponsored NGO, the Asia-Pacific Economic Exchange Foundation (APECF), and claims proximity to Chinese President Xi Jinping. Simon Kei Shek Ming accompanied Xiao

Wunan when he travelled to Dharamsala in August 2012, and in a rare accomplishment met the Dalai Lama, Ughyen Thinley Dorje, who is a claimant to the throne of the Gyalwa Karmapa, and the "Sikyong" Lobsang Sangay, all in one day.

The APECF, incidentally, was also the first Chinese outfit to reveal its interest in Lumbini—the Buddha's birthplace—when it unveiled a US$ 3 billion plan for redevelopment of the city. In December 2014 reports suggested that the Nepal government's Social Welfare Council (SWC) had initiated proceedings against the APECF to blacklist it for, among other reasons, lack of transparency and failure to submit its audit reports. In the process the SWC uncovered that while the APECF had made inroads into rural areas adjoining Lumbini like Dolakha, Sindhupalchowk, Rasuwa and Nuwakot, it had not informed the SWC of the year-long education and three-year-long agriculture projects run from 2013 to 2017 in these districts.

In her interview to "Yazhou Zhoukan," Prof. Jin Wei was categoric in her assertion that China must ensure that the Dalai Lama's reincarnation is found "inside China" and China must "make every possible effort to avoid the embarrassment of the 'twin Panchen Lama' event." She was critical of past policies and, advancing a new framework for talks, said it was necessary "to put aside disputes and break the current impasse" and acknowledge that the Dalai Lama is considered a "living god" by six million Tibetan people. China's dealings with him, she said, "affects the feelings of thousands and thousands of Tibetans," and therefore, "we cannot simply treat him as an enemy." She described the Dalai Lama as a "key figure" in Tibet-related issues and recommended restarting the talks with his representatives that have remained suspended since 2010.

Her views were swiftly and sharply rebuffed by Yu Zhengsheng, Politburo Standing Committee (PBSC) member and Chairman of the Chinese People's Political Consultative Conference (CPPCC) and Zhu Weiqun, presently Director of the CPPCC's Ethnic and Religious Affairs Committee and former Vice Minister of the CCP CC's UFWD. Zhu Weiqun said, "when we refer to Mr. Tenzin Gyatso as the Dalai Lama we are recognising his spiritual rank. However, in the course of time, he has acquired another label which we should never forget. Because of his efforts to split China he has become a political refugee."

Prof. Jin Wei's continuance at the Central Party School despite the opposition generated by her interview suggests that her views have approval at some high level. This has been implicitly confirmed in the past few months with Prof. Jin Wei having apparently been drafted by the CCP to publicise its "new thinking" on the Tibet issue in influential circles abroad.

In late 2014, she travelled quietly to the US where she had closed-door meetings with select think tanks and, more significantly, with some of the Dalai Lama's key supporters in Washington DC and New York. More recently, she spoke at Oxford and addressed the School of Oriental and Asian Studies (SOAS) in London on November 11, 2014. It is understood that she will very shortly be travelling again to London at the invitation of SOAS.

Prof. Jin Wei's remarks in the UK were interesting and hinted that Beijing could be re-evaluating its policy of aid to the Tibet Autonomous Region (TAR). In her talk at SOAS entitled, "Opportunities and Challenges in Western China—a case study in Tibet," she expressed doubts about the benefits of Beijing's financial assistance to TAR. Noting that the autonomous region's GDP had grown steadily since the "peaceful liberation" of Tibet in 1951, Prof. Jin Wei observed that the region had taken "initial steps" in establishing a "modern economic base." Tibetans now had access to "basic" health care and education, good quality housing, usually with electricity and gas, and life expectancy had risen by 31.5 years. She highlighted, however, that Beijing's top-down economic policies in the TAR had created what she described as a "two-way dependency."

She gave the following break-up of projects undertaken in the TAR:

Year	Number of projects	Investment in TAR (in 100 million RMB)
1984	43	4.8
1994	62	48.6
2001	117	311
2005	24	64.2
2007	188	137.8
2011	236	419.2
2014	670	599.9

Her analysis of figures highlighting investment in TAR by the Central Government and provincial authorities revealed that only RMB 7 out of every RMB 100 spent by the TAR authorities came from local revenues. This was despite TAR having the second highest expenditure of any province.

She said that despite the increasingly large amounts being invested in TAR, the rate of increase in GDP growth had plateaued. She hinted that Beijing should discard established policies and explore new ones. She concluded that while aid to Tibet and high-levels of central investment need to continue, the authorities need to tailor these to local conditions and the needs of Tibetans. While Prof. Jin Wei said that not all projects had failed, she asserted that almost 70 per cent of the projects started in TAR had become bankrupt or been forced to close down. Citing examples of the failure of the top-down policy of development assistance, she mentioned a wool processing plant in Naqu in northern TAR which had been forced to close down due to poor management and lack of a market for the wool; a "new" hospital where, because of the heavy cost of maintenance that local authorities could not afford because of inadequate local revenue, the roof leaked so badly that the patients had to shelter under plastic sheeting; and the Potala Square in Lhasa, which is the centrepiece of Beijing's massive urban redevelopment of Lhasa, where the work unit in charge of the square had told Prof. Jin Wei that they lacked the funds to maintain the road surface which was badly potholed and cracked.

Prof. Jin Wei said she had often travelled to Tibet since 1984 and on each occasion she had been touched and moved by the Tibetan people's belief in religion. She disclosed that this has raised major concern among scholars and leaders in China. Prof. Jin Wei pointed out that in 1950, the year before the PLA entered Lhasa, there had been a total of 2,711 temples and monasteries in the TAR and 114,103 monks and nuns. This had fallen to 553 and 6,913 respectively in 1965 but had increased to 1,787 and 46,000 respectively by 2014. Commenting on the issue of controls over monasteries and nunneries in China, Prof. Jin Wei observed that though the number of monasteries and monks in TAR had increased since 1965, most officials in TAR saw monks as "troublemakers."

Commenting on the issue of the tightening controls over monasteries and nunneries in China, she said that the new policies introduced in 2011 included linking monasteries with towns by road, providing them electricity, requiring them to display photographs of Chinese leaders, fly the Chinese flag, and enrolling monks and nuns in social security schemes. She said, "the most significant reform" had been to place more officials inside monasteries and nunneries and on the Monastery Management Committees. She disclosed that for every six monks and nuns in the TAR, there was one official based in the monasteries across TAR. Stating that the officials stationed in the monasteries felt marginalised and did not like the job, Prof. Jin Wei described the policy as "unsustainable" but implied that there was little chance that the authorities would change their approach since most officials in TAR saw monks as "troublemakers." Prof. Jin Wei commented that "policymakers" and those who "oversee policies on religion" were themselves not religious which also made it difficult for them to formulate "ideal" policies. She acknowledged that these reforms had increased "internal tensions."

Within weeks of Jin Wei's visit, TAR Chairman Lobsang Gyaltsen led a high-powered 8-member delegation to Canada and the US from November 30 to December 6, 2014. It was the ninth overseas trip by Tibetan legislators since 2009. The delegation included two Deputies of the National People's Congress (NPC) as well as Tenzin Lhundrup (Ethnicity: Tibetan) Deputy Secretary General TAR People's Government; Phuntsok (Ethnicity: Tibetan), Deputy of the TAR People's Congress and Director of the Standing Committee of Ngari (Ali) Prefectural People's Congress; and Zhang Yanqing, (Ethnicity: Han) Mayor of Lhasa and Deputy of the TAR People's Congress. The delegation visited five cities in North America. Tenzin Lhundrup, Deputy Secretary General of the TAR government and a member of the delegation, told *Global Times* that the "Tibet question groups" set up by more than twenty Western parliaments to assist "Tibet independence" forces were "the key targets of, as well as barriers to, our communication efforts."

In Vancouver, Toronto and Ottawa they met overseas Chinese, Tibetans and Canadian officials. Lobsang Gyaltsen met Daniel Jean, acting Canadian Minister of Foreign Affairs and Victor Oh, Canadian Senator and Chairman of the China-Canada Parliamentary Association in Ottawa, who officially invited the delegation.

During his meeting with the Canadian officials, Lobsang Gyaltsen explained the CCP's Tibet policy and the "tremendous" social and economic progress that Tibet has made under the CCP's leadership. He reaffirmed that, "Tibet is an inalienable part of China since time immemorial" and that the "CCP liberated Tibet peacefully" more than 60 years ago. Lobsang Gyaltsen stressed that the TAR authorities fully adhere to the policy of religious freedom, promotion of religious harmony and strengthening the management of religious affairs according to law. He described the current situation in Tibet as the best period in its history and appealed to Canadian officials to take an impartial view of Tibet and recognise the importance and sensitivity of the Tibet issue. He requested them not to provide any scope for anti-China activities in order to cement the healthy and friendly relations between the two nations.

Welcoming the delegation led by TAR Chairman Lobsang Gyaltsen, Canadian officials affirmed that Tibet is an inalienable part of Chinese territory and that Canada does not support the "independence" of Tibet and is not willing to see the Tibet issue obstruct the development of relations between the two countries.

Lobsang Gyaltsen left for the US on December 2, 2014, where he visited Washington and New York. He spoke at the Brookings Institute and met journalists, overseas Chinese and overseas Tibetans.

Interesting too are the reports circulating in the US and West which, quoting reliable Chinese sources, state that Xi Jinping had conveyed to the Government of India that he would like to meet the Dalai Lama during his visit to India in September 2014. These sources claim that the Indian government did not respond.

In a fresh development laden with political overtones, on January 29, 2015, Xiao Wunan, a former provincial level official of the CCP's United Front Work Department (UFWD) and Chief Executive of the APECF, released a videotape of his meeting with the Dalai Lama in August 2012 through the British Broadcasting Corporation (BBC). It clearly depicts Xiao Wunan informing the Dalai Lama that there is a void at the top in China's Buddhist religious circles. He suggests that this could be filled by the Dalai Lama and offers the Dalai Lama the job. The video also attempts to portray that China allows a modicum of personal religious freedom by showing a room in Xiao Wunan's house that has been set aside as a shrine for worship of the Buddha.

The video shows that in this room a photograph of the Dalai Lama has been given pride of place. It is obvious that the release of such a video, which is unprecedented, has been "cleared" at a high level in the CCP.

It is perhaps the first time that there has been such a brazen and publicised propaganda push to lure the Dalai Lama back to China. The video reveals that the main objective of China's efforts and of Xiao Wunan's visit to Dharamsala in 2012, was to persuade the Dalai Lama to return to Beijing to a religious post. It is interesting too that Xiao Wunan, who refers to himself in the video as a practising Buddhist, is described as a "former official" and that he has been able to inject the suggestion that he has a family relationship with Chinese President Xi Jinping.

China has in recent months seemingly stepped up engagement with foreigners on the Tibet issue. Examples include the participation by foreigners in the Tibet Forum in Lhasa in mid-August 2014, tour of Beijing-based foreign military attachés to Tibet the following month and the release in late January 2015 of Xiao Wunan's video via the BBC. Simultaneously, Chinese officials appear to be trying to bring increasing pressure to bear on Tibetans. During a visit to Nepal in October this year, TAR Chairman Lobsang Gyaltsen asserted that, "China doesn't have any refugee as such" and those crossing the border into Nepal are "illegal." This appeared to hint that China could at some point question the status of "political refugees" accorded to escaping Tibetans.

Separately, members of Chinese think tanks have been noticed raising the Tibet issue during meetings with their Indian counterparts in India and abroad since late 2014. They generally observe that the Dalai Lama's presence in India is an obstacle to India-China relations and that while the "Dalai Lama has a religious colour," the "present person" is a political individual indulging in anti-Chinese activities.

(The article was published in The Institute of Peace and Conflict Studies, New Delhi, June 24, 2013).

40

China's "Big Two" Sessions Signal Policy Shift on Dalai Lama

A definitive shift was discernible in Beijing's policy towards the Dalai Lama at the 4th plenary session of the 12th National People's Congress (NPC), China's version of a parliament, that concluded in Beijing on March 15, 2016. China additionally utilised the Chinese People's Political Consultative Conference (CPPCC) and NPC sessions—popularly called the "Big Two"—to subtly continue its efforts to drive a wedge between the Dalai Lama and the various Tibetan Buddhist sects in the bid to undermine his influence and isolate him. Remarks by officials of the Tibet Autonomous Region (TAR) on the sidelines of the "Big Two" clarified that there would be no relaxation in the tough policies being implemented in Tibet.

Tibet has been a major preoccupation of the Chinese Communist Party (CCP) leadership, but interestingly, CPPCC Chairman and Politburo Standing Committee (PBSC) member, Yu Zhengsheng, did not make specific mention of Tibet in his 16-page report to the 2,200 delegates attending the opening session of the CPPCC in Beijing on March 3, 2016. He merely said: "We promoted ethnic unity and religious harmony to bring together the will and strength of the people." The CPPCC, incidentally, is China's top political advisory body overseeing work relating to national minorities and specifically Tibet and Xinjiang as well as non-Communist Party organisations. Nonetheless the Tibet issue figured directly in remarks by Deputies during the sessions and also in the days around the "Big Two" sessions.

CPPCC Chairman Yu Zhengsheng did, however, mention "religions" sixteen times in the report, six times more than last year according to the Hong Kong-based *Ta Kung Pao*. One major development is that the report asked delegates to "actively work to guide religions adapting to the socialist society, make suggestions and proposals on the implementation of the Regulations on Religious Affairs, policies on real estate property held by religious groups and the development of philanthropy work by religious communities." The reference to "policies on real estate property held by religious groups" is intriguing. The report, also for the first time, proposes the concept of "religious philanthropy."

In its despatch on March 3, 2016, the authoritative official news agency Xinhua reported that Yu Zhengsheng had echoed a recent Qiushi article in his address and "urged CCP members within the CPPCC National Committee to enhance their consciousness of the ideology, the whole, the core and the line." The article in the CCP Central Committee's theoretical journal "Qiushi" (*Seeking Truth*) exhorted that faithfulness to the core leadership of the Party is characterised "by staunch loyalty to the CPC Central Committee, [its] General Secretary Xi Jinping as well as to Party theories, guidelines, principles and policies" and it declared that "all the society must be united under the advocacy of Xi on the Chinese dream of national rejuvenation."

As if to affirm their loyalty to the CCP, the 18 delegates from TAR to the CPPCC and NPC sessions wore two badges displaying the photographs of five Chinese leaders. One showed Mao Zedong, Deng Xiaoping, Jiang Zemin, Hu Jintao and President Xi Jinping, and the other only depicted Xi Jinping. Monasteries and temples in Tibet have displayed photographs of Mao Zedong, Deng Xiaoping, Jiang Zemin and Hu Jintao since 2011. Though one Tibetan Delegate said they had been wearing the badges after the 50th anniversary of the founding of TAR in 2015, their display during the sessions sparked criticism as an attempt to project Xi Jinping's image. The delegates appeared without the badges at the closing ceremony on the final day!

Some interesting developments around the time of the "Big Two" sessions ensured attention to the Tibet issue. Just days before commencement of the CPPCC and NPC sessions, China's official news agency Xinhua (March 1, 2016) sought to project a favourable image of the CCP's engagement with Tibetan religious affairs. It publicised that Sun Chunlan, Politburo (PB) member and head of the CCP CC's United Front Work Department (UFWD), received Gyaltsen Norbu, the Chinese-appointed Panchen Lama, on his return to Beijing from a sojourn in Tibet. It quoted Gyaltsen Norbu as saying he "will bear in mind the care from the CPC Central Committee and the central government as well as Xi's instructions" and as vowing to work hard to help "Tibetan Buddhism (get) better incorporated into socialist society." He said he would promote Tibet's prosperity and harmony.

In contrast, the US-based Radio Free Asia (RFA) pointed to the restiveness in Tibet and reported the first such incident of self-immolation in China this year. This was by Kalsang Wangdu, a young Tibetan monk of the Retsokha Aryaling monastery in the Kardze Tibetan Autonomous Prefecture's Nyagrong (Xinlong) county, Sichuan province, on February 29, 2016. The report was later denied by a TAR official. Another RFA report claimed that on March 1, 2016, a 33-year-old Tibetan woman had been taken into custody in Ngaba county's Meruma township in Sichuan province for holding up "a photo of the Dalai Lama and (having) shouted slogans challenging Chinese policies."

Support to the Dalai Lama received a fillip when on March 10, 2016, the Geneva Graduate Institute ignored a written protest from the Chinese Embassy dated March 8, and received the Dalai Lama along with other Nobel Laureates at an event sponsored jointly by the US and Canada. The communication from the Chinese Embassy said, "China resolutely opposes the 14th Dalai Lama's separatist activities in whatever capacity and in whatever name in any country, organisation or event." It urged addressees, "not to attend the above-mentioned event, nor meet the 14th Dalai Lama and his clique." At the event, which coincided with the 57th anniversary of the Dalai Lama's flight from Tibet and riots in Lhasa, the US, Canada and eleven other countries sharply criticised China's mass arrests of lawyers.

There were a couple of intriguing developments as well. On March 10, 2016, Ms. Nancy Pelosi and Jim McGovern, members of the first US Congress delegation to visit Tibet in eight years in 2015, issued a statement saying, "the deteriorating human rights situation throughout China is deeply troubling. However, our trip has led us to believe there is a narrow but real opportunity to encourage the Chinese government to re-evaluate its policy toward Tibet." They asked that, "It must be a prominent part of our conversations with the Chinese government at every level. Our country has a responsibility to speak out in support of human rights in Tibet and elsewhere in China." The observation that, "there is a narrow but real opportunity to encourage the Chinese government to re-evaluate its policy toward Tibet," suggests that quiet back-channel contacts have possibly been at work.

The sudden announcement by the International Shugden Community (ISC) on March 10, 2016—the 57th anniversary of the Dalai Lama's flight from Tibet and riots in Lhasa—that it had decided to "completely stop organising demonstrations against the Dalai Lama" and dismantle its website, is also an as yet inexplicable development. Giving some credit to a Reuters investigative report on the activities of the Shugden group which he described as "something complete, holistic sort of presentation, it was very helpful," the Dalai Lama curiously said he was aware of the ISC's decision but "don't know" what was behind the group's announcement.

An important indication of the shift in the Chinese government's stance towards the Dalai Lama was the remark by Padma Choling (Baima Chilin), the 64-year-old TAR Deputy Party Secretary. He categorically told journalists that the Dalai Lama, "was no longer a religious leader after he defected his country and betrayed its people. If the Dalai Lama wants to return to China, he must give up 'Tibet independence,' and must publicly acknowledge Tibet and Taiwan are inseparable parts of China and that the People's Republic of China is the only legitimate government." Padma Choling's remarks are significant and, as observed by Zhang Yun, a researcher at Beijing's Research Centre on Tibetology, show that,"the legitimacy of the Dalai Lama's status as a religious leader was no longer acknowledged by the central government as he has failed to fulfil his obligation to inherit and spread Buddhism and continued his separatist activities." Zhang Yun added that, "the reconsideration came about after the central government realised the Dalai Lama's commitment to oppose the Chinese government, and his support of separatism was unlikely to change." Xiong Kunxin, a Professor of Ethnic Studies at China's Minzu University reiterated to the state-run *Global Times* "that Baima Chilin's (Padma Choling) remarks show the central government's attitude towards the Dalai Lama's identity, who had long been considered a religious leader."

Separately talking to reporters on March 7, 2016, Padma Choling implicitly expressed China's opposition to the Dalai Lama's visits abroad. Expressing "firm opposition" to the Dalai Lama's visit to Taiwan, he said, "We strongly oppose anyone who is in power (in Taiwan) to invite the Dalai Lama to visit Taiwan. Everyone clearly knows what kind of person the Dalai Lama is. The Dalai Lama must give up his secessionist stance and stop all activities to split the motherland."

This policy shift follows the declaration by the CCP CC PBSC, after a week-long closed-door "conclave" on June 30, 2015, that, "The authority of the central government has always been important in the reincarnation process. Historical precedents have clearly shown the central government's vital role in the process." The authoritative official Xinhua news agency report added, "all confirmations of the Dalai Lama have required approval by the central Chinese government, which has deemed the process an important issue concerning sovereignty and national security." An anonymous source was cited by Asia News as saying that Xi Jinping had said at the meeting that the Communist Party would pick "the next Dalai Lama, period! If things do not go well, we are ready to take corrective action."

Pertinent is the accusation that the Dalai Lama "defected" and "betrayed" the Chinese people. The first time that China alleged the Dalai Lama was "anti-national" and "unpatriotic" was after he affirmed that Arunachal Pradesh and Tawang are part of India. It made the accusation during the Sixth Round of talks between Chinese officials and the Dalai Lama's special representatives from June 29 to July 5, 2007, which was also the first occasion they raised the India-China border issue in these talks.

Notable was the apparent deliberate effort to single out the Dalai Lama for criticism at these sessions. Though a Mainland Chinese singer and two actors had visited Bodh Gaya in India on February 14, 2016, for an event connected with the Karma Kargyu sect of Tibetan Buddhism, the TAR Deputy Party Secretary, Wu Yingjie, chose to raise the issue only on March 7, 2016. Speaking to reporters in Beijing on the sidelines of the NPC, he criticised renowned Chinese singer Faye Wong, actor Tony Leung Chiu-wai and actor Hu Jun for attending the event in Bodh Gaya to commemorate the 92nd birth anniversary of the late predecessor of the 17th Gyalwang Karmapa. He said,

"As celebrities, especially superstars, they are public figures that bear certain social responsibilities. We hope the celebrities to take the responsibility for their own deeds. We firmly oppose all celebrities, however influential they are, and whatever purpose they have, to make any contact with the 14th Dalai clique, or even help him spread his ideas." China's official media similarly criticised the celebrities. The actors Faye Wong and Tony Leung Chiu-wai did not comment, but in a statement on his social media account, Hu Jun wrote that he did not know there were any "separatists" present. Important is that while the Dalai Lama and his "clique" were singled out for criticism and visitors warned to avoid contact with them, any critical reference to the Gyalwa Karmapa, who heads the Karma Kargyu sect of Tibetan Buddhism, was carefully avoided. In its effort to undermine the influence of the Dalai Lama, Beijing is distinguishing between the Dalai Lama and other Tibetan Buddhist religious leaders and attempting to wean the latter away.

As part of this policy Nepal, with Beijing's tacit approval, in mid-2014 loosened restrictions to allow Tibetan Buddhist sects to organise functions in Lumbini. The first beneficiary was the Sakya tradition and its various sub-sects who, after decades, were permitted to organise Monlam celebrations there. The policy accentuates divisions among Tibetan Buddhist religious sects and undermines the authority of the Dalai Lama who, Kathmandu has said, will not be allowed to visit Buddha's birthplace till he effects reconciliation with the CCP leadership in Beijing. Meanwhile, the Nyingmapa sect last year opted to recognise Beijing's authority and get its recognition for Penor Rimpoche's reincarnation.

There were other developments with the potential to impact India. The Chinese Deputy Director of the TAR Tourism Development Commission, Hong Wei, was quoted by the English-language *China Daily* as saying, "Tibet will be more open to domestic and foreign tourists in the next five years. We will simplify the procedure for foreigners to obtain travel permits and cut the waiting time." TAR Deputy Party Secretary Padma Choling clarified that the permit system requiring non-Chinese foreign travellers to obtain a special Tibet travel permit to tour the region, in addition to a Chinese visa, will not be abolished completely. Tibetans criticised the relaxation as intended to facilitate migration of Hans to Tibet. The NPC also approved a new railway line linking Chengdu in Sichuan province with Lhasa. Obviously a strategic military project the railway, which will go via Nyingchi, a large military and missile base opposite Arunachal Pradesh, has limited commercial viability. Approval was also accorded to extension of the Lhasa-Shigatse railway line to Kyirong on Tibet's border with Nepal.

China's stance suggests it no longer views the Dalai Lama as a religious figure and may not continue contacts with him. By setting preconditions for the Dalai Lama in case he wants to return to China, it is also trying to reduce his room for manoeuvre. The developments could have implications for India. At the same time, China appears to have begun to more overtly woo high-ranking monks and heads of other Tibetan Buddhist sects.

(The article was published by the Centre for China Analysis and Strategy (CCAS) and Vivekananda International Foundation (VIF), New Delhi, April 2016).

41

China's New Appointments and the New Tibet Party Secretary

Weeks after the annual conclave of senior leaders of the Chinese Communist Party (CCP) at the Beidaihe seaside resort, China's official news agency Xinhua on August 28, 2016, announced the appointments of six new Party Secretaries. Priority appears to have been given to the Autonomous Regions with three of them getting new leaders. Of interest to India are the appointments of Wu Yingjie as the new Party Secretary for the Tibet Autonomous Region (TAR), Chen Quanguo as the Party Secretary of the Xinjiang-Uyghur Autonomous Region (XUAR) and 62-year-old Chen Hao as the Party Secretary of Yunnan.

Other appointments include those of 59-year-old Li Jiheng as Party Secretary of Inner Mongolia, 1955-born Du Jiahao as the Party Secretary of Hunan, 1958-born Li Jinbin as Party Secretary of Anhui and Li Xiaopeng, son of former Chinese Premier Li Peng (from 1987 to 1998) at the time of the army crackdown in Tiananmen in 1989, as China's new Transport Minister.

There is speculation that Zhang Chunxian, who was born in 1953 and has been replaced after six years as Xinjiang Party Secretary by former TAR Party Secretary Chen Quanguo, is likely to move to Beijing as Deputy Chairman of the Central Leading Small Group on Party Building Work and later take over as its Chairman from Politburo Standing Committee (PBSC) Member Liu Yunshun. He is a Politburo Member and in the running for promotion to the PBSC. Some reports, however, claim that his past association with former PBSC Member Zhou Yongkang and friendship between their wives who worked together at CCTV, will mar his future prospects. They also cite the appearance, during the National People's Congress (NPC) session in March 2016 of a letter critical of Xi Jinping on a XUAR government-maintained website, as an added factor.

The appointments reflect Chinese President Xi Jinping's preference for appointing cadres who have either worked with him or have a "Red" lineage, army background or professional expertise, to sensitive positions. The new TAR Party Secretary and Transport Minister are "Red Descendants" while Chen Quanguo's background includes service in the People's Liberation Army (PLA). Sixty-one-year-old Chen Quanguo, incidentally, was reliably learnt to have been appointed as TAR Party Secretary at the express behest of Xi Jinping, who was then China's Vice President. Chen Hao and Du Jiahao have both worked under Xi Jinping in Shanghai. Chen Quanguo and 59-year-old Li Jiheng have both been moved from one autonomous region to another indicating that they had successful tenures and their career graphs continue to rise. Both are presently members of the 18th CCP Central Committee (CC) and likely to be elevated to the Politburo at the 19th Party Congress late next year. The norm for retirement for provincial level cadres is 65 years.

Of specific interest is the new TAR Party Secretary, Wu Yingjie. It would be difficult for the CCP to find another ethnic Han cadre who is as "Tibetan" as Wu Yingjie. The last Han cadre fluent in Tibetan and who was regarded as a "Tibetan" was former PLA General Yin Fatang, who served as Party Secretary of TAR from 1980 to 1985.

Till his elevation, Wu Yingjie was one of four TAR Deputy Party Secretaries, with the others being Padma Choling (Tib), Lobsang Gyaltsen (Tib) and Deng Xiaogang (Han). While Padma Choling and Lobsang Gyaltsen were ranked higher, Wu Yingje was designated the Executive Deputy Secretary. Indication that Wu Yingjie was earmarked for promotion was his being sent to attend the Central Party School in Beijing from March 2000 to January 2001. He studied in the CCP Central Party School's Research Institute, focusing on Party history.

Wu Yingjie has an impeccable "Red" pedigree. His father, Wu Ziming, was a member of the Party committee and Secretary of the Communist Youth League of Changyi County Shandong Province. Wu Ziming was transferred to Tibet from Shandong's Changyi county in 1956 before Wu Yingjie's birth and assigned work in Golmud. All his family members along with Wu Yingjie came to settle with him in Golmud in 1958.

Born in Changyi County in Shandong Province in December 1956, Wu Yingjie graduated from a high school in Shandong in 1974. He first came to TAR as an "educated youth" under the Tibet Aid programme and worked in Nyingchi. In October 1977, Wu Yingjie came to live in Lhasa and became a worker at a power plant in the western part of the region. He stayed on in Tibet for the next over 40 years and joined the CCP in May 1978. Three years after the Chinese government resumed the all-China college entrance exam, Wu Yingjie enrolled in the Chinese Language and Literature Department of the Tibet Nationalities Institute, Xianyang in Shaanxi in 1979.

After graduating from University in August 1983, he was assigned the post of clerk in the Board of Education of the TAR. In 1986, Wu Yingjie was promoted to Senior Staff and in April 1987 was appointed the Deputy Director of the Primary and Secondary Education Department of the Tibet Autonomous Region Science and Technology Education Commission. Through the 1990s, he held the posts of Deputy Director as well as Director of the Assistance Office and was later promoted as Deputy Director of the Board of Education in the Tibet Autonomous Region Board of Education. By the time he reached 43 years of age in May 2000, Wu Yingjie was appointed the Director of the Tibet Education Department. Credible reports state that during his tenure in the TAR Board of Education, Wu Yingjie "worked hard to promote the development of education in Tibet" and made "important contributions" to the Tibetan schools.

In January 2003, Wu Yingjie was promoted to the level of a Deputy Provincial cadre and appointed Vice Chairman of the TAR Government. Since then Wu Yingjie served in the TAR Party Committee as Director of the TAR Party Propaganda Department and later as Deputy Chairman of the TAR Government. In November 2011, Wu Yingjie was appointed Deputy Party Secretary of the Autonomous Region, Deputy Chairman of the Autonomous Region Government Executive and Deputy Secretary of the leading group of the Party. In April 2013, he succeeded Hao Peng as Governor of Qinghai Province and was concurrently Deputy Chairman of the Autonomous Region Government's Executive.

As Director of the TAR Propaganda Department, Wu Yingjie received special credit for the propaganda work during the TAR's 40th anniversary celebrations in 2005. The Region's propaganda work was praised as "smooth and fast." At the time of the March riots in Lhasa in 2008, he would have worked closely with Liu Yunshun, then Director of the CCP CC's Propaganda Department, in shaping a decisive role for the CCP's propaganda apparatus which for the first time introduced a schism between the Han majority and Tibetans. Liu Yunshun is currently a Member of the PBSC. Official Chinese media reports state that "a resounding success of patriotism education was seen" during Wu Yingjie's tenure as Director of the TAR's Propaganda Department.

Some interesting remarks have been made by Wu Yingjie in the past. When meeting a group of seven South Asian journalists including four from India being hosted by China's State Council Information Office on a tour to showcase developments in Tibet, TAR Deputy Secretary Wu Yingjie disclosed to the journalists in Lhasa on August 25, 2014, that talks were on with the Dalai Lama. He clarified that these were being held through "personal envoys" and limited to discussing the possibility of his return to Tibet. He said, "All Tibetans, including the Dalai Lama and the people around him, can return if they accept Tibet and Taiwan as part of China, and give up 'splittist' efforts."

Earlier in October 2009, he told US diplomats travelling in Tibet that the Dalai Lama and his "clique" masterminded the "March 14" incident as part of a bid to take back feudal power in Tibet. He claimed that during the 11th Five-Year Plan the TAR had invested a lot of money in restoring religious sites and protecting Tibetan culture, and the many people praying at temples in Lhasa testify to the government's protection of religious freedom. He added that tax exemptions for farmers and herders, free medical care, subsidised housing, education and vocational training, and investments in protection of traditional Tibetan culture had improved the lives of ethnic Tibetans. Wu Yingjie also said, "Nearly all rural Tibetans can read, however, one-quarter of Tibetans still live without electric power." He asserted that, "Tibetans are not economically marginalised and discrimination based on ethnic background is illegal."

Also in October 2009, Wu Yingjie asserted that "the "Dalai" uses his religious role for political purposes and that the "March 14th Incident" was masterminded by the Dalai in order to destroy the Beijing Olympics. The Dalai just doesn't want to lose his power." He added that, "In the old days, five per cent of the people controlled 95 per cent of the land. The Dalai wants to restore his feudal rule, but the serfs have already been liberated. America freed all the black slaves and people welcomed that, but China freed all the Tibetan slaves under the 'Dalai Clique,' and some people are not happy." Wu Yingjie added, "I don't know why." He said,"some foreign countries also give money to the Dalai and send high-level delegations to Dharamsala. For example, US Speaker of the House Pelosi and a White House senior staff member special emissary both went to Dharamsala to see the Dalai Lama."

He said, "The Dalai is asking China to withdraw its People's Liberation Army (PLA), and other non-Tibetan people from the region, and is trying to create a so-called 'Greater Tibet' that would include ethnic Tibetan areas of Sichuan, Qinghai, Yunnan and Gansu. No sovereign state could accept such demands, which would divide the country."

Wu Yingjie additionally disclosed that, "After the March 14th (2008) incident, 950 people were arrested and 80 of them were sentenced … Two hundred monks from outside of the TAR who were in the TAR without legal documents were sent back to their home areas, but no monks or nuns are missing. The government views the monasteries as public units (gonggong danwei). Therefore, the government provides the monasteries with free medical care, drinking water, and electricity, and also builds and maintains roads to the monasteries." He also said that, "During the 11th Five-Year Plan the TAR has invested considerable money in the protection of Tibetan culture. For example, the government invested 380 million RMB in repairs of the Potala Palace, and the Sakya, Norbulinka, and Tashi Lhunpo Monasteries." He said the government had built many hospitals of traditional Tibetan medicine and protected about 100 kinds of Tibetan customs as part of the PRC's "national intangible cultural heritage."

Wu Yingjie explained that, "The TAR government has undertaken a series of policies to benefit Tibetans. Tibetan language education is well developed in the TAR. Rural children receive free compulsory education. The TAR offers free tuition, free food, and free accommodation for students who need to reside at school. The TAR covers up to 1,300 RMB (US$ 190) in annual expenses for primary school students and 1,400 RMB (US$ 206) for middle school students. Many rural schools teach classes in both Tibetan and Chinese. Some rural schools even teach English. With support from the Ministry of Information Industry, new technology has been developed to make the Tibetan language easier to use on computers." Wu Yingjie also said, "the TAR would like to teach courses in the natural sciences in the Tibetan language at the university level." He added, "before 'liberation' only five percent of Tibetan people went to go to school; now, 80 per cent of them are getting an education." He said, "over 98 per cent of rural youth and middle aged people are literate—that is, they are able to read the Tibetan language edition of the Tibet Daily. The government also sends many Tibetan students to inland China to study for free. Generous stipends are provided to students from the TAR who are accepted into a university in inland China."

In response to a question by the US Consul General at Chengdu about the economic marginalisation of ethnic Tibetans in the TAR and a sign on a Lhasa shop that only an ethnic Han would be hired for a particular job, Wu Yingjie declared that, "Tibetans are not economically marginalised," and, "I don't know why people say such things." Stating that it is impossible to develop such a rapidly growing economy without the participation of ethnic Tibetans, he pointed out that in TAR, 70 per cent of the civil servants are ethnic minorities and only 30 per cent are ethnic Han.

Wu Yingjie is reputed to get along well with colleagues and be good at delegating work. He is 1.83 metres, or just over six feet, tall and a good athlete who has played basketball and volleyball.

Wu Yingjie's appointment suggests an effort by Beijing to adopt a more sensitive and understanding approach towards Tibetans. While his predecessor Chen Quanguo focused more on tightening security and enhancing the Party's presence and surveillance throughout Tibet, Wu Yingjie is likely to give more importance to the TAR's propaganda effort. He can be expected to retain the focus on education.

The appointments also indicate that decisions have been taken to fill the anticipated more than 90 vacancies in the CCP Central Committee at the 19th Party Congress. There will also be 5 clear vacancies in the PBSC and 6 among the 18 full members of the Politburo. Xi Jinping will try to fill as many of these as possible with loyalists.

(The article was published by the Centre for China Analysis and Strategy (CCAS), New Delhi, September 2016).

42

China's Ambitions in the Asia-Pacific

This decade has been marked by pronounced Chinese assertiveness for reinforcing its territorial claims—whether on land or sea—and for dominance over what it claims as areas within its sphere of influence. China's growing economic and military might, especially in the wake of the global economic crisis, have given it increased heft in international affairs and the confidence to advance its claims more forcefully. Beijing's perception that the US is on the decline, albeit gradually, makes this period a window of opportunity. Beijing's assessment that this window could begin to close in approximately 5 years gives its push added impetus. China has chosen the Asia-Pacific as the region where it will first further its ambitions.

The US is central to the realisation of China's ambitions especially as most of the rival claimants for maritime territories are closely tied to the US including through long-standing security arrangements. While Beijing is pushing the boundaries to assert its claims it does not desire either confrontation with the US or to spark a conflagration with rival claimants. The latter have the potential to escalate and derail China's current effort to modernise its economy, improve the well-being of its citizens and modernise the military, all of which are essential for the Chinese Communist Party (CCP) to retain its legitimacy.

Beijing's assessment of US capabilities was encapsulated by China's Ambassador to the US, Cui Tiankai, in remarks a couple of weeks ago to a US audience. These simultaneously underlined the important role of the US in the region. Cui Tiankai called for shifting the orientation of Sino-US relations from one of "crisis management to opportunity management" on the ground that using coercive language is not constructive. He also frankly acknowledged that "the United States is a powerful and very strong country…

the most powerful and strongest country in the world, and will remain so for many many years to come."

Current tensions in the Asia-Pacific and their effect on Sino-US relations were naturally extant in Cui Tiankai's remarks when, referring to the interests of both countries in the Asia-Pacific, he asserted that Beijing is not about to withdraw its maritime territorial claims. He said, rather diplomatically, that the "United States presence, interests, and influential role in the Asia-Pacific is fully and widely recognised" and that China welcomes a "constructive role by the United States in the region." Equally important was his observation that, "China is also a Pacific country, and China is also an Asian country. Geographically, China is just situated in the centre of the Asian continent. And we have been here for centuries, perhaps a little bit longer than the whole history of the United States. So I think it may be fair to say that neither Chinese nor Americans are aliens from Mars in the Asia-Pacific, but we are somehow more indigenous than you are." He warned that, "any attempt to manage or manipulate the regional affairs at the expense of China's legitimate interests in the region, cannot be justified, and would indeed be detrimental to the stability and prosperity of the entire region, and eventually will serve nobody's interests."

Similar sentiments were echoed, but far less diplomatically, by Shanghai-based Chinese venture capitalist and commentator, Eric X. Li, recently in Seoul. He emphasised that China had not erred in its actions regarding the territorial disputes in the South China Sea and East China Sea and that history will "probably prove" that China had been pre-eminently agile in dealing with these situations. He declared that China's strategic objective in the region is to change the status quo, which it did not have the power to influence when it was being established, to its advantage while avoiding military conflict. He concluded by stating that China has, and always will, act in its own best national interests and that China's "world view is to keep out barbarians and not invade them."

Viewed from a geopolitical perspective, the current dispute between China and Japan over the Diaoyu (in Chinese), or Senkaku (in Japanese), islands is really not a territorial dispute, but a more fundamental one involving China's national identity and is about China's place in the sun. China, which seeks to cast off humiliations of the past and regain its "lost" territories and self-perceived rightful status, views repossession of the disputed territories as recognition of its predominance in the region. Its economic and military "rise" has given it confidence that the time is opportune to assert its claims and wrest international recognition of its predominant position in the Asia-Pacific. Pertinent are its assertions at the 18th Party Congress and, more recently during the CCP Central Committee's (CC) Third Plenum in November 2013, that China is a maritime power.

Re-energisation by the US since 2010, of its presence and relationships in the Asia-Pacific are viewed with concern by Beijing. These have served to reinforce the Chinese communist regime's lack of trust in the US and conviction that it is intent on effecting the "containment" of China and is therefore attempting its encirclement by "unfriendly" powers. The sentiment has been expressed by senior Chinese Communist Party (CCP) leaders at important Party functions, including Party Central Committee plenums. The US concept of the "Asian Pivot" and the TPP and TTIP are seen as additional deliberate attempts to disadvantage China strategically and supplement the US strategy of containing China and placing limits on its influence in the region.

The Trans-Pacific Partnership, or TPP, is a revised version of the US strategy to maintain its lead over other countries and preserve its status as the pre-eminent world power. The TPP is a serious effort to change the rules of the game, as it were, in matters of global trade regulations and laws. It is intended to ultimately replace the GATT and WTO. The US has thus far had detailed discussions on the TPP with the UK, Europe and Japan. Details of the discussions have not been made public and neither have details of the TPP. In fact, there is criticism in Japan that details of the TPP are being closely held by a small group within the government. Concerned that the rules governing the international economy and global trade will change appreciably, disadvantaging China which has benefited from them over the past couple of decades since it joined the WTO on September 17, 2001, Beijing has sought clarity on the subject. It was a subject of discussion during Xi Jinping's first visit to the US as China's President for a "working Summit" with US President Obama in June 2013. It was disclosed after the Summit that Beijing would be briefed on the

TPP and regarding its details. In any event, talk of the military component of the US proposed "Asian Pivot" has receded after discussions on the TPP gained momentum. The implication is that the US and West plan, in preference to a military strategy, to recast international trade rules to their benefit and to deny China the benefits it has thus far obtained thereby retarding its economic growth. China is, however, actively considering joining the TPP.

In this backdrop, tensions have continued to escalate in the maritime zone surrounding the Sea of Japan and South China Sea particularly over the past year. China's strategic policy on the South China Sea disputes, formulated way back around 1989, is now being put to the test. Beijing's policy remains one of conducting bilateral negotiations with rival claimant nations while steadfastly opposing a regional approach. To implement this policy, it is using economic and other levers to cow down rival claimant nations.

As part of "Sanzhong Dafa" (or the "Three Warfares," involving legal, propaganda and psywar) to further its claims, China has over the years also been assiduously constructing a sort of legitimacy for its maritime and land territorial claims. Quite ignoring the fact that the strength and influence of all countries and empires with a long history have waxed and waned over the years, the Chinese communist government has taken China's largest territorial extent as the basis for its claims. As in the case of other territorial and sovereignty claims, China has sought to "construct" a legitimacy for its maritime claims on the basis of descriptions of sea voyages by the eunuch, Admiral Zeng He, historical maps published in April 1935 and February 1948 and, more recently, the legislation passed, or enacted, by the National People's Congress (NPC)—China's version of a Parliament. As Mohan Malik pointed out in *The Diplomat* (August 30, 2013), it is ironic that in its territorial disputes with its neighbours like India, Myanmar, and Vietnam, Beijing always insisted that its land boundaries were never defined, demarcated, and delimited. However, in the case of its maritime claims in the South China Sea, it claims otherwise. China's claim that its land boundaries were historically never defined and delimited is in sharp contrast with its stance that China's maritime boundaries were always clearly defined and delimited. This basic contradiction (ji ben mao dun) in China's stand on land and maritime boundaries is untenable.

Since Deng Xiaoping launched the Modernisations Programme in December 1979, the acquisition of naval power consonant with China's anticipated global stature has been a goal. The "recovery" of China's sovereignty over its land and maritime territories and the sea frontiers claimed by it has been an unwavering priority item on China's strategic agenda. Deng Xiaoping initiated the process by planning the modernisation of the People's Liberation Army Navy (PLAN) and hand-picked his confidant, Admiral Liu Huaqing, then the only senior PLA officer with a Navy rank, for the job. Admiral Liu Huaqing's immediate focus was to build a credible deterrence that would facilitate unification of Taiwan with Mainland China in case the use of force became unavoidable and, thereafter, to allow Chinese naval activity in the Asia-Pacific region. China's military strategic planners and the PLAN higher command has over the years adhered to the plans and doctrine drawn up by Admiral Liu Huaqing. The concept of the first and second Island chains took shape from around this time. Recent examples of this, and the Chinese military's growing confidence, are the unveiling of the DF-21 Anti-Ship Ballistic Missile (ASBM) when tension with the US was high over its planned largest-ever joint exercises with the Republic of Korea (ROK) and Japan in 2010, and revival by China of its claims over the Ieodo Rock off ROK and James Shoal off Thailand in the midst of escalating tension in the South China Sea and East Sea.

As was to be expected tension has risen in the region and China's relations with Vietnam, the Philippines and Japan have been damaged. The other South East Asian countries are seriously apprehensive now of China's "rise" and talk in South East Asian capitals of its "rise" being benign has given way to looking for other big powers to take an interest in the region. China is aware of these concerns, but is choosing to ignore them. The internal debate on the continuing benefits of the policy advocated by Deng Xiaoping of "daoguang yanghui" (lie low, bide your time), apparently failed to get adequate support and has died down. The finalisation by Beijing last year of China's Asia Policy would have contributed to the end of such debate.

Beijing has instead chosen to opt for a policy of applying a blend of economic, diplomatic and military pressure on the Philippines and Japan. After an initial show of resistance, Vietnam has presently chosen to lie low and use the "fraternal" links between the Communist Party of Vietnam (CPV) and the Chinese Communist Party (CCP) to keep bilateral relations in a state of decent repair. The Philippines, unable to withstand Chinese military and economic pressure but unwilling to acquiesce to China's maritime territorial claims, opted to internationalise the issue. It took the matter of the disputed maritime territories to international arbitration. For this it earned China's ire, which was amply and publicly exhibited in the remarks of Ruan Zongze, the Vice President of the Chinese Institute of International studies (CIIS), while on an official trip to Manila on April 3, 2013. He warned the Philippines, quite pointedly while on Philippines soil, to prepare for a rough four years as a consequence of its action.

Japan is the largest and most powerful country in the region and for various reasons is viewed by Beijing as a serious challenge. Beijing has, therefore, focused on Japan. It banned the export of rare earth minerals and metals to Japan for three months and later whipped up anti-Japanese campaigns. PLAN ships have sailed past Okinawa into the Pacific and sorties by PLAN aircraft over waters claimed by Japan have prompted Japanese military aircraft to scramble to intercept them. The incidence has increased each year over the past two years with no signs of Beijing backing off from its harsh stance vis-à-vis Japan. Beijing also set up an "Office to Respond to the Diaoyu Crisis" under the direct leadership of Xi Jinping and took things a step further by promulgating the Air Defence Identification Zone (ADIZ). In response, Japan's new Premier Shinzo Abe declared, after his first visit to the US as Prime Minister in this term, that Japan is not and will not ever be a second-rate power, and also initiated a series of tough measures.

After 11 years of decline, Japan's defence budget for 2013 rose by 0.7 per cent to US$ 47 billion (4.68 trillion yen). The first Defence White Paper of Prime Minister Shinzo Abe's government, published in July 2013, stressed the need for further strengthening ties with the US. It additionally stated that Japan anticipates greater threats to its national security which require enhanced military capabilities. The tense territorial dispute with China along with North Korea's increasing belligerence was identified among the threats. The paper also hinted at a possible change in the role of the Japanese military from that of a purely "Self-Defence Force." These include the development of Japan's ability to launch pre-emptive attacks on enemy bases abroad and creation of an amphibious force similar to the US Marine Corps. Soon after release of the Defence White Paper, Japan's Defence Minister Itsuno Onodera said that Tokyo needs to be wary of China's maritime expansion in the South and East China Sea. He said, "China has made more and more advancement into the seas," and that, in the event of a conflict in Asia, Japan could be a key participant. "Japan therefore needs new equipment and must reconfigure its defence. It needs a good defence to protect the country, which means new equipment, new aircraft, defence systems or cyber protection."

The increase in the defence budget will accelerate modernisation of Japan's Self Defence Forces (SDF). Indication of Japan's intent is already available, albeit subtly, in that Japanese Navy ships deployed in the Gulf now do not refer to themselves as the SDF Navy but only as the Japanese Navy. The Japanese Navy is also already well equipped—such as with the Aegis Class Destroyers—and quite openly confident of taking on and defeating the PLAN. Japan's Asahi Shimbun last year reported that Japan's Defence Ministry is planning a new protocol to deal with foreign unmanned aircraft that approach Japan's airspace, like the Chinese military drone that ventured near the disputed Senkaku Islands on September 9. The protocol will include provisions for "necessary measures," or shooting down a drone, if it continues to violate Japan's airspace and poses a serious and immediate danger to the lives and property of the Japanese public. Japan's Defence Minister Onodera described the drones as a "major risk." Escalating tension has led to a drop in Japan's exports to China, which fell by 16.7 per cent to their lowest in the period January-June 2013 for the past four years, as compared to 14.8 per cent in the previous six months July-December. Imports by Japan from China registered a similar downward trend. This reduction in Japan's exports and imports away from China has been deliberate and occasioned by the deterioration in bilateral relations. According to JETRO, while Japan's direct investments in China for January-June fell 31.1 per cent from the previous year to US$ 4.9 billion in 2012, there was a simultaneous 55.4 per cent increase to a record US$ 10.3 billion for the Association of Southeast Asian Nations (ASEAN). This trend, according to JETRO Chairman Hiroyuki Ishige, is likely to continue as Japanese companies seek a safer political environment as well as lower labour and business costs in ASEAN and elsewhere.

Recent developments, however, point to quiet efforts to ease escalating tensions and the sense of crisis. This follows Japan's decision to increase its defence budget. Among the steps taken in recent months to defuse tension, Japanese Prime Minister Shinzo Abe decided not to undertake the usually controversial visit to the Yasukini Shrine in mid-August though at least three Japanese Cabinet Ministers visited the Shrine. Hong Kong authorities meanwhile denied permission to the group of "anti-Japan" Chinese protestors from sailing to the Senkakus.

The real possibility of the Arctic Route opening for commercial shipping is a new dynamic that offers China an alternative route for seaborne cargo which is also shorter and more economical. With a distance of 2,936 nautical miles (5,437 kilometres) China's ships could sail through the Bering Strait through the East Siberian Sea and Vilkitsky Strait before docking at any of the various European ports. Qi Shaobin, a Professor at the Dalian Maritime University, observed that the route will significantly shorten the distance between Chinese, European and North American markets. The Chinese ports of Dandong, Yingkou, Qinhuangdao and Tianjin ports will particularly benefit. The Polar Research Institute forecasts that China's sea trade will grow to US$ 6.7 trillion by 2020. The new shipping route will directly benefit China's plans to develop the economy of its northeast provinces.

More concretely, Beijing too appeared to have decided at the highest levels to adopt a policy of easing tension. At the end of July 2013, China's entire 25-member Politburo (PB) met in a special session to discuss maritime power. Xi Jinping presided. He repeated the resolutions of the 18th Party Congress that China must become a major maritime power and develop its maritime resources. At the same time, however, he resurrected Deng Xiaoping's prescription that, "sovereignty remains ours; shelve disputes, pursue joint development." Xi Jinping also appeared to echo the policy articulated by China's then President Hu Jintao in 2006, when Hu Jintao had referred to the equal importance of managing the domestic and international overall situations. Xi Jinping said at the recent Politburo meeting that China must "plan as a whole the two overall situations of maintaining stability and safeguarding rights". The phrase seems to give equal importance to maintaining regional stability (weiwen) and safeguarding China's "maritime rights and interests" (weiquan). Some days later China's new Foreign Minister, Wang Yi, during a tour of South East Asian countries, said that final resolution of the disputes would take time. He also added that a code of conduct could meanwhile be discussed for minimising maritime problems and disputes, but without outside interference. The latter was clearly a reference to the US and action by the Philippines.

Despite these indicators, China's public stance as articulated by its official media has not relented. It has "boasted" about its navy's circumnavigation of Japan and disclosed that Chinese ships have spent a record number of hours in territorial waters administered by Japan. In a mandatory training begun in October 2013, the CCP CC's Propaganda Department instructed all Chinese journalists not to be supportive of Japan when writing about territorial and historical issues between the two countries. Nonetheless, a senior official from the Asian Division of China's Ministry of Foreign Affairs is learnt to have secretly met a high-ranking Japanese counterpart in Japan in early October. During the APEC Summit in Indonesia also in early October, while Beijing declined a formal meeting between the two leaders to discuss the island dispute, Japan's Prime Minister Shinzo Abe shook hands with Chinese President Xi Jinping. People-to-people contact has also increased with a record number of Chinese tourists travelling to Japan last year and two-way trade continuing to register an increase. Beijing at the same time has opted for a "no official contact" policy which, reports indicate, will remain in force so long as Shinzo Abe is Prime Minister.

It is more than likely that the US has, from behind the scenes, urged Tokyo and Beijing to tone down rhetoric and reduce tensions. At the same time, Tokyo's decision to enhance its defence budget would have raised anxiety in Beijing and given it cause for pause. Beijing certainly does not want to see a rearmed Japan on its doorstep especially if it decides to go nuclear. Meanwhile, Beijing's plans to modernise the PLAN and add at least two more aircraft carriers to its fleet to secure dominance over the South China Sea and Sea of Japan are moving ahead. Beijing's pause should correctly be viewed as a temporary stalling and reduction of belligerent rhetoric to gain greater future strategic advantage.

(The article was published by the Centre for China Analysis and Strategy, New Delhi, September 2016).

43

Beijing's Strategies Towards South China Sea

Tensions have escalated in the maritime zone surrounding the Sea of Japan and South China Sea since 2009, and particularly in the past few months. China's strategic policy on the South China Sea disputes, formulated way back around 1989, is now being put to the test. Beijing's policy is of bilateral negotiations with rival claimant nations and opposes any regional approach. Its adherence to this policy is evident in its use of economic and other levers to cow down rival claimant nations.

Viewed from a geopolitical perspective, the current dispute between China and Japan over the Diaoyu (in Chinese), or Senkaku (in Japanese), islands is really not a territorial dispute, but more fundamental involving China's national identity and is about China's place in the sun. China, which seeks to cast off humiliations of the past and regain its "lost" territories and self-perceived rightful status, views repossession of the disputed territories as recognition of its predominance in the region.

Its economic and military "rise" has given it confidence that the time is opportune to assert its claims and wrest international recognition of its predominant position in the Asia-Pacific. Pertinent is its assertion at the 18th Party Congress that China will be a maritime power. Japan is similarly unwilling to yield its position in the region and views sovereignty over the uninhabited rocks as symbolic. Japan's Prime Minister Shinzo Abe spelt out his country's position recently in Washington, when he said: "Japan is not, and will not be, a second-tier country."

The recent round of escalation in tension has come about during the interregnum when the US is widely perceived as a power on the decline—or at least stretched to the limits of its capacity because of the financial and material strain of its involvement in Iraq and Afghanistan—and which coincides with China's rise. A complication for countries in the region as well as the US is China's growing economic and military might combined with the considerable influence that it wields in East Asia, which has made the majority of countries dependent on its goodwill. It simultaneously means that these countries are unwilling to choose between the US and China, though they would like to see US power stay.

Beijing's Quest for South China Sea

China has for decades eyed the South China Sea islands and waters and regarded them as China's maritime territories. In fact, China lays claim over large portions of these waters and China's official media at regular intervals asserts that at least "3 million sq. km" of the South China Sea is Chinese maritime territory. As in the case of other territorial and sovereignty claims, China has consistently used history to bolster its claims and the estimates of huge reserves of oil and natural gas have seen reinforcement of these claims. China claims that its naval forces began to patrol and exercise jurisdiction over the area, establishing China's maritime boundary in the South China Sea, and cited maps published in April 1935 and February 1948, as evidence. "Sanzhong Dafa" (or the "Three Warfares," involving legal, propaganda and psywar) to further claims, is part of Chinese strategy.

The 4,982,900-square kilometres maritime area in the Asia-Pacific is poised to remain a cockpit of tension in the coming decade. Though Chinese President Hu Jintao deliberately avoided categorising the South China Sea as one of China's "core interests" along with Taiwan and Tibet when he visited the US in January 2011, and China was compelled to acquiesce to the US being designated as an Asia-Pacific power in the joint communiqué issued in January 2011, China has not given up its quest to "recover" its "lost" maritime territories.

As China accelerated its bid to secure international acceptance of its dominance in this region, it was prompted by mixed signals emitted by the US, or miscalculation of its own strength and its perception of the decline of US power. Signals possibly misinterpreted by Beijing as US recognition of its pre-eminent status in the region include Kissinger's remarks to Chinese

Foreign Minister Huang Hua in the 1970s, then US President Clinton's speech in Beijing in 1991, and a senior Chinese Navy officer's remark about sharing the area west of Hawaii made to visiting US Admiral Keating in 2009. This region has, meanwhile, attracted the renewed attention of major powers.

The US Chairman of the Joint Chiefs of Staff, Admiral Mike Mullen, on February 8, 2011 signed the US National Security Strategy, a document in which China's influence is implicitly present throughout. It states that US "strategic priorities and interests will increasingly emanate from the Asia-Pacific region," and that the US will "seek new ways to catalyse greater regional security cooperation," including with "traditional Chinese allies" like Vietnam. "Assured access to and freedom of manoeuvre within the global commons—shared areas of sea, air, and space—and globally connected domains" is declared as of enduring interest to the US.

Separately and soon thereafter, Russian Defence Minister Anatoly Serdyukov said on February 26, 2011, that Russia would deploy troops on the disputed Kurile Islands to ensure the security of the islands which are "an inalienable part of Russia." Russia will deploy military units on the Iturup and Kunashir islands which are part of the Kurile Island chain. Coincidentally, Russia and China are co-founders of the Shanghai Cooperation Organisation (SCO).

Securing South China Sea: Beijing's Strategies

The Chinese leadership, however, remains intent on restricting the scope of activity of the US and other powers in Asia-Pacific waters. China's ambition is to dominate at least the area within the "first Island chain," which is bounded between the Chinese mainland up to southern Japan along the Philippines and down to Brunei and Vietnam. The maritime area of serious Chinese interest comprises large areas of the Sea of Japan (978,000 sq. km), Yellow Sea (380,000 sq. km), East China Sea (124,900 sq. km) and the South China Sea (3,500,000 sq. km).

On the sidelines of the Eleventh National People's Congress held in Beijing in March 2011, a Xinhua news agency despatch reiterated that China's maritime resources extended over 3 million square kilometres of offshore waters, adding that these contained proven marine oil reserves of 24.6 billion tonnes and 1.6 billion cubic metres of natural gas. The statement was an important reassertion of Chinese sovereignty.

As China's leadership stays focused on ensuring the security of vital energy sea lanes and on "recovering" sovereignty over claimed maritime territories, "deterrence" and "reach" will remain the guiding philosophy for the Chinese Navy through this decade. Beijing's determination to achieve its national objective of "recovering" claimed maritime territories and dominating the region was discernible in its response to the joint military exercises conducted in April 2010 by the US with South Korea, and later with Japan.

Quite significantly, and as part of its strategy, China made a differentiation at the time between the US and other neighbouring countries. In a move which highlighted the importance of the US to China, Beijing eased off on its angry rhetoric before it could damage Sino-US relations and ensured a good atmosphere for President Hu Jintao's visit to the US in January 2011, which was quite pointedly not called off at any time during this period. China's Party and military leadership additionally publicly asserted that China had no intention of "confronting" or "challenging" the US. This position remains unchanged.

In contrast, China showed no such softening of stance against the neighbouring countries. Japan was subjected to protracted pressure with Beijing insisting on the release of the Captain of a fishing vessel and demanding an apology from Japan. Beijing's pressure was reinforced with the suspension of exports of vital rare earths to Japan and all shipments were halted ostensibly due to procedural delays in Customs. Japan is entirely dependent on these rare earth exports, which are essential ingredients for the manufacture of a variety of items ranging from hair dryers to iPods to missile guidance systems. Exports were resumed after almost three months. Though this was the first time that China used rare earth exports as an economic weapon, the action has wider implications and indicates that Beijing would not hesitate to take similar steps in future when considered necessary.

Japan, also because it is the larger regional power, has been singled out for special attention and China's pressure on Japan has been sustained. On August 29, 2011, China's official news agency Xinhua reminded Japan's new Prime Minister, Yoshihiko Noda, that he "should take concrete and substantial steps to promote its relations with China, and respect China's core interests." It accused Tokyo of managing "its relationship with Beijing without due respect for China's core interests" and emphasised that "Japan needs to show enough respect for China's national sovereignty and territorial integrity, especially when it comes to matters concerning Diaoyu islands, which are an integral part of China's territory." At the same time, it said China "would like to settle its differences with Japan through candid dialogue ..." and is "willing to shelve differences and jointly explore … the resources in the surrounding waters of the Diaoyu Islands, on condition that Tokyo recognised China's complete sovereignty over the archipelago." The term "core interests" reappeared in the Chinese official media after many months.

This caution was strengthened on September 17, 2012, when China's solitary official English-language *China Daily* published an article by Jin Baisong, Deputy Director of the Department of Chinese Trade Studies at the Chinese Academy of International Trade and Economic Cooperation affiliated to the Ministry of Commerce. He described the tension as a "well-orchestrated plan" by Japan and recommended strong countermeasures, especially economic sanctions. Listing potential retaliatory measures, he observed that the US$ 345 billion two-way trade was crucial in helping Japan avoid another recession in 2013 and was giving Japan's economy impetus. He cautioned that China held short-term and long-term Japanese government bonds worth US$ 230 billion by the end of 2011 and had become Japan's largest creditor in 2010.

In early 2013, tension has escalated with Chinese vessels regularly and deliberately intruding Japanese-claimed waters or patrolling off the Diaoyu Islands. Earlier, Beijing had taken steps to tackle the issue on a substantive level and established a new "Office to Respond to the Diaoyu Crisis." Headed by Xi Jinping, it includes Dai Bingguo, several military officers and possibly the Commerce Minister as members. While the officials in this office will change following the 12th NPC, this Office has reportedly already formulated a series of step-by-step responses for possible contingencies with the goal of compelling Tokyo to, at the minimum, accept Chinese sovereignty over the Islands.

Purchase by Tokyo of the disputed Islands provoked Beijing to begin enforcing its sovereignty. Chinese civilian law enforcement vessels now patrol the area around the Senkaku/Diaoyu islands and cross into the 12-nautical-mile territorial zone around the islands, with the intention of "protecting" China's sovereignty. Aircraft of both nations are engaged in close patrols. Serious was the provocation when Japan accused a Chinese Navy frigate of "locking" its radar on a Japanese vessel. China has promised an enquiry but denied that the incident occurred.

South China Sea, Beijing and the Philippines

The Philippines was also marked out for Beijing's attention. China has periodically asserted its claims, but just before Philippines President Aquino's arrival in Beijing, the official Chinese news agency Xinhua on August 31, 2011 warned that bilateral relations cannot be boosted only through trade but are dependent on a commitment to "proper settlement of the maritime disputes in the South China Sea." It declared, "China has always made itself loud and clear that it has indisputable sovereignty over the sea's islands and surrounding waters, which is part of China's core interests." Stating that Beijing is willing to shelve differences and seek joint development, it "urged the Philippines to halt its action deemed detrimental to China's maritime sovereignty and interests in the South China Sea and to cease releasing irresponsible remarks."

During the stand-off in July 2012 between the Philippines Navy and armed Chinese vessels around the contested Scarborough Reef, Beijing prohibited the import of bananas and pineapples from the Philippines and instructed Chinese tour operators to cancel tours to the Philippines. Manila lost 400,000 jobs and its economy was adversely impacted. The US brokered an end to this stand-off between China and the Philippines.

However as soon as the Philippines withdrew its ships, Chinese Navy vessels returned and placed a chain marker demarcating their claimed area. This elicited no reaction from the US. China had effectively demonstrated its ready willingness to use economic ties and military might as coercive instruments of foreign policy.

Conclusion

India was also brought into the orbit to warn New Delhi against drawing too close to the US. Official media articles critical of the military exercises in 2010-11, bracketed Japan, India and Vietnam as countries that were drawing closer to the US to "contain" China. Some articles observed that history had imposed limits on the extent to which China's relationship with Japan and India could develop, while others observed that China would have to ultimately use military means to settle outstanding border disputes and that India will likely be the first choice. Muscle was added to these warnings with the People's Liberation Army (PLA) and People's Liberation Army Air Force (PLAAF) staging major exercises across the Line of Actual Control (LAC). Directly related were the Chinese warnings to INS *Airavat* and the ONGC survey vessel off Vietnam.

The purpose of warning India and Japan would be threefold: to demonstrate to other countries in the region that it would be of no use, and possibly even counterproductive, to forge close relations with either of these bigger countries in the region against China; that the US would be unable to come to the assistance of these countries in time; and that China will be unchallenged in the region.

This policy of being tough with neighbours was amplified in a signed article published in Qiushi (*Seeking Truth*), the authoritative theoretical magazine of the Central Committee of the Chinese Communist Party (CCP). Published on December 10, 2010, the article detailed its perception of the US strategy against China and how China should counter it. It listed seven types of US pressure on China and China's countermeasures. Asserting that: "the US seems highly interested in forming a very strong anti-China alliance ..." It said, "countries like Japan, India, Vietnam, Australia, the Philippines, Indonesia, and Korea are trying to join the anti-China group because they either had a war or another conflict of interest with China. They are attempting to gain benefits by using the US, and these are the countries that surround China ..." It concluded that, "China must adhere to a basic strategic principle: We will not attack unless we are attacked; if we are attacked, we will certainly counter-attack. We must send a clear signal to our neighbouring countries that we don't fear war, and we are prepared at any time to go to war to safeguard our national interests. China's neighbouring countries need China's international trade more than China needs them … Therefore, they, but not China, will suffer greater damage by antagonising China … This is also the most effective means to avoid a war."

Tension in this region is unlikely to reduce early as China will push the envelope to ascertain the US's "red line" and simultaneously coerce Japan to back down. China's determination was spelt out by the Jiefangjun Bao on July 27, 2012, which said, "… the People's Republic of China is facing a very grim situation … More than half of the three million sq. km of waters that should fall under China's jurisdictions according to the UN Convention on the Law of the Sea are under demarcation disputes with peripheral countries."

Washington's action in brokering a defusing of tension between China and the Philippines and, more recently, to unsuccessfully reduce tension between China and Japan have been carefully monitored in the region's capitals and have raised doubts about US willingness to abide by Security Treaty commitments. Future trends are uncertain, however. Japan could, if pushed unduly, decide to become a nuclear power. Estimates are that this would take not more than 10 months. It could also amend its "Peace" constitution citing threats from Beijing and Pyongyang as justification. The US could, in turn, try and accelerate creation of a coalition combining Japan, South Korea, Indonesia, Australia and India, but back that by some guarantees.

(The article was published at The Institute of Peace and Conflict Studies, New Delhi, May 2013).

44

China-South Korea Presidential Summit: Fait Accompli?

The three-day (January 9-11, 2012) visit by South Korean President Lee Myung-bak to Beijing came at a time of heightened tension in the Korean Peninsula and political sensitivity for Beijing, following the untimely demise of North Korean leader Kim Jong-il. Over the past year, China's relationship with South Korea has also been subject to strain due to sovereignty and territorial issues. Geopolitical and economic compulsions have however, motivated successive South Korean administrations to keep relations with China on an even keel.

During his sixth visit to China, his second since he became the President in February 2008, Lee Myung-bak, President of the Republic of Korea (ROK), was received with due protocol. In his meeting with the top three leaders of China, the South Korean President was accompanied by a delegation of high-level dignitaries.

Since the 2008 elections, his administration has adopted a tough stance towards the Democratic People's Republic of Korea (DPRK). It has consistently declined the passage of food or humanitarian aid unless Pyongyang explicitly admits to two provocations in 2010, namely, the sinking of an ROK Navy warship and artillery firing on an ROK island which killed 50 people. Resumption of aid has been made dependent on progress in efforts to get Pyongyang to give up its nuclear programme.

Lee Myung-bak did not relent on this stance even when Kim Jong-il died on December 17, 2011 and Seoul sent no condolences or official delegation for the funeral, prompting harsh criticism and threat of unspecified retaliation by the North. The situation plummeted when, recently, the official

North Korean website, Uriminzokkiri, for the first time denounced ROK's Minister for Unification by name. Meanwhile China has also found South Korea's posture disconcerting, since it does not want tensions to derail the smooth transition of power to Kim Jong-un in which it has a large stake. In fact, reduction of tension on the Korean Peninsula was China's top priority during the visit.

Assuaging China's concerns, Lee Myung-bak struck a conciliatory note. After Kim Jong-il's death, he said, a "big change is expected" and the "situation on the Korean Peninsula is now entering a new turning point." Despite North Korea's belligerence and amidst rumours of a likely third nuclear test by Pyongyang in the first half of this year, South Korea's President assured, "it is South and North Korea, before anyone else, that must try to achieve the task of building peace, security and reunification on the Korean Peninsula." He asserted that South Korea is "leaving a window of opportunity open. If North Korea shows its attitude of sincerity, a new era on the Korean Peninsula can be opened."

Coincidentally, Beijing had initiated steps to ease tensions on the Korean Peninsula just a few days prior to Kim Jong-il's unexpected death. On December 14, 2011, Beijing quietly arranged a meeting between the US special representative on Korean policy, Glyn Davies, China's Foreign Minister, Yang Jiechi, Assistant Foreign Minister, Liu Zhenmin, and Special Representative for Korean Peninsula affairs, Wu Dawei. It was hinted that Li Gun, Chief of the American Affairs Bureau of the DPRK Ministry of Foreign Affairs, met Glyn Davies. Later, South Korea's nuclear envoy, Lim Sung-nam, visited Beijing on December 23 and met Wu Dawei. Following these meetings, China expressed the hope that these contacts could create favourable conditions for resumption of the Six-Party talks.

In addition, a recent report disclosed that during this meeting the DPRK had requested the US to resume supplies of food aid instead of milk powder and supplements. The US is yet to respond though DPRK has offered to stop the enrichment of uranium domestically. Separately, on January 9-11 a secret contact took place between Hiroshi Nakai, former Head of Japanese efforts to settle the abductees issue, and DPRK representative, Song Il Ho, allegedly by Chinese involvement. China had also offered, as an incentive, to start negotiations with Seoul for a Free Trade Agreement (FTA).

Reduction of tensions on the Korean Peninsula figured prominently in the joint statement signed on January 10 at the conclusion of the Presidential Summit. Both agreed to make efforts to "maintain peace and stability in the region and realise lasting political stability," and create conditions to resume Six-Party talks. They agreed to try and boost bilateral trade to US$ 300 billion by 2015 from the current US$ 200 billion, sign economic agreements and establish a hotline between the two Foreign Ministries.

The US-ROK security relationship will, however, remain a factor in Beijing's policy towards Seoul particularly because of recent US activism in the Asia-Pacific. South Korea's Institute for Foreign Affairs and National Security also predicted that while Six-Party talks are likely to resume in the first half of the year, there will be no real progress.

Beijing, however, was keen on a successful visit to reduce tensions on the Korean Peninsula at this critical time. Another objective was to lessen strains in the relationship following the largest ever US-ROK navy exercises in 2010. Reports publicised by the South Korean newspaper, Dong-A Ilbo, that the ROK Navy plans to create a fleet for the Korean Islets of Dokdo (Liancourt Rocks) and Ieodo, were accordingly played down. From Beijing's perspective, the Summit succeeded in easing tensions on the Peninsula.

(The article was published in The Institute of Peace and Conflict Studies, 2012).

45

China Articulates Sharp Suspicions about US Intentions

As the Chinese Communist Party (CCP) prepares for the transfer of power at the highest echelons this October, suspicion of the US among China's leaders has become more acute thereby sharply heightening tension in the bilateral relationship. The US is viewed as persisting with its "Cold War mentality," trying to "contain China's rise" and "meddling" in the South China Sea. A series of recent authoritative signed articles in the official Chinese media reflect these concerns.

The articles have been sought to be balanced, however, by others which highlight the collaborative aspects of Sino-US relations. China's official news agency Xinhua, for example, while reporting the meeting in Beijing between Chinese President Hu Jintao and visiting US National Security Adviser Tom Donilon on July 24, 2012, in this vein observed that both had specifically described Sino-US relations as "the most important relationship in the world."

Three recent signed articles, that unusually and bluntly articulated the suspicion at the highest levels in the Chinese leadership of USA's perceived clandestine efforts to bring about the collapse of China from within, merit special attention. Written by Ministerial-level Party cadres they also laid bare the Chinese leadership's frustration at USA's apparent unwillingness to dispel the ambiguity that surrounds its policy of re-entering the Asia-Pacific.

China's expert on American affairs, 60-year-old Vice Foreign Minister, Cui Tiankai, authored one such article which exceeded 5,000 words. Entitled, "Sino-US Relations in the General Mapping of Chinese Diplomacy in the New Era," it was published in China International Strategic Review—2012. Publication of the article coincided with US National Security Adviser Tom

Donilon's important two-day (July 24-25, 2012) visit to Beijing. No doubt because his name is circulating in Washington as a possible successor to US Secretary of State Hillary Clinton, Beijing accorded Tom Donilon a red-carpet reception. He was received by Chinese President Hu Jintao, Vice President Xi Jinping, State Councillor Dai Bingguo and Military Commission Vice Chairman General Xu Caihou.

Reviving memories of the time when, immediately after the collapse of the erstwhile Soviet Union in 1989, suspicion of perceived covert efforts by the US to bring about China's downfall from within was at its height in the top echelons of the Chinese Communist Party, Cui Tiankai used the term "peaceful evolution" twice in the article. The term has not been noticed being used in the official Chinese media for many years. "Peaceful evolution" is a descriptive shorthand that the Chinese used to refer to the USA's perceived clandestine actions intended to: dismantle the CCP; introduce multiparty democracy; and replace the socialist economy with free-wheeling capitalism. Cui Tiankai used it in the context of the US interfering in China's internal affairs on the issues of Tibet, Xinjiang, democracy and human rights. Acknowledging that "in a multi-ethnic country with a huge population it is not difficult to find dissatisfaction," he cautioned that if this is perceived by those "obsessed" with "peaceful evolution" as an opportunity to engage in "colour revolution," then they are committing a major strategic error. As if to convey the enduring, long-term nature of China's policy towards the US enunciated in this article, a younger co-author, Pang Hanzhou, was named. Pang Hanzhou has been identified as a Second Secretary posted in the Chinese Embassy in London around 2008. Some reports emanating from Beijing, incidentally, speculate that Cui Tiankai is likely to be appointed China's next Ambassador to the US.

Referring to China and the US as "self-confident" nations, Cui Tiankai emphasised that China is focused on its domestic development and has steadfastly pursued a peaceful policy of cooperation. He wrote that "the road of peaceful development is a strategic choice made by the Chinese collective leadership, the ruling party and the overwhelming majority of the masses." He added that China and the US have "no territorial claims against each other, therefore there is no important source of antagonistic conflict between the traditional powers."

Emphasising their mutual economic interdependence, Cui Tiankai observed that over 60 platforms of bilateral engagement exist between the two countries, that economic and trade exchanges had become an important link and US capital and technology play an important role in China's development. He underlined that the relationship benefited the US. China and the US are now each other's second largest trading partners with the bilateral trade volume in 2011 reaching US$ 446.6 billion, or an increase of 182 times since diplomatic relations were established. He cited US-China Trade Committee statistics to show that US exports to China increased 468 per cent between 2001 and 2010, and that this trade directly supported between 4 million and 8 million jobs in each country. In the same period, imports of low-cost Chinese goods saved US consumers US$ 600 billion. By the end of 2011, US investment projects in China totalled 61,068, with a contracted amount of US$ 162.3 billion and an actual investment of US$ 67.6 billion. He referred to an American Chamber of Commerce report that enterprises in China generated a 60 per cent higher profit margin than the global average. The non-financial direct investment of Chinese companies in the US had accumulated to about US$ 6 billion. He reminded that, "China is a huge market with over 1.3 billion consumers and the next five years will create US$ 10 trillion worth of demand for imports."

The Chinese Vice Foreign Minister thereafter acknowledged that as two "great powers" neither China nor the United States "will give up their own deeply-rooted historical and cultural traditions, beliefs, values and social systems, and will firmly safeguard their own interests." However, he warned that "the strategic long-term cost of any misjudgement of each other's strategic intentions may be bigger than a war." He declared that China has "no intention of challenging the status of the United States and no intention of competing with US hegemony," and that it would be incorrect to make such an assumption.

He then asserted that in "recent years the United States had chosen not to solve certain problems with a pragmatic attitude, but instead exaggerate them and, worse still, speculate about China's intent." He questioned the "true intentions" behind the US policy of "return" to the Asia-Pacific, "greatly strengthening the alliance system," "promoting the Asia-Pacific Anti-Ballistic Missile system," implementation of the Air-Sea Battle concept, and "intervening in differences between China and its neighbours." He said, "not only the Chinese but other countries in the region are also uneasy." It was therefore necessary, he insisted, for the US to "make clear" its true intentions and ensure that the "core interests" of both countries are safeguarded. China, he added, "has always respected the reasonable interests and concerns of the United States" in the Asia-Pacific.

Indirectly referring to the South China Sea dispute as "some of the problems in areas surrounding China," he projected China as "not the initiator, but the victim." He reiterated that China will never seek a dominant position in the Asia-Pacific region. In conclusion, he said the "US policy of military expansion" and forging "Cold War type military alliances" had aroused public concern and that countries in the Asia-Pacific region are "unwilling to be forced to choose between the US and China."

The second equally important article was written by Yuan Peng, Director of the Institute for American Studies at the China Institutes for Contemporary International Relations (CICIR), which is directly subordinate to the powerful Ministry of State Security. Entitled, "China's Real Challenge Is the Next 5-10 Years," it was published in the Party mouthpiece *People's Daily* on July 31, 2012. This article assessed that China's real strategic contest with the US and West will start only after 5-10 years when its economy overtakes that of the US and its military and sci-tech capacities had risen appropriately. There will be no military conflict, but the contest will be in the non-military realm. Very interesting was the article's frank assertion that China intended to settle all issues of sovereignty and territorial integrity by military force.

Yuan Peng said the US strategic community is already debating three fundamental questions regarding China. These are: how to respond to the resource, energy and economic demands of a great power with 1.3-1.5 billion people; how to respond to the successful alternate political system, developmental model and cultural values of a socialist great power; and, "how to respond to the military challenge posed by a socialist great power that has not yet settled all its issues of sovereignty and territorial integrity." This last statement is of great import for India and China's other neighbours who have unsettled territorial issues. It also has implications for Tibet, Xinjiang and Taiwan.

Assessing that after the US and Europe tide over the current difficult phase they will witness an explosive growth of technology and productivity, he said they will then close China's window of strategic opportunity. Over the next 3-5 years the US will strive to revive national power and ensure its "hegemonic status." The "pivot" to the East will reinforce its leadership of the Asia-Pacific. The US will avoid a militarily confrontation with China, but instead exploit the latter's sovereignty and territorial differences with other countries.

Identifying sectors such as finance, the Internet, and legal activists as attractive to the US, the article detailed the methods that the US will employ to "contain China" or "disrupt its rise." Convertibility of the RMB, it said, will be used to open China's financial and insurance markets and enter China's services sector to reap "huge economic and financial" benefits and "control the lifeblood of China's development." Using "Internet freedom" as a slogan, the US will attack "top-down" governance to advocate "liberal democracy." It warned that the US will use "human rights lawyers," "underground" religion, dissidents, "Internet heroes," and disadvantaged social groups as the core forces to push for a "bottom-up" grass-roots approach to governance for changing China. In foreign affairs, the US will attempt to weaken and split China's ties with North Korea, Pakistan and Myanmar. It will offer these countries alliances or cooperative partnerships. It will seek to rebuild US-Russia relations to isolate China and constrict its diplomatic space. In conclusion, it said that to weaken China's ability to compete or strategically challenge the US, the latter will promote dialogues on subjects like the "global commons" of sea, air and space as well as cyber.

The third article was written by Ye Xiaowen, who is Vice President of the Central Institute of Socialism, which is equivalent to a Minister, and an alternate member of the 17th CCP Central Committee. It was released around the same time as the other two. Published by the *People's Daily* on July 24, 2012, it was captioned: "Do not let Strategic Anxiety lead to Strategic Misjudgements." Stating that as the sole superpower the US had acquired "unrivalled power as well as conceited, arrogant, domineering and meddlesome ways," the article assessed that when the US suddenly found itself on the decline and another power rising to catch up, it had become anxious. It cautioned the US against making strategic misjudgements, prompted by strategic anxiety, and trying to "contain China."

The appearance within the span of a week of three signed articles authored by Ministerial-level cadres is unusual in China. They obviously convey the views of China's top Party and government leadership. The articles signal the serious suspicion among top Chinese leaders that the US intends to try and engineer the collapse of the CCP and China from within and prevent it from rising internationally to its true potential. They additionally reveal that China's leadership is feeling vulnerable. At the same time, it is evident the Chinese leaders are keen that the Sino-US relationship is kept in a state of good repair. The views would appear to be shared by the new generation of Chinese leaders who will soon enter the CCP CC's Politburo and Politburo Standing Committee.

(The article was published in The Centre for Air Power Studies, August 2012).

46

The Xi Jinping-Obama Submit

Though not a "state" visit, Chinese President Xi Jinping's first visit (June 7-8, 2013) to the US as President has been described by the US as "unique" and "enormously important." The Summit received close international attention, particularly because of the new Chinese leadership's demonstrably increasing assertiveness, including in the Asia-Pacific. Beijing declared that Xi Jinping would discuss a "new type of great power relationship." High on the US agenda were the issues of cyber theft, the Asia-Pacific, North Korea, climate change and human rights.

The tone for the visit was sought to be set by China's Ministry of Foreign Affairs whose spokesperson, Qin Gang, announced that the Chinese and US leaders will "have an extensive and in-depth exchange of views on bilateral relations as well as international and regional issues of common interest." Underlining its strategic significance, she added, "It is believed that this meeting is important to the long-term, sound and steady development of China-US relations as well as regional and international peace, stability and prosperity."

Separately, *Global Times*, the racy nationalist subsidiary of the Chinese Communist Party (CCP) mouthpiece, *People's Daily*, also emphasised the strategic aspect of the Summit. It declared that, "China is growing into a bigger and more far-reaching power," and that Xi Jinping will discuss a "new type of great power relationship" with US President Obama. The remarks tried to project the Summit as one between leaders of the world's two most powerful countries and point to Chinese President Xi Jinping's desire to deal with the US as an equal partner. Importantly, they could equally signal an impending shift in China's attitude and behaviour towards other countries, which it does not consider as "major powers."

Highlighting the importance of the visit, Chinese analysts, including Sun Zhe, Director of the Centre for US-China Relations at Beijing's Tsinghua University, said the visit's aim was to nurture trust and simultaneously project self-confidence. They claimed that despite widespread wariness of US intentions, China's leadership is genuine in its desire to build a stable and productive relationship.

The agenda's focus on security and strategic issues was framed after Tom Donilon, who remains US National Security Adviser till July, quite unusually travelled (May 26-28, 2013) to Beijing to finalise preparations for the visit.

Prior to the visit, China's official media sought to portray that a "self-confident" Chinese leadership was engaging the US. It publicised Xi Jinping's decision, to eschew ceremonial trappings usually associated with visits by high-level Chinese leaders and meet US President Obama on a working visit, as evidence of self-confidence. Xi Jinping also indicated to Tom Donilon his preference for free-wheeling discussions without notes during the six hours of meetings scheduled with Obama.

Xi Jinping and US President Obama had slightly over 8 hours of talks spread over two days in the informal setting of the 200-acre Annenberg Estate desert retreat in Mirage Ranchero near Los Angeles. The Chinese leader, his wife and entourage, however, stayed at the nearby Hyatt hotel reportedly to avoid eavesdropping. Both leaders were keen to meet early as in the normal course they would have met only this September on the sidelines of the G-20 meeting in St. Petersburg.

Xi Jinping, who is not fluent in English, was accompanied by State Councillor, Yang Jiechi, China's Commerce Minister, translators and 57-year-old Politburo member Wang Huning. Wang Huning, who was in attendance throughout, is Head of the Chinese Communist Party's (CCP) Central Research Office but, more importantly, is a member of Xi Jinping's "brains trust." Like Yang Jiechi, Wang Huning is an America expert. He is also reputedly a staunch Marxist. Xi Jinping's decision to first visit Trinidad and Tobago, Costa Rica and Mexico—all three in the US's backyard—on a well-advertised influence-buying tour was publicised as indicative of the leadership's "confidence."

China's "self-confidence" and firm stance on issues of sovereignty and territorial integrity were reinforced by the remarks of senior Chinese military officers on the sidelines of the Shangri-la Dialogue in Singapore held over the last weekend of May 2013. They were buttressed by at least two articles published in the Chinese Communist Party (CCP) mouth piece, *People's Daily*. These together outlined Beijing's goals for the visit.

Again, articulating China's long-held objections to the surveillance of China's coastline and EEZ by US aircraft and ships, a Senior Colonel of the People's Liberation Army (PLA) divulged at a working session on maritime security that China had "thought of reciprocating" by "sending ships and planes to the US EEZ," and had actually done so "a few times." While reports have been in circulation for some time that PLA Navy (PLAN) vessels had been detected around Okinawa and Guam, this is the first occasion when a Chinese military official confirmed such reports. The disclosure reveals that Beijing's maritime policy is set to shift towards increased assertiveness. It implies that as China's military might continues to increase and its economic and strategic interests expand, China will imitate US behaviour. It will accord to itself the right to carry out surveys and gather intelligence inside the EEZ's of other countries.

Ni Lexiong, Director of the Sea Power and Defence Policy Research Institute at the Shanghai University of Political Science and Law, confirmed that this reflected the "changing concept of maritime affairs" of China's leaders, "following the rapid development of China's maritime industry and rising strength of its naval force in the past decade." The remarks also suggest that Beijing could be reviewing its interpretation of the UN Convention on the Law of the Sea.

Meanwhile, coinciding with US National Security Adviser Tom Donilon's stay in Beijing, Xinhua (May 28, 2013) publicised a report of the Centre for National Defence Policy (CNDP) of the PLA's Academy of Military Sciences (AMS). Entitled "The Strategic Review 2012," it observed that "amid strategic competition among the big powers, the fierce oceanic competition and frequent regional conflicts, the complexity, sensitivity and uncertainty of China's security environment loom large." It asserted that the US has accelerated the eastward shift of its strategic focus and that competition for maritime rights had increased. "Territorial disputes between China and its neighbours have escalated in recent years, with relations between Beijing and Tokyo damaged by their claims to the Diaoyus, the East China Sea archipelago known to Japan as the Senkakus. Disputes between China and several Southeast Asian countries in the South China Sea have also soared." Assessing that the stand-off between Beijing and Tokyo over the Diaoyus will last a long time with cycles of heightened tension, it warned that there could be a risk of armed clashes prompted by Japanese fighter jets flying close to Chinese civilian patrol flights. Commenting on the review, retired PLA Colonel Yue Gang said China is facing major "strategic pressure" centring on territorial disputes and that "any compromise in these disputes will trigger a wave of nationalist movements in the relevant countries." Ni Lexiong, of the Shanghai University of Political Science and Law, said China's expansion in the South China Sea had irked the United States and "the United States has resorted to containing China by forging ties with China's neighbours, making the dispute more complicated."

Of the two articles in the *People's Daily*, one (May 28, 2013) was written by Jiemian Yang, Dean of the Shanghai Institute of International Studies (SIIS) and younger brother of Chinese State Councillor and former Foreign Minister, Yang Jiechi.

Crediting Xi Jinping with "innovative thinking"—unusual praise for China's top leader so early in his term—he hinted that China was now thinking like a world power. The increase in China's comprehensive national strength had given its new leaders more confidence in dealing with the international community. He asserted that China will adhere to its own theories, systems and path of development. Mian Yang emphasised that this "self-confidence" has enabled China's leaders to be "very firm" in safeguarding sovereignty and territorial integrity while simultaneously being flexible in dealings with smaller countries. He revealed that they will focus more on the neighbourhood and travel oftener in the region. He cited the establishment of a "strategic partnership" between China and Brunei as an example of China's flexibility and effort to seek cooperation and common development for building confidence to settle regional disputes.

China's new leaders have also exhibited a willingness to deal with "hot" foreign policy issues, like steps to ease tensions in the Korean Peninsula. He said China needs to develop relations with the US, consolidate ties with Russia and improve relations with BRICS countries. He said it needs to "normalise relations with Japan." Listing the "many maritime disputes" as among China's major challenges, he said China must strive to prevent and manage crises that may arise. He recommended that it show greater tolerance to the international community. Making an important distinction between China and other countries, he observed that, "as long as China and the United States, other major powers, neighbouring countries and other members of the international community" cooperate and support China, "it will eventually emerge as a very peace-loving, powerful and prosperous nation."

The second article was published on June 4, 2013, and written by Li Wen, a scholar from the Centre for Research on the Theory of Socialism with Chinese Characteristics of the Chinese Academy of Social Sciences (CASS). It said Beijing wanted cooperative relations with major powers and that the "win-win of the new power relations" is essential for "common prosperity and a harmonious world." It advised major powers to discard "Cold War" ideas and hegemonic policies, adding that emerging powers do not seek hegemony and conflict was no longer inevitable. The article said that depicting a country as a "strategic competitor" and seeking to "contain it," is unrealistic and that it is necessary to "let true intentions" be known to avoid catastrophe. It urged major countries to "show more kindness and less hostility, and respect each other's core interests."

US President Obama lent a positive colour to the Summit when, at the end of the first day's meetings, he told journalists, "we had an in-depth, sincere and candid discussion on the domestic and foreign policies of China and the United States, on our joint work to build a new model of major country relationship, and our international and regional issues of mutual interest. And the President and I reached important consensus on these issues."

Speaking to reporters at the conclusion of the visit (June 8), US National Security Adviser Tom Donilon hinted that the US had adopted a more cooperative stance for the Summit. He described the discussions as "strategic" and said they had taken place at a time when the US faces "an intense range of bilateral, regional and global challenges on which US-China cooperation is critical." He labelled the over 8 hours of deliberations as "quite unique and important" and said they covered virtually every aspect of the US-China relationship. He said the Summit aimed to start building a "new model of relations between great powers."

China has again not succeeded in getting the US to acquiesce to its pre-eminent status in the Asia-Pacific. Instead, Donilon noted that the US aimed for a "stable security environment and a regional order rooted in economic openness and peaceful resolution of disputes, and respect for the universal rights and freedoms in Asia." He defined the "rebalancing strategy" as having a "number of elements: strengthening alliances, deepening partnerships with emerging powers, empowering regional institutions, helping to build regional economic architectures that can sustain shared prosperity" with TPP at the core. China, he disclosed, had shown interest in details of the TPP. Rebalancing, he added, includes "building a stable, productive and constructive relationship with China."

China's *Global Times* tried to put a positive spin on the issue, but could not conceal that differences continue to exist. It quoted Xi Jinping as reiterating that, "the Pacific Ocean is vast enough to accommodate the development of two great powers in the world." He also said that the Summit is "to map out a blueprint for the development of China-US relations and engage in cooperation across the Pacific Ocean."

Considerable progress has been claimed on the issue of North Korea and Pyongyang's timely offer, just prior to the Summit, to resume talks would have contributed. Both leaders stated that North Korea has to denuclearise and neither country will accept North Korea as a nuclear-armed state. President Obama stated the "United States will take any steps that we need to take to defend ourselves and our allies from the threat that North Korea presents." Both agreed to continue to apply pressure to halt North Korea's ability to proliferate and impress upon it that its continued pursuit of nuclear weapons is incompatible with its economic development goals. Positive mention was made of China enhancing enforcement of sanctions and the public statements of senior Chinese leaders. Absent, though, was mention of any tangible steps by China to move the process forward.

US concerns on the issue of cyber theft have not been assuaged despite cyber theft and economic issues being extensively discussed. The US President made clear that the threat posed to economic and national security by cyber-enabled economic espionage was unacceptable and that resolving this issue is really key to the future of US-China economic relations. The Chinese agreed to "look at this" and engage in a dialogue with the United States on norms and rules in the realm of cyberspace.

In a bid to blunt US complaints at the Summit, the official English language *China Daily* on June 5, observed that "cyberattacks from the US are as grave as the ones the US claims China has conducted." Huang Chengqing, Director of the National Computer Network Emergency Response Technical Team/Coordination Centre of China (CNCERT), said "we have mountains of data if we wanted to accuse the US, but it's not helpful in solving the problem." US agencies and the US Congress have accused Chinese military and other entities of cyber theft valued at billions of dollars. US officials have described cyber theft as a major obstruction to the development of bilateral relations to their full potential. With intriguing timing, the left-leaning British newspaper *Guardian* front-paged an exposé the very day that Xi Jinping landed in California on the "illegal" monitoring by the US's National Security Agency (NSA), under a programme named "PRISM," of all communications worldwide. More intriguingly, Edward Snowden, the CIA computer expert who leaked the information is currently in Hong Kong Special Administrative Region (SAR), thus raising the question as to whether Beijing will accede to a US request to extradite him.

Among other issues discussed at the Summit were climate change, which yielded an agreement, human rights and Sino-US military relations.

China and the US appear to have reached consensus on strategic issues at the Summit, but neither received tangible satisfaction on some key issues. Chinese President Xi Jinping has gained, including domestically, with China appearing to have been accepted by the US as a major world power with the prospect of enhanced involvement in resolution of international and regional issues. The US has, however, shown it is unwilling to surrender authority in any part of the globe as noticeable in China's failure to secure acceptance of pre-eminent status in the Asia-Pacific. China also did not give firm commitments on issues like North Korea and cyber theft.

(The article was published in The Institute of Peace and Conflict Studies, June 2013).

47

Chinese President Xi Jinping's First State Visit (September 23-28, 2015) to USA

Chinese President Xi Jinping's first state visit to the US later this month is important and comes amidst escalating testiness in the Sino-US bilateral relationship and growing wariness in the higher echelons of the Chinese leadership about US intentions. Cybersecurity, Yuan appreciation, China's maritime claims, Taiwan, Japan, North Korea and human rights are among the issues creating turbulence and will be on the agenda. Viewed in Beijing as China's most important bilateral relationship, the visit will be carefully monitored inside China and other world capitals. Countries around the South China Sea and particularly Taiwan and Japan will evaluate it with an added sense of immediacy.

The visit is slated to begin in Seattle on September 23, 2015, with a series of engagements after which Xi Jinping will proceed to Washington for summit talks and a formal state banquet with US President Obama on September 24-25. He will conclude his sojourn in the US with a speech at the United Nations on September 28.

Prior to commencement of the visit and to restore some of the sheen lost by the rout in the Shanghai stock market which highlighted the vulnerabilities in the Chinese economy, Xi Jinping has taken care to project that China's economy is sound and the leadership is strong. China's maritime ambitions have also been unambiguously spelt out. Beijing is also putting a positive spin on the visit with influential Chinese analysts and academics asserting that, "Xi's visit is as important as the US visit of Deng Xiaoping in 1979, which changed American views on the Chinese overnight." China's Ambassador to the US, Cui Tiankai, also told reporters that the outcomes of Xi Jinping's visit would be "a pleasant surprise when made public."

The sudden jolt to the economy caused by the wiping out of just under US$ 1 trillion in two weeks in Shanghai has been halted. Last month the IMF independently endorsed China's economic policies and China's banks just early this week announced that funds totalling between Yuan 1.2 trillion (US$ 188 billion) to Yuan 1.5 trillion would soon be injected to revive investment projects. Official forecasts are that China's GDP will grow at seven per cent.

At the same time, Xi Jinping reviewed a well choreographed grand military parade in Beijing on September 3, 2015, where over 800 weapons and at least 6 IRBMs and ICBMs were displayed publicly for the first time and where 120,000 soldiers goose-stepped 25-abreast with precision. Intended mainly to appeal to nationalist sentiments of a domestic audience, the parade was designed to simultaneously project China's military might and diplomatic influence. China's official media highlighted that 30 heads of state attended. To evoke Mao nostalgia and remind people about the Chinese Communist Party's (CCP) leadership role and traditions, Xi Jinping appeared dressed in a grey Mao suit—all other senior leaders on the podium were dressed in western-style suits—and reviewed the parade in the iconic Chinese communist Hongqi (Red Flag) limousine.

Significant was the attendance at the parade of former Chinese President Jiang Zemin. Following the arrests and detention over the past year of many of Jiang Zemin's protégés on charges of corruption, Beijing had for months been abuzz with reports that Jiang Zemin and his family had also been placed under house detention. A very unusual commentary front-paged in the CCP mouthpiece *People's Daily* on August 10, 2015 had warned "senior retired cadres" against intervening in the organisations they formerly worked for as this made new leaders feel that "their hands and feet were fettered" and they had to work with "unnecessary concerns." This has been widely interpreted as targeting Jiang Zemin. Jiang Zemin's presence next to Xi Jinping now is undoubtedly intended to dispel such speculation as well as send a signal prior to his visit to the US that Xi Jinping continues to enjoy the support of the veteran cadres. He also utilised the opportunity to demonstrate his firm grip on the People's Liberation Army

(PLA) by announcing a troop reduction of 300,000 personnel thereby signalling a definite push to major military reforms.

The US-China relationship is comprehensive and extensive with over 85 points of strategic contact and dialogue that entail meetings between officials of the two countries almost daily. There are 200,000 Chinese students in the US and over 5,000 American students in Chinese universities. In a wide-ranging interview to the official English-language *China Daily* on September 11, 2015, Chinese State Councillor and former Foreign Minister Yang Jiechi described both countries as "very important." Pointing to last year's two-way trade valued at US$ 550 billion and two-way cumulative investment totalling almost US$ 120 billion, he said the new visa arrangement between the two countries facilitates visits by businessmen and students. Observing that military contacts continue, Yang Jiechi said these show "that a new model of major country relationship between our two countries will work in the best interest of China."

A major agenda item for Xi Jinping's talks with US President Obama will be to push Washington to acquiesce to Beijing's new formula for "a new type of major power relations." Put forward in June 2013 and again in July 2014 and November 2014, the main objectives of this are that: US and China should have no conflict or confrontation; should emphasise dialogue and treat each other's intentions objectively; and, most importantly, that both powers should acknowledge and respect each other's "core interests." In other words, Beijing wants Washington to acknowledge and accept Beijing's claims over areas it defines as within its "core interests" and which it maintains are non-negotiable. The US has thus far declined to accept the formulation.

Beijing presently lists Taiwan, Tibet and Xinjiang as China's areas of "core interest," but since Beijing has left open the possibility of expanding its definition of "core interests" this will, in future, probably include the South China Sea and other claimed territories.

Pertinent in this context is former Chinese State Councillor Dai Bingguo's official definition of "core interests." In August 2009, when he was China's principal interlocutor with the US and Russia and with India for the boundary negotiations, he said: "China's number one core interest is to maintain its fundamental system and state security; next is state sovereignty and territorial integrity; and third is the continued stable development of the economy and society." Beijing also wants that the US and China should discuss and jointly be the arbiters on major international, regional and subregional issues.

Indications are that Xi Jinping is travelling to the US with an agenda that is not defensive but designed to robustly engage with US business, the technology and IT sector as well as US politicians. In a move that caught the US Administration offguard, China has sought to pre-empt any proposed cybersecurity-driven US sanctions and counter accusations that state-backed Chinese hackers "stole" the personal data of 21 million US Federal employees, by organising a high-level meeting with technology leaders in Seattle on September 23, 2015. The lure of China's economy and vast market for the IT industry ensures that the meeting will be attended by top Chinese and US tech companies such as Alibaba, Baidu, Apple, IBM, Facebook and Google. Chinese analysts expect that this will nudge "State senators and representatives from those states that heavily rely on economic cooperation with China" into "remaining neutral about controversies with China, avoiding harsh criticism over their trading partner." Bill Gates is hosting Xi Jinping to dinner on September 23 evening. Former US Treasury Secretary Henry Paulson's Paulson Institute is also hosting a CEO RoundTable for Xi Jinping in Seattle.

The selection of Seattle as the venue is deliberate. While Washington State is China's largest merchandise trade partner, it is also home to the Boeing Company which secures huge orders from China for civilian passenger aircraft and whose factory Chinese Presidents and Premiers usually visit while on visits to the US. In Seattle, Xi Jinping will visit Boeing's headquarters and tour its Everett factory where a new deal for Boeing to open a "delivery and completion centre" in China is expected to be announced. China had considered Hawaii and Detroit as possible venues but dropped Hawaii because of the US Pacific Command's critical attitude towards China on the South China Sea issue and Detroit because of security concerns.

Meanwhile on September 11, Obama made tough remarks on cyber theft asserting that, "There comes a point at which we consider this a core national security threat and will treat it as such." He added, "we have been very clear to the Chinese that there are certain practices that they are engaging in, that we know are emanating from China and are not acceptable." In a symbolic gesture the US Administration separately disclosed that Obama will this year not be staying at the Waldorf Astoria Hotel in New York consequent to its purchase by China's Anbang Insurance Group. The Chinese insurance company purchased the hotel, where the US President traditionally stays during UNGA sessions, for US$ 1.95 billion last year.

Underscoring the importance of Cybersecurity and describing the US and China as "countries with highly-developed Internet technology," the authoritative official Chinese news agency, Xinhua, on September 12 emphasised the importance of enhancing mutual trust and cooperation in this sphere. It additionally reported that consensus on combating cybercrimes was reached during the four-day (September 9-12, 2015) visit to Washington of Chinese President Xi Jinping's special envoy and CCP Politburo member, Meng Jianzhu. Meng Jianzhu, who heads China's security apparatus, met a number of US officials including US Secretary of State John Kerry, Secretary of the Department of Homeland Security Jeh Johnson and NSA Susan Rice. A US official disclosed on September 15 that an agreement had been reached during Meng Jianzhu's visit and "there are not going to be any sanctions" before Xi Jinping arrives on September 24.

While maritime territorial issues and China's activities in the South China Sea will certainly figure near the top of the agenda for discussions between US President Obama and Chinese President Xi Jinping, China has not resiled from its maritime territorial claims and assertive stance in the South China Sea. It has, instead, chosen to opt for what can best be described as a strategic pause by announcing a unilateral halt to land reclamation on the various shoals, islets and islands in the waters of the South China Sea claimed by it. Also on hold are its plans to build military facilities on these features and announcement of its Air Defence Identification Zone (ADIZ) over the South China Sea, though reports claim that plans are ready. These announcements could follow the visit. On the other hand, Beijing chose to restate its wider maritime ambitions when the People's Liberation Army Navy (PLAN) conducted exercises in May with the Russian Navy in the Mediterranean Sea for the first time and when five PLAN ships sailed through US territorial waters close to the Aleutian Islands out into the Bering Sea again for the very first time earlier this September.

China has taken steps to diffuse other potential areas of criticism by the US. On the issue of Human Rights and the proposed stringent regulations governing NGOs, a senior Chinese official has stated that a draft law is before the National People's Congress (NPC)—China's version of a parliament—and it is for the NPC to decide and not the government. Separately, a coalition of US-based NGOs addressed a letter to Obama on September 9, appealing that he take up the issue with Xi Jinping. Regarding the Dalai Lama and resumption of stalled negotiations, which US President Obama has said he will urge Xi Jinping to resume, China has already clarified its position and drawn the parameters for any future negotiations with the issue of the White Papers on Tibet and its "liberation" and the resolutions of the Tibet Work Forum. It has also set preconditions for the Dalai Lama.

China's effort will be to preserve stability and a cooperative tenor in Sino-US relations, though it is unlikely that there will be any major breakthroughs during the visit. The US is unlikely to endorse the "new type of major power relations," but despite its critical rhetoric it will probably continue to remain hesitant in its actions in the South China Sea. This will allow China to steadily advance and consolidate its claims over the 3 million sq. km of these waters claimed by it. In addition to bilateral issues, among the international and regional issues that both leaders will discuss in Washington will be terrorism, Afghanistan, Pakistan and India. Xinhua's reporting on the recent visit of US National Security Adviser Susan Rice to Beijing to prepare for the Obama-Xi Jinping summit noted that she had discussed international and regional issues with Chinese officials. Her stopover and remarks in Islamabad were indicative of the areas of discussion. Likely areas of agreement could be on climate change and a Bilateral Investment Treaty.

(The article was published in the Centre for China Analysis and Strategy, New Delhi, September 2015).

Index

Y